Cognitive Behavioural Preventio
Suicide in Psychosis

This practical and informative text lays out the product of a number of years of clinical research into suicide behaviour and its prevention. While the focus is on non-affective psychosis and the schizophrenia-spectrum disorders, the mechanisms underlying suicide behaviour in this group may well underlie or at least influence suicide behaviour in other disorders. The authors describe methods of assessment through individual formulation, and a cognitive behavioural intervention through case studies, to reduce the risk of suicide.

This book argues that:

- Suicide behaviour lies on a cognitive behavioural continuum from ideation, through intention to action.
- Mechanisms based on biased information processing systems, the development of suicide schema, and appraisal styles are likely to be fruitful in explaining suicidal thoughts and behaviours.
- A psychological theory of suicide behaviour is needed in order to develop a mechanism of suicide and to understand the components of suicidal thoughts and behaviours.
- Suicide risk can be reduced through the use of the intervention methods described within the text.

Cognitive Behavioural Prevention of Suicide in Psychosis evaluates practical applications of contemporary research on this topic, and will therefore be of interest to practitioners, postgraduates in training and researchers studying suicide and/or psychosis.

Nicholas Tarrier is Professor of Clinical Psychology at the Institute of Psychiatry, Kings College London, UK. From 1991 until 2011 he was Professor of Clinical Psychology at the University of Manchester and Consultant Clinical Psychologist in the NHS. He has pioneered the development and evaluation of cognitive behaviour therapy for schizophrenia and other psychological disorders.

Patricia Gooding is a Senior Lecturer at the University of Manchester. Her research focuses on understanding the psychological mechanisms that lead to suicidal thoughts and behaviours, and also on understanding the psychological mechanisms that confer resilience to suicidality.

Daniel Pratt is a Lecturer in Clinical Psychology at the University of Manchester and a Clinical Psychologist for Manchester Mental Health and Social Care NHS Trust. For the past ten years, he has conducted research investigating psychological models and interventions to prevent suicidal behaviour. Dr Pratt is currently conducting a feasibility trial of a psychological therapy for suicidal prisoners.

James Kelly is a Senior Clinical Psychologist working at Lancashire Care NHS Foundation Trust within the Early Intervention Service. He has published on the use of mobile phone technology to scaffold the delivery of cognitive behavioural suicide prevention therapy in real world settings. He has an interest in suicide prevention, cognitive therapy for psychosis and compassion focused therapy.

Yvonne Awenat has been involved in mental health research for the past four years following early retirement due to ill health from her former position as a Consultant Nurse. She now uses her personal experiences of mental distress combined with prior expertise as a NHS clinician to promote mental health research and services that reflect the needs of people with mental health issues. She is Honorary Research Fellow, School of Psychological Sciences, University of Manchester, UK.

Janet Maxwell is a Clinical Psychologist whose doctoral research focused on cognitive behavioural and family interventions for psychosis. She has worked in private practice and public mental health services in Australia and also as a research therapist in the United Kingdom, delivering psychological therapy aimed at preventing suicide in individuals experiencing psychosis.

Cognitive Behavioural Prevention of Suicide in Psychosis

A trea

Nichol
Daniel
Yvonn

Routledge
Taylor & Francis Group

LONDON AND NEW YORK

First published 2013
by Routledge
27 Church Road, Hove, East Sussex BN3 2FA

Simultaneously published in the USA and Canada
by Routledge
711 Third Avenue, New York, NY 10017

Routledge is an imprint of the Taylor & Francis Group, an informa business

British Library Cataloguing in Publication Data
A catalogue record for this book is available from the British Library

Library of Congress Cataloging in Publication Data
    Tarrier, Nicholas, author.
    Cognitive behavioural prevention of suicide in psychosis :
    a treatment manual / Nicholas Tarrier, Patricia Gooding,
    Daniel Pratt, James Kelly, Yvonne Awenat, and Janet Maxwell.
    pages ; cm
    Includes bibliographical references and index.
    1. Suicidal behaviour—Treatment. 2. Cognitive therapy.
    3. Suicide—Prevention. I. Title.
    RC569.T37 2013
    616.891425—dc23
    2012031936

ISBN: 978-0-415-59732-6 (hbk)
ISBN: 978-0-415-65870-6 (pbk)
ISBN: 978-0-203-06688-1 (ebk)

Typeset in Times New Roman
by Swales & Willis Ltd, Exeter, Devon

MIX
Paper from
responsible sources
FSC
www.fsc.org   FSC® C004839

Printed and bound in Great Britain by
TJ International Ltd, Padstow, Cornwall

Contents

Illustrations

Preface

Introduction to the science and practice of Cognitive Behavioural Suicide Prevention for Psychosis (CBSPp)

Executive summary

> - *Suicide behaviour is a continuum from ideation, intention and action to suicide.*
> - *All aspects of this continuum are important.*
> - *Effective interventions are best derived from understanding theoretical mechanisms.*
> - *Understanding general and disorder specific mechanisms is more important than diagnostic label.*
> - *Understanding theoretical mechanisms helps the clinician understand individuals and formulate individual-specific and relevant interventions.*
> - *In clinical practice aim to build up positives and limit and manage negatives.*

Suicide is final, there is no return. To attempt to take one's own life and to want to cease to exist indicates a deep despair and suffering. This self-evidently signifies that suicide and its antecedents of ideation, intent and attempts are of enormous clinical, social and public concern. To understand the underlying psychological causes and mechanisms and by doing so to be able to prevent suicide and suicide behaviour is one of the challenges, if not the paramount challenge, to psychological and mental health science and its practice. A successful suicide will result in the death of the individual, but also in *'collateral damage'* to all those around that person, including their family, friends and professionals. For some the damage will be permanent, their lives will never be the same and they will never recover. The occurrence of suicidal behaviour can have similar effects on others. The not knowing whether it will happen again and if so when, can be devastating because of its unpredictability for all those involved or affected. An individual's behaviour never exists in isolation, and the ramifications of something so serious and irrevocable as suicide behaviour can be immense.

A considerable amount is known about the general characteristics of those who are suicidal and those who attempt suicide successfully. But these characteristics tend to be population characteristics, and much less is known about the individual and what leads a particular person in specific circumstances to want to end their life. Current risk and behaviour is frequently predicted by past behaviour; a history of past suicide attempts is a predictor of future attempts, but the exact psychological nature of this and other risk factors remains obscure. We have very little understanding of how these psychological mechanisms work so as to map onto a model or template the characteristics of an individual so as to intervene and bring about change to reduce risk in the future.

In this book we will lay out the product of a number of years of clinical research into suicide behaviour and its prevention, mainly with those suffering psychosis although the principles and methods may well be more widely applicable. Our ultimate goal is to produce a rigorous and helpful clinical guide to allow clinicians to intervene with high-risk individuals to reduce the risk of suicide. We have adopted a systematic approach to achieving this goal by devoting considerable effort into developing and testing psychological theory to further understand the mechanisms that underlie suicide behaviour. We have then formulated our intervention based upon our theoretical position. We strongly hold the view that by equally developing theory and practice in tandem we strengthen both and significantly improve our ability to intervene and prevent suicide behaviour.

It is very well established that the experience of mental disorder is associated with suicide behaviour. Affective disorders, such as depression, and psychotic disorders, such as schizophrenia and bipolar disorder, have much higher rates of suicide and suicide behaviour than the general population. But merely equating suicide risk with the presence of a diagnostic group is unhelpful as it tells us little about the underling mechanisms, the motivation and thought processes that have brought an individual to the brink of taking their own life. Many people who have been diagnosed with a mental disorder such as depression or schizophrenia may be very distressed but they do not consider suicide. Thus a diagnosis in itself does not predict with any precision who will and who will not become suicidal. The traditional view that suicidal behaviour is a symptom of a mental illness is similarly unhelpful for the same reasons. The observation that the accrual of psychiatric diagnoses, that is, those who are diagnosed with more than one formal mental disorder, is associated with further increased risk suicide behaviour is of interest but suffers similar problems in terms of advancing understanding and explanation. Suicide risk is higher in those who suffer from PTSD and depression compared to PTSD alone (Panagioti, Gooding & Tarrier, 2009); suicide risk is higher in those suffering schizophrenia with depression and hopelessness compared to schizophrenia alone; suicide risk is higher in those suffering schizophrenia, dual diagnosis and PTSD compared to those with schizophrenia and dual diagnosis alone (Picken & Tarrier, 2011; Tarrier & Picken, 2011). These findings are intriguing but again tell us little of the psychological processes or further understanding of individual cases unless we look beyond the diagnostic labels. Group characteristics of elevated risks may give clues to these processes but they do not in themselves reveal the mechanisms. An important issue relates to the specificity or generality of these mechanisms. There are a number of possibilities: (1) Is there an underlying mechanism to suicide behaviour irrespective of the diagnostic group or nature of the clinical problem – a transdiagnostic mechanism? That is, the same mechanisms will be operating irrespective of whether a person is diagnosed with depression, schizophrenia or personality disorder; (2) The mechanism is disorder-specific. That is, the underlying mechanism will be different depending on the disorder, so that the psychological mechanism leading to suicide will be dependent on the clinical problem and different for each; (3) The mechanism results from a common clinical problem such as depression or hopelessness. That is, suicide behaviour might be elevated in those suffering from schizophrenia or PTSD but only occur in those who are hopeless because it is the psychological mechanisms of hopelessness that result in suicide behaviour and not schizophrenia or PTSD themselves; (4) Some interaction between a common and specific mechanism. That is, there may be a specific mechanism that results from a common problem or mental state, such as hopelessness, but this is influenced in different ways by the specific disorder. That is, hopelessness and schizophrenia is different from hopelessness and depression or hopelessness and PTSD.

It is important to point out that a diagnostic label tells us very little about the mechanisms underlying it. Generally, we have adopted a pragmatic view that there is most likely to be an interaction between general or non-specific mechanisms and disorder-specific factors. Such the burden of particular experiences associated with a disorder, such as persistent hostile auditory hallucinations, flavours general mechanisms associated with suicide as an escape from unrelenting stress.

The focus of this book is non-affective psychosis or the schizophrenia-spectrum disorders, however, as we have indicated above, the mechanisms underlying suicide behaviour in this group may well underlie or at least influence suicide behaviour in other disorders. Furthermore, people often suffer a range of problems that would involve more than one diagnostic label or suffer from co-morbidity. Thus it is not uncommon to find people diagnosed with schizophrenia also suffering from depression or PTSD. From a scientific point of view it is important to understand how these factors interact, and from a pragmatic point of view how to intervene effectively with co-morbidity. We would also emphasise that a disorder such as non-affective psychosis has primary consequences such as the symptoms associated with the disorder but also secondary consequences such as reduced social networks, reduced social mobility, stigma, poorer employment prospects and reduced access to community, economic and social resources. It may well be these secondary consequences rather than the disorder itself that increase the risk of suicidal behaviour.

Without a better understanding of psychological processes we remain in the dark about understanding individuals and in our ability to develop preventative interventions. For these reasons we have emphasised the importance of a theoretical understanding being the driver to the development of effective intervention and prevention. We accept that the only real future for any scientific theory is to be disproved and refuted, but in being so abandoned new and more precise theoretical understandings are arrived at. For the clinician theory functions as a clinical heuristic, which may be proved imprecise in the future, but it is the best explanation we have at the present time and it usefully drives and innovates clinical practice.

We argue that:

1. Suicide behaviour lies on a cognitive behavioural continuum from ideation, through intention to action.
2. Although successful suicide is less frequent than suicidal thoughts and attempts it is determined and preceded by thoughts and actions.
3. Thus suicide can best be prevented by understanding and intervening with its antecedents.
4. All aspects of suicide behaviour are in themselves distressing, disruptive and undesirable and important targets of preventative treatment.
5. Trying to treat suicide behaviour by focusing on population and risk factors alone will be ineffective.
6. Assuming that suicide behaviour can be treated by solely treating the specific symptoms of a psychological disorder will result in ineffective interventions.
7. Describing psychological characteristics of populations with elevated risk of suicide behaviour will lack the depth to provide an understanding of such behaviour that can be translated into an effective clinical intervention.
8. A psychological theory of suicide behaviour is needed in order to develop a mechanism of suicide and to understand the components of suicidal thoughts and behaviours.

9. Such mechanisms need to account for general and disorder-specific factors and their interactions.
10. Once the mechanism is understood, then treatments can target the processes underlying the mechanism.
11. Mechanisms based on biased information processing systems, the development of suicide schema and appraisal styles are likely to be fruitful in explaining suicidal thoughts and behaviours.

Over the last six or so years we have adopted a strategy to understand and develop a coherent and testable theory of suicide behaviour and from this to develop a clinical manual to be evaluated through clinical trials. This strategy will now be outlined and this book is its product. The realisation of this strategy has involved:

1. Investigation of potential candidate psychological mechanisms of suicide behaviour through an audit and critical review of existing models (Bolton et al., 2007).
2. Further development of a theoretical model through (i) refining and integrating existing models (e.g. Johnson et al., 2011; Taylor et al., 2011); (ii) data mining to develop and test theory (Tarrier et al., 2007); (iii) development of specific models to psychosis (Schematic Appraisal Model of Suicide, SAMS, Johnson et al., 2008).
3. Experimental studies to test the model (e.g. Taylor et al., 2009; Johnson et al., 2010; Taylor et al., 2010a; b; c).
4. Development of preventative interventions based upon the current general prevention literature and the developed theoretical model. This has been achieved by combining the results of a systematic review of current CBT interventions for suicide behaviour in general (Tarrier, Taylor & Gooding, 2008) with the intervention development based upon new theoretical model.
5. Development of a treatment manualfor CBSPp (Tarrier & Gooding, 2008).
6. An evaluation of the preventative intervention. Initially this is through a feasibility trial, which aims to evaluate the potential to engage participants, the acceptability of the intervention and the feasibility of its delivery as well as an understanding of its efficacy. An important aspect of this evaluation is the participant feedback and the personal testament of service users as to their experiences in general and of the intervention in particular.

This has allowed us to build on both existing theory and practice and to integrate these into a new approach, which will be the topic for this book. The results of this research strategy will be expanded in subsequent chapters in which the reader can find a more detailed account of the issues involved and a critical appraisal of the relevant research results and literature.

As we have said, we feel it is important that the reader who intends to embark upon clinical interventions to reduce the risk of suicidal behaviour has a good understanding of theory and potential psychological mechanisms underlying such behaviour. We are of the opinion that there is a very sound clinical purpose behind this. The grasp of psychological theory and understanding of psychological processes and mechanisms allow the clinician to have a template at their disposal by which they can attempt to understand each patient as an individual and upon this understanding or formulation arrive at an individually relevant intervention.

In most psychological treatment approaches, and especially in cognitive behaviour therapy, the individual or case formulation is the mechanism by which the individual's problems are understood and a suitable treatment strategy derived.

Although the underlying basic psychological processes that exist in all of us may be pretty similar we are all different, and although individuals and clinical problems can be usefully put into categories we still retain our individual differences because the actions and interactions of the processes and the interactions with each individual's circumstances will be different. Thus it is our view that it is extremely important to understand this variability and variation. It is the theoretical template that helps us understand these individual differences. Thus we advance the case for an understanding of psychological mechanisms as a way of understanding individual difference and variation so as to formulate an individually designated intervention.

It is important to remember that individual variation does not just encompass differences in negative aspects of a person but must also include positive characteristics such as resilience, skills and abilities. Such positive characteristics, whatever the nature, extent or configuration of negative characteristics, should be the clinical platform from which to launch interventions to compensate for these negatives. So our philosophy for intervention, if it can be so grandly described, is not to eradicate all negative characteristics but to build up positives so as to overcome or manage the negatives. Negative experiences will always occur – there is nothing we can do about that, however much we wish it otherwise –and our aim here is to reduce, limit and manage their consequences. It is important to always remember that people are social beings who live within a social context. The ability to relate to others, to be valued by others and to contribute something of value to others are important reasons for living and rewards of life. We put great importance in aiming to facilitate such social action and social reciprocity and not just trying to reduce negative affective states.

In this chapter we have tried to lay out some of the principles and issues that have challenged us in carrying out our clinical research and practice in aiming to reduce suicide behaviour in people suffering non-affective psychosis and other mental disorders. We have not found these challenges easy to resolve or in some cases even clearly to define, but they do encompass what we feel are essential aspects of our endeavour. These themes will persist throughout the book and hopefully guide the reader in their practice.

Chapter 1

Suicide

The problem

1.1. Introduction

- Every year, almost one million people die from suicide; that's one death every 40 seconds.

- In the UK, the suicide rate for men is three times that for women.

- Those aged between 25 and 44 years are most at risk.

- Social factors shown to influence suicide rates include unemployment, divorce and religion.

- Having a mental health problem makes a greater contribution to a person's risk of suicide than any social factor, with 9 out of 10 suicides experiencing mental health problems.

- The risk of suicide is particularly elevated for individuals experiencing depression, psychosis, traumatic stress, substance misuse or personality disorder.

- Experiencing multiple 'co-morbid' mental health problems further compounds this risk.

- A history of previous suicide attempts remains one of the most important and clinically relevant risk factors, which persists throughout an entire lifetime.

1.1.1. Rate of suicide

- Every year, almost one million people die from suicide; that's one death every 40 seconds.
- Over the past 60 years, the rate of suicide in the UK has remained stable at between 7 and 13 deaths per 100,000 persons.
- Suicide rates are relatively higher in Scandinavia and former Soviet Republics and lower in Mediterranean countries.
- Social factors shown to influence suicide rates include unemployment, divorce, substance misuse and religion.

According to World Health Organization (WHO) estimates, each year approximately one million people die from suicide and 10 or 20 times more people attempt suicide worldwide. This represents one death every 40 seconds and one attempt every 3 seconds, on average (www.who.int/whosis).

In the UK, suicide is the third largest cause of death. In 2008, there were 5706 suicides, an increase of 329 (6%) from the previous year. However, over the past sixty years, the total number of suicides in the UK has changed little. In 1950 there were 4660 self-inflicted deaths, a difference of only 20% from 2008. Despite slight variation each year, the suicide rate over this time period has remained between 7 and 13 persons per 100,000 persons since 1950 (ONS, 2010).

The rate of suicide varies widely across and within the different continents of the world. Table 1.1 provides the suicide rates per 100,000 of a small selection of countries from the various Regional Offices of the WHO. Within some regions, all countries seem to maintain similar rates. For example, in the Western Pacific region, which includes Australia, New Zealand, China and Hong Kong, all countries have average suicide rates per 100,000 for 1990–2000 of between 12 and 15 persons per year. Similarly, Argentina and Brazil have an average rate of 6.5 and 3.7 persons per year, respectively. And yet, also in the Americas region, Cuba has an average rate of over 20 persons per 100,000 per year (WHO, 2004).

In Europe, variation across countries is also quite marked. For instance, Denmark has an average rate of over 18 persons per 100,000 per year, much in line with its Scandinavian neighbours. Even higher rates have been observed over the past few years in Russia and many of the former Soviet Republics, with rates of more than 40 persons per 100,000 per year. Conversely, the southern European countries of Italy and Greece have observed much lower suicide rates of 7.6 and 3.6 per 100,000 persons, respectively.

It must be noted, as seen in Figure 1.1, that little data is collected from countries on the African continent. Therefore, little can be reported on how these particular countries compare to the rest of the world.

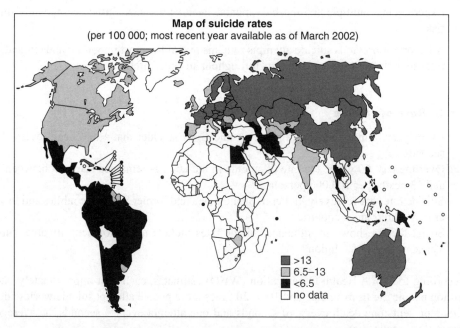

Figure 1.1   Map of suicide rates (Source: www.who.int/mental_health/prevention/suicide/ suicideprevent/en/index.html [accessed 20 July 2012])

Table 1.1 Suicide rates (per 100,000) by country

	1950	1955	1960	1965	1970	1975	1980	1985	1990	1995	2000	1990–2000 average
Americas												
Argentina				9.4	9.9		7.1	6.6	6.5	6.4		**6.5**
Brazil							3.3	3.1	3.2	4.1		**3.7**
Cuba						17.2			21.3	20.2		**20.8**
USA	7.6	10.2	10.6	11.1	11.5	12.7	11.8	12.3	12.4	11.9	10.4	**11.6**
South-East Asia												
India							6.3	7.1	8.9	9.7	10.7	**9.8**
Thailand		2.8	3.5	3.5	4.2	4.7	7.4	5.8		4.0		**4.0**
Europe												
Denmark	23.3	23.3	20.3	19.3	21.5	24.1	31.6	27.9	23.9	17.7	14.3	**18.6**
France	15.2	15.9	15.8	15.0	15.4	15.8	19.4	22.5	20.0	20.6	17.5	**19.4**
Greece			3.8	3.2	3.2	2.8	3.3	4.0	3.6	3.5	3.6	**3.6**
Hungary		20.6	24.8	29.8	34.8	38.6	44.9	44.4	39.9	32.9	32.6	**35.1**
Italy	6.3	6.6	6.1	5.4	5.8	5.6	7.8	8.3	7.6	8.0	7.1	**7.6**
Russia							34.6	31.2	26.5	41.5	39.4	**35.8**
UK	9.5	10.7	10.7	10.4	7.9	7.5	8.8	9.0	8.1	7.4	7.5	**7.7**
Eastern Mediterranean												
Kuwait						0.5	0.7	1.0		1.5	1.6	**1.6**
Western Pacific												
Australia	9.3	10.3	10.6	14.9	12.4	11.1	11.0	11.6	12.9	12.0	12.5	**12.5**
China								17.6	14.5	14.5	13.9	**14.3**
Hong Kong		10.5	11.1	8.2	13.6	12.3	13.5	13.2	11.5	11.8	13.2	**12.2**
New Zealand			9.6	9.1	9.6	9.5	10.8	10.3	12.4	15.3	11.9	**13.2**

(Source: WHO, 2002)

Over the past 100 years, the rates of suicide across nations have varied although the rank ordering of countries has remained relatively constant (Diekstra, 1995). This suggests that suicide rates are likely to be determined by persisting cross-national differences including traditions, customs, religions, social attitudes and climate.

Durkheim (1897) suggested that suicide rates may be influenced by the extent to which individuals are integrated within society, arguing that 'social integration could be achieved through family support together with religious, political and work affiliations'. This theory has been extensively researched over the past 100 and more years, with supportive evidence stressing the importance of social factors such as unemployment, divorce, substance misuse and religion, in explaining national differences and trends in suicide (Gunnell et al., 1999a; Lester, Curran & Yang, 1991; Makela, 1996; Lester, 1997). Societal changes, such as economic crises or periods of war, have also been recognised as contributing to changing patterns of suicide. A number of studies have identified an association between a country's economic and societal factors with time trends in overall population suicide rates (Weyerer & Wiedenmann, 1995; Low et al., 1981; Lester & Yang, 1991).

With respect to religion and its influence over suicide, Durkheim concluded that suicide rates should be lowest among followers of those religions that closely integrate the individual into collective life. For example, among Christians, Protestants would be less protected against suicide than Catholics, due to the higher state of individualism in Protestantism. Neeleman et al. (1997) investigated whether a negative association between religion and suicide is attributable primarily to social cohesion provided by religious organisations (Durkheim, 1897) or to an association of religious belief with reduced tolerance of suicidal behaviour (Stack, 1983; Stack & Lester, 1991). Religious and socio-demographic variables were obtained from a random sample of adult participants of all 19 non-Eastern bloc European countries, Canada and USA (total n = 28,085), which took part in the 1990/1 World Values Survey (WVS Study Group, 1994). The study reported that suicide rates relate more strongly to levels of religious belief and suicide tolerance than to church membership or attendance. The findings supported the religious commitment or cognitive dissonance model, which states that 'commitment to a set of personal religious beliefs may be more important in guarding against suicidal behaviour than social integration in religious groups' (Neeleman et al., 1997, 1169).

It is, however, unlikely that one single factor can be clearly implicated as having sole influence over suicide rates, since the causes of suicide are thought to be complex and multi-factorial with all such factors more likely to represent fundamental societal changes (Gunnell, et al., 2003).

1.2. Suicide and social factors

1.2.1. Gender and age

- In the UK, the suicide rate for men is three times that for women.
- Historically, older people experienced higher rates of suicide, although more recently, those aged between 25 and 44 years have become the most at-risk age group.
- This shift in risk associated with age has been attributed to increases in the rate of unemployment, divorce, substance misuse and alcohol consumption in the younger age groups.

In the UK in 2008, the suicide rate for men (18 suicides per 100,000) was more than three times that for women (5 suicides per 100,000) (ONS, 2011). On a global scale, this difference in rates between males and females has been steadily increasing over the past 50 years (see Figure 1.2). The global suicide rate for females has remained almost constant at around 5 suicides per 100,000 per year. However, the rate for males has increased from 16 per 100,000 in 1950 up to 25 per 100,000 by 1995, an increase of nearly 60% (WHO, 2002).

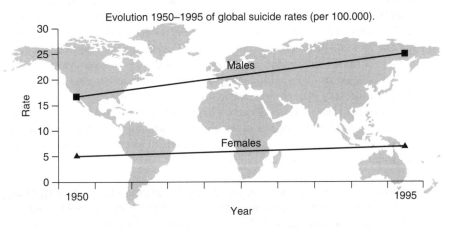

Figure 1.2   Evolution 1950–1995 of global suicide rates (per 100,000) (Source: www.who.int/mental_health/prevention/suicide/evolution/en/ [accessed 20 July 2012])

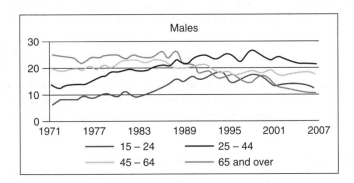

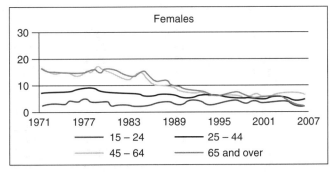

Figure 1.3 Suicide rates by sex and age (per 100,000) (Source: ONS, 2011)

Trends in suicide rates have varied by age and sex in the UK, although in each age group, males generally have a higher suicide rate than females (Figure 1.3). In the 1970s and 1980s, there was a steady increase in the rate of suicide by men across all age groups. This increase was particularly noted in the 15–44 year age group (Table 1.2), although older men maintained the highest suicide rates. During this period, older women also had the highest suicide rates for females, although the rate for females aged 45–64 years was only slightly less. In more recent decades, the suicide rate for older men has declined, with the rate for 2007 of 12.3 per 100,000 men being less than one-half of its peak. The rates for women aged 45 and over have also declined during this time. In more recent decades, there has been a decrease in the suicide rate for males across all age groups; however, the fall in the younger age groups has not been as dramatic as previous increases, leaving the 25–44 year age group with the highest rate of suicide in males. In females, the rate of suicide has also fallen in all age groups, with an especially marked decrease in the older age groups.

The difference between these rates can be explained in various ways. Schmidtke et al. (1996) suggested the lower suicide rate in females is misleading since men have a higher rate of completed suicide, whereas women have a higher rate of attempted suicide. This suggestion is underlined by Mann (2002), who observed that

> men tend to use means that are more lethal, plan the suicide attempt more carefully, and avoid detection. In contrast women tend to use less lethal means of suicide, which carry a higher chance of survival, and they more commonly express an appeal for help by conducting the attempt in a manner that favours discovery and rescue.

The preferred choice of method could be influenced by gender differences in the occurrence of impulsive–aggressive personality traits, a potentially important risk factor for suicide (Dumais et al., 2005).

The shift towards a younger high-risk age group has been observed on a global scale. According to the WHO, in 1950, 60% of suicides occurred in persons aged 45 years and over. By 1998, this proportion had fallen to 45%. Several explanations have been put forward for this new high-risk age group, including increases in male unemployment, increases in the number of divorced men who had not remarried, increases in the rate of substance

Table 1.2 Suicide rates for UK: by age and sex (per 100,000)

	1971	1981	1991	2001	2007
Males					
15–24	6.8	10.8	15.8	14.7	10.6
25–44	13.6	19.6	24.8	23.3	21.1
45–64	19.7	23.0	20.4	19.0	17.5
65 and over	24.9	24.1	18.7	15.4	12.3
Females					
15–24	3.2	3.4	3.9	3.6	2.6
25–44	7.7	7.9	5.9	6.2	5.0
45–64	15.7	14.9	8.3	6.7	6.5
65 and over	16.5	15.7	8.5	5.5	4.7

(Source: Office for National Statistics; General Register Office for Scotland; Northern Ireland Statistics and Research Agency)

misuse and alcohol consumption, and the changing role of women to becoming more independent, more likely to be lone-mothers and preferring to get married older (Pritchard, 1992; McClure, 2000). All of these factors may have consequential effects on the mental health of young men and the rate of suicide.

1.2.2. Unemployment

- Suicide is related to unemployment, especially for younger age groups.
- Being unemployed is associated with an eight-fold increase in suicide risk compared to full or part-time employment.
- The increased risk associated with unemployment may reflect an important relationship between poor social integration and suicide.

In Great Britain, male suicide rates increased during economic recession but the opposite occurred in females (Crombie, 1989; Charlton, et al., 1992). This increase was in line with most other European Community countries (Pritchard, 1992). To examine the association between unemployment and suicide over a period spanning 'the two great economic recessions' of the last century, Gunnell et al. (1999) identified all suicides, in 15–44 year old men and women, between 1921 and 1995. A time-series analysis of this data identified an association between suicide and unemployment in males and females aged 15–44 years. The association was observed to be most highly significant in the younger age bands for both males (15–24 years: coeff. 0.20, 95%CI 0.05–0.35, $p = 0.011$; 25–34 years: coeff. 0.18, 95%CI 0.08–0.28, $p = 0.001$) and females (15–24 years: coeff. 0.46, 95%CI 0.18–0.73, $p = 0.002$). However, Gunnell et al. (1999) highlight the ecological fallacy that the association found for population data cannot be used to imply that individuals who complete suicide are themselves unemployed.

In another study of suicide and employment, Hawton et al. (2001) examined all suicides aged 15 years and over in the Oxfordshire area, between 1985 and 1995. A significant association was found between male suicide rates and a measure of socio-economic deprivation, which included the proportion of unemployed persons, although this effect was attenuated when controlling for a measure of social fragmentation, which included population turnover and the proportion of unmarried persons.

Finally, Duberstein et al. (2004) reported on a case-control study of the association between suicide and social integration among those aged over 50 years. The study identified 137 suicides in two counties within the state of New York, USA, between December 1996 and January 2001. Adopting a psychological autopsy approach, the authors interviewed informants for almost two-thirds of the suicides (86, 63%) along with informants for a group of randomly selected controls matched to cases on age, gender, race and county of residence. In terms of employment status, Duberstein et al. (2004) found the risk of suicide associated with being unemployed was more than eight times that of those in full or part-time employment (OR = 8.27, 95%CI 2.90–31.61).

In summary, there appears to be support for unemployment as a risk factor for suicide. However, whether unemployment is a cause of suicide, per se, or more of an indicator of lower social integration remains to be shown.

1.2.3. Marital status

- Married people are less likely to die from suicide than single, divorced, separated and widowed persons.

- For women, being a parent of a young child may actually be the protective factor, rather than being married per se.
- Being widowed at a younger age elevates a person's suicide risk, more so than at an older age, as it is viewed as an 'off-time' event with greater personal adjustment required.

Another demographic factor frequently cited as linked to suicide is that of marital status, with married persons experiencing lower suicide rates than single, divorced, separated and widowed persons. The relationship between suicide and marital status has been found across various populations, including the UK (ONS, 2010), the USA (Kessler, Borges & Walters, 1999; Kposowa, 2000), Finland (Heikkinen et al., 1995) and Denmark (Qin et al., 2000). However, there may be subtle gender differences within this relationship, since being a parent of a young child appears to explain the apparent protective effect of marriage for women rather than married status, per se (Hawton, 2000; Duberstein et al., 2004). Why such differences occur between divorced men and divorced women has attracted some theoretical interest. It may be that marriage confers health advantages that divorced persons lack. Perhaps marriage offers security and social support, and as a result, the married may be happier than the divorced (Verbrugge, 1979).

Durkheim (1897) explained the relationship between marriage and suicide using the concept of social integration, referring to 'the strength of the person's ties to society and the stability of social relations within that society, marriage being one of them'. Consequently, when a marriage ends, a sudden and unexpected change occurs in a person's social standing. The divorced or widowed person no longer feels a sense of cohesiveness and support as was once provided by married life. A consequence of this loss is an increased risk of suicide. The increased risk of suicide among divorced and widowed people may also be related to the new circumstances associated with a change in marital status, e.g. loss of integrative family unit following a divorce, and bereavement in widowhood.

One criticism of Durkheim's theory is that it does not explain the differences observed between the suicides rates of divorced men compared to divorced women. Kposowa (2000) suggested that women tend to form a much broader and stronger support network of friends and confidants. Therefore, should the woman's marriage break down, they have a greater source of emotional and social support to draw from in a time of need. It may be that men form less meaningful and fruitful supportive social bonds and networks, such that, if his marriage ends, a man has fewer people to turn to for support.

The protective effects of marriage have been found to more pronounced for younger age groups (Luoma & Pearson, 2002). At younger ages, being widowed, as compared with being divorced, was associated with a higher risk of suicide. At older ages, however, this pattern reversed, with divorce associated with higher suicide rates rather than widowhood. The point at which this pattern reversed appeared to occur at around 50 years of age. The differential effect of marriage could be explained from a life course perspective, where being widowed has very different meanings and effects at different points in a person's life course.

> When a younger person loses a spouse, it is considered an 'off-time' event, and the personal adjustment following the loss is more difficult than for older groups. . . . In contrast, loss of a spouse may, for an older person, be expected and considered 'on time', resulting in a relatively easier adjustment.
>
> (Luoma & Pearson, 2002)

So it seems that married persons are less likely to complete suicide than those who remain single or who have been widowed. Indeed, such a notion has been a longstanding tenet in the sociological literature on suicide (Durkheim, 1897). This notion has since been empirically examined and confirmed in many studies. From the empirical and sociological literature, we can conclude that people who become more socially integrated within their community, by being married and having children, are offered a greater number of reasons to live and therefore a reduced likelihood of suicide.

1.3. Suicide and mental health problems

- Having a mental health problem makes a greater contribution to a person's risk of suicide than any social factor.
- Nine out of every 10 suicides will have experienced a diagnosable mental health problem at some time in their life.
- The risk of suicide is particularly high for depression, psychosis and substance use disorders.

While certain socio-economic factors, such as unemployment and marital status, have been shown to have strong associations with an increased risk of suicidal behaviour, perhaps the most important risk factor is the presence of mental health problems. Mortensen et al. (2000) conducted a population-based nested case control study using national registers of data collected on a random 5% sample of the population in Denmark, aged 16–78 years between 1980 and 1994. In total, 811 suicides were identified and a random sample of 79,871 living controls. When adjusted for age and sex only, Mortensen et al. (2000) reported an increased risk of completing suicide in people who were single, unemployed or in the lower income bracket. However, perhaps the more interesting finding came from a second regression model that included all variables: age, sex, employment status, education, marital and familial status, income bracket as well as psychiatric admission and any diagnosable mental illness, with each variable adjusted for each other's effects. In the second analysis, the effect of most of the socio-economic risk factors was decreased, eliminated or even reversed. From the results of this latter model, Mortensen et al. (2000) argued that 'studies of socio-economic risk factors of suicide that do not take the distribution of mental disorders into account are likely to yield confounded results where the effects of these risk factors will tend to be over-estimated'.

Qin, Agerbo & Mortensen (2003) conducted a much larger study using data sourced from the same national databases in Denmark and repeated similar analyses using the same variables, with 21,169 persons who completed suicide and 423,128 living controls. Family histories of suicide or psychiatric admission were also added to the analysis in order to investigate the phenomenon of suicidal behaviour clustering in families. Similar results were observed, with 40% (95%CI = 39.7–41.0) of suicides associated with a previous psychiatric admission, 26% (24.6–26.9) with being single, and 9% (8.4–9.2) with the lowest income bracket.

In addition to the 'group-level' approach to investigating suicide, a more 'individual-level' approach has been frequently adopted in order to ascertain the personal meaning and reasons behind the suicidal act. The obvious obstacle to gaining this understanding is that the victim cannot be interviewed. The *psychological autopsy method* proposes to overcome this obstacle (Schneidman, 1981). This method aims to collect and collate sufficient information about the person and the circumstances of their death in order to piece together as full and accurate a picture of the deceased as possible, along with an understanding of the reasons for the suicide. Such information is usually collected from interviews with the family members and friends closest to the deceased, from hospital and general practice case notes, social work reports, inquest files and other criminal and legal records.

In a landmark study of suicide and mental illness, Barraclough et al. (1974) reported on 100 cases of suicide recorded by coroners in the counties of West Sussex and Portsmouth, during 1966, 1967 and 1968. Psychological autopsy techniques were employed including interviews with key informants, 83% of whom were first relatives of the deceased. Interviews were also conducted with expert witnesses such as pathologists, pharmacists and social workers, where relevant, with an average of 4.5 interviews for each suicide case. Supporting evidence was collated from psychiatric hospital notes, medical records and post mortem reports. A control group was also identified, matched to the cases on age, sex and marital status.

Ninety-three out of 100 suicides were diagnosed with a psychiatric disorder, including 70 who received a diagnosis of a depressive illness, 15 alcohol dependence and 3 schizophrenia. Most suicides were in contact with medical services (80%), receiving psychotropic medication (80%), and had given some form of warning of their suicidal thinking (55%).

Since the publication of this study, other cultural, social-economic and environmental factors have become recognised as important variables that should now be included in any examination of risk factors for suicide, e.g. employment status, recent life events. However, the strong association between suicide and mental illness reported by Barraclough et al. (1974) has since been replicated by subsequent studies.

Cavanagh et al. (2003) reviewed 75 psychological autopsy studies, which included 53 case series reports and 22 case control studies. In the case series reports, the median proportion of cases with any mental illness was 91% (95%CI = 81–98%), with the majority of cases of mental illness having a depressive disorder (median = 59%, 95%CI = 45–70%). In the case-control studies, the proportion with mental illness was 90% (88–95%) in cases and 27% (14–48%) in controls. The reviewers also quantified the impact of mental disorder on rates of suicide, reporting that between 47% and 74% of the suicides examined were attributable to mental disorder, leading to the conclusion that between half and three-quarters of suicides could be prevented if adequate and effective treatment of mental illness could be made available. Although these findings are based only on younger age groups, if we assume that the importance of mental illness in suicide increases with age (Conwell et al., 1996) then these proportions would represent underestimates of the true fractions.

Harris & Barraclough (1997) conducted a meta-analysis of the many follow-up mortality studies of mental disorders determining the associated standardised mortality ratios (SMRs) for each disorder. A total of 249 papers fulfilled the stringent inclusion criteria for the analysis. Reporting on 44 mental disorders, 36 were found to have a significantly raised SMR for suicide. Suicide was found to be significantly related to a number of mental disorders with suicide risks for major depression, schizophrenia and substance use disorders were 20, 8 and 6 times that expected, respectively.

1.3.1. Depression

- Between 6 and 9 of every 10 suicides has a depressive disorder.
- Depression is a necessary but not sufficient condition for suicide.
- Although 1 in 10 people experiencing depression complete suicide, it remains difficult to identify those that attempt suicide from those that do not.

While between 60% and 90% of completed suicides had a depressive disorder at the time of death, Wulsin et al. (1999) reviewed 35 studies that reported rates of suicide in people with depression, and found a mean of approximately 10% rising to 16% when considering psychiatric patients alone. Therefore, it appears that depression could be a necessary but not sufficient condition for suicide. This point raises the clinically important questions of 'which persons with a depressive disorder are more likely to complete suicide?' or 'how can we identify those 10% of depressed persons who are most likely to kill themselves?'

Mann and colleagues (1999) conducted a nested case-control study of patients, aged 14–72 years, who were admitted to a university psychiatric hospital in the USA. Psychiatric diagnoses were made, where applicable, and a number of observer and self-rated measures of psychopathology were completed. The sample of 347 patients was split into two groups according to their history of previous suicide attempts. A total of 184 (53%) had made a previous suicide attempt, of which 118 (64%) had made multiple attempts. Attempters and non-attempters only differed on the *subjective* ratings of depression, hopelessness and severity of suicidal ideation. The *objective* measures of symptoms did not distinguish the patient groups. Such a finding has important implications for the clinician's intuitive use and, perhaps, reliance on observer-rated measures of psychiatric symptoms as an indicator of suicide risk.

1.3.2. Psychosis

• Suicide is the main cause of premature death among individuals experiencing psychosis.
• Four in ten people experiencing psychosis report suicidal thoughts, at least two in ten attempt suicide, and one in ten die from suicide.
• The 'revolving-door' pattern of frequent psychiatric admissions increases suicide risk.
• Suicide risk is doubled during the first week following discharge from hospital.

Psychoses, such as schizophrenia, are relatively common mental disorders, affecting around 15 persons per 1000 of the general population (Kendell & Zealley, 1993). Suicide remains the main cause of premature death among individuals experiencing a psychosis. Approximately 40% of patients diagnosed with schizophrenia report suicidal ideation, 20 to 40% make at least one suicide attempt during the illness phase and 5 to 13% end their lives by suicide (Barraclough et al., 1974; Caldwell & Gottesman, 1992, Meltzer & Fatemi, 1995; Harris & Barraclough, 1997; Palmer, Pankratz & Bostwick, 2005). De Hert & Peuskens (2000) highlighted that patients with schizophrenia who complete suicide share many of the general risk factors common for all suicidal patients, including single males, living alone with a family history of suicide and previous suicide attempts.

In an extensive review of previous studies of suicide in schizophrenia, Caldwell & Gottesman (1992) proposed three different categories of risk factors for suicide in schizophrenic patients:

1. Common risk factors for suicide in general and schizophrenia populations, including male, white, socially isolated.
2. Personal risk factors for suicide in general and schizophrenia populations, including depressed, sense of hopelessness, history of suicide attempts, familial history of suicide, recent loss.

3.   Specific risk factors for suicide in schizophrenia populations, including chronic illness, numerous episodes, high level of psychopathology, functional impairment, expectation of deteriorating illness, history of psychiatric admissions.

Rossau & Mortensen (1997) conducted a nested case-control study of psychiatric in-patients to identify specific risk factors for suicide in patients with schizophrenia. The authors expressed a particular interest in those factors related to the patient's course of hospitalisation and to investigate when the patient would be more amenable to intervention. This large record-linkage study identified subjects from the Danish Psychiatric Case Register between April 1970 and December 1987 with a diagnosis of schizophrenia. Cases (n = 505) for the study would also be found on the Danish Register of Death Certificates. Ten live controls per case were selected, matched to cases as having schizophrenia at the suicide's date of death. In agreement with the proposed risk factors from Caldwell & Gottesman (1992), the general risk factors for suicide from this study were found to include depressed males with a history of suicide attempts. More specific to suicide in schizophrenia, the study identified an increased risk during the first six months after first admission compared to subsequent admissions. Furthermore, patients who had more admissions in a year were much more likely to complete suicide. The study reported patients with more than 8 admissions had an 11-fold risk over patients who had not been admitted during the year. The authors conclude that the revolving-door pattern of admissions increased the suicide risk considerably.

The study also observed the risk of suicide during the first 5 days after discharge from hospital to be double the risk during the first 5 days after admission. They also found that patients who have endured schizophrenia for a greater time were significantly less likely to complete suicide than those who were within their first year of diagnosis. This suggests a period of acclimatisation following diagnosis with a 'coming-to-terms' with the effects of the illness and hospitalisation and developing appropriate coping strategies.

1.3.3. Psychosis and depression

• Depressive symptoms are a major risk factor for suicide in psychosis.
• Subjective feelings of depression are a better predictor of suicidal behaviour in psychosis than a prior diagnosis of a depressive disorder.

Depressive symptoms have consistently been identified as a major risk factor for suicide in psychosis, with a multitude of studies confirming this association over the past 40 years (Warnes, 1968; Roy, 1982; Heila et al., 1997; Walsh et al, 2001). These studies have characterised the high-risk individual as a young man in the early stages of a psychosis with frequent episodes and relapses, and with several admissions to psychiatric wards. However, it could easily be argued that since so many people fit this description, it is of little help to clinicians attempting to target care and supervision where most needed.

Heila et al. (1997) conducted a nationwide psychological autopsy study of suicide victims with schizophrenia in the general population in Finland, between April 1987 and March 1988. During this time, 1397 suicides occurred and, for each person who completed suicide, interviews were held with a next-of-kin informant, a healthcare professional and the individual's last health or social care contact. Based on information provided to the study, 92 (7%) individuals were retrospectively diagnosed with schizophrenia.

Perhaps the most interesting and clinically useful findings came from the analysis of co-morbid symptoms and disorders. Depressive symptoms were found to be highly prevalent immediately before suicide (64%), a history of suicide attempts was very common (71%), and alcohol abuse or dependence was reported in over a fifth of suicide victims (21%). However, the prevalence of these three risk factors varied according to age and sex, with young and old men suffering more often with depressive symptoms and middle-aged men more likely to abuse alcohol. Conversely, depressive symptoms were more likely to be found in young and middle-aged women than among older women.

In a similar study, Harkary-Friedman et al. (1999) compared the demographic and clinical characteristics of 52 individuals diagnosed with schizophrenia or schizo-affective disorder who had attempted suicide with those of 104 individuals diagnosed with similar disorders who had not attempted suicide. Those attempting suicide did not differ from the non-attempters with respect to a history of major depression, although the most frequent reason for a suicide attempt was that the person felt depressed (32%). Furthermore, suicidal ideation during a current depressive episode occurred twice as often in the suicide attempters than in the non-attempters. The authors concluded that, while a prior history of depression did not differentiate the groups, current feelings of depression were more likely to increase the risk of suicidal behaviour in those that had previously attempted suicide.

In conclusion, if we return to Caldwell & Gottesman's (1992) category of specific risk factors for suicide in schizophrenic populations, we have seen evidence of increased risk during the first six months after first admission and also the 'revolving-door' pattern of admissions and its propensity to increase the likelihood of suicide (Rossau & Mortensen, 1997). In addition to hospitalisation risk factors, we have also seen that subjective reports of depression were found to be highly prevalent immediately before suicide (Heila et al., 1997; Harkary-Freidman, et al., 1999).

1.3.4. Post-Traumatic Stress Disorder

- Individuals diagnosed with PTSD are 3 times more likely to think about or attempt suicide than those without PTSD.
- Completed suicide rates for individuals diagnosed with PTSD are 10 times higher than for those without PTSD.

Post-Traumatic Stress Disorder (PTSD) is commonly conceptualised as an anxiety disorder with an inherent requirement of exposure to a traumatic event that is perceived as highly threatening or intensely distressing. The event initiates a response characterised by fear and traumatic memories. Whether PTSD emerges or not depends on the individual's ability to modify this fear response. Estimates from general population samples indicate that PTSD is a common disorder, with a lifetime prevalence ranging from 7% to 12% and the incidence of the disorder being twice as common among women as men (Breslau, Kessler, Chilcoat, Schultz, Davis & Andreski, 1998; Kessler, Sonnega, Bromet, Hughes & Nelson, 1995; Panagiati et al., 2009; Seedat & Stein, 2001).

A strong connection has repeatedly been demonstrated between suicide-related thoughts and behaviour and PTSD, across various types of trauma and samples (Panagiati et al., 2009). In a nationally representative, cross-sectional psychiatric survey conducted in the USA, individuals diagnosed with PTSD were almost three times more likely to report suicidal ideation (OR = 2.8, 95%CI 2.0–3.8) or to attempt suicide (OR = 2.7, 95%CI 1.8–3.9) (Sareen,

Houlahan, Cox & Asmundson, 2005). Similarly, in a study examining suicidal behaviour after severe trauma, Ferrada-Noli et al. (1998) found 57% of participants diagnosed with PTSD reported suicidal behaviour compared with 29% of participants with other psychiatric diagnoses (e.g. depressive disorders, anxiety disorders, personality disorders).

To examine the association between PTSD and completed suicide, Gradus and colleagues (2010) conducted a large record-linkage study with data obtained from the nationwide Danish health and administrative registries for all completed suicides between 1994 and 2006. Controls were selected from a sample of all Danish residents, matched to cases on gender, date of birth and time. Of the 9612 suicides, 38 (0.4%) were diagnosed with PTSD compared to 95 (0.05%) of the 199,306 controls. This study found the rate of completed suicide for individuals increased 10-fold in the presence of a diagnosis of PTSD (OR = 9.8, 95%CI 6.7–15). This elevated suicide risk remained after controlling for psychiatric and demographic confounders (OR = 5.3, 95%CI 3.4–8.1). The authors concluded that a diagnosis of PTSD should be seen as a risk factor for completed suicide.

1.3.5. Psychosis and PTSD

- Between 1 and 4 in 10 people experiencing psychosis also report PTSD symptoms.
- People diagnosed with PTSD are at a greater risk of suicide if they also experience positive psychotic symptoms.
- Similarly, people experiencing psychosis with co-morbid PTSD are at a greater risk of suicide than those without PTSD.
- The combination of psychosis and traumatic stress/PTSD compounds a person's risk of suicidal behaviour.

Since suicidal ideation and behaviour has been found to be significantly, but separately, associated with both psychosis and PTSD, a growing number of studies have investigated how the elevated risk of suicidality in people experiencing psychosis may be further compounded by the effects of traumatisation and co-morbid PTSD.

Estimates of co-morbid PTSD in individuals experiencing psychosis range from 10% (Neria, Bromet, Sievers, Lavelle & Fochtmann, 2002) to 38% (Tarrier, Khan, Cater & Picken, 2007), which exceeds the lifetime prevalence of PTSD in the general population of approximately 6% to 8% (Breslau et al., 1998; Frans et al., 2005).

With PTSD as the primary diagnosis, Sareen, Cox, Goodwin & Asmundson (2005) examined the relationship between PTSD and positive psychotic symptoms, and their effects on suicidal ideation and behaviour. Individuals diagnosed with PTSD and co-morbid positive psychotic symptoms were significantly more likely to report lifetime suicidal ideation (OR = 1.67, 95%CI 1.12–2.49) and lifetime suicide attempts (OR = 2.10, 95%CI 1.23–3.57). However, after adjusting for socio-demographics, mental disorders and general medical co-morbidity, these associations became non-significant.

Strauss and colleagues (2006) reported on a study of 165 male veterans whose primary diagnoses were schizophrenia or schizo-affective disorders. The authors found individuals with co-morbid PTSD were significantly more likely to report suicidal ideation than those without PTSD (68.0% versus 33.3%, 95%CI 20–49%, p < 0.0001). The incidence of suicide attempts was also increased among individuals with co-morbid PTSD, but this result failed to achieve statistical significance (14.1% versus 5.8%, 95%CI–1–18%, p = 0.07).

In a sample of 35 patients hospitalised for their first episode of non-organic psychosis, Tarrier, Khan, Cater & Picken (2007) identified 58% of those participants who met caseness for PTSD were suicidal compared to 35% of those who did not meet caseness, although this difference was not significant. However, suicidal behaviour was found to be significantly associated with the experience of prior trauma (chi^2 = 4.88, df = 1, p = 0.036), but not the severity of that trauma.

In another recent study from this group, Tarrier & Picken (2010) found individuals with co-morbid PTSD reported significantly more suicidal ideation and behaviour than those without co-morbid PTSD (median = 6 versus median = 2; U = 673, p < 0.01). A mediational analysis was conducted to analyse the effect of hopelessness, a known predictor of suicidality, on the relationship between traumatic stress and suicidal behaviour. This analysis identified a highly significant relationship between traumatic stress and suicidality; however, when the effect of hopelessness was controlled for, the relationship was no longer significant. Therefore, the impact of traumatic stress on suicidality was mediated by hopelessness.

In conclusion, although the existing literature on the impact of PTSD plus psychosis in suicidal behaviour is limited, findings from initial studies suggest that among individuals experiencing psychosis, co-morbid traumatic stress and/or PTSD appears to further elevate the risk for suicide.

1.3.6. Alcohol misuse

- Alcohol consumption is positively related to suicide mortality.
- This relationship is influenced by the drinking culture of a country, with drier cultures at greater risk than wetter cultures, due to a lack of alcohol tolerance.
- Alcohol use disorder elevates an individual's risk of suicide.

High levels of alcohol consumption in a population is proposed to lead to higher numbers of alcoholics and abusers with consequential negative effects on social integration and an increased risk of suicide. Skog (1991) also argued that an acute state of intoxification may reduce self-control and increase impulsivity, which leads to increased likelihood of suicidal behaviour. In order to test this hypothesis, Caces & Harford (1998) conducted a time series analysis of data on alcohol consumption and suicide mortality in the USA, from 1934 to 1987. The study also included possible confounders such as unemployment, income and divorce rates, and explored any age- or gender-specific effects. Alcohol consumption was shown to steadily rise after the Second World War from around 11 litres of ethanol per person per year in 1940 through to almost 15 litres per person per year by 1985. The overall suicide mortality rate also appeared to increase after 1945, and the study identified a significant, positive relationship between alcohol consumption and suicide mortality. Caces & Harford (1998) also found that suicide rates in the young were increasing; in middle age rates stabilised and then decreased; and in the elderly rates generally declined.

In Europe, it is recognised that there is great cultural variation in the pattern of alcohol use. Norström (1995) suggested that the association between alcohol consumption and suicide would be stronger in 'dry' drinking cultures than in 'wet' drinking cultures. Dry cultures were typified by Nordic countries with low average consumption per capita, heavy binge drinking at weekends and a restrictive alcohol control policy. Wet cultures were typified by Mediterranean countries with a high general level of drinking distributed evenly throughout the week with few, if any, restrictions on the availability of alcohol. Norström (1995) also recognised individual as well as cultural factors involved in the relationship between alcohol and suicide. While it could be expected for each country to have similar proportions of individuals with a predisposition to become heavy drinkers, Norström (1995) argued that people in dry cultures would experience substantially less exposure to alcohol than those in wet cultures. Consequently, an individual with a weak predisposition for alcoholism may well become a heavy drinker if he lives in a wet culture, while a person with a strong individual predisposition may not in a dry culture. Therefore, Norström (1995) hypothesised that there is likely to be a greater overlap between alcohol abusers and those at risk of suicide in dry compared to wet drinking cultures.

In order to test this hypothesis, Ramstedt (2001) conducted a time series analysis of alcohol consumption and suicide mortality data in 14 Western European countries, between 1950 and 1995. To obtain reliable estimates of alcohol consumption from regions that were assumed to represent similar drinking cultures, the countries were divided into three groups according to alcohol consumption figures. The 'low-consumption' group comprised of Finland, Norway and Sweden; the 'medium-consumption' group of Austria, Belgium, Denmark, Ireland, the Netherlands, the UK and West Germany; and the 'high-consumption' group of France, Italy, Portugal and Spain. The time series models of association revealed a positive and significant relationship between per capita alcohol consumption and suicide rates in the low-consumption region of Northern Europe (men: pooled estimate = 0.086, $p < 0.001$, women: pooled estimate = 0.114, $p < 0.001$). In the high-consumption region of Southern Europe, this relationship was weak and non-significant (men: pooled estimate = –0.006, p = ns, women: pooled estimate = 0.005, p = ns). Ramstedt (2001) supported the hypothesis that the suicide rate tends to be more responsive to changes in per capita alcohol consumption in dry drinking cultures than in wet. An increase in alcohol consumption of 1 litre per person increased the suicide rate by 2–7% for France, 2–5% for Denmark, 2% for Portuguese men and 5% for Finland, thus indicating a strong and consistent link between alcoholism and suicide.

McCloud et al. (2004) reported on the prevalence of alcohol use disorder in a psychiatric in-patient sample and its association with suicidality. Almost 200 in-patients consented to take part in the study, which required them to complete a lifestyle survey of demographic, quality of life, smoking, alcohol and substance use questions. Of the 199 persons in the study, 105 (53%) were men, with no significant age differences between men and women. Suicidality was indicated if a patient's case notes contained references to self-harm, thoughts or plans of self-harm or suicide (n = 104). Hazardous or harmful alcohol use was found to be strongly related to suicidality, and suicidality was also found to be associated with illicit drug use in the previous 30 days, especially so for women.

1.3.7. Personality disorder

- Three in ten suicides have a diagnosable personality disorder.
- Personality disorder is associated with a 10-fold increase in suicide risk.
- Emotionally Unstable/Borderline Personality Disorder have the highest suicide rates.
- As in psychosis, feelings of depression immediately precede episodes of suicidal behaviour.

Barraclough et al. (1974) described 100 completed suicides who were retrospectively diagnosed with psychiatric disorders based on key informant interviews and medico-legal records. Of the 100 completed suicides, 27 were classified as having an 'abnormal personality', which suggests personality factors may play a key part in suicide. While the definitions of personality disorders have changed during the past 30–40 years, an estimated prevalence of personality disorder in the general population of 10–15% (Hawton & Van Heeringen, 2000) does raise the important question of how personality disorder could be related to suicidal risk. In a more recent meta-analysis of suicide as an outcome for various psychiatric disorders, Harris & Barraclough (1997) reported on five studies of psychiatric in-patients diagnosed with personality disorder, some followed for up to 14 years. When combined, the population of over 3000 in-patients gave a suicidal risk seven times that expected.

Foster et al. (1999) conducted a case-control psychological autopsy study comparing suicides with controls matched on age, gender and marital status. Interviews were conducted with the bereaved informants of 117 completed suicides and their GP and mental health professional, where relevant. Also, information was obtained from GP files, psychiatric and general hospital records and coroners' inquest files. Similar interviews and information sources were analysed from the control subjects. This study identified cases that were 15 times more likely than controls to have at least one diagnosable Axis II disorder.

Cheng, Mann & Chan (1997) also investigated the association between personality disorder and suicide in a psychological autopsy study of all consecutive suicides from three ethnic groups in Taiwan, between July 1989 and December 1991. Of the 113 suicides, 70 (62%) were diagnosed with a personality disorder, compared to 53 (24%) of the 226 matched controls. There was a positive relationship between the presence of traits suggestive of personality disorder and risk of suicide, since individuals diagnosed with more than one personality disorder were eight times more likely to complete suicide than those with one personality disorder.

In a more recent report of this sample, Cheng et al. (2000) reanalysed the data including a number of psychosocial risk factors for suicide: marital status, unemployment status, early parental deprivation, concurrent physical morbidity, history of suicidal behaviour and life events in last 12 months. Even after adjustment for all these known risk factors for suicide, a diagnosis of emotionally unstable personality disorder was four times more likely among suicide victims. Other significant risk factors also identified from this analysis included major depressive episode, a loss of health, a person, a cherished idea, employment and/or material possessions, and suicidal behaviour in first-degree relatives. It would appear that psychosocial risk factors may act as a concomitant or as a consequential factor.

Yen at al. (2003) suggested an alternative means of investigating the predictive utility of psychiatric disorders. In a multi-site, naturalistic, prospective study, comparisons were made between four different personality disorder groups – schizotypal, borderline, avoidant and obsessive-compulsive – and group participants with major depressive disorder without any personality disorder. In total, 668 subjects were interviewed at baseline, 6 months, 1 year and 2 year follow-ups. At each follow-up assessment, the longitudinal course of psychiatric disorders and functioning including suicidal behaviours was assessed, in order to identify specific changes in the course of a disorder prior to a suicidal event.

At baseline assessment, 621 participants had at least 1 year of follow-up data, with the following personality disorder diagnoses: 304 (49%) avoidant, 248 (40%) obsessive-compulsive, 220 (35%) borderline and 92 (15%) schizotypal. A total of 287 (46%) met criteria for major depressive disorder. Almost a third (31%) of participants were diagnosed with more than one disorder. Of the 621 participants, 58 (9%) made at least one suicide attempt, and women were significantly more likely to make an attempt than men. A total of 45 (78%) of the suicide attempters met criteria for borderline, 31 (53%) for avoidant, 14 (24%) for obsessive-compulsive and 6 (10%) for schizotypal.

In order to better understand the effect of a distressing Axis I disorder on the risk of suicide, a proportional hazards regressions analysis was conducted using weekly Psychiatric Status Ratings (PSRs) for each Axis I disorder present at baseline diagnosis. PSRs ranged from PSR6 (full criteria/severe symptoms) to PSR1 (full remission/no symptoms). For each of the 58 participants who had attempted suicide in the follow-up period, average proportions of PSRs at each of the six levels were calculated for the 12 months before and after the attempt. Figure 1.4 depicts PSR changes of major depressive disorder relative to the month of the suicide attempt (month 0).

We can see from this group average data that symptoms of major depressive disorder appear to worsen several months prior to the suicide attempt, with a sharp deterioration immediately prior to the attempt. There then appears to be an immediate improvement in depressive symptoms, which continues for at least six months. The pattern of deterioration prior to suicide attempt and improvement following the attempt was also observed in the PSR scores for alcohol use disorder and drug use disorder. The PSR ratings for all three of these Axis I disorders observed near the time of the suicide attempt were significantly different from the general level of changes in all other months. Therefore, it would appear that proximate changes in the course of an Axis I disorder may have important predictive utility (Yen et al., 2003).

In summary, individuals with a diagnosable personality disorder are at 10-fold increased risk of suicide (Foster et al., 1999; Barraclough et al., 1974). Furthermore, certain types of personality disorder have higher suicide rates than others, notably emotionally unstable and borderline personality disorders (Cheng et al., 2000). Specifically, individuals with pronounced impulsivity traits are more vulnerable for suicidal attempts in response to negative life events and stress (Mann et al., 1999; Cheng et al., 2000). With respect to Axis I and Axis II co-morbidity and its prevalence in patients completing suicide, we have seen how the suicide risk in the presence of at least one Axis II disorder remains significantly high, even after the adjustment of Axis I disorders (Foster et al., 1999).

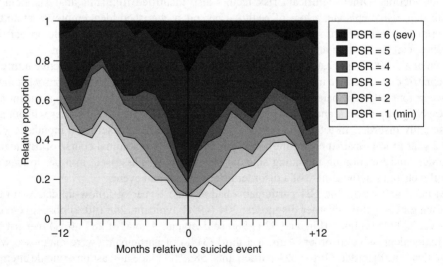

Figure 1.4 Major depressive disorder psychiatric status rating (PSR) scores from PSR 1 (minimal) to PSR 6 (severe) in relation to month of suicide attempt (Source: Yen et al., 2003)

Despite this literature on suicide and personality disorder, as already discussed with suicide and depression, the base rates of suicide are relatively low compared to the base rates of Axis I and Axis II disorders. Therefore, diagnoses alone are of limited use when attempting to identify the individuals most likely to attempt suicide. One solution to this dilemma can be seen within the study by Yen et al. (2003), who identified measurable changes in individuals' symptomatology in the periods leading up to and following a suicide attempt. This approach could help to assist timely interventions for those persons who are already at increased risk of suicide identified via a diagnosis of personality disorder.

1.3.8. Co-morbidity

- Half of suicides have two or more diagnosable mental health problems.
- Experiencing two mental health problems elevates a person's suicide risk 90-fold.
- The most common co-morbid problems include depression, substance use and personality disorder.

It is possible that some of the association between mental disorders and suicidal behaviour is due to the co-morbidity of certain disorders with other disorders that, independently, contribute to suicidal behaviour.

(Beautrais et al., 1996)

In order to investigate the prevalence and co-morbidity of mental disorders among completed suicides, Henriksson et al. (1993) used data from a nationwide suicide prevention project. In this study, 229 subjects were randomly selected from the project's total sample (n = 1397) of all suicides in Finland between April 1987 and March 1988. Using psychological autopsy techniques, mental health professionals conducted interviews with family members, close friends and healthcare professionals of the deceased. Other information was collected from medical, social agency and police records. Retrospective diagnostic evaluations were conducted by psychiatrists.

In keeping with other studies, Henriksson et al. (1993) reported that 93% of the individuals completing suicide received at least one Axis I diagnosis, most commonly depressive disorders (59%) and alcohol dependence (43%). The study also found that 44% of the completed suicides had two or more diagnoses, with co-morbidity more common among males than females. Among the 71 completed suicides with a primary diagnosis of major depression, 20 (28%) also had alcohol abuse/dependence, and 22 (31%) also had a personality disorder. Only 11 (15%) suicides with major depression were without any co-morbidity.

In another study investigating the prevalence and co-morbidity of mental disorders in suicidal behaviour, Beautrais et al. (1996) identified a consecutive series of 317 individuals who had attempted suicide and then presented for emergency hospital treatment, between September 1991 and May 1994, of which 302 (96%) agreed to take part in the study. A comparison group of 1028 participants was selected from electoral roles, stratified by age and gender to be representative of the population as a whole.

Beautrais et al. (1996) reported significantly higher rates of all mental disorders, except for non-affective psychosis, in the suicide attempters with an overall rate of psychopathology of 90%. Depressive disorders were present in 77%, substance/alcohol misuse disorders in 39% and anxiety disorders in 24% of suicide attempters. Personality disorders were also present in 31% of cases. Depressive disorders were most strongly related with suicidal risk for older subjects. Substance misuse disorders were associated with increased suicidal risk across all ages and both genders. Furthermore, elimination of depressive disorders was predicted to have led to an 80% reduction in the risk of a serious suicide attempt. In terms of comorbidity, cases with one mental disorder were 17 times more likely than cases with no disorder to have attempted suicide, and those with two mental disorders found to be 90 times more likely. These results highlight a very substantial elevation of suicide risk for individuals with two or more mental disorders.

1.4. Suicide and previous self-harm

*   A history of previous suicide attempts is one of the most important and clinically relevant risk factors.
*   Individuals who have previously harmed themselves are more than 30 times likely to kill themselves than the general population.
*   Although a significant risk factor, previous self-harm is absent in the majority of suicides, especially males.
*   Previous self-harm indicates an enduring risk of suicide that persists throughout an individual's entire life.

Within their meta-analysis of follow-up mortality studies of mental disorders, Harris & Barraclough (1997) identified nine studies from the USA, Sweden, England and Denmark reporting figures on previous attempted suicide as a risk factor for completed suicide. With a combined sample size of 2700 and a follow-up period of 20 years, these studies gave a suicide risk 38 times that expected; it was higher than the risk related to any specific psychiatric diagnosis. The sheer size of this finding has led many clinicians to consider a history of previous suicide attempts as one of the most important and clinically relevant determinants of suicide risk.

Cheng (1995) reported that 21% of suicides had previously attempted suicide according to the bereaved family's accounts, and Conwell et al. (1998) found 42% of suicides had a history of previous suicide attempts. So, it appears that while previous suicide attempts are not uncommon among suicide victims, such a history is absent in the majority of cases. In order to more fully investigate the relationship between completed suicide and previous attempted suicide, Isometsa & Lonnqvist (1998) used a database of 1397 suicides in Finland. The authors found it was not uncommon for completed suicides to have made a number of previous suicide attempts before finally achieving a fatal outcome, although males were significantly more likely to die at their first attempt than females. Also, females were found to make subsequent suicide attempts sooner than males, with 39% of female suicides making the fatal suicide attempt within a year of a preceding attempt, compared to 19% of male suicides.

In a systematic review of published follow-up data on repetition of self-harm, Owens, Horrocks & House (2002) reported that, of those patients attending a general hospital as a result of an episode of self-harm, approximately 2% will complete suicide within a year, and over 5% within nine years of the initial act of self-harm. So we can see that compared to a national rate of suicide of about 10 per 100,000 persons per year in the UK, individuals with a history of self-harm can be hundreds of times more at risk of suicide.

In order to assess how long this increased suicide risks persists, Suominen et al. (2004) reported on a long-term follow-up study of 100 consecutive self-poisoned patients in

Finland. The authors aimed to determine the rate of suicide among this cohort of patients who had previously attempted suicide. The follow-up period was from 1963 to 2000, during which time 54 of the 98 patients identifiable at the end of the follow-up period had died. Thirteen had completed suicide. Eight of the 13 suicides (62%) occurred at least 15 years after the suicide attempt, with mortality found to be significantly higher among the men. Consequently, Suominen et al. (2004) concluded that 'a history of a suicide attempt by self-poisoning appears to be an indicator of high risk for completed suicide throughout the entire adult lifetime' (p.563).

The important finding of a persistent and enduring risk of suicide among individuals with a history of self-harm is in accordance with findings found in a similar group within the UK. Jenkins et al. (2002) traced a consecutive sample of 223 patients for 22 years after they presented to a central London hospital following an episode of self-harm. Using data held by the Office for National Statistics, 140 (63%) patients could be traced, of whom death certificates revealed 3 suicides and 9 probable suicides (4 open verdicts and 5 accidental deaths). The rate of suicide throughout the follow-up period varied from zero to 680 per 100,000 persons per year. Perhaps most importantly, the authors found this suicide rate did not decline with time, thus underlining the persisting risk of suicide for people with a history of attempted suicide.

In one of the most recent investigations of the association between suicide and self-harm, Cooper et al. (2005) identified a cohort of 7968 patients who presented to one of the four emergency departments in Manchester and Salford following an episode of deliberate self-harm, between September 1997 and August 2001. For each patient a standard assessment form was completed, which included details of the self-harm episode, demographic and clinical data and information regarding the patient's mental state. Using mortality data provided by the National Confidential Inquiry into Suicide and Homicide by People with Mental Illness (Appleby et al., 2001), Cooper and colleagues identified that 60 of the 7968 subjects had subsequently completed suicide. Consistent with previous research, the number of suicides by people who had previously self-harmed was 34 times that expected in the general population, when matched on age and gender. The risk of suicide was 50 times higher than expected for females and 29 times higher than expected for males.

In summary, persons who have previously harmed themselves have been shown to be considerably more likely to kill themselves in the future, with studies reporting a risk of suicide more than 30 times higher than experienced by the general population. Female self-harmers were found to be at greatest risk. Furthermore, the increased risk of suicide associated with a history of self-harm has been shown to persist for several years after the self-harming episode; indeed, the risk may endure throughout the rest of the person's life.

Chapter 2

A theoretical approach to understanding suicide

2.1. Executive summary

- *Trying to treat suicidality by focusing on risk factors will be ineffective.*

- *Assuming that suicidality can be treated by treating the specific symptoms of a psychological disorder will be ineffective.*

- *Describing psychological characteristics of suicide will lack the depth to provide an understanding of suicide that can be translated into an effective clinical intervention.*

- *A psychological theory of suicide is needed in order to develop a mechanism of suicide and to understand the components of suicidal thoughts and behaviours.*

- *Once the mechanism is understood, then treatments can target the processes underlying the mechanism.*

- *Mechanisms based on biased information processing systems, the development of suicide schema and appraisal styles are likely to be fruitful in explaining suicidal thoughts and behaviours.*

2.2. Why do clinicians need a theory of suicide?

We need a theoretical approach to understanding suicide for four main reasons. First, as we have seen in the previous chapter, the risk-based approach to understanding suicide is simply not specific enough (Bolton, Gooding, Kapur, Barrowclough & Tarrier, 2007). It results in too many false positives. That is, people are identified as at risk of suicide when in fact they are not thinking of, or planning, suicide. Consequently treatment approaches based only on risk factors will be ineffective and inefficient.

A second and related reason is that that an epidemiological approach identifies factors that are hard to change. So, being male, being young, going through a divorce and having financial difficulties cannot be targeted by psychological therapies nor any other kind of intervention or treatment. One of the roles of the clinician is to facilitate helpful behaviour change. This means that risk factors, if they are to be countered, need to be formulated in terms of psychological appraisals. For example, if an individual has a chronic disease such as multiple sclerosis, the progression of this disease cannot be targeted by psychological therapies. However, the way in which an individual appraises this disease progression can be targeted.

The third reason leads on from this point. To be able to facilitate behaviour change, we need to have an idea of the psychological factors that underlie the unwanted behaviour, in this case suicidality. Once we have identified possible psychological factors that underlie suicidality, the next thing we need to do is use them to build a mechanism that can explain suicidal thoughts and behaviours. For instance, we have some evidence that (a) having a negative perception of the past, the present and especially the future (e.g. 'I'm just bad; I never do very well; things are going to get worse'); (b) feeling constantly stressed (e.g. 'I always feel stressed when I have to go out socially; I just can't cope'); and (c) having strong recollections of past failures ('I've never done well at anything, I always get it wrong') seem to be present in those who have suicidal thoughts and behaviours. From a clinical perspective we now need to know which of these factors manifests first because aspects of those factors may strengthen subsequent suicidal processes and need to be targeted immediately. It is plausible that negative attentional biases may be the first target of a psychological treatment (Tarrier & Gooding, 2007). This is because such information-processing biases affect what is encoded into memory and what is retrieved from memory. As a consequence, these biases affect reasoning processes that are critical to therapeutic success, such as making arbitrary inferences (e.g. 'my sister called today to say that she can't take me shopping. She doesn't care about me. I am unlovable'), failing to review numerous sources of evidence (e.g. 'I always fail at interviews' when in fact the individual does not fail 100%), and an inability to draw on previous 'successes' to solve current problems.

The fourth reason to develop a theory of suicidality is that the mechanisms being postulated can be tested. Without a test of the theory, it remains mere speculation. The theory should, of course, be amended and tested iteratively, leading to greater theoretical refinement. For the clinician, the result is a more precise profile of what thoughts and behaviours should be focused on in therapy, and in what order specific interventions should be executed.

To give an example of how predictions are built from theory in a way that can be directly translated into clinical practice, the Broaden & Build theory of positive emotions is based on work that shows that whereas negative emotions reduce attentional focus, positive emotions enhance attentional focus, encourage exploration, encourage creative processing strategies where apparently disparate sources of information are integrated, and help to build personal and social resources that confer a survival advantage (Fredrickson, 2004; Fredrickson & Levenson, 1998). For example, feelings of joy facilitate engaging with the here-and-now, which can promote the acquisition of new skills and form new social friendships or attachments (Fredrickson, 1998).

Negative emotions can reduce attentional focus, meaning that individuals may focus repeatedly on a limited number of perspectives on any situation that will probably be negative, especially for individuals with depression and feelings of suicidality. For example, anger may lead to dwelling on revenge, and depression may lead to dwelling on what has been lost. This in turn may mean that negative information is consolidated into memory, and a negative worldview becomes increasingly reinforced.

The Broaden & Build theory suggests that focusing on the positive may be able to counter the tendency for negative thoughts, feelings and memories to hijack processing resources. This theory converged with clinical observations with individuals with a diagnosis of Post-Traumatic Stress Disorder (PTSD) and depression, and led to the development of Broad Minded Affective Coping procedure (BMAC) (Tarrier, 2010). Tarrier (2010) noticed that asking clients with PTSD to recollect positive memories and to do so in a vivid manner that engaged all the senses (e.g. what could be seen, smelt, heard, touched and tasted) at the start of therapy seemed to be relaxing and also resulted in the remainder of the therapy session progressing more constructively than if this exercise wasn't used (Tarrier, 2010). This was consistent with the idea that positive recollections and positive thoughts and feelings associated with those recollections experienced in the 'here and now' can become integrated with a client's view of themselves and their 'world'. Further work has tested whether this procedure can be applied to those experiencing psychosis who are suicidal. The BMAC procedure was contrasted with a condition in which clients just listened to relaxing music, and it increased feelings of hope and happiness more so than the music condition (Johnson, Gooding, Wood, Fair & Tarrier, in press). Similar results have been found in those experiencing post-traumatic stress disorder (Panagioti, Gooding & Tarrier, 2012). Clearly these are just the initial stages of developing the BMAC procedure. The next step is to use a randomised control trial to see whether a form of Cognitive Behavioural Therapy (CBT) that incorporates the BMAC procedure leads to improved outcome variables relative to a control condition (e.g. CBT plus music). Following this an attempt should be made to investigate the BMAC procedure at the level of psychological mechanisms. It might be expected that it would result in clients being able to problem-solve more creatively and integrate evidence pertaining to themselves in more complex or ingenious ways.

2.3. Do we need a theory of suicide – will a theory of psychosis or depression not suffice?

We have seen that an atheoretical focus on risk factors is too all-inclusive to be of clinical utility. We have also seen the potential for how a theoretical model of suicidality will develop mechanisms that are testable and which develop dynamically with clinical observations. A question that arises is whether a theory of suicidality is necessary at all. One argument may well be that suicidal intent and acts are observed in a number of different psychopathologies, for example, major depression, substance abuse, bipolar disorder, PTSD and psychosis. The argument continues by suggesting that suicidality is a function of characteristics or symptoms that are specific to each of these disorders. It follows that what is needed is a way of tackling each of these disorders because suicide arises as an offshoot of each of the disorders, the dynamics of which are specific to each of them. If the disorder can be tackled then improvements in suicidal thoughts and behaviours will follow. This is an approach generally endorsed by the medical model of mental illness. An alternative approach is that suicide needs to be understood in its own right and not as an offshoot of a diagnosable mental illness.

When we first started researching suicidality it was in the context of psychosis and, to an extent, we did, indeed, expect that there would be aspects of suicidality that would be strongly tied to problems with dealing with psychosis specifically. We started by adopting a theoretical model of suicide developed by Mark Williams and colleagues called the Cry of Pain (CoP) model (Williams, 1997; Williams, Crane, Barnhofer & Duggan, 2005). The CoP model was developed from work investigating suicide in those with major depression. We were interested in the extent to which this model could apply to psychosis. At the outset we expected that symptoms of psychosis, such as hallucinations, would be strongly related to suicidality and that the CoP model would be inadequate for explaining suicidality in psychosis. In fact, what happened was the opposite to our expectations. The CoP model described mechanisms underlying suicidality that applied very well to those with psychosis. For instance, social isolation and stigmatisation apply to almost all mental illnesses, including psychosis. The specifics of social isolation related specifically to psychosis may moderate the association between social isolation and suicidality, but the impact of social isolation on suicidality appears to be transdiagnostic (Bolton et al., 2007). Experiences of psychosis are unique to that disorder but they also manifest as a major stressor. Stressors are a key element of the CoP model. The only factors that we found that may be related to specific aspects of psychosis and suicide were delusions (Bolton et al., 2007) and suspiciousness (Taylor, Gooding et al., 2010), and even then the number of studies that investigated the effects of these symptoms directly were sparse. Hence, we concluded that there is no added advantage in developing a model of suicidality in psychosis as opposed to developing a transdiagnostic model of suicidality. This highlights the need to focus on mechanisms of suicidality in order to devise treatment interventions rather than taking the approach that treating specific diagnoses will be adequate.

A year or two later we became interested in suicidality in PTSD. Given that depression is strongly co-morbid with PTSD (Panagioti, Gooding & Tarrier, 2009), we expected that suicidality in PTSD would be explained mainly by depression. Again contrary to our expectations, we found that suicidality was predicted by perceived life impairments, which was associated with perceptions of poor occupational functioning; and this, in turn, was associated with appraisals of poor social functioning. The analysis that we performed was a path analysis, and the analysis indicated that depression should not be included in the path to suicidality (see Figure 2.1). Interestingly, none of symptom clusters associated with PTSD, that is, re-experiencing the trauma, numbing and avoidance, and hyper-arousal, predicted suicidality, but they did lead to depression (Panagioti, Gooding, Dunn & Tarrier, 2011). So, again, suicidality in those with PTSD does not appear to be specific to the symptoms of PTSD nor was it related to depression. This means that it would be a fallacy to think that suicidal thoughts and feelings are just a side effect of depression and/or PTSD symptoms, and that by treating the symptoms of these disorders that feelings of suicidality will be ameliorated.

2.4. Overview of theories

A challenge to any theory of suicidality is being able to explain the way in which factors, at a number of different levels, interact to produce suicidal thoughts and behaviours. For instance, biological factors include genetic inheritance and the role of neurotransmitters, particularly serotonin; social factors include perceptions of the agency of others and a sense

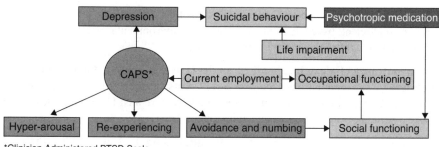

*Clinician Administered PTSD Scale

Figure 2.1 Pathways to suicidal thoughts and behaviours in those with a diagnosis of PTSD

of belongingness within a community; individual psychological factors include cognitions and meta-cognitive beliefs about the self. Consequently many theories try to have a biopsychosocial approach or a socio-cognitive approach.

From a psychological perspective, rather than a sociological perspective, the best-known theories of suicide are the Psychache model of Schneidman (1987, 1990); the Escape theory of Baumeister (1990); Joiner's Intrapersonal theory (2009); the Cry of Pain model (CoP; (Williams, 1997)), and more recently the Schematic Appraisal Model of Suicide (SAMS; (Johnson, Gooding & Tarrier, 2008)) (see Box 2.1 for a brief description of theories of suicide). We will focus on the latter two theories because, in our view, they contain the most well-developed putative socio-cognitive mechanisms underlying suicidal thoughts and behaviours.

Box 2.1 Theories of suicide

Overlap model of Blumenthal and colleagues (Blumenthal, 1988; Blumenthal & Kupfer, 1988). Five domains of suicidality are highlighted: (1) psychosocial life events and chronic illness; (2) neurochemical and biochemical variables; (3) personality traits (e.g. aggression, impulsivity, hopelessness), including personality disorders; (4) family history and genetics; and (5) psychiatric illness.

Escape theory (Baumeister, 1990). Six steps are described: (1) a perception of severely falling short of a standard or standards; (2) negative attributions of failures to the self; (3) acute awareness of the self in a negative light (inadequate, incompetent, unattractive, guilty); (4) increase of negative affect; (5) an attempt to escape from unpleasant thoughts and feelings; and (6) increased impulsivity.

Hopelessness theory (Beck, 1986; Beck, Steer, Beck & Newman, 1993; Weishaar & Beck, 1992). Hopelessness is a strong predictor of suicidal ideation and intent, and may be part of a stable schema representing negative expectations that is resistant to change.

Suicide as psychache (Shneidman, 1993, 1998). Suicide is characterised by great psychological pain (psychache); an inability to cope with, or lowered threshold for, psychological pain; death is seen as a solution or an escape; and death is seen as the only possible solution.

The suicide trajectory model (McDowell & Stillion, 1994). Focuses upon the interaction of biological, psychological, cognitive and environmental risk factors that trigger suicidal thoughts and actions at all ages.

A four-pathway clinical–biochemical model (Fawcett, Busch, Jacobs, Kravitz & Fogg, 1997). The model is based on four components: (1) increased agitation and anxiety related to cortisol levels; (2) increased impulsivity related to serotonin levels; (3) depression; and (4) hopelessness and anhedonia.

Interpersonal theory of Joiner and colleagues (Joiner et al., 2009; Ribeiro & Joiner, 2009; Van Orden et al., 2010). This theory posits that a person will die by suicide if they have both the *desire* and the *ability* to die in this way. There are three components to the model: (1) perceived burdensomeness; (2) low sense of belonging-ness (social alienation); and (3) habituation to pain, injury and death.

The Cry of Pain Model (Williams, 1997; Williams, Crane, et al., 2005). Feelings of defeat, entrapment and hopelessness are key to the model, which has six components: (1) the presence of stressors; (2) the perception of stressors as negative; (3) cognitive biases; (4) hopelessness; (5) perceptions of no rescue; and (6) means and imitation models (see section 2.4.1).

The Schematic Appraisal Model of Suicide (Johnson, Gooding, et al., 2008). This model builds on the Cry of Pain model of Williams and colleagues. It has three main components: (1) information-processing biases; (2) a suicide schema; and (3) an appraisals system (see section 2.4.2).

2.4.1. The Cry of Pain model (Williams, 1997; Williams, Crane et al., 2005)

The 'Cry of Pain' model of suicide (Williams, 1997; Williams, Crane et al., 2005) is a bio-psychosocial transdiagnostic model. A starting point of the model is that feelings of being under extreme and uncontrollable stress, from which there appears to be no respite, are a necessary component of the mechanism of suicidality. Based on ethological and evolution-ary explanations of depressive-like symptoms in animals denoting loss of social rank, and the impact of arrested flight in animals, feelings of defeat and entrapment are central to the model (Gilbert, 2001, 2006; Gilbert & Gilbert, 2003; Gilbert, Gilbert & Irons, 2004).

Six different components of the model can be identified (Bolton et al., 2007) and are shown in Figure 2.2.

Figure 2.2 Schematic representation of six components of the Cry of Pain model

2.4.1.1. The presence of stressors

The first component is that major stressors need to be present. With respect to those with a diagnosis of schizophrenia, it might be expected that major stressors are highly prominent and that they would include enforced hospitalisation, dealing with the symptoms of psychosis, and facing stigmatisation from strangers, friends and family. Such stressors would be expected to be a prelude to feelings of suicidality. It might also be supposed that those diagnosed with schizophrenia experience more negative life events. However, the evidence fails to support the idea that those with a diagnosis of schizophrenia who are suicidal face more negative life events (e.g. the loss of someone close) compared to either those with a mental illness that is not schizophrenia or to the general population (Bolton et al., 2007). Neither is there strong support for the idea that the severity of positive symptoms of psychosis (hallucinations and delusions) is associated with suicidality (Bolton et al., 2007; Fialko et al., 2006). That said, recent work by our group found that positive symptoms, particularly suspiciousness, was associated with feelings of defeat and entrapment, which then led to feelings of suicidality (Taylor, Gooding et al., 2010).

There are two difficulties with the sorts of studies that have examined the impact of life events on suicidality in those with schizophrenia. First, schizophrenia appears to be characterised by chronic stress rather than discrete negative life events (Bolton et al., 2007). Second, life event research is not targeted to the sorts of stressor that may be most pertinent to those with psychosis. For example, involuntary hospitalisation; the effects of the hospital environment, even when admission is voluntary; reactions to medication; changes of medication regimes; and a fear of psychotic symptoms returning in those who are 'well' are all stressors that do not fit well into the life events category. There is some evidence to support the idea that different sorts of stressors should be investigated in those with psychotic symptoms. For instance, both compulsory and voluntary hospitalisation can be immensely stressful (Morrison, Bowe, Larkin & Nothard, 1999), the effects of which have been poorly researched. Those with psychosis are also more at risk of developing PTSD, which can be exacerbated by aspects of the psychiatric admission process. In a sample of 47 participants with psychosis, 45% had moderate to severe PTSD symptoms that were related to psychosis and 31% of the sample had moderate to severe PTSD symptoms that were related to admission (Beattie, Shannon, Kavanagh & Mulholland, 2009).

2.4.1.2. The appraisals of stressors

The second component of the CoP model is that it is negative perceptions of the stressors, be they external (e.g. financial) or psychological (e.g. psychotic symptoms), that lead to suicidality. Negative perceptions that result in feelings of entrapment, defeat or humiliation are thought to be particularly pernicious. There is a large body of literature showing that negative interpretations of hallucinations result in psychological distress (Birchwood & Spencer, 2001; Morrison, Nothard, Bowe & Wells, 2004; Rooke & Birchwood, 1998), yet when hallucinations are interpreted in a positive way then psychological distress is reduced or negligible (Mawson, Cohen & Berry, 2010).

There is compelling evidence that illness appraisals of those who have psychosis lead to feelings of loss, defeat, entrapment, being under threat and humiliation (Birchwood, Iqbal & Upthegrove, 2005; Rooke & Birchwood, 1998). Rooke and Birchwood (1998) found that perceptions of loss and entrapment, in particular, at baseline and follow-up assessment windows were the main predictors of whether individuals with psychosis developed depression. It is, as yet, unknown the extent to which these sorts of appraisals predict feelings of sucidiality in those with psychosis (however, see section 2.4.2.2 for recent work on appraisals of defeat and entrapment in psychosis). Relatedly, it has been suggested that beliefs about relapse of psychosis (e.g. 'it is uncontrollable'; 'it will come back') contribute to the development of feelings of depression, hopelessness and helplessness (Mawson et al., 2010). Although the relationship between anticipated relapse of a psychotic illness and suicidality has not been tested directly, it seems plausible that these sorts of perceptions could lead to feelings of entrapment and defeat because of an irreversible and deteriorating illness.

2.4.1.3. Cognitive biases and problem-solving difficulties

The third component of the CoP model is that suicidal individuals will see themselves and their world in a negative light. In addition, they may find it difficult to reason and problem-solve effectively, they may find it hard to stop themselves attending to negative information, and their ability to recollect certain aspects of their lives may be impaired. From a clinical perspective, trying to alter or change the way people think, the way that they allocate attention, and the evidence that they endorse, may be a challenge unless these cognitive processes are first of all improved.

2.4.1.3.1. COGNITIVE BIASES

A vast majority of research has shown that those suffering from major depression evidence a negative cognitive processing bias (see Box 2.2), some of which have been observed even in remitted samples (Fritzsche et al., 2010; Karparova, Kersting & Suslow, 2007).

There have been two prominent types of cognitive biases associated with psychosis. The first is a reasoning bias whereby individuals make decisions on less than optimal evidence

---

Box 2.2 Examples of a negativity bias in those with major depression

- better recall of negative information and inability to use positive information to repair negative moods (Joormann & D'Avanzato, 2010);
- false recall of negative words (Joormann, Teachman & Gotlib, 2009);
- negative interpretation of ambiguous stimuli (Gollan, Pane, McCloskey & Coccaro, 2008; Lawson, MacLeod & Hammond, 2002);
- increased reaction times for negative emotional faces (Gollan et al., 2008);
- inability to inhibit processing negative material (Joormann & Gotlib, 2010; Joormann, Yoon & Zetsche, 2007);
- inability to disengage from negative facial expressions (Gilboa-Schechtman, Ben-Artzi, Jeczemien, Marom & Hermesh, 2004), especially sadness (Gotlib, Krasnoperova, Yue & Joormann, 2004);
- negative information interferes with updating the contents of working memory (Joormann & Gotfib, 2008).

(Broome et al., 2007; Freeman, 2007; Freeman, Pugh & Garety, 2008; Glockner & Moritz, 2009; Warman, Lysaker, Martin, Davis & Haudenschield, 2007), are unable to use disconfirmatory evidence (Buchy, Woodward & Liotti, 2007; Freeman, 2007), and have a liberal acceptance bias in which a conclusion is accepted based on weak evidence (Moritz et al., 2009; Moritz, Woodward, Jelinek & Klinge, 2008). The second type of bias is an external attribution bias in which private thoughts and feelings (Janssen et al., 2006; Lepage, Sergerie, Pelletier & Harvey, 2007), and social interpersonal events (Levine, Jonas & Serper, 2004), are attributed to an external source, which may be exacerbated by a lack of focus and emotionality of the material (Ensum & Morrison, 2003). Both of these biases may, in part, be explained by psychosis resulting in difficulties in binding together contextual cues (Diaz-Asper, Malley, Genderson, Apud & Elvevag, 2008).

Whilst there is some evidence that negative cognitive biases in depression are linked to suicidality, there is a scarcity of evidence linking cognitive biases in psychosis with suicidality. That is not to say that the link does not exist, but future research needs to address this issue explicitly. This is a difficult task because most individuals with psychosis will show signs of cognitive processing biases and difficulties. What needs to be demonstrated is that people with psychosis who are also suicidal have more cognitive biases and cognitive processing problems than people with psychosis who are not suicidal. This means that tests of such biases and problems need to be sensitive enough to differentiate between these two groups, both of which have the deficits, but in one group the deficit is more profound. Many tests of cognitive processing ability lack this kind of sensitivity.

2.4.1.3.2. PROBLEM-SOLVING DIFFICULTIES

A feature of those who are depressed and suicidal is that they have a difficulty with problem-solving, especially when the problem to be solved is of an intra-personal or social nature (Grover et al., 2009; Pollock & Williams, 2004; Williams, Barnhofer, Crane & Beck, 2005). Problem-solving ability is most often assessed with the Means–End problem-solving task (Blankstein, Flett & Johnston, 1992) in which a problem is presented followed by the desired end point (e.g. Mary has just moved house and is lonely . . . Mary makes friends) and the task is to generate steps that lead from the problem to the end point (e.g. Mary goes to the local library to find clubs she can join and meetings taking place in the community; she scans local newspapers for events; she looks in the window of the local newsagent for things she might be interested in). It has been suggested that problem-solving difficulties are linked with problems with over-general memories. If specifics of past events are not consolidated into memory, then those specifics will not be available to use when solving current problems. For example, individuals cannot think back to a previous time when they faced a similar problem to the one that they are facing now, and recall how the problem was solved in the past. Although there is some evidence that those with psychosis also have these sorts of problem-solving difficulties (Addington & Addington, 2008; Hoff & Kremen, 2003), the link between problem-solving difficulties and suicide has not been made convincingly in this population.

2.4.1.4. Perceptions of hopelessness

Feelings of hopelessness are an established predictor of suicidal ideation and behaviours in a number of clinical samples, including those with major depression (Beck, 1986; Beck et al.,

1993; Bolton et al., 2007; Williams, 1997) and psychosis (Cohen, Lavelle, Rich & Bromet, 1994; Nordstrom, Schalling & Asberg, 1995). For example, a study examining Chinese individuals with a diagnosis of schizophrenia found that in those who had attempted suicide (38/5000) three predictors were key, namely, hopelessness, positive symptoms and age (Ran et al., 2005). A meta-analysis examining the relationship between aspects of personality and suicide found that hopelessness, neuroticism and extraversion were important predictors (Brezo, Paris & Turecki, 2006) in illustrating the role of hopelessness in the pathway to suicidality even in non-clinical samples. A recent study examined predictors of suicide over a seven-year follow-up period in those with first episode psychosis (Robinson et al., 2010). A total of 282 individuals participated, and 61 of those (21.6%) attempted suicide, 12 of whom completed suicide. Baseline predictors of suicidality for this group were history of self-harm, history of alcohol abuse, depression and hopelessness. In older participants (those aged 40 or over) past suicide attempts and hopelessness continued to be a predictor of currently experienced suicidal ideation (Montross et al., 2008).

One means by which psychosis may lead to hopelessness is through insight into the consequences of having this disorder possibly mediated by depression. For example, in a sample of African-American women who did not have a psychiatric history attending a non-emergency medical walk-in centre, depression was indeed found to mediate the relationship between psychoticism and hopelessness (Compton, Carter, Kryda, Goulding & Kaslow, 2008). This is an important study because this pattern was found in those with no diagnosis of psychosis, and supports continuum models of psychosis (Garrett, Stone & Turkington, 2006). It also underscores the value of offering interventions early on. A review investigating the role of insight in schizophrenia indicated that good insight into the progression of the illness leads to depression and hopelessness, which in turn leads to suicidality (Drake, 2008). Other aspects of schizophrenia that may be linked to suicidality because they increase hopelessness include a negative attributional style, negative self-evaluations, a history of abuse and experiences of stigmatisation (Bolton et al., 2007). These aspects warrant further investigation.

There is a distinction with respect to hopelessness that is important, namely the perception that the future is negative versus the perception that the future brings nothing positive. The latter factor appears more indicative of suicidality. For example, some studies have shown that low expectations that something positive will happen in the future was more predictive of suicidality even when controlling for depression (Hunter & O'Connor, 2003; O'Connor & Cassidy, 2007; O'Connor & O'Connor, 2003).To date, examining these two different aspects has not been attempted with those with schizophrenia who are currently, or have been, suicidal.

2.4.1.5. Lack of social support and feelings of 'no rescue'

The CoP model highlights the importance of individuals who are suicidal feeling that they are socially isolated and that the probability of being helped or rescued is small (Williams, 1997). In those with a diagnosis of schizophrenia, as might be expected, social isolation is related to suicide risk (Tarrier, Barrowclough, Andrews & Gregg, 2004). Those with poor or no contact with their families are more likely to feel suicidal. It is hard to quantify poor family contact. Early work reported that, for those with schizophrenia, having less than five hours contact per week with a relative or significant other was associated with higher levels of suicidality across the lifespan (Radomsky, Haas, Mann & Sweeney, 1999). Given that schizophrenia is characterised by positive symptoms that accentuate avoiding social contact (e.g. paranoia) or negative symptoms (e.g. withdrawal or emotional blunting), both of which impair social skills, it is little wonder that people with schizophrenia have limited social networks, with only a small number of people attempting to offer social support in a number of ways compared to those without a mental illness. An additional issue, which has received scant attention from researchers, is whether subjective appraisals of social support differ from an objective evaluation of available social support.

A substantial literature shows that people with a diagnosis of schizophrenia have greater relapse rates, more severe psychotic symptoms and an increased negative evaluation of themselves when their relatives express criticism of them, are hostile towards them, are overly involved with them and exhibit less warmth towards them (e.g. an individual may be perceived as being lazy if they appear reluctant to engage with tasks; as anti-social if they don't want to go out; as 'difficult' if they complain about the effects of their medication and so forth) (Barrowclough & Hooley, 2003). The term for these kinds of negative and overly critical perceptions and responses is 'high expressed emotion' (high EE). The relationship between high EE relatives in those experiencing psychotic symptoms is, again, under-researched. One seminal study investigated these relationships (Tarrier, et al., 2004) and found two distinct pathways to suicide risk in a sample of 59 (see Figure 2.3).

As can be seen from Figure 2.3, hopelessness is a central component in the pathway to suicide risk. However, two largely independent pathways impact on hopelessness. One arises from critical comments of relatives associated with negative symptoms, which leads to negative self-evaluations and then feelings of hopelessness. The other path arises from social isolation, which in turn emerges from positive symptoms, age, illness duration and being unemployed. This is an interesting study because it shows that the route from social isolation to hopelessness and then suicide has a different underlying mechanism from that involving negative criticisms from relatives. Hence, it cannot be assumed that negative criticism leads to social isolation, which in turn leads to hopelessness and suicidality. The mechanisms underlying the two separate pathways must each be tackled.

An additional, although related, issue that applies to relatives and health professionals is their attitude towards expressions of suicidality in those experiencing psychosis. For example, an early study looked at the way in which significant others responded to communications about

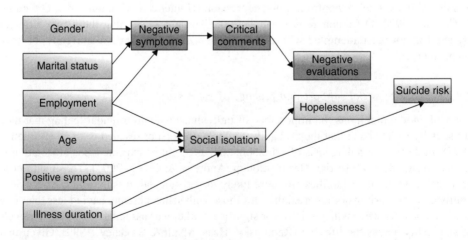

Figure 2.3 Pathways to hopelessness and suicidality

suicide by individuals who had been admitted to psychiatric wards because of suicide attempts (Wolkwasserman, 1986). Only six people in their sample were experiencing psychosis. However, in this group if the patient talked about suicide then this was considered a normal and expected aspect of their mental illness by relatives and significant others. Relatives tended to respond to such communications about suicide with silence. Relatives also seemed to believe that they should not initiate any discussion about suicide with the patients, possibly because they felt that this might elevate or trigger suicidal feelings or lead to distress.

Similar concerns are also voiced by ethical committees about any study that directly addresses suicidality, either through interviews or questionnaire measures. Again, the fear is that engaging clients in overt discussion of their suicidal feelings may lead them to feel more distressed and so amplify any suicidal feelings they may be experiencing. We addressed this issue directly in a qualitative study that used thematic analysis (Taylor, Awenat et al., 2010), and found that individuals with psychosis expressed a number of positive reasons for participating in suicide research that overtly asked them about suicidal thoughts and feelings. Their responses fell into four themes of Altruism (e.g. 'If it helps other people in the long run then it's worth it', 'Happy to help others'); Value of being involved in research (e.g. 'It's something that needs to be done, psychology is in its infancy', 'Should be more research'); Catharsis (e.g. 'Didn't bother me, glad to get it out of my system', 'Great. The talking did me good'); and Enjoyable experience (e.g. 'I really enjoyed it, remembered a lot of things in my life', 'Alright, enjoyed doing it'). Overall, negative feedback about being a participant in our studies was rare, occurring in 2.5 to 15.2% of responses. In contrast, positive feedback was more frequent, occurring in 45.6 to 60.8% of responses.

A further issue is that health professionals and clinicians may interpret symptoms of depression and suicidality as 'normal' and 'expected' in those diagnosed with schizophrenia. This may be particularly important if depression leads to social withdrawal. There is some work indicating that in these instances health professionals and clinicians showed a loss of professional concern for the client (Saarinen, Lehtonen & Lonnqvist, 1999). Clearly, quite the opposite approach is needed. The therapeutic relationship needs to be made even more secure and reassuring, and health professionals need to be proactive in nurturing this relationship. Of relevance to group therapy, there is some evidence from a thematic analysis of transcripts documenting focus group discussions of women with schizophrenia that intra-group support in such groups may be in issue. It was found that when one woman initiated a discussion about suicide another group member attempted to suppress that discussion (Chernomas, Clarke & Chisholm, 2000).

2.4.1.6. Availability of the means of suicide and imitation models

Having access to a means of suicide is the final component of the CoP model. This fits with evidence showing that suicide attempts are predicted by both a previous history of suicides and being close to someone who has attempted to or succeeded in killing themselves (Hawton, 2010; Hawton, Sutton, Haw, Sinclair & Deeks, 2005; Hawton & van Heeringen, 2009). Clearly, a knowledge of how to commit suicide, and how to do so reliably, is crucial to the success of suicide attempts. There is an abundance of literature showing the utility of limiting means of suicide, such as, detoxification of the gas supply to houses, preventing paracetamol from being bought in bulk or installing barriers on railway lines (Law et al., 2009), and adding barriers on bridges (Jacobs, 2010). Knowledge of a means of suicide is important when individuals move from suicidal ideation to suicidal planning (Hawton et al., 2005).

The intra-personal theory of suicide (Joiner et al., 2009; Ribeiro & Joiner, 2009; Selby et al., 2010; Van Orden et al., 2010) takes this one step further. This theory is based on three components (see Box 2.1): feelings of being a burden; feelings of not belonging; and habituation to the physical, violent and probably painful means of suicide. Joiner and colleagues argue that this last component is crucial in driving suicide attempts, as contrasted with suicidal ideation. They observed that suicide attempts are more frequent in those individuals who have habituated to violent deaths, for example, combat veterans.

One question that emerges is to what extent people with psychosis have access to a greater variety of potential means for suicide. One assumption might be that those with a diagnosis of schizophrenia have greater potential access to medication, which they can use as a form of poisoning. However, there is little evidence to support this assumption. With respect to the second question, people diagnosed with schizophrenia do seem to adopt violent means of suicide (Dumais et al., 2005). For example, a UK-based study examining suicides in England and Wales found that 13% of suicides by the mentally ill died after jumping from a height or jumping in front of a moving vehicle. This figure was doubled (27%) in those with schizophrenia (Hunt et al., 2006). A study of individuals who had survived self-inflicted gunshot wounds or stabbing, that is, used a violent method of attempting suicide, in an inner city area of Australia, found that 37/88 (42%) had a psychotic illness and 18 (49%) of those individuals had not received treatment (Nielssen & Large, 2009). A study of 505 suicides in the Netherlands found that those with psychotic disorders mainly chose to jump from heights (Huisman, van Houwelingen & Kerkhof, 2010), again a choice of a violent method.

The issue, then, is why individuals experiencing psychosis attempt suicides by violent methods. One prediction is that such individuals, perhaps because of frequent hospital admissions or exposure to family members who have been, or are, suicidal, are exposed to other people who have plans of a violent suicide attempt. One study interviewed 20 people who had attempted suicide by throwing themselves under London underground trains (Odonnell, Farmer & Catalan, 1996). It was found that 75% of these individuals had been receiving psychiatric treatment at the time of their suicide attempt, and schizophrenia was the most common diagnosis. When asked why they had chosen this method of suicide 45% of participants said that they knew of someone who had committed suicide in this way. Knowledge of fellow patients who had used this method seemed to make it an acceptable choice, supporting the idea that certain methods of suicide may become part of a folklore within some psychiatric institutions.

A second prediction relates to impulsivity and drug or alcohol abuse. It is known that drug and alcohol abuse increase impulsive behaviours (Dick et al., 2010). There is also good evidence that impulsivity is related to violent suicides, especially when it co-occurs with lifetime experiences of aggression (Dumais et al., 2005). It follows that violent suicides in those with schizophrenia may be mediated by three factors: (1) a subculture in which plans of suicide are perceived as normal; (2) a history of aggression, either as the aggressor or as the perpetrator of aggression; and (3) impulsive behaviours fuelled by substance abuse. This prediction remains to be tested in those experiencing psychosis.

2.4.2. The Schematic Appraisal Model of Suicide

The CoP model is an important model with a number of strengths (Johnson, Gooding & Tarrier, 2008). For instance, the model attempts to bring together the effects of cognitive-emotional processes and social factors; it attempts to explain both suicidal ideation and completed suicide; all components of the model are potentially empirically testable; and it can be translated into therapeutic interventions. However, the model also has limitations (Johnson, Tarrier & Gooding, 2008).

One of the most important of these limitations concerns the role of defeat and entrapment. While there is excellent support for defeat and entrapment playing a role in depression, the evidence is less strong for the role of defeat and entrapment in suicidality, because only eight studies have to date examined defeat and entrapment in suicidality directly and none of those studies had a longitudinal design that makes disentangling cause and effect difficult (Taylor, Gooding, Wood & Tarrier, 2011). Furthermore, even though the concepts of defeat and entrapment are derived from separate theories it becomes difficult to define them in such a way that the distinction is compelling. Added to this is the difficulty that defeat, entrapment, hopelessness and no rescue appear conceptually synonymous (Johnson, Tarrier et al., 2008). Recent work from our group has shown that defeat and entrapment are best conceptualised as one factor (Taylor, Wood, Gooding, Johnson & Tarrier, 2009), although it should be acknowledged that this was based on a student sample. We have also shown that when defeat and entrapment were treated as one factor, then this factor predicted suicidal ideation in a sample of participants with schizophrenia spectrum disorders (Taylor, Gooding, Wood, Johnson & Tarrier, 2011).

A second limitation is that although concepts of defeat, entrapment, hopelessness and no rescue are important to the model and also seem accurate descriptors of some of the phenomenology of suicide, the psychological mechanisms by which they occur are not well elucidated. For example, it is unknown whether defeat and entrapment lead to problems with information processing, or whether it is biases in information processing that lead to feelings of defeat. We recently tested this experimentally by inducing feelings of success and defeat in participants and then asking them to recall a story. Defeat caused a recall impairment (Johnson, Tarrier et al., 2008). The sample comprised undergraduate students. Usually, work with students lacks clinical applicability. However, in this case it was a strength because the participants were relatively 'healthy' and did not have extreme feelings of defeat at the outset of the experiment. Hence, we knew that it was the defeat induction manipulation that had produced the recall problems.

The Schematic Appraisal Model of Suicide (SAMS) builds on the strengths of the Cry of Pain model, but it attempts to provide a framework from which to understand the development of psychological mechanisms that drive suicidal thoughts and behaviours. Rather than concentrate on concepts such as defeat, entrapment and hopelessness, the SAMS attempts to specify the psychological mechanisms that lead to suicidal thoughts and behaviours. There are three components of the SAMS (depicted in Figure 2.4), namely those that are concerned with information-processing problems and biases, the development of a suicide schema and an appraisal system. The information-processing component is based on the same approach as the Cry of Pain model (see section 2.4.1.3), so this component will not be elaborated on further in this section. The notion of suicide schema and an appraisal system will, however, be expanded upon.

2.4.2.1. Suicide schema

The idea of schemata in psychology stretches back to the work of Henry Head and Bartlett. A schema was seen as a way of representing an individual's view of themselves and their world and incorporated different types of information. Schema include many different types of

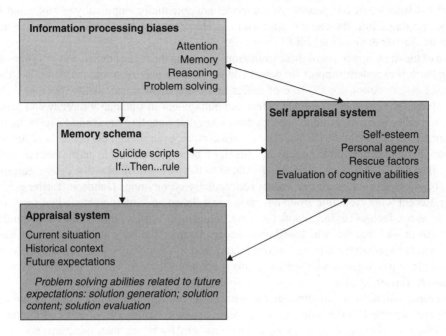

Figure 2.4 The Schematic Appraisal Model of Suicide (Johnson, Gooding & Tarrier, 2008)

elements, for example, representations of things, actions, beliefs, judgments, images, emotions, social dynamics, temporal information (i.e. when something happened) and spatial context (i.e. where something happened). Typically, these elements are depicted as being linked in a complex web of interacting nodes. Specific models of schema have described the ways in which moods and concepts about the self and the world could be associated.

With respect to suicide, the differential activation theory elaborates on the idea of suicide schema (Lau, Segal & Williams, 2004). It is suggested that nodes representing suicidal thoughts and behaviours become associated with other nodes representing numerous sensations, cognitions and emotions, including a linkage between suicide and forms of escape (Lau et al., 2004; Williams, Crane et al., 2005). According to spreading activation theory, each time an association between suicide and a concept such as escape is triggered then that association is strengthened. As more concepts become associated with suicidal thoughts and behaviours, the greater is the potential for a wide range of mood states, images, thoughts and sensations to become associated with suicidality, and to activate the suicide schema (Williams, Crane et al., 2005).

The development of suicide schema is an important component of the SAMS. We suggest that as thoughts of suicide occur they become associated with other thoughts, feelings and behaviours (e.g. suicide is associated with feelings of relief). This then creates a feed-forward loop whereby these associated thoughts and feelings can trigger ideas of suicide, which in turn become associated with yet more thoughts and feelings (e.g. suicide is associated with feelings of relief; relief is associated with a lack of tension; suicide becomes associated with a lack of tension). The more volatile the emotional states experienced by the individual the more extensive the suicide schema becomes because many different experiences and behaviours become associated with suicide. Some work even suggests that individuals who are suicidal may have flash-forwards to how they might kill themselves (Hackmann & Holmes, 2004; Holmes & Hackmann, 2004; Holmes & Arntz, 2008; Holmes, Crane, Fennell & Williams, 2007). This imagery may then become incorporated into the suicide schema. As a result of this feed-forward loop, it is expected that in those who are suicidal seemingly disparate thoughts and feelings can trigger a suicide schema. This may help to explain so-called impulsive suicides where outwardly trivial or minor events lead to suicide attempts in individuals who do not seem to be actively suicidal (Johnson, Gooding et al., 2008; Tarrier et al., 2007).

The converse is also true, which is that a less extensive network of associated thoughts and feelings should be part of a less extensive suicide schema in those who are not suicidal. Although the idea of schema has an intuitive appeal, testing the presence of schema is notoriously difficult. We were able to advance this to some extent by examining suicidal thoughts and behaviours in individuals displaying negative symptoms of psychosis, that is, blunted affect and emotional withdrawal. These negative symptoms represent less emotional lability. Hence, we expected that suicide schemas would incorporate fewer links to different thoughts and emotions in these individuals, and that they would be less suicidal. We found that in a sample of 278 individuals with recent onset schizophrenia, in line with our predictions, emotional withdrawal was negatively associated with suicidal behaviour (i.e. the more someone displayed signs of emotional withdrawal, the less likely were they to be suicidal). This suggests that restricted emotional lability is indicative of a reduced suicide schema, and reduced concomitant suicide risk (Tarrier et al., 2007).

We were able to further investigate the notion of suicide schema using a method called Pathfinder Analysis (Prescott, Newton, Mir, Woodruff & Parks, 2006), which is a way of determining the structure of semantic memory by looking at how close items are when they are generated by individuals. For example, if participants were asked to generate mammals, if dog is generated first followed by cat by most participants, then this suggests that dog and cat are prototypical examples of mammals and that they are closely semantically related. Figure 2.5 illustrates the way in which semantic closeness is calculated using pathfinder analysis.

One task that we used to investigate suicide schema in 84 participants with a diagnosis of non-affective psychosis recruited from community mental health services (Pratt, Gooding, Johnson, Taylor & Tarrier, 2010) was open-ended and asked participants to generate any association with suicide that came into their head. Pathfinder analysis provided us with a visual depiction of the structure of suicide schema derived from this data, which is shown in

	Cat	Dog	Pig	Lion	Tiger
Cat	0	1	2	3	4
Dog	1	0	1	2	3
Pig	2	1	0	1	2
Lion	3	2	1	0	1
Tiger	4	3	2	1	0

Figure 2.5 An example of the calculation of proximity scores

Figure 2.6 (Pratt et al., 2010). In accord with the predictions of the SAMS model, the suicide schema of those experiencing psychosis who were also suicidal was more extensive than the suicide schema of those who were not suicidal. There was also evidence that this schema was more entrenched (Pratt et al., 2010).

2.4.2.2. Appraisal systems

Four types of appraisal are highlighted by the SAMS. These are appraisals of the current situation, appraisals of the past, appraisals of the future, and appraisals of the self (Johnson, Gooding et al., 2008), and they will be examined in turn.

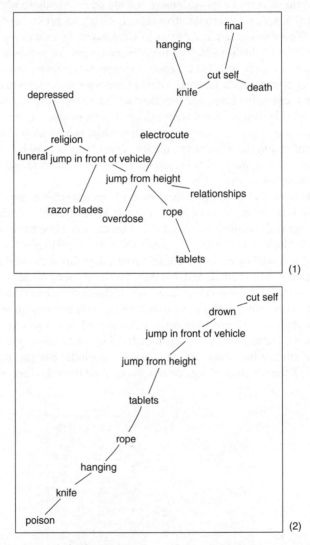

Figure 2.6 The structure of suicide schema in those who were suicidal (diagram 1) and were not suicidal (diagram 2) using the generation task

2.4.2.2.1. APPRAISALS OF THE CURRENT SITUATION

A body of research has shown that it is not the presence of a mental illness per se that causes distress but the way in which aspects of the illness are perceived (e.g. hallucinations) and the way in which an individual's ability to cope with aspects of the illness is appraised that is important (Birchwood et al., 2007; Fortune, Barrowclough & Lobban, 2004; Kinderman, Setzu, Lobban & Salmon, 2006; Lobban, Barrowclough & Jones, 2004; Lobban, Haddock, Kinderman & Wells, 2002; Moses, 2009; Rooke & Birchwood, 1998). For instance, people with psychosis often feel inferior to the voices that they hear. Birchwood and colleagues demonstrated that this is an appraisal of that individual's social rank in a wider context (Birchwood, Meaden, Trower, Gilbert & Plaistow, 2000). Related to this, perceptions of a mental illness as being stigmatising can worsen symptoms and lead to considerable distress (Morrison et al., 1999). Recent work by our group specified one possible mechanism by which negative mental illness appraisals lead to suicidality. The SAMS proposes that negative appraisals increase feelings of defeat and entrapment. In a sample of 78 people experiencing psychosis we found that this was indeed the case. Perceptions of the severity of psychotic symptoms, suspiciousness in particular, led to feelings of defeat and entrapment, which in turn led to feelings of suicidality (Taylor, Gooding et al., 2010).

Perfectionism, especially social prescribed perfectionism, is an important factor in the pathway to suicidality (O'Connor, 2007; O'Connor, Fraser, Whyte, MacHale & Masterton, 2009; Rasmussen, O'Connor & Brodie, 2008). Socially prescribed perfectionism describes a situation in which an individual feels that they are looked down upon, disapproved of or considered not good enough by their social peers. This demonstrates the far-reaching impact that negative appraisals of the current situation can potentially have on suicidality, ranging from illness and health appraisals to appraisals relevant to social situations.

2.4.2.2.2. APPRAISALS OF THE PAST

Multiple suicide attempts and knowing someone who has attempted suicide are strong predictors of a completed suicide attempt (Hawton, 2010; Hawton & van Heeringen, 2009). Perceptions of this kind of history as a template for providing an escape route or a solution to seemingly intractable problems relate to the development of an entrenched suicide schema. Similarly, over-general memories in which details of success or achievements are missing but details of failures are prominent will likely lead to a negatively biased appraisal system and contribute to a suicide schema (Williams, Barnhofer et al., 2005; Williams et al., 2006).

As will be elucidated later in this book, it is important from a clinical perspective to determine the sorts of 'rules' that individuals who are suicidal use to frame or reframe their history from the stance of viewing this personal history as an appraisal. These appraisals then need to be formulated in a way that is not related to content but to 'rules of thinking', with the premise that such rules can be countered and changed.

> *Annabelle presented with a number of 'rules of thinking'. For instance, she engages in black or white thinking and tended to 'catastrophise'. The smallest sign of a setback was blown out of proportion and appraised as a terrible failure. Annabelle made a number of appraisals about the past such as 'nothing has ever gone my way' and 'everybody leaves me'. The therapist worked with Annabelle to understand the origins of these appraisals of the past and her thinking styles. Annabelle had a strict father who was cold towards to her. His father had struggled for work and had experienced a number of periods of*

depression throughout Annabelle's childhood. Annabelle remembered him responding warmly on a couple of occasions, when she had come top of her class. These memories seemed to explain Annabelle's tendency for 'black or white' or dichotomous thinking – she had to be the best and achieve or she was worthless. Annabelle's catastrophic thinking seemed to be routed in her experiences with her mother, who had lost her own mother when she was very young. Her mother worried when Annabelle went out with her friends and wanted her to be in earlier than them, to make sure she was safe. Identifying how appraisals were linked to an underlying tendency helped Annabelle greatly, and charting these tendencies to events in her past allowed her to identify that they were no longer useful for her. Annabelle spontaneously commented that, like a snake, she needed to shed her skin. Annabelle developed simple verbal reframes such as, 'I am catastrophising, like my mum, but it'll be ok'. Work on reducing perfectionism and accepting not doing things perfectly helped her with her fixed rules about achieving and, through self-esteem work, Annabelle began to incorporate being a caring and loving mother into her image of self-worth, guarding against global appraisals of being worthless.

Changing appraisals based on a seeming unshakeable history of failures, disappointments and distressing and/or humiliating experiences can seem daunting. Indeed, the author is sad to note that some colleagues have said that they dislike working with older people because their 'schema', their 'rules', seem inflexible because of repeated experiences of failure and loss. Therefore, it would seem important to be able not necessarily to alter appraisals of the past that are related to experiences and content but rather to limit the damage that entrenched appraisals can have on perceptions of current situations and evaluations of the future.

When discussing Jade's past experiences with her, the therapist noted a number of 'global appraisals' about her past, such as 'nothing ever goes right for me', 'everybody who has loved me has left me'. The therapist worked carefully with Jade to understand the origins of these appraisals; her mother had undermined her frequently as a child, and this linked into a sense of thwarted goal-directed behaviour. Jade was bullied at school and had a pattern of forming very close friendships with a small number of people. Unfortunately, one of her best friends had died when she was 11, in their first year of high school. Jade had a friend who was murdered when she was 18. The therapist worked with Jade to identify how these past experiences led her to withdraw from social situations, believe every sign of a setback was evidence of abject failure and to be wary of forming relationships with people because of expected pain and grief. These appraisals were understandable given her past experiences. However, Jade and the therapist talked about how they were flavouring current experiences and how they had created a set of 'blinkers', restricting her from seeing situations that were not negative. Jade had recently submitted a piece of poetry about her feelings to a local competition and it had been shortlisted. Jade was a passionate musician and had taught herself to play the guitar. She also managed a flat by herself, working 3 days a week and paying her bills. Jade acknowledged that these were signs of being competent and of having abilities. The point here was that this was quickly discounted when some setback occurred. Jade liked the idea of keeping her 'self-worth' spread across a number of accounts and began to pursue activities that developed different elements of self-worth, such as being a good aunt, taking guitar lessons and gradually increasing her confidence through social experiences. These regular appointments gave Jade specific and positive future events to look forward to, despite the difficult experiences of the past.

2.4.2.2.3. APPRAISALS OF THE FUTURE

Rather than focusing on hopelessness, the SAMS tries to identify mechanisms by which appraisals of the future may lead to feelings of hopelessness. Seven components of future appraisals were identified and are shown in Figure 2.7.

The ability to generate solutions to both current difficulties and difficulties that are considered likely to occur is the first step, and is based on a large literature showing that people who are suicidal find generating solutions difficult (Pollock & Williams, 2004; Williams et al., 2006). It might be predicted that problem-solving is likely to lead to hopelessness, particularly if an individual feels a pressure to solve problems because of expectations of friends, family and colleagues.

The next three components focus on the content of the solutions generated, the evaluation of the solutions and the ability to implement the solutions. Solutions with a negative content, such as, 'I embarrass my friends, therefore I won't go out with them tonight so save them that embarrassment' are likely to result in feelings of hopelessness, as are evaluations of solutions as being not good enough or uncontrollable. One feature that we predict to be important is people's appraisals of their own ability to carry out a solution. Perceptions of personal attributes and personal characteristics are likely to impact on such appraisals, as are perceptions of available social support, through family, friends and health professionals. The relationships between these aspects of appraisals of the future, hopelessness and suicidality defines a comprehensive research programme and remains to be tested.

2.4.2.2.4. APPRAISALS OF THE SELF

In the SAMS, negative self-appraisals are viewed as feeding into the three other systems in a continuous and interactive manner. These negative self-appraisals can perhaps be broken down or categorised further into appraisals of:

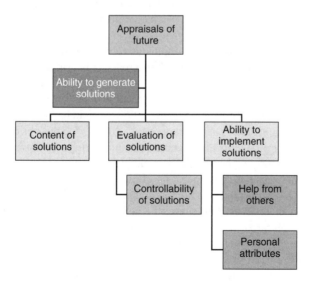

Figure 2.7 Psychological components of appraisals of the future

1. Personal characteristics, e.g. feelings of self-worth, self-esteem.
2. The ability to achieve and to attain goals.
3. Other people's perceptions of the individual as being able to make a contribution to society.
4. Cognitive abilities.

2.5 Challenges to theories and models of suicide

Six major challenges can be identified, and these are summarised in Box 2.3.

Box 2.3 Challenges to theories and models of suicide models of suicide

1. Include multiple levels of explanation.
2. Account for impulsive suicides.
3. Integrate clinical experience into theory.
4. Ensure service-user involvement.
5. Demonstrate the transdiagnostic utility of theories.
6. Use convergent methodologies.

The first challenge is the incorporation of a number of different levels of explanation into theories of suicide. There is an understandable tendency to concentrate on the level of the individual in suicide research. However, theories, as they become more sophisticated, need to include a psychobiological level of explanation and understanding in addition to a socio-cognitive psychological perspective. One area ripe for development is the role of group identity in suicidality. Although it is clear that social isolation is a risk factor for suicide, what is unknown is whether the dynamics surrounding group membership may be protective of suicide. For example, a preliminary analysis of qualitative data relating to resilience to suicide in those with psychosis points to being a member of a religious group as being helpful.

The second challenge is accounting for impulsive suicides. The SAMS attempts to explain impulsive suicides in terms of an extended schema that can be triggered by seemingly trivial events. However, issues of co-morbidity and neuropsychological impairments need to be addressed. Impulsive behaviours are increased with alcohol and drug use (Elizabeth Sublette et al., 2009; Lejoyeux et al., 2008; Wojnar et al., 2009). Such behaviours are also observed in those with damage to prefrontal cortex (Raust et al., 2007). One possibility that needs to be the focus of a research initiative is that mechanisms underlying impulsive suicides are quite different from those underlying non-impulsive suicides.

The third challenge relates to incorporating clinical models and observations of suicidal behaviour into theoretical models. Our Suicide Research Group in the School of Psychological Sciences in the University of Manchester is, perhaps, fortunate in that it includes clinicians who are active researchers, and academics who can view their work from clinical and applied perspectives. The challenge for the future is to maintain this collaborative venture and to encourage this kind of practice widely.

A fourth challenge is to ensure that the research underlying theory developments is informed by clients who have experienced suicidality at every point of the research process, from formulating research questions, to designing the research through to implementation and dissemination. Again, our group in Manchester is lucky in that we have dedicated individuals, who have experience of feeling suicidal and attempting suicide working with us and who also have a wealth of academic experience.

Fifth, we have indicated that the SAMS is transdiagnostic in nature. The SAMS was developed partly as a response to understanding suicide in psychosis. Currently, we are working on whether it applies to those with a diagnosis of PTSD. Initial findings are positive. We have plans to test the SAMS in adolescents with depression and anxiety, and in those who are incarcerated. It is a large undertaking, and therefore a substantial challenge, for any theory of suicide to demonstrate that it can be usefully applied to suicidal thoughts and behaviours experienced across a variety of clinical samples.

The sixth challenge is adopting a convergent methodological approach. The strongest conclusions can be drawn from evidence which converges, which is drawn from qualitative and quantitative methodologies and which uses a number of different designs, for example, cross-sectional, longitudinal, experience sampling, focus groups, semi-structured interviews and so forth. The next stage in our research at Manchester is to design longitudinal studies and experience sampling studies focusing on suicide.

Chapter 3

Does Cognitive Behavioural Therapy for suicide work?

3.1. Executive summary

- *CBT is highly effective at countering suicidal thoughts, feelings and behaviours, particularly in adults.*

- *The effects of CBT may last for two years and, possibly, longer.*

- *Interventions that were delivered in a one-to-one format in addition to interventions that included individual sessions together with group sessions were the most effective.*

- *Psychological interventions should be targeted at suicidality and not, for example, the symptoms of depression.*

- *Randomised controlled trials of poor quality tended to over-estimate effect sizes. Nevertheless, when that was controlled for, the positive effects of CBT still remained.*

- *The most recent studies published from 2009 to 2011 support the conclusions of the 2008 meta-analysis, which is that CBT is effective in reducing suicidal thoughts and behaviours.*

3.2. What is Cognitive Behavioural Therapy?

Cognitive Behavioural Therapy can be thought of as an umbrella term to include a range of therapeutic methods, techniques and processes based upon the cognitive and behavioural sciences. Originally, behaviour therapy had its roots in learning theory (classical and operant conditioning) and in social learning theory. Over the last three decades or more cognitive, or thought processes have taken a much more prominent position in both theoretical and experimental work and in therapeutic processes and procedure. Such mental processes can include cognitive content, cognitive processes such as attention, and underlying beliefs and assumptions about the world, or schema through which information and experience are filtered. Clinical and emotional problems are hypothesised to arise from faulty or maladaptive thought patterns and behaviour. How the individual structures their experience and infers meaning to the events in their life is viewed as of prime importance to the origin and maintenance of these problems. Interventions are aimed at resolving these problems through a collaborative process between the client and clinician to change appraisals of events and experiences, which can be implemented through altering thoughts, feelings, images, memories and actions. Clearly, in preventing and reducing the risk of suicidal behaviour addressing how the client views themselves, their world and their circumstances is going to be crucially important. In CBT for suicidality, as in the treatment or interventions for myriad other disorders, a wide range of variants and configurations of CBT approaches, methods and procedures have been developed. Although it would be wrong to regard CBT as a homogeneous entity there are certainly many overlaps between the treatment approaches that have been used in the studies we have evaluated in this chapter. In evaluating the efficacy of psychological treatments to reduce suicide risk and behaviour we have focused on CBT because it has an underpinning of evaluation, being evidence-based and operationalising the intervention procedure, which clarifies what was actually done and aids replication and dissemination.

3.3. How to find out whether Cognitive Behavioural Therapy for suicide works

The gold standard approach for determining whether a treatment works, whether it be psychological, medical or pharmaceutical, is considered to be a randomised control trial (RCT), although there are alternative views (Cartright, 2007; Simon, 2001). This is because participant characteristics are randomised over treatment and control conditions, meaning that those characteristics cannot bias treatment effects. To illustrate, let us compare RCTs to patient preference trials, where individuals choose whether to opt for the treatment or control condition, or, if two treatments are being compared, which type of treatment to opt for. Imagine that the patient preference trial is comparing cognitive analytic therapy and Rogerian counselling for depression and anxiety in university students. Further imagine that Rogerian counselling fares better when the outcome variables are analysed. It would be incorrect to reach any conclusions about the relative merits of Rogerian counselling compared to cognitive analytic therapy because it may have been the case that those individuals with more severe and/or enduring symptoms opted for cognitive analytic therapy. Clearly, such individuals pose a greater therapeutic challenge.

3.3.1. Randomised control trials and CBT

In a simple RCT for CBT effectiveness, there is usually a *treatment condition*, which consists of the CBT, and a *control condition*. Often, this control condition is treatment as usual or a waiting list control. Sometimes, although more rarely, CBT is contrasted with a different type of treatment, for instance, supportive counselling. Quality assurance in RCTs is measured by the extent to which certain procedures are in place (see Box 3.1).

CBT is unique in that it has been tested with RCTs more than any other psychological therapy (Tarrier, 2002). That said, there are problems with relying on any one published report of an RCT of CBT. One problem is the sample size. RCTs require sample sizes in the hundreds. Typically, there are neither the resources (usually financial) nor the recruitment potential to satisfy such large sample size requirements. Indeed, some RCTs are small-scale and address, predominantly, issues of feasibility. In these cases, the sample size in each condition may not exceed 30 participants. An additional problem is that CBT is very much

---

Box 3.1 Indicators of quality in RCTs

- participants are randomly assigned to either the treatment condition or the control condition;
- the randomisation procedure is scheduled by external experts;
- primary outcome measures are stated in advance of statistical analyses taking place;
- primary outcome measures are defined in terms of efficacy and/or effectiveness;
- measuring attrition rates from initial recruitment to the start of the therapy, and from initial recruitment to the end of the therapy;
- determining whether participants who drop out of the trial are significantly different from participants who complete the trial;
- having stringent inclusion and exclusion criteria;
- having manualised treatment protocols, and checks that those protocols are adhered to;
- ensuring that statistical analyses are performed by a statistician rather than the person leading the study or the therapist(s);
- for psychological treatments, having a measure of therapist efficacy/fidelity;
- for psychological treatments, the qualifications/experience of the therapist(s) should be stated;
- outcome assessors should not be the therapists;
- outcome assessors should be blind as to whether a participant was in the treatment or control condition.

---

an umbrella term. For example, some forms of CBT may focus on psycho-education. Others may use a mixture of therapies such as motivational interviewing combined with CBT. A related issue is that the number of therapy sessions differs across RCTs, as do the length of therapy sessions, and the timings of such sessions (e.g. one weekly session, two sessions per week, one session every fortnight, and so forth). In addition, some CBT RCTs may adopt therapy delivered in a one-to-one format between the client and therapist, others may use a group format, and still others may use a mixture of the two. Modern technologies also mean that CBT may be delivered, or supported, by various forms of e-technologies (e.g. email messages, instant chatting, texts). A further issue concerns the outcome measure(s) used. For instance, if an RCT is being conducted to alleviate depressive symptoms, the outcome measure may be the Beck-Depression Scale, the Hospital Depression and Anxiety Scale, the CES-D or the Depression Anxiety Stress Scale. There may be many more valid scales. The issue is which one of these is optimal. These sorts of issues means that relying on one published RCT of CBT may be misleading.

3.3.2. Meta-analysis

Meta-analytic techniques overcome some of the problems listed above. A meta-analysis combines the results of all studies that are relevant to a particular research question (Rosenthal & Dimatteo, 2001), for example, all RCTs that examine the effectiveness of CBT for suicidality. This means that by using sub-group analysis and meta-regression techniques the data can be probed for the effects of factors, such as the type of therapy delivered, the way in which the therapy was delivered (e.g. group, individual, mixed), the number of sessions of therapy, and so forth (Borenstein, Hodges, Higgins & Rothstein, 2009). In addition, a measure of the quality of the RCTs can be applied to the analyses.

A meta-analysis works by converting the results of all relevant studies into a common effect size metric. This allows all of the effect sizes to be combined across studies. It is then possible to determine whether the combined effect size is significantly different from chance (Borenstein et al., 2009). Essentially, the result of each study is treated as an independent data point, which is conceptually similar to the way in which data points from individual participants are treated in experimental or questionnaire studies.

3.3. A meta-analysis of CBT for suicidality: Conceptual methodological and clinical issues

We conducted a meta-analysis to see whether CBT was effective in ameliorating suicidal thoughts and behaviours, which was published in 2008 (Tarrier, Taylor & Gooding, 2008). There were a number of conceptual, methodological and clinical issues that had to be addressed prior to identifying published papers and conducting the analysis. These issues are described briefly below.

3.3.1. The definition of suicide

We adopted a continuum view of suicide, in which suicidality is thought to increase in severity from suicidal ideation or thoughts through to the formation of concrete suicidal plans, attempted suicide and, finally, completed suicide (Baca-Garcia et al., 2011; Johnson, Gooding & Tarrier, 2008; Scocco, de Girolamo, Vilagut & Alonso, 2008; ten Have et al., 2009; Yoder, Whitbeck & Hoyt, 2008). Of course, we acknowledge that some individuals will not pass through the stages of this continuum as laid out, but many will do so. Thoughts and ideas about suicide can be highly distressing, and as such, we would argue, they should be the focus of psychological treatment interventions. That said, it must be pointed out that not everyone agrees that suicidal thoughts and behaviours lie on a continuum. For instance, there is some discussion as to whether impulsive suicides can be accounted for by continuum models (Dick et al., 2010). We believe that these sorts of suicide fit the idea of a suicide schema (Tarrier et al., 2007). However, this idea needs to be tested.

3.3.2. Search strategy, inclusion and exclusion criteria

One source of anxiety when conducting meta-analyses is whether all relevant published papers have been identified. In some cases, for instance, examining suicidality in prisons, it may be necessary to access the 'grey literature' because peer-reviewed literature is sparse. The 'grey literature' refers to reports that are not published in peer-reviewed scholarly journals but that are reported by, for example, the Department of Health. We took the decision to include only papers in peer-reviewed journals because the peer-review process attempts to provide some reassurance about the quality of a publication. The inclusion and exclusion criteria that we used to select papers for our meta-analysis are shown in Box 3.2.

Box 3.2 Inclusion and exclusion criteria

Inclusion criteria:

- published in a refereed journal;
- had a treatment group that consisted of a form of CBT;
- had a control or comparison group of any kind.

Exclusion criteria:

- °case studies;
- clinical descriptions;
- reviews;
- discussion articles;
- the absence of a control group (e.g. just pre- and post-intervention measures);
- published before 1980;
- not published in English.

3.3.3. Evaluation of quality of the studies

Tarrier and colleagues (Tarrier & Wykes, 2004) developed the Clinical Trials Assessment Measure (CTAM) to measure the quality of psychologically based RCTs. The CTAM provides a quantitative evaluation of the quality of a study. It comprises 15 items, which assess six areas of trial design, namely, recruitment method, sample size, allocation to treatment, treatment descriptions, assessment of outcome measures, control groups, and methods of data analysis. Although measures of quality were available for RCTs at the time that the CTAM was developed, these measures tended to be medically oriented or targeted for pharmaceutical rather than psychological trials. Hence, the CTAM is an important instrument from a psychologically perspective. Previous work had shown that trials with poor methodological rigour produce findings that exaggerate treatment effects by up to 40% (Moher et al., 1998; Schulz, Chalmers, Hayes & Altman, 1995). We wanted to see whether a similar bias was operating in RCTs investigating CBT for suicide.

3.4 The types of treatment used in the studies included in the meta-analysis

One thing that was apparent when we first started doing this meta-analysis was the enormous variability in the treatment techniques that were used and the way in which they were delivered. For example, some studies used standardised forms of CBT that were accompanied by manuals and on occasion training procedures. In other studies, a project-specific intervention had been developed. Although the techniques were diverse, there were nevertheless commonalities in therapeutic approaches at both the strategic and process mechanism levels.

Dialectical Behaviour Therapy (DBT) was the most frequently used standardised treatment programme. It was originally developed for the treatment of borderline personality disorder and has been described as:

a manualized treatment that combines treatment strategies from behavioral, cognitive, and supportive psychotherapies. . . . It includes concomitant weekly individual and group therapy that is conducted for one year. Individual DBT applies directive, problem oriented techniques (including behavioral skill training, contingency management, cognitive modification, and exposure to emotional cues) that are balanced with supportive techniques, such as reflection, empathy, and acceptance. . . . The emphasis is on teaching patients how to manage emotional trauma rather than reducing or taking them out of crisis. . . . Group therapy met once each week for two and a half hours and followed a psychoeducational format. Behavioral skills in three main areas were taught as follows: 1) interpersonal skills, 2) distress tolerance/reality acceptance skills, and 3) emotional regulation.

(Linehan et al., 1999)

DBT was used in this standardised manner by four studies. However, in three studies the version described above was shortened to six months, three months or a two-week intensive programme aimed at adolescent inpatients. An additional study combined DBT with problem-solving skills and psychodynamic psychotherapy. Manual-assisted Cognitive Behavioural Therapy merges components of DBT with Beck's cognitive therapy and bibliotherapy (Weinberg, Gunderson, Hennen & Cutter, 2006). Three studies used this form of CBT. A supplementary component of the therapy in these three studies was problem-solving. For a further 11 studies, training in problem-solving skills was a core element.

Nine studies used cognitive therapy or cognitive restructuring as a key element of the intervention. In some cases this was based on the established format of Beck's cognitive therapy for depression. In others, it addressed issues that are highly relevant to psychological suicide prevention. For example:

Cognitive therapy aimed at vulnerability factors, including hopelessness, poor problem solving, impaired impulse control, treatment non-compliance and social isolation, and relapse prevention.

(Brown et al. 2005, 564)

Training clients in the use of adaptive coping strategies or skills to manage dysregulated affect was the focus of three studies. Improving social competencies through the use of social skills training was a major focus of two studies.

In the majority of studies, treatment was delivered on a sessional outpatient basis, although there was, of course, variability in this. An intensive treatment programme was used by four studies, delivered to inpatients or day hospital patients over 10 to 14 days. In contrast to this intensive approach, one study delivered brief solution-focused treatment by telephone with no face-to-face contact between therapist and client (Rhee, Merbaum, Strube & Self, 2005). Brief therapist contact of up to six or seven sessions was used by three further studies, which delivered a self-help manual version of CBT developed by Schmidt and colleagues (Schmidt, Davidson et al., 2004). One study, however, used longer-term therapist–client contact, and over two years delivered an assertive community treatment programme, which included medication, psycho-education and social skills training (Nordentoft et al., 2002). Patients were most frequently seen in hospitals or clinics. That said, at least two studies provided treatment via home visits.

Most studies conducted therapy on a one-to-one basis between the therapist and patient. However, five studies included parents or families in the treatment programme. The way in which the family programmes were delivered ranged from highly structured behaviour therapy (e.g. Liberman & Eckman, 1981), to a small number of parent-only sessions (e.g. March & Team, 2004), to including parents in therapy groups if thought appropriate by the therapist (e.g. Rathus & Miller, 2002).

Various professionals with quite different levels of clinical training and experience delivered the therapy. These included nurses, specialist nurses, counsellors, psychiatrists and clinical psychologists. In some cases, the therapy was delivered by individuals who were relatively junior and inexperienced, for example, Master's-level psychology students. Only seven studies indicated that frequent supervision was provided to therapists during the course of the study. The studies also differed with respect to the number of therapists delivering therapy (range = 1–41). It can be speculated that this may have depended on the financial resources available.

3.5. A meta-analysis of CBT for suicidality: The results

The interested reader is directed to our 2008 paper for a detailed account of the results of this meta-analysis (Tarrier, et al., 2008). We will try to express the key points below.

3.5.1. The effects of CBT up to three months after therapy cessation

Twenty-five studies were included in the main analysis, which evaluated whether CBT was effective in countering suicidality immediately after therapy ceased, or up to three months after therapy cessation. We used an effect-size metric known as Hedge's g. The bigger the effect size then the bigger the effect of CBT compared to the control. Figure 3.1 graphically represents the effect sizes across all included studies.

As can be seen from the figure, the effect size for all studies were to the right of zero, meaning that the treatment group had better outcome scores than the control group.

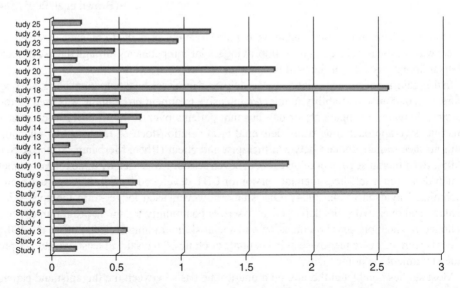

Figure 3.1 Effect sizes (Hedge's g) up to three months after therapy cessation

The overall effect size taken across all studies was significant (Hedge's g = 0.59, p < .0001).

We were also interested in investigating different aspects of this data. For example, although CBT was effective overall at countering suicide, when participants were adolescents it was ineffective. Seven of the studies had used Dialectical Behaviour Therapy, and when we examined the effect sizes of just these seven studies then the results were highly significant (Hedge's g = 0.697, p < .005) and comparable to results with the studies that had used CBT with no DBT component (Hedge's g = 0.56, p < .0001). We contrasted effect sizes for interventions that had been delivered in a one-to-one format with delivery in group format. Delivery in a group format was ineffective, but individual sessions either alone or in tandem with group sessions were highly effective.

Nine studies had used a measure of suicidal ideation as the outcome measure, and 13 studies had used suicide plans and attempts as the outcome variable. We found that CBT was highly effective regardless of which type of suicide measure was used as the outcome measure. That it was effective for suicidal ideation seems promising, first because it will alleviate the high levels of distress often associated with suicidal ideation, and second, because it has the potential of preventing suicidal thoughts from progressing to the formation of concrete plans. Some studies had examined measures of suicidality as well as measures of hopelessness. Hopelessness has been found to be a better predictor of suicidality than depression. When we analysed the data on hopelessness together, again we found that CBT was effective at ameliorating feelings of hopelessness.

Twenty-one of the included studies had focused on the alleviation of suicide, but for four studies alleviating suicide was an indirect effect, with countering distress, the symptoms of schizophrenia and the symptoms of depression being the focus. Interestingly, the effect size for these four studies was not significant (Hedge's g = 0.23, p = 0.32). This suggests that the development of psychological interventions for suicide based on CBT should be focused on aspects of suicidal thoughts, plans and behaviours (see also van Beek, Kerkhof & Beekman, 2009). This contrasts with some medical or psychiatric approaches in which it seems to be assumed that if depression is the focus of treatment, say with antidepressants, then suicidality will also be treated. Data from this meta-analysis is clear and does not support this approach.

Finally, using meta-regression techniques, we examined relationships between the duration of therapy and the effect sizes, the number of sessions of therapy and effect sizes, and the quality of the study (as measured with the CTAM) and effect sizes. Not all studies provided clear information about the number and duration of therapy sessions. However, the estimated mean number of sessions was around 26 (SD = 33, range = 3–104), the median was 11, and the mean hours of therapy was estimated as 43 (SD = 60.5, range = 3–191), and the median was 12. The number and hours of therapy were not related to the effect sizes. When we looked at the CTAM data we found that the CTAM scores were significantly and negatively associated with the effect sizes, and, as we had predicted, those studies that were poorest in quality were associated with larger effect sizes (see Figure 3.2).

3.5.2. The effects of CBT at follow-up

Some studies measured outcome variables at a follow-up time point, which were six months, 12 months and between 16 and 24 months. Effect sizes were strongest for the longest follow-up time point of 16–24 months (Hedge's g = 0.3, p < .05). Results approached significance

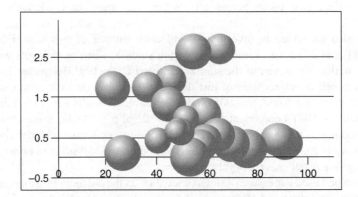

Figure 3.2 CTAM scores are along the X axis and hedge's g effect sizes are on the Y axis. The area comprising the points is indicative of the study weights

for the 12 months follow-up period and were promising at the six-month time point. The difficulty with these last two time points is that very few studies (three and four) contributed to the analyses, which compromises power.

3.6. Studies that have been published since 2008

Recent peer-reviewed publications that reported the effects of an RCT that included CBT to address suicidality were identified for the period of January 2009 to November 2011. Eight studies that met our criteria for the meta-analysis were identified.

Based on evidence that hopelessness levels are high in those dealing with the aftermath of a traumatic brain injury, and that hopelessness is a strong predictor of suicidality, one study offered a 20-hour manualised CBT programme in group format (10 weekly, two-hour sessions) to participants who had suffered traumatic brain injury, had experienced traumatic amnesia for more than a day, and had moderate to severe levels of hopelessness (Simpson, Tate, Whiting & Cotter, 2011). Hopelessness scores improved post-intervention in the CBT group (n = 8) compared to a waiting list control group (n = 9), and there was a strong trend for levels of suicidal ideation to improve also.

An Australian study examined whether DBT was effective in reducing suicidal behaviours in those with a diagnosis of borderline personality disorder being cared for via a routine public mental health service (Pasieczny & Connor, 2011). DBT was delivered over a six-month period to the treatment group. The control group was treatment as usual, and, compared to this group, the treatment group had lower levels of self-injury, visits to the emergency department, and psychiatric admissions. The authors do point out that therapists with intensive DBT training had the greatest success rates in reducing suicidal behaviour compared to therapists with only four days of basic DBT training.

Another UK-based study also targeted those with a diagnosis of borderline personality disorder (Davidson, Tyrer, Norrie, Palmer & Tyrer, 2010). This study, however, examined six-year follow-up data. The CBT programme that was delivered was tailored to issues experienced by this patient group. After one year, those in the CBT group were found to have less-suicidal behaviours, and this finding was also observed after six years. It is important to note that attrition at this six-year follow-up period was only 18%.

A third study compared the effects of DBT with what was termed 'general psychiatric management' in those with borderline personality disorder (McMain et al., 2009). General psychiatric management included psychodynamically oriented therapeutic skills in addition to symptom management through the use of medication. After one year of treatment, there were significant improvements in both groups, including measures of self-harm and suicidal behaviours. However, there were no group differences reported.

A fourth study compared CBT (n = 33) and Rogerian counselling (n = 32) in participants with a diagnosis of borderline personality disorder (Cottraux et al., 2009) after one year of therapy. After six months, hopelessness was more reduced in the CBT group than the Rogerian group. Retention rates were, in general, better for the CBT group than the Rogerian group.

Finally, one study assessed the effects of mentalisation-based treatment compared to a structured therapy framework which did not involve mentalisation for those with a diagnosis of borderline personality disorder (Bateman & Fonagy, 2009). Mentalisation was described as a psychodynamic treatment founded on attachment theory and CBT. Therapy was delivered over 18 months of weekly sessions that combined individual and group work. After 12 months of treatment, the number of six-month periods tht were free of suicidal behaviours was greater for the mentalisation group.

Based in Norway, the goal of one study was to determine whether an intervention would be effective in reducing repeat suicide attempts in those not receiving psychiatric treatment for schizophrenia, bipolar disorder and severe depression including psychotic depression (Hvid et al., 2011). The acronym for the intervention was OPAC, representing outreach, problem-solving, adherence and continuity. The control group received treatment as usual. A total of 8.7% of 65 participants in the treatment group repeated a suicide attempt compared to 21.9% of 59 participants in the control group.

A study in the UK examined whether CBT for psychosis delivered by non-expert clinicians who were, nevertheless, supervised reduced measures relevant to psychosis (Peters et al., 2010). One such measure was identified as emotional problems, suicidal ideation and self-esteem. After six months, that is, at therapy cessation, suicidal ideation was reduced in the treatment group (n = 36) compared to the control, treatment-as-usual group (n = 38). However, this difference was not observed at follow-up, three months after therapy cessation.

In conclusion, studies published between 2009 and 2011 appear to support the general conclusion of the meta-analysis, which is that CBT-type intervention approaches are successful in reducing suicidal thoughts and behaviours.

Chapter 4

Pre-therapy

Engagement and assessment

4.1. Executive summary

- *Engagement is the most important aspect of early therapy and assessment.*

- *Barriers to therapy should be identified and worked upon to aid engagement.*

- *The CBSPp assessment is specifically focused on the suicide-specific elements of psychological difficulties and experiences of psychosis.*

- *An appropriate level of goal setting will allow clients to identify goals in order to inspire hope rather than activating hopelessness linked to a lack of goals or confidence in achieving them.*

- *The assessment of factors leading to suicide should be informed by the Cry of Pain and SAMS models, placing emphasis on factors associated with Defeat, Entrapment, No Rescue appraisals and the Suicide Schema.*

- *The assessment should attempt to identify factors associated with resilience or the inhibition of suicidal states, including positive schematic-appraisal networks.*

- *An important outcome of the assessment is an overall assessment of risk.*

Many people experience psychosis. Some people go on to have suicidal thoughts and some go further, attempting to, or actually killing themselves. An understanding of a person's experiences of psychosis per se is therefore not enough to explain their suicidal behaviour. A thorough assessment is needed to identify the factors that are specifically implicated in suicidal behaviour. These may be directly or indirectly linked to experiences of psychosis, their consequences, or to a wide range of non-psychotic experiences. Pre-therapy refers to the engagement and assessment stage that precedes therapy. Therapy refers to the idiosyncratic formulation of suicide and resilience (Chapter 5) and the delivery of the CBSPp intervention (Chapter 6).

Engagement is an important task. In order to provide information for the assessment and formulation, the client needs to talk about their experiences of suicide. This may be extremely difficult for come clients; it may tap deeply held beliefs about the danger of talking about these experiences. Such difficulties may reflect the core processes locking a person into the states of defeat and entrapment that make suicide more likely. This isn't the case for all clients, and our research shows that talking about suicidal experiences in a research setting can be cathartic (Taylor et al., 2010). We have found that to be the case for people in therapy. However, people who can talk about their experiences are perhaps further forward in their journey towards gaining agency over these experiences. The point here is that potential barriers to therapy may need to be dealt with prior to direct CBSPp work. For this reason, Chapter 10 addresses a number of specific barriers to therapy and how to address these with clients in order to engage them with therapy.

Once a client has engaged, the CBSPp assessment may take place. The rationale for the assessment is to (1) assess current levels of risk to inform risk management; (2) collect information about factors that leave the client vulnerable to suicidal behaviour; and (3) identify factors that may be harnessed to reduce vulnerability to suicidal behaviour and improve resilience. An understanding of such factors can allow the therapist and client to proceed with the CBSPp formulation (Chapter 5), plan for future events that may confer risk, and implement intervention strategies (Chapter 6). An important aspect of CBSPp is to build upon a person's natural strengths and to identify natural inhibitors or regulators of suicide.

The twin processes of engagement and assessment then provide the foundations for the development of an individual case formulation (Chapter 4). This is an individualised model of a person's suicidal behaviour, with clearly identified putative psychological mechanisms that are amenable to change through a range of psychological interventions. The formulation also identifies the mechanisms involved in the prevention of suicidal behaviour (Chapter 6). In order to outline the engagement and assessment processes, we will refer to the cases of Catrina and Max. These cases will be followed throughout the formulation and intervention chapters, to highlight how the different stages of CBSPp were applied to their unique presentations.

4.2. Engagement

In CBSPp we are hoping to create a safe environment where the client is able to share some of the most difficult times of their lives. From the outset, it is therefore very important to develop a collaborative and empathic, trusting relationship with clients. Commencing therapy with a gentle, warm and relaxed conversation about a general topic of interest can facilitate engagement and build rapport. Normalising experiences and distress, as well as the difficulties of entering into a new relationship with the therapist, can assist clients in feeling understood and diffuse fear or angst associated with therapy. Maintaining engagement and the therapeutic relationship throughout therapy is essential, and important clinical decisions must always consider this point.

For many, having the opportunity to talk about their experiences of suicide is a tremendous relief, something they have not previously had the chance to do. This is borne out in the literature, with a number of studies showing that participants in research studies investigating the suicidal experience found that clients did not tend to find this distressing; rather, it was a positive experience (Cukrowicz, Smith & Poindexter, 2010; Jorm, Kelly & Morgan, 2007; Taylor et al., 2010).

The rationale for CBSPp is that many people during recovery from psychosis are overcome with feelings of despondency and hopelessness, which may lead to suicidal thoughts or acts (Birchwood, Iqbal, Chadwick & Trower, 2000; Gumley & Schwannauer, 2006). The aim of the intervention is to try to reduce vulnerability to these feelings in the future. Feelings of 'not wanting to go on' can be very distressing for the client and their friends and family and also interfere with valued aspirations and future goals. Thus, the intervention aims to reduce such distress and impediments to achievement. These points, if explained appropriately, should aid engagement.

In situations where the initial engagement is problematic the best strategy is to 'roll with resistance', that is, be patient and try to alleviate any agitation but maintain contact and return at another time. It is important to validate the client's experience but not necessarily agree on the cause or with their interpretation. To further build engagement it is important not to dispute or argue with the client, especially at this early stage, if the client is not convinced that there is any benefit to be gained from therapy.

If engagement continues to be difficult, we have found that exploring barriers to talking about these experiences may reveal particular psychological mechanisms that actually maintain the suicidal schema; for example, beliefs that thinking about suicide will make a person feel suicidal again. It may also reveal barriers to sharing things with other people; for example, a sense of shame and stigma. Some people fear that they may harm other people or burden them by telling them about their difficulties. These barriers can sometimes be linked to the fears of 'no rescue' that are central to the Cry of Pain model (Williams, 1997; Williams, Crane, Barnhofer & Duggan, 2005). These fears are discussed in Chapter 10, along with specific strategies to address them.

In summary, it is important that the clinician embodies the characteristics of empathy, unconditional acceptance, warmth and genuineness in order to engage clients and to develop and maintain a strong therapeutic relationship. Clients need to feel accepted and understood, and this is particularly true for people who have had experiences of psychosis, who may have been dismissed or misunderstood as a result of their experiences. Time spent addressing fears about the therapy, and exploring strategies to reduce these, form the foundation of the assessment, formulation and intervention.

Box 4.1   The case of Catrina

Catrina was referred for CBSPp by her social worker. The referral stated that she had been subject to a sustained and violent sexual assault by a number of perpetrators a number of years previously. Although this had been investigated, no charges had been made. She heard multiple voices and attributed these to her attackers.

Catrina was very wary of meeting with the male therapist. Engagement began with a phone call to her. Catrina explained that she did not want to talk about her previous experiences but wanted to feel better. The therapist reassured her that therapy would proceed at her own pace. She was also told that she had a 'virtual stop button', which she could press at any time if she found a conversation too difficult. An agreement was made to meet the therapist in person to discuss the therapy and to see if she wanted to continue. She reported that she felt reassured because of the therapist's kind voice.

Upon meeting the therapist, Catrina seemed tense but relaxed as the conversation progressed. The therapist and Catrina discussed what it would mean to feel better. She described a feeling of calm and of not being bothered by her voices any more. Catrina reported an ongoing re-experiencing of the trauma, and her voice-hearing experiences made her want to kill herself. She consented to exploring ways of working towards these goals while being in control of what she disclosed to the therapist. She reported feeling better for meeting with the therapist and was happy that he had listened to her needs.

Box 4.2 The case of Max

Max was referred to CBSPp by his Care Coordinator. He had an enduring belief that an entity controlled him and some aspects of the world around him. He was unsure whether other people were real or were placed there by the entity.

Upon meeting, Max explained to the therapist that he was constantly scanning the environment for signs from the entity that he might become ill again. He explained that if he became ill again he couldn't cope and would either have to kill himself to escape because it would be unbearable or he would kill himself under the control of the entity.

Max explained that the more he talked to the therapist the more real he seemed. He wanted to spend more time doing the things he enjoyed but was constantly being distracted by the signs from the entity and the entity speaking to him, and his subsequent fears of becoming suicidal again. The therapist told Max that the therapy involved exploring together what would help with his feelings of wanting to kill himself and to increase his ability to spend more time doing the things that he wanted to do.

Max reported that this sounded good but he had managed 'on an even keel' for years now and didn't want to 'rock the boat' by starting therapy. The therapist used a cornfield analogy to show how therapy may work to increase pleasurable experiences. Max could then decide how much he wanted to engage with thoughts of the entity. Max thought that this was a reasonable place to begin therapy.

The cases of Catrina and Max provide some important insights into the task of engagement. Firstly, the interpersonal style of the therapist is important in creating a safe environment; Catrina responded to the tone of the therapist's voice on the phone. Max relaxed in the therapist's company, leading to an increase in his belief that the therapist was real and was not a creation of the entity. Secondly, the therapist explained how CBSPp focuses on developing strengths and resilience. Thirdly, engagement is boosted by setting meaningful goals that outweigh a person's perceived barriers. For Catrina, the balancing act was one of freeing herself from ongoing traumatic experiences against the potentially traumatic experience of discussing this with the therapist. For Max, the goal of increasing his range of positive experiences was limited by a fear of 'rocking the boat' and disrupting the stability he had established over the years.

4.2.1. Interviewing style and process issues

The therapist may begin by asking broad, open-ended questions about the client's experiences and then switching to closed questions to obtain the information required. Once the details of an experience have been elicited, the therapist can then validate the client's experience with appropriate expressions of empathy, while also drawing links to corresponding elements of the CoP and the SAMS model. The therapist and client work together on the joint task of building an understanding of how life events have conspired to leave a person feeling defeated. Clients may find it hard to provide answers in a structured way, and it is important to allow them to tell their story. However, applying a structure to this story, using the different elements of the CBSPp formulation, can be the first step to increasing a sense of control over events rather than being a passive observer. The introduction of defeat, entrapment and no rescue as normative processes can provide the basis both to validate a client's perspective but also to provide mechanisms that are modifiable. Over time, therapists may encourage clients to use the model to report their experiences.

A second core element of CBSPp is to identify factors that inhibit suicide behaviour. Events that occurred in the past to reduce states of defeat can provide the foundation for the formulation and intervention. The early identification of such events at the assessment stage can introduce a sense of agency over situations, thoughts, feelings and internal states that were hitherto considered defeating.

Particular attention should also be paid to the language used in session. The client may have his or her own terms for states of defeat/entrapment. Clients may use terms such as 'the point of no return' or other expressions to indicate that there is a point after which they have no choice. These assumptions can be gently challenged as the assessment and formulation begin to identify modifiable processes that lead to these states. Directing attention towards events that did result in a shift away from these states is also a powerful technique; clients may then be encouraged to use a different term that does not indicate a final state, and to begin using terminology that emphasises personal choice and volition.

4.3. Repairing the roof when the sun is shining: The use of metaphor in CBSPp

Catrina and Max both found the prospect of CBSPp challenging because they had been able to establish a sense of 'equilibrium'; they managed ongoing feelings of threat and suicidality and were wary of introducing change for fear of worsening their experiences. This fear of 'rocking the boat' may be a bigger barrier for those clients who are currently functioning well, especially if they have adopted a 'sealing over' coping strategy (Tait, Birchwood & Trower, 2003). The client should not be considered in isolation here – it is often families who trigger help in times of crisis, and they may be contributing to and influencing a client's decision as to what 'risks' they take with goal-directed behaviour measured against the risk of relapse. However, in terms of harnessing strengths and resilience, this may be the optimal time for intervening. We have used the following quote from President John F. Kennedy to illustrate this;

> 'The time to repair the roof is when the sun is shining.'
> (J.F. Kennedy, 87th State of the
> Union Address, 1962)

Clients are then encouraged to discuss the pros and cons of working on a problem when it is not currently causing them distress. The main advantage to be explored is the value in adopting a careful, methodological approach to understanding the problem and developing a long-term solution as opposed to dealing with crises as they occur. A useful follow-up question can be:

> 'What would be difficult about fixing the roof when it is raining?'

The client is then asked to reflect on the advantages and disadvantages of attempting to develop resources and a prevention plan when they are in a crisis.

4.3.1. Cornfield metaphor

An essential element of CBSPp is that the development of alternative, positive schema can inhibit the suicidal schema. This can be a difficult concept to explain in abstract terms. We have found that discussing clients' dilemmas using a corn circle metaphor can provide a rationale for developing new skills and abilities. We begin as follows:

Imagine walking through a cornfield in a circle just once. How much corn would you flatten down? Would you be able to find the path again? . . . It may be difficult. How long do you spend thinking about your difficulties a day? How long have you been doing this for? Ok, imagine walking round the cornfield for X minutes/hours a day for X days/ months/years. How strong would the pathway through the corn become? If you zoomed up and looked down on the pathway, what would you see? How much corn would be flattened down? This is a little bit like how the brain learns: the more time spent thinking about something, the stronger the pathway. How strong is the pathway linked to thinking about your difficulties?

The therapist may want to draw out a field of corn (just a series of straight lines on paper) in the file and then add a thick circle into it. The therapist then draws another field of corn.

Ok, how long have you spent thinking about your abilities to cope or in developing new ways of coping with your difficulties? How long have you spent dwelling on positive experiences? It may be that it is hard to remember such experiences. Imagine if you spend X minutes a day for X days/months/years walking through this pathway. This new pathway can contain memories of good experiences, times when you coped well, a confidence in being able to cope with difficult situations in the future. What would your 'positive' pathway look like? How strong would this pathway through the corn be? If you were spending your time walking through this pathway, what would be happening to the old pathway? Which would be the thickest pathway? What do you make of that? How would this help with your difficulties?

This metaphor can be found within the neuropsychological literature to explain the development of neural pathways. We have adapted it to explore the idea that the development of new pathways can inhibit older pathways. It is intended to instill hope and to illustrate the idea that our view of the world and way of seeing things develop through experience. Exposure to new experiences and actively processing them may inhibit existing (suicidal) schemata.

CBSPp works best when it builds on, and increases access to, existing resources and coping strategies. The following may then be added.

Of course, you haven't only just started this new pathway. We want to build on all the hard work you have already done, to increase access to memories of good times and when you have coped well. By thickening the pathway and spending more time reflecting upon these times, you might be able to remember them and apply them more readily when you are experiencing difficulties in the future.

Box 4.3: The use of metaphor with Catrina and Max

Catrina

Catrina thought that the time of her assault was like a thunderstorm, whereas now, although it did rain from time to time, there were times when she felt good. The corn circle metaphor was used to demonstrate how Catrina's attention and thoughts fixated on her experiences of being assaulted, and if she spent the same time thinking about her wonderful experiences with her grandchildren she would feel better. Catrina was not sure that it was possible to escape the old pathway, but was willing to try. Later in therapy, Catrina developed her own metaphor of changing the videotape in her mind.

Max

Max related to the corn circle analogy in that regardless of whether the entity existed or not, there were times when he did not think about it, and these were times when he did not think about suicide. This was time spent in the other circle. Max thought it would be a good goal to spend less time thinking about the entity and doing more of the things that he enjoyed, such as watching DVDs and playing snooker.

4.4. Mode and aims of CBSPp assessment

4.4.1. Model-driven assessment

CBSPp may be considered to be a recovery-focused intervention. It is therefore important to establish a person's Recovery goals, hopes and aspirations for the future (Pitt et al., 2007). Progress towards Recovery goals may reduce processes that lead to suicide. Suicide may also come to be understood as a transgression of cherished personal goals. An assessment of current risk should be undertaken, driven by the empirical literature, and informed by psychological models such as the CoP and the SAMS (see Figure 2.2). This provides the basis for a comprehensive risk assessment and the foundations for the case formulation. The assessment should also attempt to identify factors that reduce or inhibit suicidal behaviour.

4.4.2. Mode of assessment

A comprehensive assessment should be based on as many sources of information as possible. The therapist may want to speak to family members, friends and members of the clinical team. Speaking to others in the client's broader network can help to identify:

- Objective sources of threat.
- Levels of expressed emotion in the environment.
- The breadth of the client's social network.
- Factors that either exacerbate or reduce difficulties.

However, in many cases, the clinician may only have access to the client's own reports of their experiences. The essential elements of a psychological assessment should include psychometric assessments and a semi-structured interview conducted with the client.

4.4.3. Recovery goals

Recovery from psychosis has been conceptualised, by service users, as working towards cherished life goals of developing the self, developing hope and working towards an important future (Pitt et al., 2007). Instilling hope is a vital component of CBT in general (Kuyken, Padesky & Dudley, 2009) and in suicide prevention work in particular. The themes developed by Pitt et al. (2007) offer a potential framework to guide the process of goal setting and in developing hope.

The function of suicidal behaviour can be understood in much more detail when we understand how a person's appraisals of how their cherished life goals, values and aspirations have been transgressed. Focusing and increasing the appraised likelihood of achieving important life goals can therefore reduce the function of suicide; we are thickening the alternative pathway through the corn.

Goal setting is particularly important with clients prone to hopelessness. Setting realistic, achievable and specific goals can begin the process of changing appraisals about the future. However, the therapist should also be cautious not to overstretch, leading the client to the experience of failure and potentially to a state of feeling defeated. The therapist should therefore aim for an approach of cautious optimism, maintaining a sense of respect and validation of past and current experiences while introducing choices and the concept of change into future appraisals. As demonstrated by the case of Catrina, the process of balancing goal setting while overcoming defeat cycles triggered by the suicide schema is a delicate process that may continue throughout therapy. We return to this in the formulation section.

Box 4.4 The elicitation of Catrina's goals to reduce hopelessness

Catrina presented with chronic voice hearing – believed to be the voices of people who had abused her in the past. During therapy Catrina contracted a viral disease and could not have contact with her grandchildren for two weeks. Catrina experienced a sharp increase in depression and voice hearing. Through careful questioning, Catrina observed that time spent with her grandchildren reduced her distress. Catrina further expressed the goal of returning to her position as matriarch of the family and fulfilling her role of grandmother. This goal served as a driving force behind all interventions; for example, reducing time spent attending to voices would allow her to spend more time attending to her grandchildren. Critically, Catrina realised that she had been attributing her ongoing depression to her past experiences. Catrina reattributed her depression to the consequence of isolating herself because she felt she needed to concentrate on the voices, and to the task of distinguishing reality from 'psychosis'.

4.4.4. Recovery measures

Scales measuring Recovery from psychosis may be particularly useful for identifying goals and personal resources that may be harnessed by the person to prevent future suicidal behaviour.

4.4.4.1. Questionnaire about the Process of Recovery (QPR; Neil, Kilbride, Pitt, Nothard & Morrison, 2009)

The QPR was developed using information collected from interviews about recovery from psychosis with service users. It was subsequently checked for face validity and received input from a steering committee of service users. The scale consists of 22 items measuring both intrapersonal and interpersonal processes. The scale correlates with measurements of empowerment and quality of life and also shows good test-retest reliability.

4.4.4.2. Service User Experience of Psychosis Scale (SEPS, Haddock et al., 2009)

The SEPS is a 45-item questionnaire measure developed jointly by clinicians and service-users. It was subsequently checked for face validity and received input from a steering committee of service users. It focuses on the positive and negative impact of experiences (as defined by the client) on a client's interpersonal and intrapersonal functioning.

4.4.5. Risk assessment

Once the client has been appropriately engaged, it is important to assess their current level of suicidal behaviour. A semi-structured interview should supplement questionnaire data in assessing current risk.

4.4.5.1. Semi-structured interview

An initial risk assessment provides the clinician with baseline data against which to assess changes in risk throughout therapy. It also allows the therapist to make decisions around the suitability for CBSPp; if the client is actively suicidal, strategies for immediate suicide prevention are necessary (see Cooper & Kapur, 2004; Wenzel, 2009).

4.4.5.2. Number of past attempts

The clinician should assess for past attempts as this is continually noted as an important risk factor. The details of this should be established and the impact upon the client assessed. Questions as to how these experiences relate to a client's own experiences can be useful.

4.4.5.3. Family history

Family history of suicide is an important predictor of suicide (De Hert & Peuskens, 2000; Murphy & Wetzel, 1982; Sorenson, 1991). It is important to assess for the impact of this event(s) upon the individual. A person may be more likely to consider suicide as an escape if they have observed this in others. For example, one client reported that his father attempted suicide when he got into debt, leading the client to internalise this experience as an if-then rule, 'if I get into debt then I will kill myself'.

4.4.5.4. Psychiatric diagnoses

Holding a psychiatric diagnosis or multiple diagnoses has been identified as a risk factor for suicide. Negative experiences in relation to psychiatric difficulties may be reconceptualised as a potential trigger or stressor for suicide where appropriate.

4.4.5.5. Current problems/stressors

The first stage of the assessment is to assess for current difficulties or stressors. The therapist may consider whether suicidal behaviour is mainly attributable to current and extreme personal circumstances. If this is indicated, the therapist may choose to adopt a problem-solving approach to reduce external stressors before addressing top-down schematic processes. Essentially, the therapist is assessing the extent to which difficulties reflect natural reactions to ongoing events and the extent to which these experiences are being maintained by schematic-appraisal processes. Current stressors that may need prioritising are as follows (Linehan, 1993a, b; Persons, 2008):

- homelessness;
- significant substance misuse;
- homicidality;
- criminal behaviours that may lead to jail;
- high-risk sexual behaviours;
- living with an abusive partner;
- living under high risk if personal attack/current danger;
- unemployment: Note, this is very common in people with experiences of psychosis, especially in times of economic downturn. Finding employment may be a goal for some, giving a person a sense of value and purposeful activity as well as routine and structure.

4.4.5.6. Life events

The clinician should also assess for life events that were stressful, distressing or traumatic and that could be impacting upon current experience, for example:

- bereavement and/or loss;
- conflicts;
- illnesses or medical conditions;
- living conditions and lifestyle;
- relationship difficulties;
- poor social networks (or dysfunction within those networks);
- family dysharmony and/or criticism from family members;
- job-related difficulties;
- trauma.

There may be particular stressors associated with experiences of psychosis. Examples are as follows:

- enforced hospitalisation;
- dealing with the experiences of psychosis (see section 4.5);
- facing stigmatisation from strangers, friends and family;
- effects of the hospital environment, even when admission is voluntary;
- reactions to medication;
- changes of medication regimes;

- a fear of psychotic symptoms returning in those who are 'well';
- changes in staff patterns leading to a lack of consistency and a loss of stable relationships.

4.4.5.7. Recent experiences of suicide

The clinician begins by assessing suicidal ideation, its frequency, duration, level of associated distress and triggers. Useful questions are listed below:

> *Over the past month have things ever got on top of you, so you felt that you couldn't cope?*

> *At these times, did you have thoughts of harming yourself, or of taking your own life?*

> *Please can you tell me a little about what happened?*

4.4.5.8. Information processing

At the risk assessment stage it is important to identify cognitive processes that may increase the likelihood of suicide. Common processes that can lead to negative appraisals are indicated in Box 4.5.

Box 4.5 Information processing biases operating to maintain Suicidal Schematic Appraisal Systems

- *Jumping to conclusions:*
  - ○ Deriving conclusions rapidly without considering all information available to an individual.
- *Catastrophising:*
  - ○ A tendency to dwell on the worst possible outcome and appraise it as highly likely to occur.
- *Maximising/minimising:*
  - ○ This refers to an over-inflation of risk and threat and underplaying the positives in a situation.
- *Selective abstraction:*
  - ○ The tendency to focus on situations that are suicide schema-relevant and not processing situations that are incongruent with suicide schema.
- *Personalising:*
  - ○ To assume that events are related to the self when there is no objective reason for doing so.
- *Mind reading:*
  - ○ To imagine negative appraisals from others about the self when there is no reason to believe that this is so. This may be a tendency that leads to specific barriers in asking for help, thus affecting rescue appraisals.

The clinician may identify such process from the client's report or by working through a summary sheet with the client with the aim of identifying how they may be currently operating. Information processing may also be influenced by problem-solving and autobiographical memory functioning. These factors are considered further in Chapters 5 and 6.

4.4.5.9. Suicidal ideation

It is important to assess suicidal ideation or 'suicide-relevant cognitions' as these are an important predictor of suicidal acts. Suicidal ideation is a broad term covering thoughts, images and hallucinations (Wenzel et al., 2009). With regard to hallucinations, these are likely to be auditory or visual. Hallucinations are classed as suicidal ideation if the content depicts suicidal behaviour. They may also be considered as suicidal ideation if the *interpretation* of these cognitions indicate or increase the chances of suicidal acts.

4.4.5.10. Interpretation of suicidal ideation

It is important to understand the appraisals or interpretations an individual makes about their suicidal ideation. Some clients have a well-elaborated suicidal schema and/or a rich delusional belief system. The case of Max illustrates this point; images of a post office were appraised as indicative of suicide because he had felt suicidal outside a post office. Such thoughts were therefore believed to be symbolic of suicide and to have originated from the 'entity'. In addition, some cognitions may be explicitly suicidal in their content but are not appraised to be indicative of suicide. For example, one client reported seeing repeated images of a noose. However, after receiving normalising information about the nature of intrusive thoughts (Rachman & de Silva, 1978), they reappraised these images as a normal experience of spontaneous, unwanted thoughts, *with no suicidal meaning*.

4.4.5.11. Suicidal intent

It is important to assess a person's reported level of motivation to kill themselves. This is an important predictor of subsequent suicidal acts and deaths (Krupinski et al., 1998; Goldstein et al., 1991). The therapist should assess:

- The person's current motivation to act.
- How likely it is that the person thinks they will act.
- How resilient a person is to setting a contract with the therapist not to act on suicidal intentions.
- What further stressors would lead to the client acting?
- Is motivation contingent upon an event? For example, a particular feared event, such as not getting benefits or an argument.
- What is the likelihood of this happening?
- What does the person predict will happen if they carry out this behaviour?

Obtaining an accurate assessment of suicidal intent may be difficult if a person does not wish to fully convey their level of intent. Concealment of intent is a particularly strong indicator. The clinician should therefore assess for behavioural indicators of intent, such as whether a person took precautions not to be found, mental state leading up to attempt and the person's previous history of attempts (Wenzel et al., 2009).

4.4.5.12. Defeat/entrapment appraisals

It is important to assess for current levels of defeat and entrapment and the level of recent variability in these states. As discussed by Johnson et al. (2008), there are a number of different states that may be classed as defeat. In order to simplify this for clinical use, we have summarised elements of the defeated and entrapment states as follows:

Defeat refers to:

- feelings of failure;
- a sense of not being able to bear or tolerate a particular state;
- a sense of failed struggle and loss of rank.

Entrapment refers to:

- a state where a person signals to themselves and others that they are not going to take on any more challenges.

The elicitation of recovery goals prior to the risk assessment can help a clinician develop an understanding of the values and belief systems a person holds in order to understand why particular events are defeating. For instance, if a person holds a strong desire to be a good parent, shame over letting their children down may be a strong indicator of defeat. The clinician should assess for situations that give rise to such states and the likelihood of these situations occurring in the future. Situations where recovery goals may be transgressed may be an indication of triggers and should, therefore, be carefully and thoroughly explored with the client.

4.4.5.13. Hopelessness/no rescue

An important risk factor for suicide is hopelessness. This refers to a sense of pessimism about the future. This may be characterised by not seeing any positive events occurring in one's future, and/or believing that one's future will be negative. The clinician should assess whether there is a general sense of negativity or whether the person believes specific negative events are going to occur.

Hopelessness has overlap with the concept of 'no rescue'. For the sake of simplicity, we operationalise 'no rescue' clinically as a person's sense that external help can be sought to reduce the sense of defeat/entrapment. The clinician may build up a picture of internal/external sense of agency – how much a person believes they are able to cope with or ameliorate their sense of defeat and/or the extent to which they rely on the presence/intervention of others. As discussed at the start of this chapter, there may be specific blocks to talking about suicide or in accessing help. These should be identified as they pose a barrier to 'rescue appraisals'. The clinician should also assess how no-rescue appraisals change at times of suicide, for example, appraisals of suicide harming one's family may change to thoughts of 'they'd be better off without me'.

4.4.5.14. Plans of suicide

An important predictor of risk is the extent to which a client has made a plan of suicide (Hawton et al., 2005). In terms of understanding the schema, it is also important to understand whether these plans are longstanding or change with each new episode of suicidal experience. The clinician should assess:

- Level of planning.
- Behaviours to put plan into action.
- Has the person planned how to obtain the means of suicide?
- Plans for death (e.g. will change, family farewells).
- Method of suicide and lethality (e.g. hanging, shotgun).
- Have these plans changed over time or do they represent a longstanding plan?

The model/means of suicide is a core aspect of the Cry of Pain model. Some people report planning to commit suicide, but this is on the level of an if-then proposition; they plan to do so if a specific situation(s) occurs. Some people report a general strategy, such as overdosing. A person may also have considered the specific tactics of the plan, for example, they will take a specific substance and have planned how they will obtain it. It is thus important to assess the level of detail of the plan. However, it should be noted that some clients obsess over their plans as a means of distraction, it can become functional itself. If so, the therapist should assess time spent planning and the function for the person, which is usually linked to a sense of taking control.

4.4.5.14.1. ACCESS TO MEANS

An aspect of the Cry of Pain model is that a person may have access to a means of suicide. If the person has a specific plan, the ease by which a person can put their plan into action is a strong predictor. The clinician should therefore assess:

- Does the person have means available to act on their plan? (e.g. tablets in the house, a bridge nearby, access to knives/guns).
- What barriers are there to a person carrying out their plan?

4.4.5.15. Lethality and perceived lethality

As stated in Chapter 2, people with psychosis tend to adopt more violent methods in their suicidal acts (Dumais et al., 2005). However, objective lethality may not be a good predictor of intent as the person may have a poor understanding of the likely consequences of their act. The clinician should therefore assess the person's appraised consequences of their act – *how likely was this to result in death?* If the act was perceived as high-risk then the person may be more vulnerable to future suicidal acts.

4.4.5.16. Factors increasing likelihood

There are a number of factors that may increase the likelihood that a person may make a suicidal act. Beck et al. (1972) referred to these as *mitigating circumstances* and suggested that such factors either decreased a person's awareness of the consequences to their actions or increased the likelihood of self-destructive behaviour. Examples may be:

- substance use and toxicity;
- changes in social circumstances;

- feared future events and specific if-then rules, for example, 'if I get into debt I will kill myself'.

4.4.5.17. Impulsivity

A person's level of impulsiveness should also be assessed. As stated in Chapter 2, strong links have been found between drug and alcohol abuse and impulsive behaviours (Dick et al., 2010). There is also good evidence that impulsivity is related to violent suicides especially when it co-occurs with lifetime experiences of aggression (Dumais et al., 2005). The clinician should therefore assess the following:

- To what extent were previous attempts planned?
- Did previous attempts occur within the context of a number of 'mitigating factors'?

  o   Emotional disturbance, e.g. in response to arguments, fights, etc.

- Is suicidal behaviour considered normal within a person's subculture?

  o   The extent to which this is perceived as a natural consequence of a given set of events.

- The level of aggression a person has displayed or experienced.
- Interactions between a number of mitigating factors.
- Was the person's plan of suicide made on the 'spur of the moment'?

Work by our own team has established that the ease of activation of the suicide schema may give rise to impulsivity (Pratt, Gooding, Johnson, Taylor & Tarrier, 2010). The amount of 'diffuse triggers' and the level of activation of the suicide schema in response to these triggers may also be considered as an index of impulsivity. We suggest that a latent suicide schema underlies ostensibly impulsive acts, processes that can be elucidated through the formulation process. This may reveal (1) the nature of the schema, and (2) the 'cognitive reactivity' of the schema (Pratt et al., 2010; Teasdale, 1988); for some, the threshold for activation may be low.

4.4.5.18. Factors decreasing likelihood

It is also important to assess for deactivators or inhibitors of suicide. The presence of such factors is also an important predictor of overall risk. These deactivators may be proximal, like a family member coming to stay or a brief happy period. Distal factors may include not wanting to harm family members or religious belief systems. This is an important aspect of the assessment as CBSPp aims to elaborate and build upon natural inhibitors in order to prevent suicide.

4.4.5.19. Reasons for killing self

The interviewer should be inquisitive as to the ultimate reason a person has for wanting to kill themselves. It can be helpful to operationalise such states as cognitive or affective states, allowing for specific contingency plans to be put in place. The limits of what a person can tolerate may be defined, for example;

- unending worry;
- frequency 5 or 6 times a day;
- duration 2 to 3 hours;
- emotion: anxiety;
- distress 7/10.

The function of suicide is vital to CBSPp, and the level of understanding develops and grows throughout therapy; these behaviours become contextualised within a person's experiences and relationships.

4.4.5.20. Capability to resist

The person's strengths and resources are also a vital aspect of the CBSPp formulation. A person may be able to indicate their capability to resist certain stressors, for example, being able to resist worry or strong threat-based emotions. If possible this should be objectified, for example:

I can resist anxiety at 8/10 for 2 hours before I begin to think I can't cope any more.

4.4.5.21. Criteria for living

An important aspect of the risk assessment is to ask the client to objectify the conditions under which they would no longer want to kill themselves. For example, the person may state that a reduction in distress would lead to such a change. In the above examples, the person may be able to state reducing the frequency, duration and/or the emotional intensity. This can often begin the process of goal setting. For instance, the person above may set their goal to reducing anxiety to 4/10 with an hour's duration.

4.4.5.21. Reasons for not killing self/protective factors

It is common for people to be ambivalent about killing themselves (Wenzel et al., 2009; Zerler, 2009). Despite reasons for wanting to do so, people may also have strong reasons for not doing so. These may be interpersonal reasons such as family ties, not wanting to hurt family members, missing family members, etc. A person may not be fully convinced about their reasons for killing themselves. Cognitive Therapy techniques can be used to explore any alternative sources of evidence that reduce the strength of thoughts or beliefs stated as reasons for killing oneself. For instance, if a person believed their worry to be never-ending, the person may also be able to identify times when they haven't worried. The assessment of such times is continued throughout therapy, in as much specific detail as possible, to encourage the client to review and reassess global appraisals such as 'my worry is unrelenting'. The factors leading to the alleviation of worry can inform the formulation and be generalised to other, similar situations as part of a strategic intervention.

4.4.5.21. Reasons for living

A broader set of criteria for living may also be established. It can be useful to return to recovery goals here. Movement towards certain life goals may reduce the amount of anxiety or the state of defeat a person experiences, or it may mean that the person can tolerate such experiences because they have something else to live for; Catrina actively faced her distressing voices because she wanted to spend more time with her grandchildren. Other examples may be spending time with friends and family or achieving important life goals such as getting back to work.

4.4.5.22. Experiences of psychosis and immediate risk

A CBSPp risk assessment should also assess for the specific links between experiences of psychosis and suicidal behavior, for example, command hallucinations and any associated risk behaviours or conciliatory actions, or harm-related delusions. Again, this should be objectified in terms of the meaning of these experiences, their frequency, duration, intensity and distress. Critically, the component(s) of these experiences that lead a person to then appraise their situation as unbearable should be clarified. A more thorough examination of the links between the experiences of psychosis and the suicide schema is considered in Chapter 5.

4.4.5.22.1 PSYCHOMETRIC ASSESSMENT OF SUICIDE

There are numerous psychometrics for measuring level of risk and suicidal behaviour. A number of measures enable a multi-dimensional and comprehensive assessment. This reduces therapist drift and provides an index of change against which to measure the efficacy of therapy.

4.4.5.22.2 THE BECK HOPELESSNESS SCALE (BHS)

The Beck Hopelessness Scale (BHS; Beck & Steer, 1988) is a 20-item self-report scale for measuring negative beliefs about the future. It is designed to measure three domains: hopelessness; feelings about the future; loss of motivation, and expectations.

4.4.5.22.3 THE BECK SCALE FOR SUICIDE IDEATION (BSS)

The Beck Scale for Suicide Ideation (BSS; Steer & Beck, 1991) was designed to evaluate suicidal ideation, planning and intent. It consists of 21 items and participants are asked how much they endorse each item on a 3-point scale. The scale distinguishes between actively intending to commit suicide versus a low desire to stay alive in risky situations – what may be called 'passive suicide'.

4.4.5.22.4 THE SUICIDE PROBABILITY SCALE (SPS)

The Suicide Probability Scale (SPS; Cull & Gill, 1988) is a self-report measure for predicting suicidal behaviour. It consists of 36 items rated on a 4-point Likert-type scale. This scale is useful as it produces a probability score of future suicidal behaviour. Clients are classified into Subclinical (0 to 24%); Mild (25 to 49%); Moderate (50 to 74%) and Severe (75 to 100%).

4.4.5.22.5 THE ADULT SUICIDAL IDEATION QUESTIONNAIRE (ASIQ), THOUGHTS ABOUT LIFE

The (ASIQ; Reynolds, 1991) is a self-report scale measuring thoughts and level of preoccupation with death, dying and suicide. Items reflect the number and frequency of recent and more distal suicidal thoughts. Higher scores reflect higher levels of suicidal ideation. High internal consistency, high test-test reliability and satisfactory validity have been reported.

4.4.5.22.6 BRIEF PSYCHIATRIC RATING SCALE (BPRS) – SUICIDALITY

This is a widely used, 16-item, self-report measure and includes symptoms such as somatic concern, anxiety, depressive mood, hostility and hallucinations. These are rated from 0 (not present) to 6 (extremely severe).

4.5 Baseline levels of psychosis and assessment of impact upon experiences of suicide

There are numerous ways that experiences of psychosis may influence suicidal ideation. Such experiences may be one of the primary triggers to defeat appraisals. For example, clients may experience command hallucinations that directly order a person to kill themselves or a delusional belief that they need to kill themselves immediately. However, for others, an experience of psychosis may not contribute to an appraisal of defeat, but the sequelae of such experiences, for example, hospitalisation or social stigma may increase the level of stress the person experiences. The person's appraisals of their experiences of psychosis are likely to influence the extent to which they are distressing. This is consistent with research suggesting that defeat and entrapment appraisals represent transdiagnostic mechanisms fit for purpose for use with people with psychosis (Bolton et al., 2007).

It is therefore important to assess for current experiences and history of psychosis. A number of good texts exist to guide the clinician in the assessment of psychosis (e.g. Morrison et al., 2004). The aim within CBSPp is to explore the specific links between experiences of psychosis and states of defeat/entrapment and subsequent suicidal behaviour; that is, the specific elements of psychosis that increase or decrease the chances of suicide. As reported by Tarrier et al. (2004), there may be different pathways for positive and negative symptoms. The assessment should therefore focus on each experience and how it influences appraisals of defeat, and how suicide may serve as an escape behaviour with potentially multiple functions.

4.5.1. Psychometrics

4.5.1.1. Positive and Negative Syndrome Scale (PANSS; Kay & Opler, 1987)

The Positive and Negative Syndrome Scale (PANSS) is a semi-structured interview schedule with subscales assessing positive and negative 'symptoms' of psychosis; a general psychopathology scale is also included. It is a useful addition to a CBSPp assessment as it offers comprehensive coverage of different experiences of psychosis, which can then be assessed in terms of their links to suicide.

4.5.1.2. Psychotic Symptoms Rating Scale (PSYRATS; Haddock, McCarron, Tarrier & Faragher, 1999)

The Psychotic Symptom Rating Scales (Haddock et al., 1999) are semi-structured interviews designed to assess the subjective characteristics of hallucinations and delusions.

The scales have been shown to have excellent inter-rater reliability and good validity as measured against the Positive And Negative Symptom Scale (Kay & Opler, 1987) both in first-episode (Drake, Haddock, Tarrier et al., 2007) and chronic psychosis (Haddock et al., 1999).

The auditory hallucinations subscale (PSYRATS-AH) has 11 items: for frequency, duration, controllability, loudness, location, severity and intensity of distress, amount and degree of negative content, beliefs about the origin of voices, and disruption.

The delusions subscale (DS) has six items: duration and frequency of preoccupation, intensity of distress, amount of distressing content, conviction, and disruption. A five-point ordinal scale is used to rate symptom scores (0–4). The scale has good reliability and validity with sensitivity to change.

4.5.2. Positive symptoms

The assessment should screen for the presence and history of hallucinations and delusions. This is for the following reasons:

1. *Assess potential barriers to CBSPp work.*
   Positive symptoms may present an initial barrier to therapy, for example, suspiciousness intrudes upon the therapeutic relationship; hallucinations reduce working memory capacity, instruct the client not to talk to the therapist or threaten punishing the client if they do so.
2. *Assess the extent to which these experiences lead to suicidal behaviour.*
   When experiences of psychosis lead to distress, the extent to which they lead to defeat/ entrapment appraisals and suicidal behaviour should be assessed.

4.5.2.1. Hallucinations

In terms of potential barriers to therapy, the clinician should assess the extent to which hallucinations may (1) actively instruct a person not to engage with the therapy, and/or (2) reduce the available resources to attend to the therapy. As discussed in Chapter 6, the clinician may revert to CBTp to reduce such barriers, while being mindful of the CBSPp formulation, capitalising on positive changes and encouraging links to be drawn to appraisals of coping and the reduction of defeat appraisals.

The clinician should also assess:

- Suicide-specific or related content.
- Which aspect(s) of the voice-hearing experience (i.e. the content, the beliefs about the voices, the frequency of the voice, etc.) are the most distressing?
- How are the voices appraised?
- How threatening does the individual appraise these experiences to be?
- Do these experiences increase or decrease defeat/entrapment appraisals?
- How does this relate to experiences of being suicidal?

The purpose is to understand the elements of the voice-hearing experience that are likely to be the main triggers of the suicide schema. The specific pathways between appraisal and threat-based affect are explored in more depth in the formulation chapter (Chapter 5).

4.5.2.2. Suspiciousness

The clinician should assess whether suspiciousness poses a barrier to engagement. If the PANSS and PSYRATS suggest that suspiciousness is likely to impact upon the therapeutic relationship, the clinician should consider using standard CBTp engagement strategies. Again, similar to working with hallucinations, the clinician should be mindful of linking changes in level of suspiciousness to appraisals of personal efficacy, control and personal qualities and resources. It is also possible that suspiciousness may be directly related to defeat and entrapment. Consider the case of George, as follows:

> *George believed that drug dealers in the local area wanted to harm him. George also believed that he was stigmatised for previously being a heroin addict, which was seen in the drug use subculture as being lower in rank to cocaine use. George explained how his levels of suspiciousness increased when he became stressed. This led to a mutually reinforcing cycle of increased distress, increased psoriasis and a sense of being exposed. These factors, especially the sense of being exposed, led to increased suspiciousness and a firmer belief that he would be assaulted. George would then avoid populated areas and avoid looking into people's eyes. These conspiring factors increased until he felt that they were unbearable – leading to a sense of being defeated, both by his feelings and his sense of being 'bottom of the barrel' in his social world. At this point, George would remember previous suicide attempts and begin to think about shooting himself – to make sure he was successful after previous failed attempts.*

The clinician should therefore assess the links from experiences of psychosis to subsequent states of defeat and suicide.

4.5.2.3. Negative symptoms

Negative symptoms may be incorporated within a pathway to hopelessness that is distinctive to the pathway characterised by positive symptoms (Tarrier, Barrowclough, Andrews & Gregg, 2004). The PANSS provides a comprehensive assessment of negative symptoms. The domains of interest are as follows:

4.5.2.3.1 NEGATIVE OR DIMINISHED AFFECT AND ENGAGEMENT WITH ACTIVITIES

The PANSS provides an assessment of 'blunted affect', in essence, diminished emotional expression. This can lead into specific difficulties with expressing or talking about suicidal experiences (see barriers). This can increase the appraisals of 'no rescue'. The therapist may also consider exploring ways of helping the client to express their difficulties to those around them.

It is also important to assess 'emotional withdrawal', a lack of interest/involvement/commitment to life's events and 'passive/apathetic social withdrawal'. A lack of emotional engagement and a passivity to engaging with activities is a vital component of the suicide assessment; if a person is no longer experiencing rewards or is no longer driven to participate in activities, this becomes a focus for intervention (see Chapter 6).

4.5.2.4. Affective activities monitoring

An element of CBSPp is to create a positive feedback cycle of anticipating, initiating and savouring activities associated with positive affect (see Chapter 6). This therefore requires an assessment of the amount of activities a person finds rewarding. This can be done through retrospective assessment as part of the semi-structured interview or through a structured activity scheduling sheet (see Appendices). It is important to record the emotions associated with these activities and their intensity.

4.5.2.5. Flexibility of thought

An important element of CBSPp is to increase flexibility of thought in order to allow the generation of alternative options to presenting difficulties. If the client is to internalise these processes, they require the skills to think in abstract terms. The PANSS assesses both difficulty in abstract thinking and stereotyped thinking. As discussed in Chapter 10, if more pervasive difficulties are indicated, the therapist should consider ways of amending the intervention strategy for the client. Generating a number of concrete alternatives to behaviours currently activated in their suicidal cycle may be one option. The formalisation of an if-then schedule becomes particularly useful in such circumstances. The therapist may also consider alerting other people to specific points/triggers connected to the suicide cycle.

One client, who successfully engaged in CBSPp, achieved a score on the Autistic-Spectrum Quotient (AQ; Baron-Cohen et al., 2001) indicative of high functioning Autism or Asperger Syndrome. An aspect of this difficulty that affected the delivery of therapy was a rigid thinking style and a limited ability to generalise the application of new coping techniques developed during the course of therapy. The impact of this difficulty was overcome through the collaborative development of a 'mood-management plan'. The first part of the plan was for the client to regularly rate their mood from 1 out of 10, indicating extremely low mood through to 10 for extremely high mood. The second part of the plan comprised of a series of idiosyncratic activities that the client had previously experienced as mood-enhancing. One or more of these activities were selected by the client whenever their mood was rated as 3 out of 10 or less. In addition to the immediate mood-lifting experience, this plan also provided the client with a perceived increase in control over the emotional impact of their daily life and also contributed to their blossoming belief that they were able to look after themselves, even when they felt low (a belief previously known to trigger access to their suicide schema).

4.6. Resolution of suicide experiences

Increasing a person's sense of control and agency over situations hitherto deemed defeating is a key aim of CBSPp. This is achieved explicitly through specific formulation-driven interventions (Chapter 5). However, this is also achieved through every exchange with an individual. The assessment offers the first opportunity to begin to increase a person's sense of agency over defeating experiences and the suicidal experience itself. Traditional risk assessments begin with triggering incidents and end with the elicitation of suicidal behaviour. However, we have found that identifying how long a period of suicidality lasted for and an indication of the factors that resolved this issue, where possible, can be an important aspect of the assessment. This is illustrated in Figure 4.1.

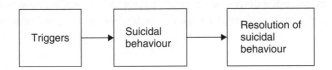

Figure 4.1 From trigger to resolution of suicidal ideation and behaviour

4.7. Evaluation of risk and risk management

Once the assessment has been completed, the overall level or risk should then be formulated and appropriate action taken. If the client presents with suicidal ideation and they have a high level of intent to kill themselves, strategies for risk management and immediate risk reduction are indicated. We outline interventions that may be used to reduce immediate risk in the intervention chapter (Chapter 6).

4.8. Assessment of strengths and resilience

A key element of the CBSPp assessment is an analysis of a client's strengths and resilience factors. There are two main aims: (1) to identify factors that may be harnessed to prevent suicidal behaviour; and (2) to assess the level of suicide schema activation: the ease of identification of strength and resilience factors is an excellent indicator of the level of elaboration and/or activation of the suicide schema.

4.8.1. Persistent behaviours

As discussed by Kuyken et al. (2009), clients can often forget or find it hard to draw upon their strengths and coping strategies when they are very distressed. We suggest that an elaborated suicide schema increases the breadth of suicide behaviour as a coping behaviour, effectively reducing access or inhibiting problem-solving potential or alternative functional behaviours (Johnson et al., 2008; Pratt et al., 2010). In cases with an elaborated suicide schema the therapist should remain aware of any evidence of positive/functional behaviours. Kuyken et al. (2009) provide the following examples:

- Personal hygiene/appearance (clothing choices, hair, shaving).
- Going to work.
- Caring for a pet.
- Keeping a garden.
- Attending sports/commitments.
- Parental behaviour.
- 'Any common daily activity maintained during distress can be viewed as a strength. These values and strengths may only be implicit, and clients may minimize them through the cognitive biases that are typical of emotional disorders' (Beck, 1979).

These behaviours should be highlighted by the therapist throughout the therapy. The comments should be realistic or else they may trigger self-criticism; this information is likely to be incongruent with the suicide schema and emergent appraisals of defeat and entrapment, and may therefore prompt a defensive reaction. Biases in information processing should be noted as they occur, and the therapist should use their judgement in highlighting these to clients.

4.8.2. Resilience

Kuyken et al. (2009) suggests that resilience means '. . . the psychological processes through which people draw upon their strengths to adapt to challenges'. So, resilience to suicide factors are those factors that a person can draw upon to reduce suicide schema activation. Ann Masten (2001, p. 234) described resilience as 'ordinary magic', arguing that resilience arises from '. . . connections to competent and caring adults in the family and community, cognitive and self-regulation skills, and motivation to be effective in the environment' (p. 234). Johnson et al. (2008) suggested that specific resilience factors in the prevention of suicide in psychosis were positive self-appraisals (see Chapter 6, the intervention chapter).

4.8.3. Personal values

Kuyken et al. (2009) suggested that a vital component of a resilience formulation is an analysis of a client's personal values. Values are defined as important beliefs that are relatively enduring across a number of situations in a person's life. It is often only when one understands how a situation transgressed a person's deeply held values that one can understand the factors that led a person to feel defeated.

4.9 Creating a summary of assessment and obtaining informed consent

The client should be presented with a summary of the assessment and an overview of CBSPp before informed consent is taken (Rudd et al., in press). The assessment should summarise:

- recovery goals;
- current levels of risk;
- factors impacting upon risk;
- protective factors;
- inhibitory factors/natural exits from suicidal states.

The client should then be given an outline of CBSPp, which may be as follows:

> In this therapy we would work together to understand your experiences of suicide better. We would look at how your life experiences and challenges have led you to feel defeated and that you could not escape. We can explore together how your thoughts are influenced by your mood as well as your attention and memory. Then, we can begin to think about how we might work together to plan for life's hurdles in the future. We start by exploring how the way we look at the world is influenced by our mood, and we can try some techniques that can help you to move your attention to the positive things in your life (information processing). We then look at the role of thoughts and how these can make you feel worse (appraisals). Then we can think about how your mind has learnt to think of suicide as a way out of these situations and how we can learn alternative ways

of dealing with them (suicide schema). Throughout this therapy we will help to identify all the things you have done in the past to deal with these situations and build on them together.

This introduction should be amended to the individual's own frame of reference by adopting the language that they have used to talk about their experiences. The client is then offered the choice to proceed with therapy. As discussed in Chapter 6, some clients may not choose to work on their experiences directly. The following overview may be provided:

I understand that you find it hard to talk about some of your experiences. We can work together to explore these difficulties. This is understandable, there can be many reasons why a person may find this difficult. We can work together to make this easier for you.

The clinician then begins to address the difficulties of direct CBSPp work, as discussed in Chapters 4 and 6. Once a client feels ready to talk about their experiences of suicide, they are offered the choice to consent to direct CBSPp work. This can be a symbolic moment in their sense of agency over such experiences.

Chapter 5

Formulating the prevention of suicide

5.1. Executive summary

- *A CBSPp formulation identified the psychological mechanisms that increase the activation of the suicide schema and those mechanisms that are influenced by this schema to increase the probability of suicidal ideation, intent and behaviour.*

- *The formulation also identified specific thoughts, feelings, behaviours and schemata involved in the inhibition of suicide.*

- *The formulation identified the idiosyncratic function of suicide as an escape.*

- *Functional alternatives to suicide as an escape are hypothesised.*

- *Three stages are identified:*

  ○ *information processing;*
  ○ *appraisals;*
  ○ *schema.*

- *The formulation leads to strategic interventions to (1) attenuate suicide-specific processes and (2) increase suicide inhibitory processes.*

The preceding chapters have considered the role of various risk factors for suicide in the context of psychosis. An explanatory framework has been presented: The suicide schema seems to provide a mechanism to explain the development, perseveration and elaboration of states of defeat and hopelessness and to prime suicide as an escape behaviour from such states. It is therefore the task of the clinician to develop a case formulation with the client, arriving at a shared understanding of how this schematic appraisal system may be operating to maintain a client's suicidal state or how it may be activated in the future to increase the probability of suicidal behaviour.

The schema is thought to be a network of interrelated appraisals and emotions; elaboration leads to an iteratively expanding web of potential triggers (Pratt, Gooding, Johnson, Taylor & 2010). The function(s) of suicidal behaviour are conceptualised to be the core element of the suicide schema and are therefore central to the formulation. According to the CoP model (Williams, 1997, 2005) the function of the schema and suicidal behaviour will be to escape from a state of defeat. Our team have speculated that once a suicide schema becomes elaborated (Pratt, Gooding, Johnson, Taylor & Tarrier, 2010), suicidal behaviour may also function to *prevent* a return to a defeating experience(s). The client may also have a desired state they believe they can *escape to*, for example, some people imagine a return to a sense of calmness experienced after a previous suicidal act or imagine death to be a peaceful state free from worry or frightening experiences.

The case formulation represents a synthesis of theoretical knowledge applied to the unique situation and history of the presenting client. It makes hypotheses about what causes and maintains the client's suicidal behaviour, and the likely origins of these difficulties (Persons, 2008). The reader is invited to take some time to think about clients they have worked with and to reflect upon what function suicidal thoughts and behaviour had for them: what were they trying to escape from? What would they gain from ending their lives?

Key point 1

The fundamental aim of formulating suicidal behaviour is to understand its function as an escape/avoidance behaviour. In order to do this, the formulation should capture what the client believes they need to escape from or what they want to avoid; the processes that lead to this state and the processes that maintain it. It should also capture what the person's desired state is; what they want to escape to.

Research has suggested that there are multiple pathways to suicidal behaviour. Suicide may also serve multiple functions for the same person. As discussed in Chapter 2, Tarrier and colleagues (Tarrier et al., 2004) identified two different pathways in people with psychosis; one pathway was mediated by positive symptoms such as hallucinations and delusions, and the other pathway was mediated by negative symptoms, characterised by asociality and withdrawal. Suicide research suggests that defeating (Williams, 1997, 2005) or unbearable (Joiner, Brown & Wingate, 2004; Rudd, 2004) situations may be separated from hopelessness as predictors of suicide. A third factor has found to be the degree of isolation a person feels from others. Psychosis may also lead to an increased sense of stigma and experiences of discrimination, either real or perceived. This may further increase a person's sense of isolation, defeat or hopelessness and avoidance of mobilising social resources, that is, a failure to seek help and support. The formulation should therefore identify the specific nature of the experience that leads a person to suicide, whether this is a sense of defeat, hopelessness, isolation or a combination of all three; and how experiences of psychosis may be associated with these experiences.

Key point 2

There may be multiple pathways to suicide. Hallucinations and delusions along with a host of other non-psychosis related stressors may be associated with high levels of threat. This may result in feelings of defeat. Withdrawal and asociality may be linked to a sense of hopelessness, which in itself could lead to suicidal thoughts. Psychosis can lead to stigma and discrimination. This may be a factor in a sense of isolation, which is a third factor that may increase suicidal behaviour.

Another key aspect of the suicide prevention formulation is resilience (Johnson, Gooding, Wood & Tarrier, 2010; Johnson et al., 2010; Johnson, Wood, Gooding, Taylor & Tarrier, 2011; Masten, 2001). In tandem with formulating the suicidal schema, the therapist should begin to formulate hypotheses as to what reduces or inhibits a client's suicidal behaviour. The likely origins of such factors may also be conceptualised as alternative schemata (Kuyken at al., 2009). The formulation may therefore identify schematic appraisal networks that can be developed and integrated to provide functional alternatives and/or to inhibit the suicidal schematic appraisal network.

The formulation should combine knowledge of suicide and resilience schemata, and provide a hypothesis of how intervention should proceed. This may work in two ways. Just as a heart surgeon conducting a transplant will be concerned with isolating the blood flow into the existing heart and redirecting this temporarily, the therapist is concerned with identifying and reducing the factors that lead to and maintain suicidal behaviour.

However, the surgeon must also identify a new heart, keep this healthy and implant it at the right time, connecting it to each artery. Similarly, the therapist also formulates processes that will inhibit the suicide schema and build on existing links to these processes, enabling them to be activated in previously defeating situations. Therapy proceeds by developing functional alternatives for each step in the chain of events that can lead to suicidal behaviour.

Again, think of clients you may have worked with. What has led to a reduction in their suicidal behaviour? Why was this meaningful for them? What changed?

Key Point 3

The fundamental aim of formulating and developing resilience factors and developing natural inhibitors is to provide functional alternatives to suicidal behaviour or the chain of events that may lead to it.

5.2. Formulating resilience – mapping the suicide schema and resilience factors

As discussed in Chapters 3 and 4, there may be numerous pathways that lead to both increases and decreases in suicidal thoughts and behaviour. The process of mapping difficulties and resilience factors is therefore introduced early in therapy as a collaborative task between client and therapist. The links between problems, underlying cognitive behavioural mechanisms and their origins are then explored using the full CBSPp formulation.

After grouping problems into clusters, the therapist may then use a diagram to explore with the client the relationship between each of their difficulties and, ultimately, their links to suicidal thoughts and behaviour. In some cases, the process of mapping these links can be tremendously empowering for clients as it helps to demystify the relationships between different experiences and can increase the understanding of both the client and therapist as to what are the important processes involved in suicide. This can then inform the goals of therapy. This process can also lead into an exploration of the function of suicide behaviour.

An example of a diagram that may be drawn with a client is presented in Figure 5.1. It can be seen that different problem clusters activate the suicide schema at different levels. Clusters of problems or difficulties that have previously triggered suicidal acts may be most strongly linked to the suicide schema, represented as Problem Cluster 1. Problems that were hitherto manageable may become potential triggers once the suicide schema has become activated as schema activation may spread the inhibition of problem-solving/coping strategies to other domains. For example, command hallucinations (problem 1) telling a person to kill themselves may be made worse by arguments with a partner (problem 2). Arguments with a partner may trigger isolation, which may then become more strongly linked to suicidal

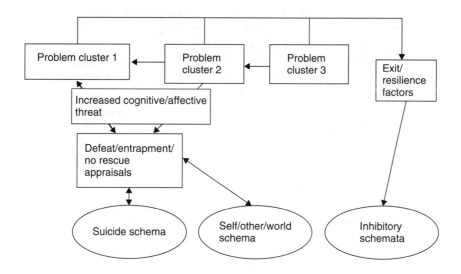

Figure 5.1 Mapping the relationship between problems and resilience qualities

thoughts/behaviours. Other problems impact upon suicidal behaviour indirectly, by impacting upon other mechanisms (problem 3). An example here may be financial pressure only leading to such thoughts if it increases tension in a person's relationships. Modelling the relationship between problems in this way can help with the prediction of future situations that could be problematic. Intrinsic to the development of the suicide schema is a person's beliefs about themselves, other people and the world that are linked to the suicidal schema. These then become a focus for the intervention.

Figure 5.1 also includes exit points. These may be things that naturally occur to attenuate difficulties. It is important to understand the key mechanism that is attenuated in such circumstances. For instance, spending time with a family member may reduce their sense of sense of loneliness and of being a burden on others. The nature of exit points and the underlying inhibitory/resilience schemata should be mapped onto this diagram.

We may then take each experience of psychosis and explore how it may activate the suicide schema. If suicide is a circumscribed reaction to a particular experience of psychosis and does not occur in response to other stressors, the intervention will then formulate the specific appraisals that then lead a person to conclude that this situation is intolerable and unrelenting.

5.2.1. Case example

For Bob, the suicide schema was most strongly triggered by thoughts of getting into debt. This was based on a childhood experience of his father getting into debt and then attempting suicide. Bob developed the rule from an early age that he would not be able to cope if he was to get into debt and that he too would attempt to kill himself. Subsequent periods of financial difficulties had indeed led to defeat/entrapment appraisals and to a number of overdoses. Getting into debt and worrying about this was therefore identified as a problem to be worked upon in therapy.

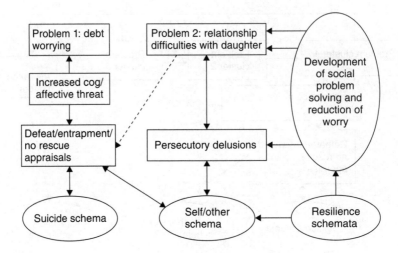

Figure 5.2 Case example of 'map' of problems and resilience factors

Bob also identified relationship difficulties as a trigger for persecutory delusions. These seemed to be based upon the view of himself as worthless and undeserving of care from others and beliefs about others as punishing and uncaring. Bob had a high tolerance for this as he had a strong relationship with his daughter. However, sporadic breakdowns with his daughter had led Bob to appraisals of being alone and 'no rescue appraisals' because he thought nobody else could or would help him. This increased his sense of defeat and entrapment. This could then lead to the activation of the suicide schema as an escape. In this way, the suicide schema becomes elaborated further and begins to represent a generic escape path for defeating situations.

This formulation allows a number of hypotheses to be made to guide intervention strategies. It would predict that reducing specific defeat appraisals with regard to worrying about debt would reduce the valence of the suicide schema. It would also predict that generic defeat appraisals of suicide as an escape may be addressed by increasing both ability and confidence in problem-solving. The appraisal that his daughter would abandon him when they had an argument also became a focus for Bob in therapy. This led to the activation of Bob's beliefs of himself as worthless and others as punishing.

Bob's persecutory delusions were formulated as a consequence of feeling isolated and ultimately because they triggered his sense that others would punish/reject him. Bob reported that they were never a primary reason for wanting to take his own life, but just compounded his sense of isolation. The specific appraisals concerning isolation at times of defeat were therefore a target for CBSPp, but general work on persecutory delusions was not. This could become a subsequent aim of CBTp.

Key point 4

The defeat, entrapment and no rescue appraisals are the gateway to activation of the suicide schema. Formulation begins by understanding how different groups of problems activate these appraisals.

5.3. The CBSPp formulation: A clinical heuristic

Once the relationships between difficulties are mapped, the therapist and client begin to identify the specific cognitive behavioural mechanisms involved in the development and maintenance of suicidal thoughts and behaviour. We have developed a clinical heuristic to provide a template for the development of a CBSPp formulation (see Figure 5.3). This formulation aggregates each cognitive behavioural cycle into a generic overview. Informed by the SAMS, this formulation is based on three main mechanisms:

1. Attention & information processing.
2. Appraisals.
3. Suicide schema.

The CBSPp model may be thought of as a suicide-specific elaboration of Tarrier and Calam's (2002) systems model of formulation, which conceptualises difficulties as a balancing of homeostatic processes. This model therefore identifies the factors that increase the probability of suicidal behaviours such as threat-focused attention, appraisals, the activation of beliefs about the self, world and other people, and the activation of the suicide schema. Maintenance cycles are also identified within the formulation such as the paradoxical role of safety behaviours and/or avoidance. The aim is to identify modifiable processes that naturally inform an intervention strategy.

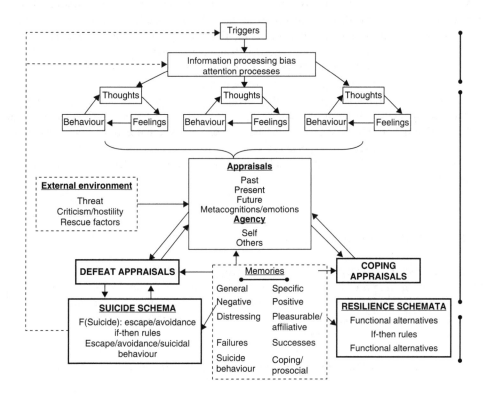

Figure 5.3 Generic CBSPp formulation

The model also includes factors that naturally attenuate, reduce or are incongruent with suicidal behaviour. This may not be clear early in therapy, especially if the client is highly problem-focused. The formulation should therefore evolve and develop throughout therapy to include 'exit' points to suicide. The end result is a plan or map to follow should a person experience a trigger to the suicide schema, with specific 'exits' or interventions to follow in such instances. We have found that the formulation becomes simplified over sessions as the client and therapist build a shared language for the processes at the heart of the formulation.

5.4. Developing a resilience narrative

The client may begin by discussing index experiences, that is, the first or most critical experience involved in the formation of schema or proto-schema (Kelly et al., in preparation), and then progressing to establish how current difficulties are linked to this underlying schema. Another option is to discuss recent and/or relatively benign events, and then progress to more traumatic memories as the client is able to do this. As discussed in the assessment chapter (Chapter 4), the therapist formulates the level of threat associated with talking about difficult/suicidal experiences. It may be that the first stage of intervention is implemented prior to the development of a full formulation to allow the client to cope with threat-based thoughts and feelings in session. The clinician and client then review specific instances of suicide and its resolution.

Increasing a person's sense of control and agency over situations hitherto deemed defeating is a key aim of CBSPp. This is achieved explicitly through specific formulation-driven interventions. However, this is also achieved through every exchange with an individual. The assessment and formulation stage offers the first opportunity to begin to increase a person's sense of agency over defeating experiences and the suicidal experience itself. We begin by outlining a standard Cognitive Therapy assessment influenced by the Cry of Pain model (Figure 2.2) before considering resilience-focused interview processes.

In the standard interview process, the therapist and client formulate the mechanisms influenced by, and influencing the suicide schema, charting them on a 'trigger to suicidal behaviour' timeline. However, as discussed above, this experience may lead a person to relive a potentially traumatic experience, resulting in the activation of the suicide schema and the experience of defeat and suicidal thoughts in session. Consider the example of Jane (Box 5.1).

Box 5.1 Case example: Jane

In the standard 'trigger-to-suicidal behaviour' formulation, J reported that she received rejecting text messages from her family. This would be appraised as one of total rejection and feeling very alone in the world. J had a history of multiple losses and experiences of rejection. The support of her family and a sense of being connected was very important to J and the sense of isolation she felt in response to these texts left her feeling very alone and defeated by the prospect of dealing with overwhelming emotions. In session, discussing these experiences was very difficult, activating a sense of isolation.

While it can be important for the formulation to activate the suicide schema in order to facilitate change, we suggest that framing accounts of previous suicidal thoughts and behaviours as experiences that were resolved in some way can reduce the strength of defeat associated with these memories and begin to connect them with a sense of agency. One approach is to extend the formulation interview to cover the period after the suicidal experience, and if possible, continuing until the person identifies a state when they were no longer suicidal (see Figure 5.4). The processes or mechanisms that led to this reduction are then identified. This may be a particular event, such as a reconnection with others. Formulating in this way may also result in the activation of the emotions associated with the resolution of such experiences. The BMAC may then be used with the aim of increasing the strength and retrievability of memories and emotions associated with specific instances of the resolution of suicidal experiences (Kelly & Welford, submitted).

Recovery from a period of suicidality may be a gradual process and the person may not be able to provide specific details. Drawing attention to the fact that suicidal feelings may not have lasted forever is still important, it may serve to reduce the finality of suicide in a person's mind. It can also reframe the autobiographical memory; the start and end points may have been the trigger and the experience of suicidal behaviour, respectively. By formulating in this way, we are attempting to move the 'end' of the memory beyond the suicidal experience to include the natural processes that may have reduced these feelings. The 'start' of the memory may be reconceptualised as earlier in the chain of events at a time when a person perceives themselves to have more choice to change the flow of events that follow (Figure 5.5).

It is sometimes possible to begin the account of suicidal behaviour with the incident that resolved it (Kelly & Welford, submitted). Clients may not be used to providing history like this or indeed thinking about their experiences in this order but there are important reasons for doing so. Once an account of a defeating experience has been elicited and the factors that resolved it established, the therapist may then bridge to other experiences by asking whether the client resolved any other experiences in this way. The value of this approach is that memories are evoked from the standpoint of an experience that was successfully

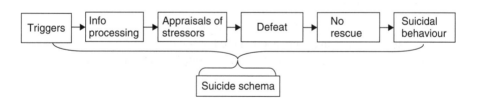

Figure 5.4 Trigger to suicidal behaviour

Figure 5.5 Resolution to behaviour to trigger

resolved. This information is 'on-line' allowing for the defeating memory to be re-processed as an experience that the client successfully dealt with. It is hoped that this will make such memories more accessible.

The exploration of naturally occurring resilience factors leads into the development of the goals for the intervention. In Jane's case, this involved solidifying memories of connection and remembering these when she felt rejected by her loved ones (see Box 5.2). We have presented checklists below of factors to assess in the development of suicidal behaviour and then in a separate section, the factors involved in the resolution of these states. This is for ease of presentation. However, in practice, the CBSPp therapist should attempt to link and weave agency appraisals and awareness of inhibitory factors into each stage of the client's story wherever possible.

Box 5.2 Jane's resilience strategy

J reported that she had recently experienced a rejecting text from a family member but had not experienced defeat appraisals or any suicidal ideation. J had been sat with her new partner when she had received the text message. J reflected that she could cope with her families rejecting text messages if she could maintain a sense of connection and not being alone with her difficulties. Whilst she had achieved this when she was in the presence of her partner, J was also able to reflect that she had received lots of rejecting texts, her family never actually rejected her absolutely, that they were often sent in the heat of the moment. One strategy for therapy was therefore to work on various means of maintaining a sense of connection at times of conflict and to address the tendency to jump to conclusions in such situations.

Box 5.3 Factors involved in the development of suicidal behaviour

Background to attempt

1. Detailed account of distal factors impacting on person
   a. E.g. life events that were pertinent to this attempt
2. Detailed account of proximal factors impacting on person (e.g. 24 to 48 hours events preceding event).

Number of attempts, then for each attempt:
Specific stressors/triggers

1. Problems (nature, duration, perceived consequences/appraisals)
   a. intrapersonal
      i. general mental health difficulties
      ii. psychosis
   b. interpersonal relationships
      i. romantic
      ii. familial
      iii. broader social network

　　c.　financial
　　d.　housing
　　e.　other

Substances
1.　alcohol
2.　other substances

Other mitigating circumstances
Information processing biases
Problem solving and
physiological experiences
Emotions
Defeat/entrapment
No rescue
Model/means:
Function of suicidal behaviour
Resolution of suicidal behaviour – proximal/distal

Box 5.4 Assessment of factors leading to the prevention of suicide

Proximal exit from suicide behaviour:

1.　nature of exit from suicide behaviour
　　a.　external (prevented by others) (likely to attribute to external sources)
　　b.　internal (strength/quality/personal rule)

Distal exit from suicidal behaviour/defeat/hopelessness:

1.　identifying processes associated with longer term reduction in suicide behaviour

　　a.　internal
　　　i.　attention switching
　　　ii.　problem-solving (external problems facing individual/appraisal of problems – 1st-tier appraisals)
　　　iii.　resolution of 2nd-tier appraisals: experiences as threatening
　　　iv.　resolution of 3rd-tier appraisals: global defeat/coping
　　　v.　role in changing relationships
　　b.　external: reduction in problem facing individual
　　　i.　interpersonal relationships
　　　　1.　romantic
　　　　2.　familial
　　　　3.　broader social network
　　　ii.　financial
　　　iii.　housing
　　　iv.　other

5.5. Cognitive Behavioural formulation of suicide

Formulation proceeds by conducting a cognitive behavioural analysis of each experience. The aim here is to elicit the role of attentional processes, information processing biases, appraisals and behaviours that are activated during experiences of hopelessness/ and suicidal thinking or behaviour. Figure 5.6 provides a framework for this assessment.

5.5.1. Triggers

The trigger to suicidal behaviour is the first event that leads to this occurring, the first domino in a chain of events. Triggers can be internal, occurring as a thought or feeling within a person; or external, an event occurring outside of a person, in their environment. We have presented triggers first for coherence. However, it may be that the therapist and client backtrack from difficult feelings and thoughts to what prompted them.

5.5.1.1. External triggers

External triggers are those in the client's environment that can activate a chain of events that could potentially lead to suicidal behaviour. Triggers may seem innocuous to the outsider (Johnson et al., 2008). It has been suggested that the more elaborated the suicidal schema the more potential triggers (Pratt et al., 2010) perhaps serving the function of an iteratively

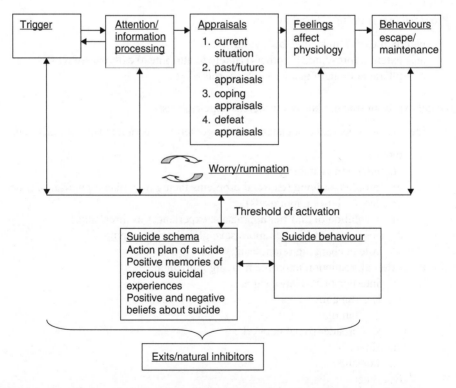

Figure 5.6 Cognitive behavioural formulation of suicide and resilience

strengthened avoidance system (Kelly et al., *if-then paper*). It is important to continue to explore how triggers become attached to the suicide schema. This may reveal implicit reasoning that underlies the elaboration of the suicide schema as a potential escape. Informing the client that this is a natural process and working with them to identify reasons why certain events have become linked to suicide may lead to the identification of further processes involved in the elaboration of the schema. The client may well be able to provide explicit reasoning as to why this is so: Max constantly scanned his environment to evaluate whether events or objects were potential signs (Chapter 4).

5.5.1.2. Internal triggers

It is vital to assess for and formulate the role of internal triggers. These may not be part of a client's natural account of their experiences. Some clients may express bewilderment as to what led to their difficult thoughts and emotions. However, providing the client with psychoeducation about the nature of internal triggers, and explicitly asking about them, can help a client to identify and describe these triggers. Internal triggers may be viewed as intrusions and may occur in any of the sensory modalities.

5.5.1.3. Diffuse suicidal triggers

We have coined the term 'diffuse suicidal triggers' to capture the network of associated environmental and cognitive events that may become linked to an elaborated suicide schema (Pratt et al., 2010). We are referring here to the triggers that a client may link to suicide but may not have an explicit reason for why this is so. There is an important clinical point here. Clients may be confused and worried by a sense of not being able to control when their feelings of defeat and periods of suicidal ideation begin. Normalising such processes and providing an explanation for how things that seem unrelated to suicide can often trigger such feelings and can begin to give the client a sense of control and agency over a seemingly defeating process.

5.5.2. Intrusions

Intrusions into conscious awareness may be a trigger for suicidal behaviour. An intrusion may be a thought, an image, a memory or a fragment of a memory, or a remembered felt-sense of threat. Intrusions have been defined as unwanted, unbidden and spontaneous (Rachman 1981; Wells & Morrison, 1994). Research evidence suggests that intrusion content is disorder-specific (Harvey et al., 2006); for example, people with GAD experience intrusions about catastrophic things that may happen in the future (Vasey & Borkovec 1992; Davey & Levy, 1998). Intrusions linked to psychotic experiences should be assessed, along with appraisals of these intrusions (Morrison et al., 1995). As discussed in Chapter 2, a number of clients experience 'flash forwards', that is, images of their imagined future suicide attempt (Holmes et al., 2007), for example, vivid images of themselves hanging from a rafter. The presence of suicide-specific intrusions/images should be assessed along with their interpretation.

5.5.2.1. Strategy for eliciting triggers/intrusions

- Where were you? What were you doing?
- What did you notice in your environment?

- What could you see?
- What could you hear?
- Could you smell anything?
- Were there any feelings (from outside)?
- Were there any feelings in your body?
- Was there an image in your mind?
- Was there a memory that triggered this?

5.5.2.2. Interpersonal triggers

- Who else was there?
- What were they doing?
- Anybody in particular?
- How did you interpret their intentions?
- How were they making you feel?
- Does this remind you of other situations?
- What do you believe about other people?
- Were you alone/in public?
- Did anybody say anything to you?

5.5.3. Attentional processes

A key component of the suicide prevention formulation is to understand how attention may be guided by the suicide schematic appraisal system and how selective attention may lead to the maintenance of this schema. The following questions may be used to elicit these attentional processes:

How much of your attention was directed inwards, to your thoughts and feelings?

Internal experience:

- How much of your attention was focused on difficult or threatening thoughts, feelings? What were they?
- How much of your attention was focused on pleasant thoughts, feelings?
- What do you make of that?

External environment:

- How much of your attention was directed towards looking for or focused upon things you find threatening in the world around you?
- How much of your attention was directed at things in the environment that are not related to your difficulties?
- What do you make of that?

Narrowed attention:

- Is it difficult to move your attention away from X?

Appraisals of attention:

- What are the advantages of looking out for X?
- What do you fear would happen if you stopped looking out for X?
- What would be the advantages of not looking for X?
- What would be the advantages of looking for 1/X – information that does not fit with what you believe might happen (i.e. incongruent information)?
- Would you find it hard to do that?
- What do you make of that?
- How do you think your attention may be influencing your experiences of hopelessness/ feeling defeated?
- How do you think that your attention influences the thought that you are defeated? Have no future?
- How do you think working on increasing your control of your attention may influence the thoughts that you are defeated? Have no future? Etc.
- Do you think you can take control over your attention and direct it away from your threatening thoughts/feelings, behaviours, memories?

5.5.4. Appraisals

The SAMS model suggests that the appraisal system both activates the suicide schema and is influenced by this schema. As depicted in Figure 5.3, we suggest that there are a number of levels of appraisal that lead to schema activation. These are as follows:

1. Appraisals of current situation.
2. Appraisals of past and appraisals of future.
3. Defeat appraisals.

Established techniques used in standard cognitive behavioural formulations may be used to establish appraisals that can lead a person to experience distress. However, specific questioning is necessary to establish appraisals that may lead to defeat and entrapment appraisals. The following set of questions may offer a guide for establishing the different components of the appraisal system. This interview process can be done for specific examples of each type of stressor. However, as discussed in section 5.5.4.3, people with a high level of distress and suicidal behaviour have been shown to use an over-general recall strategy. If the person cannot provide specific examples, then the general nature of memories may be elicited and appraisals assessed. The therapist should make a note of a person's retrieval style, whether the person provides specific information or reports a general sense of what happened without detail. This can form an important part of the formulation.

5.5.4.1 Appraisal of the current situation

It is important to assess the appraisals a person makes of their current difficulties and situation. Critically, it is important to understand how these appraisals may be linked to defeat and entrapment appraisals. These appraisals play an important role in the elaboration and maintenance of the suicide schema.

5.5.4.1.1. ASSESSING CURRENT APPRAISALS

- When you were in situation X, what was going through your mind?
- What was difficult about the situation?
- What made you feel like that?
- Downward arrow – what was so bad about that?

5.5.4.2. Appraisal of the past

A person's appraisals of the past should be formulated. These can have an important role in determining future appraisals and the speed with which a person arrives at a state of defeat. Clients may spontaneously talk about their past during the assessment, and further specific details may be elicited when difficult times in their lives are discussed. Again, it is best to begin with general questions about how a person views their life so far and then focus in on specific examples. It is also important to assess for memories of good times or times when a person feels that they have coped well. Of particular interest is how appraisals of the past are linked to defeat appraisals and thoughts and plans of suicide as a means of escape, in essence, what elements of the persons past experience come to mind when the suicide schema is activated? Contrasts should be sought for differences in appraisals in the absence of suicide schema activation.

5.5.4.2.1. OPEN/BROAD QUESTIONS

- How has life been for you?
- How would you describe the way things have gone for you?
- Can you remember good times in your past?
- In general, how do you think you have coped with difficulties?
- Do you feel that things generally go your way? What is this based on?

5.5.4.2.2. SPECIFIC SITUATIONS

- Did this situation remind you of anything?
- Did your thoughts about the past:
    - . . . influence how you saw this situation?
    - . . . make it seem more difficult or less?
- What role did your thoughts of the past have on feeling defeated, trapped, hopeless, suicidal in this situation?
- Did these thoughts affect how likely it was that you asked for help or felt able to do so?

5.5.4.3. The role of negative memories

It is important to understand the role of memory activation in the progression to suicide. It may be that they are activated when a person encounters a setback or a difficulty. If a person consistently remembers negative events from the past, it is likely to shape their appraisals of the present and their views on how things are going to work out for them. The client may have had particularly traumatic experiences of abuse, of being ill in the past, hospitalisation, suicidal acts and their consequences, etc. The therapist can then attempt to gently identify how such memories are activated given certain conditions, and how they are linked to current experiences of defeat/entrapment.

Useful questions can be as follows:

- When you are thinking like this, does it remind you of times from your past?
- Are there specific memories that come to mind?
- Or is it a general sense of what has happened to you?
- If we take some time now, can you remember what has led you to think like this?
- How recent are the memories that come to mind?

5.5.4.4. Positive memories

It may be that a person has a balance between memories of good and bad times in their lives. It is important to formulate whether good memories are stored as fragments or as specific memories. The person may not have been able to report specific positive memories but may be able to report a general sense that good things have happened.

The therapist may have discussed good times in a person's life during more relaxed moments in therapy. These should be noted and stored by the therapist. They can serve as an important signifier of a change in state when a person can no longer recall such memories or is considering beliefs such as 'nothing good has ever happened to me'. By gently reminding clients of these memories, the therapist can prepare the ground for Socratic dialogue by exploring the nature of the changes to memory systems in different states. The important point here is that clients may arrive at a conclusion that they are unlikely to remember good times in their lives when they encounter certain stressors or enter certain states, but they can gain the knowledge that this may be due to the way that their memory works rather than only bad things happening to them. We are therefore working to add shades of grey to the black or white conclusions a client may draw upon their life and past.

5.5.4.5. Appraisals of the future

Appraisals of the future are clearly very important as they will reflect optimism or pessimism regarding the possibility of change and the person's judgements about their own potency and worth as a person. This can be linked to a person's appraisals of their ability to solve the difficulties life may throw at them.

5.5.4.5.1. ASSESSING FUTURE APPRAISALS

- How do you see your future panning out?
- What do think will happen in your future?
- Can you see a future for yourself?
- Do you see the future as good or bad?
- Do you think your future will be difficult/hard?
- Are there any specific difficulties you think you will face?
- Is there anything to look forward to in your future?
- Can you think of specific things that will be good in the future?

5.5.4.6. Problem-solving appraisals

A person's ability to solve problems or their confidence in their ability to do so can be a specific factor impacting upon their view of the future. A lack of confidence in dealing with life's difficulties can make future challenges seem much more challenging. This is assessed specifically in the problem-solving stage of the intervention, but useful questions at this stage are as follows:

- When you face a difficulty, do you feel that you can overcome it?
- Do you believe that you can cope with life's difficulties?
- Can you think of ways round problems?
- Do you have confidence in approaching life's difficulties?
- How long can you persevere with a difficulty?
- Do you quickly feel defeated by difficulties?

5.5.4.7. Defeat and entrapment appraisals

The therapist works with the client to establish the factors led the person to appraisals of defeat. What was it about their appraisals of their situation that transgressed what they could tolerate? As a useful check, the appraisals of defeat and function of suicide and natural disinhibitors should match. So, if a person cites financial difficulties as the main stressor, but cites contact with their child/family/friends as a deactivator of their experiences of defeat, there is likely to be a latent or implicit appraisal of loneliness, isolation or a lack of connectedness that is not available to direct questioning of the sequence of events that led to suicidal behaviour. Within each CBT cycle, the therapist's aim is to establish the flow of events that led to an inexorable sense of defeat.

5.5.4.7.1. THE GATEWAY TO DEFEAT AND ENTRAPMENT APPRAISALS

Useful questions to elicit how a person arrived at a sense of defeat are as follows:

- What was it about this situation that made you think you could not cope?
- What happened to make you think of ending your life?
- What was it about this situation that made it unbearable?
- What went through your mind to make you then think of suicide?
- Can you describe what led you to feeling overcome by this difficulty?
- Describe what you thought when things were at their worst.

5.5.4.7.2. IDENTIFYING THE PROGRESSION OF DEFEAT THROUGH DISTINCT CYCLES

Once the factors leading to states of defeat and hopelessness have been formulated, the cognitive behavioural characteristics of these cycles can then be assessed. At this stage, the therapist may work with the client to demarcate different cycles and the thresholds that lead a person from one cycle to the next.

Typically, the first cycle may be characterised by initial thoughts, feelings and behaviour cycles in response to a setback, difficulty or an intrusion. There may then follow a secondary process such as worry or rumination, linked to the activation of the appraisal system, for example, past and future appraisals and thoughts about the self and others. Initially, these thoughts may well be non-suicide-focused. However, once some threshold is reached this may become suicide-focused, representing the full activation of the suicide schema.

The client is likely to hold both positive and negative metacognitive beliefs about processes such as worry and rumination (Wells, 2000). Within CBSPp, the therapist aims to establish suicide specific beliefs about such processes. For example, a person may believe that worrying or ruminating can stop them from encountering situations that could lead to defeat, but also believe that worry or rumination may be uncontrollable and also lead to suicide. As stated elsewhere, beliefs about intrusions are also important to establish as seemingly innocuous thoughts to the outsider may well be interpreted as suicide-specific to the client. A related point is the extent to which suicidal ideation is ego-syntonic or dystonic (related to intent) and how this may change as a function of levels of experienced defeat. For some clients, suicidal ideation represents ego-dystonic intrusive thoughts, reflecting negative beliefs about suicide. The person then appraises a situation to be beyond their coping potential, and at this point it may switch to being ego-syntonic, the positive beliefs of suicide are operationalised and the client is not caught between competing negative and positive beliefs about suicide.

It can be important to assess the frequency, duration and severity of each cycle or stage of the formulation. This can begin to provide structure to a confusing process. Inherent contradictions may be noted here that may provide opportune moments for intervention by means of Socratic Dialogue. For instance, once the suicidal schema has been activated, the content of thoughts may be, 'this feeling is unbearable and I think it's going to last forever'. If this question is then followed by an exploration of the duration of this cycle, the client often provides information that directly contradicts this, for example, 'it normally lasts for 3 hours'. An immediate exit point may then be established and an alternative thought generated, 'these experiences are difficult but do not last forever, they tend to last for 3 hours'.

5.5.5. The function of suicidal acts: Intentions and consequences (intended and unintended)

The clinician should carefully plot the expectation of a suicidal act against both the intended and unintended consequences. So, for instance, the intention for suicide may be to take the pain of a particular situation away. The actual consequences of the suicidal act may well be to reduce difficult emotions or feelings. People often report that after following a suicidal act they are filled with a sense of calmness. This can strengthen positive beliefs about suicide

The clinician should also formulate the unintended consequences to suicide. These may be positive, negative or neutral and may serve to extend the function of suicidal behaviours. Examples of positive unintended consequences are strong reactions of care from family members who do not normally express positive emotions. These may become intended consequences of future suicidal acts, although they may remain implicit or not immediately available to the interview process. Examples of negative responses to a suicidal act are traumatic experiences of being hospitalised and of emergency medical treatment. The range of consequences, both intended and unintended, the positive and negative reinforcers of suicidal acts and the subsequent development of positive and negative beliefs may therefore serve to elaborate and extend the functions of the suicide schema further (see section 5.5.8).

The clarification of the function of suicidal behaviour may reveal a person's fundamental needs. This is an opportunity to reframe these functions as goals for therapy. This is the first process in introducing the prospect of alternative means of alleviating defeating situations. For example, Bob was asked to envisage not worrying any more. Bob did not think that this was possible, but if it were, he would no longer feel suicidal. Bob agreed to work on alleviation of worry with the aim of reducing the functionality of reducing suicidal ideation/behaviour.

5.5.6. Behavioural components

It is important to understand the potential role of behaviours in maintaining a person's difficulties and experience of suicidal thoughts and behaviours. These may be safety behaviours or avoidance. Such behaviours may operate at the level of initial difficulties or in maintaining suicide schema activation.

5.5.6.1. Safety behaviours

Safety behaviours are those a person engages in when they fear that something catastrophic may occur. Emotional difficulties can be maintained when such behaviours serve a paradoxical function of maintaining catastrophic beliefs by restricting access to evidence that would disconfirm such beliefs (Clark, 1986; Salkovskis, 1991). The therapist should assess behaviours and reactions at each stage of the formulation to assess for maintenance factors in the activation of the suicide schema.

5.5.6.2. Avoidance

When a person fears a particular situation, they may avoid the situation all together. This can serve to maintain problematic beliefs by restricting access to disconfirmatory evidence. The therapist should assess for avoidance and how this may maintain the suicide schema.

5.5.7 Self/other/world schema

According to schema theory, a person's deeply held beliefs about themselves, other people and the world develop in response to early and critical experiences and can leave some people vulnerable to psychopathology (Beck et al., 1979). The operationalisation of these schemata after difficult life events may therefore lead to an increased vulnerability to suicide schema activation (Wenzel et al., 2009). This may be especially so when we consider an individual with experiences of psychosis. This group are highly likely to have experienced trauma in their formative years (Read & Argyle, 1999; Read & Hammersley, 2005), and may have had other traumatic experiences such as hospitalisation and stigma/discrimination. The formulation should establish the nature of self/world/other beliefs as a result of life experiences but, critically, how these interact with the suicide schema.

5.5.8. Suicide schema

The specific events that led a person to first consider suicide should be elicited as this provides a valuable insight into the subsequent development of the suicide schema. As discussed above, Bob first thought of suicide when he observed his father attempt to kill himself as a response to getting into debt. We may hypothesise that Bob's father provided a powerful model of suicide as an escape strategy enhancing the formation of the suicide schema. Annabelle reported never feeling loved by her mother and being bullied at school. She reported planning to kill herself every night after school and that she attempted this on a number of occasions by trying to hang herself with her school tie. Again, early experiences led her to form a strong link between life's difficulties and suicide as an escape.

Along with the development of the idea or concept of suicide, clients report developing positive and negative beliefs about suicide that may have changed over the years. For instance, Bob and Annabelle both held positive beliefs that suicide would result in an escape from their problems. For Annabelle, these difficulties were current and ongoing, while for Bob, these were imagined conditions that may occur in the future. Bob also had the belief that suicide would be an end to worry, which was a particular difficulty of his. A person's beliefs about suicide may have changed after the experience of attempting to take their own lives, leading to the development of further positive and negative beliefs regarding suicide.

This can create a conflict or a cognitive dissonance for some, and a well-elaborated suicide schema may lead to the activation of suicide with the function of an escape, but also raises strong negative beliefs that suicide is painful and should be avoided. Clients may become particularly distressed if they believe that their suicidal thoughts and images mean that they are going to lose control and become suicidal once more. The clinician is encouraged to formulate the role of these beliefs with each client.

5.5.8.1. Plan of suicide

The therapist should assess the nature of the action plan stored as a potential escape behaviour. This plan may operate at different levels of the formulation. Avoidance may serve as an escape plan for experiences of defeat. This may work in the short term. However, if this is ineffective or the level of defeat becomes intolerable, then the person may then begin to consider suicide as an escape. Clinical experience has suggested that the suicide response may be applied to an ever-increasing range of conditions. Based on clinical observation, we suggest the following levels of development:

1. Suicide may be a potential escape (widely held in society).
2. Suicide would be used in an unspecified condition, not yet realised.
3. Suicide would be used given activating condition X.
4. Suicide becomes a generalised response to problematic situations, sometimes closing down active problem-solving in other domains.
5. Suicide becomes a response to avoid threatening situations or a return to situations in the past that the person fears.

The level of the plan may be influenced by the beliefs a person has about suicide. So, for instance, negative beliefs may be that suicide is a 'coward's way out' – a commonly held belief in society. This may help a person to resist suicide, but faced with consistent pressures or difficulties, a person's self-esteem lowers to the point where they view themselves as bad, weak and cowardly, leading the person to conclude that they are a coward, therefore suicide is a legitimate option for them, effectively reversing any dissonance about them being viewed as cowardly. The therapist should assess for the details of the plan (see Chapter 4) and a person's positive and negative beliefs about this plan. It is also important to enquire about the level of control a person believes they have over this process.

5.5.8.2. Passive suicide

Some people may not plan to actively kill themselves but see little hope in their lives. This may manifest itself in a lack of motivation to save themselves from life-threatening situations. Some people may develop an increased tendency to expose themselves to life-threatening situations. For example, one client would read about the location of recent assaults or killings and then visit those areas at dangerous times (Mary Welford, personal communication). Another client would walk across a busy road without looking and think to themselves, 'Let God decide (whether I live or die)'. This type of behaviour should be enquired about specifically, and the function of dying in this way formulated by similar means to active suicidal behaviour.

5.5.9. Formulation as intervention

Clients may have specific fears about talking about suicide as this can serve to trigger the activation of the suicide schema. The task of talking about suicidal experiences in such cases can be in opposition to the avoidant function of the schema. This fear can be addressed through the development of the formulation, the process of which becomes an intervention in itself. With progressive developments of the formulation, the therapist may draw attention to or enquire about the person's increasing sense of control or ease with talking about experiences of suicide and its associated emotions. Interventions can be used in session to facilitate this, that is, relaxation, attention broadening and the BMAC before and/or after exposure to difficult emotions. The links should be made explicit, that these interventions are being used to increase control by recruiting positive emotions and broaden attention in order to regulate threat. The client may then be asked how this may help in the future. The client may be invited to reflect upon beliefs around the inevitability of suicidal thoughts or of becoming defeated by overwhelming emotions as therapy progresses.

5.5.10. Sequences of if-then propositions

Once a problem has been selected, the sequence of specific steps from trigger to defeat appraisal can be charted with the client. Standard cognitive techniques of chaining can be used here. This draws together the information from the assessment into a coherent pathway. What is important is to gain an understanding of the specific appraisals of the present, past and future that are activated by specific triggers or clusters of triggers. Although often linked in complex ways, these may be simplified in therapy into a linear sequence.

This can allow for specific exit points to be developed at each stage of the sequence. The case study below incorporates exit points that occur naturally as well as those derived therapeutically. For some clients, this formulation becomes a guide for spotting early warning signs and indications of when to activate preventative exit points, thus reducing the chances of schema activation and an experienced state of defeat.

5.6. Progressing with therapy: Setting formulation-based goals

5.6.1. Goal setting and prioritising problems

Once the therapist and client share an understanding of the conditions that lead a person to feel suicidal and of the psychological mechanisms that are involved on these processes, they can begin to set goals for therapy. The distinctive element of goal setting in CBSPp is that the goals are focused on the reduction of suicidal behavior, and may:

- Concern meaningful, cherished life goals.
- Be collaborative: Agreed upon by the therapist and the client where possible.
- Reduce problems and processes leading to suicide.

- Increase thoughts, feelings and behaviours that reduce suicide.
- Be prioritised in order of importance with regard to suicide prevention.

5.6.1.1. Concern meaningful, cherished life goals

The therapist should attempt to identify meaningful Recovery & life goals throughout therapy. This should begin at the assessment stage. Such goals may also be established by understanding a client's unmet needs, or the transgression of personal values that may have led to suicide becoming functional for them. Alternative ways of meeting these needs or values can then become a focus of therapy.

5.6.1.2. Be collaborative: Agreed upon by the therapist and the client where possible

The therapeutic goals should be agreed upon collaboratively. However, the therapist and client may hold conflicting goals; this is especially so when the client presents with suicidal ideation and intent, and the therapist's aims are to reduce such thoughts and desires. As discussed in Chapter 6, a shared goal may be to focus upon finding alternative, non-life-threatening exits from unbearable, defeating situations. The psychological formulation is particularly useful here as mechanisms underlying suicide may be identified. The therapist can proceed by asking the client to imagine life if each of the functions of suicide were to be met by another means, for example, an end to worrying could be obtained through psychological or behavioural techniques. Psychoeducation as to the effectiveness of CBT in doing this may be given. This can be a powerful means of introducing hope into the process of therapy and can lead to an increase in engagement with CBSPp.

5.6.1.3. Reduce problems and processes leading to suicide

CBSPp is a suicide-focused intervention and thus distinct from CBTp, which is a more generic approach to psychosis. The formulation should identify the extent to which processes are linked to suicide behaviour and then focus on these. While any problem may influence a person's tendency to experience suicidal behaviour, the clinician should attempt to identify underlying mechanisms rather than work with a sense of continually 'putting out fires' – a situation that can occur often with suicidal clients who may live in chaotic conditions or who have chaotic lifestyles.

An important reason for understanding the function of suicide for an individual is that goals may then be set to find other ways of meeting the needs that led to suicide in the first place. For instance, the client who remembers feeling cared for in the aftermath of a suicide attempt may believe that they will not experience this again in their lives. A possible goal here would be to look at the factors that lead a client to believe this and to explore ways of getting more out of their relationships and also of retaining a sense that people care.

5.6.1.4. Increase thoughts, feelings and behaviours that inhibit suicide

Having goals to increase access to positive states is a key aspect of CBSPp. This involves modes of processing with positive thoughts and self-appraisals – shown to be associated with resilience in suicide (Johnson, Gooding & Tarrier, 2010). Associated positive emotional states should also be identified and access to them increased. Activating a sense of connection with others and a sense of safeness is thought to trigger core regulators of threat

(Depue & Morrone Strupinsky, 2005; Gilbert, 2010), which may serve to reduce the defeat/unbearability and the sense of isolation that can occur in suicide. Formulating the patterns of activation of these naturally occurring states can be a powerful element of CBSPp (Kelly & Welford, submitted).

5.6.1.5. Be prioritised in order of importance with regard to suicide prevention

The therapist and client need to prioritise which problem(s) to work on. This 'mapping' of problems was discussed in section 5.3 and is illustrated in Figure 5.7.

The following questions are a useful way of achieving this:

1) Are there any problems/barriers that preclude direct work on CBSPp?
   a. In particular, is the client acutely suicidal?
2) Which problem cluster is linked most directly to the suicide schema?
3) Which problem does the client feel able to work on initially?
4) Which problem will reduce the valence of other problems?
5) Which problem will lead to the development of confidence in personal resilience and activate resources to approach other problems?
6) What are the advantages of working on problem X?
7) What are the disadvantages of working on problem X?

Once this information has been collected, the therapist explores potential intervention strategies, and the advantages and disadvantages of progressing with each problem.

5.6.1.6. Objectifying goals

It is important to objectify goals for therapy; for instance, 'I want to feel OK' may be operationalised as 'I want my mood stay above 3 out of 10 and I want to reduce my worry about suicide from 2 hours a day to no more than half an hour'. Appraisals of the achievability of such goals should be carefully noted and levels of hopelessness addressed.

5.7 Resilience schemata

The therapist's aim is to create a portfolio of suicide schema 'anomalies' that may then be processed at the appraisal and at the schema level, introducing a shift in deeply held beliefs about suicide as the only way of escaping from a difficult situation. Such exploration may also result in changes to a person's beliefs about themselves, other people, the future and the world that interact with the suicide schema. As discussed in Chapter 6, the therapist also aims to elaborate resilience schemata, mimicking the process of suicide schema elaboration, but this time ensuring that beliefs and thought-action repertoires concerned with more functional ways of coping are extended to other domains. These are then added to the generic formulation as therapy proceeds, the formulation in essence becoming a repository for therapeutic interventions and natural ways of coping.

5.8. Putting it all together: The case of Catrina

The goal of the formulation is to provide an explanation, in terms of psychological and social mechanisms, for the development, maintenance and inhibition of suicidal behaviour.

Furthermore, the mechanisms involved should be modifiable, providing fertile ground to embed intervention strategies aimed at reducing mechanisms increasing suicidal behaviour and increasing those involved in its inhibition. We have presented Catrina's formulation below to provide an example of a CBSPp formulation.

As discussed in Chapter 4, the assessment revealed that Catrina was experiencing prolonged critical voices and visual flashbacks, experienced as the voices of her attackers, with the belief that these voices originated from her attackers when she experienced them. These were prolonged, demanded all of her attention and were experienced as incredibly harrowing. The initial formulation to 'map' her difficulties is demonstrated in Figure 5.7.

It was noted that sustained experience of abusive voices led Catrina to fear that she was going to lose her mind and that she would need to kill herself to escape. This was identified as the primary route for activation of the suicide schema. Catrina's ongoing voice-hearing experiences led to increased depressive symptoms characterised by less interest in doing things and a drop in mood. This led to increased isolation, which further increased the amount Catrina listened to her voices. Resilience factors were identified; Catrina found great relief in spending time with her family. This served to decrease her voices and her suicidal thoughts. However, listening to her voices and the resulting increase in depression led to a decrease in motivation to spend time with her family.

5.8.1. Developing a comprehensive CBSPp formulation

The full CBSPp formulation builds upon this basic map and explores the cognitive behavioural mechanisms maintaining these cycles. At the core of Catrina's formulation was a fear of returning to the state of terror and of not knowing her own mind in the aftermath of the attack.

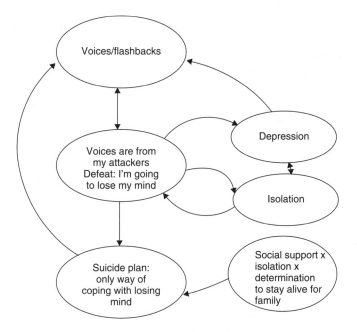

Figure 5.7 Catrina's initial map of difficulties and resilience factors

Additionally, Catrina held the belief that she had to actively monitor her mental state and distinguish between 'reality' and 'psychosis' in order to prevent a return to this state. If a fragment of a conversation reminded Catrina of this event, she switched her attention inwards to actively prompt voice-hearing experiences. This was to monitor them in order to identify whether the fragment was an aspect of the trauma memory; various rules dictated the validity of the fragment, such as which voice said it and its frequency. The fragmentary nature of the memory made this decision more difficult, with the resulting uncertainty leading to further need to monitor.

In reference to the SAMS model, Catrina's case clearly identifies the role of threat-focused attention – in this case directed towards malevolent voices with the purposes of evaluating the source of the words spoken. At the appraisal level, Catrina held meta-beliefs that she needed to monitor her internal state and understand the source of every threat-focused thought in order to keep her sanity. At the suicide schema level Catrina believed that she would be unable to cope if she didn't correctly appraise the source of her intrusive experiences and that she would return to a state of terror and lose her mind. Suicide functioned as an escape from this feared state. The voices often told Catrina to kill herself, and Catrina reported suicidal ideation. Catrina did not want to kill herself because she would miss her grandchildren growing up. As identified in the mapping stage, Catrina believed that the biggest disadvantage to her need to monitor her voices was that she spent less time with her grandchildren. This led to further depression and isolation, which led to more internal monitoring and increased voice-hearing experiences.

In terms of appraisals, the initial analysis uncovered the rules for identifying a voice-hearing experience as 'real' or 'psychosis'. However, of more interest for the intervention were the rules that directed Catrina to monitor these thoughts, which were as follows:

- I need to classify each internal experience.
- I need to listen to the voices to determine tone and consistency.
- If I don't distinguish the real world from my mind, I will lose my mind.
- If I lose my mind I will re-experience the terror of what happened in the past.

The suicide schema was also characterised by a set of rules that became a focus for intervention. These were as follows:

- Rules for present: If I let go, I will become overwhelmed by fragments of memories and return to state of terror.
- If I return to a state of terror, I will not be able to cope and I will lose my mind.
- If I re-experience this terror, I will kill myself by taking an overdose.

The development of the CBSPp formulation led to the development of an initial goal list, as follows.

5.8.1.1. Catrina's recovery goals

- Spend more time with grandchildren.
- Reduce suicidal thoughts.
- Develop ways of reducing time spent monitoring voices.
- Reduce beliefs in danger of not monitoring voices.
- Reduce fears of losing control of my mind.
- Increase sense of self as a strong and valued member of family.

In summary, the CBSPp formulation seemed to provide a set of hypotheses as to what mechanisms led to Catrina's suicidal thoughts and behaviours. The states of defeat and entrapment were clearly evident in Catrina's historical account, and her current behaviours of monitoring her internal experience seemed to function to avoid returning to this feared state. We hypothesised that when current experiences reminded Catrina of previous traumatic experiences, the suicide schema functioned to provide Catrina with a potential escape from a feared event. Suicidal ideation was experienced as thoughts and as voice-hearing experiences. CBSPp intervention would proceed by systematically addressing the psychological mechanisms thought to be maintaining the low threshold for suicidal schema activation. Spending time with grandchildren and resulting feelings of joy and connectedness seemed to inhibit the suicide schema. Strengthening Catrina's ability to experience these feelings was identified as a goal for therapy also.

5.9 Summary of CBSPp formulation

The CBSPp formulation has two aims: firstly, it aims to identify the cognitive behavioural process that leads a person to suicidal thoughts and behaviour; secondly, it aims to identify processes that serve to attenuate or inhibit suicide schema activation (Figure 5.8). The

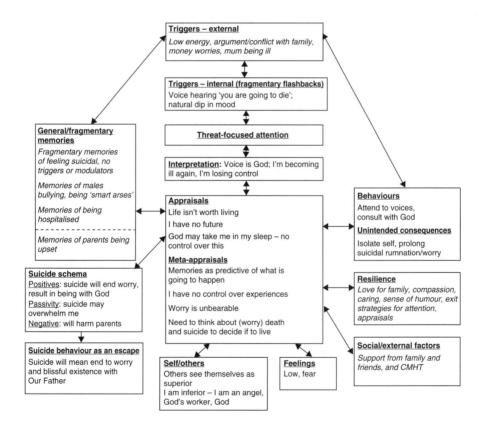

Figure 5.8 Catrina's formulation

identification of such factors may then inform the development of testable hypotheses for processes of change. This provides the basis for the strategic aims or goals of the intervention. The delivery of each intervention represents a test of hypotheses developed as a result of the formulation. Each successful reduction of a mechanism implicated in suicide schema activation or maintenance is recorded, along with resilience factors that serve to inhibit the schema. This evolves into a parsimonious representation of a person's resilience formulation that can be used to predict how a person may deal with future events, thus increasing a person's psychological flexibility and ultimately to prevent future suicidal behaviour.

Chapter 6

Clinical techniques and implementation of CBSPp protocol

6.1. Executive summary

- *The CBSPp protocol systematically addresses the mechanisms maintaining suicide, namely*
  - *information processing biases and attention*
    - *attention control*
    - *attention to imagery*
    - *stimulation of positive affect*
  - *appraisals*
  - *suicide schema.*
- *CBSPp stimulates positive emotions, thoughts, behaviours and 'self' and 'other' schemas*
- *Intervention techniques focus on verbal and behavioural reattribution techniques as used in traditional CBT.*
- *A distinctive feature of CBSPp is the use of intervention techniques such as the BMAC, to stimulate positive memories and emotions.*
- *Natural exits from suicidal processes are combined with positive emotions and schematic appraisal networks with the specific purpose of inhibiting the suicide schema.*
- *Hope for the future is generated through verbal and behavioural reattribution techniques but also by stimulating anticipatory positive emotions with the use of the BMAS.*
- *Schema change techniques are used, as follows:*
  - *self-esteem work*
  - *consolidation of suicide schema incongruent processes*
  - *consolidation of suicide schema inhibitory processes*
  - *past, present and future self perspectives.*

6.2. Introduction

The CBSPp intervention aims to systematically address and reduce the processes involved in suicide schema activation, maintenance and elaboration. This approach draws on traditional Cognitive Therapy (Beck, 1976; Wenzel, 2009). CBSP is distinctive in that is also aims to identify and amplify the processes that allow a person to deactivate the suicide schema and activate alternative and more functional thoughts, behaviours and feelings. As discussed in Chapters 2 and 4, CBSP stimulates positive emotion with the purpose of the inhibition of threat-related processes.

The CBSPp protocol systematically addresses cognitive processes in a tiered approach, moving from attentional processes to appraisals and then onto schematic processes. This is done in tandem with strategies derived from Broaden& Build principles (Frederickson &Branigan, 2005; Frederickson, Cohn, Coffey, Pek & Fingel, 2008; Frederickson & Losada, 2005; Frederickson, Mancuso, Branigan & Tugade, 2000; Garland et al., 2010). These strategies aim to disrupt the stronghold of threat activation on attention, appraisals and the suicide schema, through the stimulation of positive affect, in order to increase psychological resilience (Johnson, Gooding, Wood &Tarrier, 2010; Johnson et al., 2010; Johnson, Wood, Gooding, Taylor &Tarrier, 2011). It is also thought to increase positive goal-seeking motivations, the development of which are thought to reduce the scope and influence of the suicide schema on a person's functioning. The three phases of CBSPp, which follow the theoretical explanation of suicide behaviour (the SAMS model), are as follows:

- information processing and attention;
- appraisals;
- schema change.

6.3. Phase 1: Information biases and attention

The SAMS model suggests that the activated suicide schema patterns and shapes the way a person sees the world. So, a person's attention may be overly focused on the task of identifying potential threats in the environment. Similarly, non-threatening information in the environment may be appraised as threatening owingto information processing biases. The first step in CBSPp, then, is to reduce the valence of threat-focused attention and information processing biases in maintaining the suicide schema. This may be achieved by simple exercises or drills aimed at developing executive control over attention. Within CBSPp we also employ strategies to stimulate positive emotions in order to induce a 'Broadminded' state with the consequence of reducing threat-focused attention. The techniques used to achieve these aims are summarised in Box 6.1.

- broad minded affective coping;
- recall of problem solving strategies.

6.3.1. Attention control

A core aspect of the suicide schema is an appraisal of defeat and powerlessness to effect change. Manipulations of attentional control can be the first domain in which a person may begin to exercise personal agency. Often clients are surprised that they have a choice as to

> **Box 6.1 Phase 1 Intervention strategies to reduce information processing biases and attention to threat**
>
> **Provide exits from threat-focused attention and information processing**
>
> - Acquire attention control
>   - ◦ attention to simple external stimuli;
>   - ◦ attention to imagery.
> - Relaxation and breathing strategies.
>
> **Reduce the influence of threat on attentional processes and information processing through the stimulation of positive affect.**

what to attend to. For instance, Catrina applied these techniques and found that she was able to steadily increase her ability to switch her attention away from her voices. This highlighted to Catrina and her therapist that she was actively attending to her voices, driven by a fear that unclassified mental experience could allow her to slip into a state of mental catastrophe where she would be unable to distinguish between 'psychosis' and 'reality'.

The first stage of the CBSPp intervention is to increase a person's executive control over their attentional resources. This represents the first stage of disrupting the influence of the suicide schema over information processing. We suggest that this can then allow a person to reduce a tendency to focus on threat- and suicide-focused stimuli (internal and external). Ultimately, the aim would be able to allow clients to reduce 'attentional fixation' as experienced during acute periods of suicidal ideation or intent or when experiencing flashbacks in trauma. It is suggested that attention switching may provide an 'exit point' from such experiences. Ultimately, we suggest that acquiring attentional control can allow a person to switch their attention away from such stimuli as part of a chain of techniques and internal events, thoughts, feelings and behaviours that come to be involved in the inhibition and deactivation of the suicide schema. A participant information sheet detailing attention processes is provided in the Appendix. This information is summarised below.

6.3.1.1. Description of technique

The attention-broadening task may be explained as a means of being able to switch attention away from difficulties to neutral elements or positive elements of the environment, in order to explore whether there is a more balanced view of the world or of difficult situations.

This consists of simple attentional tasks initially. These tasks involve learning to direct attention by practising attentional focus or selective attention, sustaining attentional focus over time, and switching attention to various neutral stimuli, thus acquiring improved executive control over selective attention. Selective attention involves not only focused attention, but the ability to screen out interfering information, be that interfering thoughts (e.g. ruminations) or external sources of interference (e.g. building works). In a similar vein, switching attention requires not only a shift of focus but the ability to disengage attention.

It should be noted here that a careful assessment of a person's environment should be conducted as they may be exposed to a high level of threat.

6.3.1.2. Engagement and client rationale

If clients feel able to discuss their experiences in detail, a comprehensive formulation of the role of attention in schema maintenance and elaboration may be developed. This may occur early in therapy or later in the 'integration' stage. The case of Max provides a good example of how to construct an idiosyncratic formulation with a client that clearly demonstrates the role of attention.

Max reported that his attention rapidly alternated between external elements of the environment, which he interpreted as a sign from an entity, to his internal environment, listening to the voice of his entity discussing whether he was going to stay well or become ill and ultimately die. The latter conclusion would lead to suicidal thoughts. The therapist constructed a diagram with Max, detailing how internal and external processes make demands on attentional resources (see Figure 6.1).

This diagram shows Max in the middle with the circular shape representing his attentional resources. It illustrateshow his attention rapidly switches from internal processes (such as intrusions or voices, thoughts about his future and suicidal thoughts) to external elements of the environment (signs in the environment placed by the entity). It also highlights how no or little attention is being paid to neutral or unrelated information in the external environment. The boldness of the arrow is to reflect how much time is spent focusing on internal processes.

Importantly, the therapist can make the transition from content to process here with the client. When the client is discussing experiences, the diagram can be used to convert this into the rules directing attentional resources (Wells, 2000).

Then, to facilitate goal setting and socialise the client to the role of attention processes in their own recovery, another diagram is drawn out to highlight how acquiring attention control may lead to symptomatic relief and access to new information about the environment (see Figure 6.2).

This diagram highlights the advantages of acquiring attention control.For Max this was as follows:

- Move attention away from distressing voices.
- Move attention away from information from the entity.

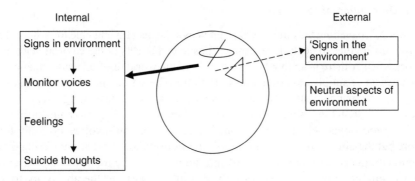

Figure 6.1 The role of attention in maintaining distress

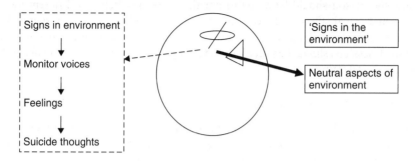

Figure 6.2 The advantages of acquiring attention control

- Reduce the frequency of the thought that the entity was considering his destiny.
- Reduce suicidal thoughts.

As stated, this intervention may also lead to the development of new appraisals about the person's sense of control over their attentional resources, and over time this may lead to changes to beliefs about the advantages/disadvantages of attending to one aspect of suicide-/threat-related internal and external stimuli as opposed to neutral, disconfirming and positive stimuli (see appraisal section).

6.3.1.3. Procedure for acquiring attention control

6.3.1.3.1. ATTENTION TO SIMPLE EXTERNAL STIMULI

To facilitate attentional focus and attentional switching, the client can be asked to relax and control their breathing. To facilitate this sometime can be allocated to brief autogenic relation and breathing control (see 6.3.2).

Clients are then asked to focus attention for brief periods of time on different objects in the room. This should be practised for periods sufficiently brief so that sustained attention is achieved. With practice, processes underlying sustained attention can be strengthened in that clients can be directed to maintain their focus of attention on each object for increasingly longer periods. Gradually, the ability to focus, maintain attention and switch attentional focus can be broadened to a greater range of objects.

Next, the client can be asked to close their eyes and focus attention on a specific sound. Initially it is easiest if the therapist makes the sound, such as rhythmic tapping. In a similar manner to attentional focus on visual stimuli, auditory attention should be switched to different sounds, with background noise also utilised. We have found that the level of difficulty can change with the speed of tapping. Some people find slow tapping fairly easy but lose concentration when the frequency increases. It is useful to vary the level of difficulty but in a gradual manner, warning the person that for some this is a difficult task. Tapping at two different rates allows the client to practise attending to more complex sounds and to switch attention from one to the other. If the client finds these tasks difficult, they should be asked not to concentrate too intensely but just to be aware of the sounds.

Clients can then be asked to be aware of tactile stimuli by closing their eyes and running their hands over different surfaces. Practice in sustaining attention and switching to an increasing number of different stimuli should be continued.

Finally, the person should be asked to practise switching between different modalities – auditory and visual stimuli, auditory and tactile etc. – and in attempting to attend to two stimuli at the same time. These tasks can be set as homework exercises. Times and duration of homework sessions should be specified, and clients asked to rate ease/difficulty and effectiveness on a 0–10 rating scale.

6.3.1.3.2 POST-EXERCISE INTEGRATION

It is important to explore the impact of the role of attention-broadening with each client. The following gives some examples of Socratic questions that may be used to do this. The key point is to establish how switching attention may be used to handle future difficulties and, in particular, experiences when a person may become suicidal.

*   How easy or difficult did you find that task?
*   If 0 was the hardest it could be, you couldn't hold attention at all, and 10 was the highest score, your attention was perfect, what score would you give yourself?
*   What sorts of things distracted you?
*   Did any thoughts go through your mind?
*   Did you think you should be able to concentrate?
*   Did this make you think about yourself?
*   Did it make you think about your problems?
*   Did you switch your attention back to the task?
*   If yes:

    o   What do you make of that?
    o   How do you think this could help in the future?

*   Looking back on the times when you have coped well in the past, can we see how your attention to threat changed? What do you make of that?

The therapist and client then look at the formulation and identify any specific ways attention-switching may be used for prevention of suicide or when it may offer an exit point from the progression from stressor to defeat appraisals and subsequent suicidal ideation. Figure 6.3 shows what was added to Max's formulation.

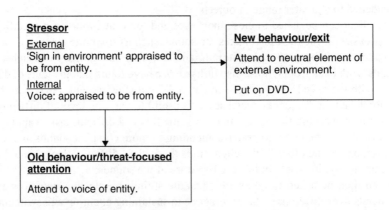

Figure 6.3 What was added to Max's formulation

Max reported that this technique had the impact of lowering his beliefs that he needed to attend to the entity (see appraisals section), and also that he was able to watch a DVD all the way through without being interrupted. The therapist and client then set a goal of watching a DVD every Sunday afternoon in order to increase the range of positive experiences and also to reduce the belief that the entity controlled every aspect of Max's life. This shows how attention-switching can be used as an exit point from suicide schema activation and also as a trigger to an enjoyable activity, which may further increase its inhibition.

6.3.1.4. Difficulties

We explore difficulties in more detail in Chapter 10, but a summary of specific difficulties with attention-broadening tasks islisted here, along with strategies for overcoming these difficulties.

Difficulty	Strategies for overcoming difficulty
Task is not relevant	Return to formulation: • Formulate past experiences from perspective of threat-focused attention. • Formulate 'natural exits' and ask about role of attention. • Set diary task to observe natural reductions in threat and level of internal/external focus. • Move to mood induction or appraisal work and then return to attention when threat is reduced.
Not applied at difficult times	• Make a CD for people to practise in home environment. • Telephone people to prompt them to do task. • Coping cards with instructions to prompt attentional switching.
Client reports that they cannot do it	• Normalise self-critical thoughts as common reaction to task. Explore from perspective of defeat appraisals. (See barriers section below.)
Long-term difficulties with task	• Break into small steps, beginning with I second, moving up at client's own pace. • Look for external triggers that switch attention away from threat, e.g. environmental stimuli, touch, smell, sounds, visual stimuli, etc.

6.3.2. Relaxation and breathing exercises

6.3.2.1. Theoretical rationale

As stated above, a distinctive element of CBSPp is the use of threat reduction as an adjunct to Cognitive Behavioural techniques. Reducing threat prior to an intervention can assist in broadening attention and access to non-threat-related information. Any intervention that effectively reduces threat should be formulated in terms of agency over a hitherto defeating process. The therapist may use techniques known to them for facilitating relaxation. We use a combination of diaphragmatic breathing and progressive muscle relaxation. Both strategies also serve to help reduce the physical aspects of stress/anxiety; provide an effective coping strategy to reduce anxiety and increase feelings of self-efficacy; offer a distraction in times of stress; and provide practice at internal focus of attention (and perceived control) that is a positive experience.

6.3.2.1.1. DIFFICULTIES

The therapist should be mindful that, for some, relaxation exercises can trigger threat and anxiety. Prior to the task beginning, the therapist may elicit some of the beliefs associated with relaxation:

- Can you relax?
- Do you always have to be on the go?
- What happens when you try to relax?
- Probe: What could happen if you stayed like that?
- Probe: What's the worst thing that could happen?

Often, attention-broadening can be used to assist with relaxation. Relaxation is then most optimally delivered as a behavioural experiment to test such appraisals, that is, that the client will lose control. It may also be framed as an exercise in switching attention to internal stimuli. We audio-record relaxation exercises and give clients a copy to practise in their own time.

In the debriefing stage, the therapist should obtain feedback about the exercise. Some clients report that they didn't relax. An all-or-nothing bias may be operating on this judgement. Some clients experience some benefits of relaxation but become self-critical of themselves if their mind wanders. This should then be normalised, as most people's attention will wander during such tasks. Clients may benefit from being advised to accept such intrusions and to gently move their attention back to the voice on the tape and the aspect of relaxation currently under focus, for example, attention to bodily experiences, sounds, etc. We have effectively combined relaxed states with attention-switching for some clients. The overall aim of reducing threat-focused attention and beliefs maintaining this should frame all such work. Obtaining feedback from any such exercise is important as it may yield important processes or beliefs that are relevant to the suicidal formulation. Processes that were not identified in the formulation stage should be explored further.

6.3.3. Attention to imagery

If the therapist and client are following a sequential progression through the protocol, sustained attention to simple external stimuli forms a foundation for then applying attention to imagery. This usually begins by a period of relaxation. The client is then asked to close their eyes. At first, the task focuses on a neutral visual image or scene. The client should practise describing the scene in detail and evoking information from other senses such as sound, touch and smell. The aim of this exercise is to acquire the ability to sustain attention to a mental image and to practise fully processing the comprehensive detail of that image. A number of different types of image should be practised. The therapist can interview the client before the experience to obtain key information. The client should practise these exercises as homework. An audio recording of the session can be presented to the client to facilitate this.

Box 6.2 Relaxation

- Introduction:
    - Invite person to become as comfortable as possible in their chair.
    - Invite person to close their eyes.
    - Invite person to become aware of their breathing.
- Attention to breathing:
    - Becoming slower and deeper.
    - A natural, relaxing rhythm.
    - Stomach rising (may want to place hand on stomach and feel it rise and fall with each breath).
    - Become aware or air entering and leaving their body.
    - Sensation of breathing out through nose.
    - Releasing any worries and tension in body.
    - Think of a word for this feeling. Can use this word at any point in the future to return to this feeling.
- Attention to body:
    - Become aware of body in chair.
    - Being supported by chair.
    - A sense of tension being released as you relax into the chair.
- Then for each area of body (head, shoulders, upper arms, lower arms, hands, back, upper legs, lower legs, feet):
    - Become aware of your body in the chair.
    - Being supported by chair.
    - A sense of tension being released as you relax into the chair.

The therapist should be sensitive to the possibility that asking the client to select a visual image from the past may trigger painful memories. It is for this reason that the therapist should take care to identify a neutral memory first. It can be useful to identify a very recent memory that can be recalled with a high level of detail. If the client is struggling to identify an event, they can schedule a 'neutral' activity and recall in detail at the next session.

The therapist should also be mindful of the benefits of this exercise, such as a prolonged break in negative experiences. For some clients, the task of sustained imagery of neutral content can be an illuminating experience as they experience a break from negative thoughts, voices, affect, etc. This should be explored fully and appraisals formed to express this. Again, appraisals of agency over internal experience can be developed. Ultimately, the idea of increasing choice over memory retrieval can be emphasised at this stage.

6.3.3.1. Socialisation to dwelling on memories to improve their strength

- Did you expect to remember that much?
- Do you think that event will be easier or harder to remember now?
- What do you make of that?

- If we spend time dwelling on memories and going over them in detail, does this make them easier or harder to remember?
- What memories have you been dwelling on?
- Has this made them easier or harder to remember?
- If we were to strengthen other memories, memories unrelated to your difficulties, what do you think would happen?
- We followed a procedure to make that memory stronger. What does this mean about choice? If you were to follow that procedure again, can you increase the amount of time you spend thinking about memories other than your difficulties?

Links to metaphors:

- If you think back to the cornfield, what pathway are we strengthening here? What would happen to the difficult pathway while we are strengthening alternative ones?
- If you think back to the horse-race metaphor, which horse won the race? Which horses have tended to win the race in the past? What do you make of that?

Development of personal appraisals:

- How could this help with your difficulties, with the chain of events that lead to you wanting to take your own life?
- What could you do to prevent this from happening again?

6.3.4. Reduce the influence of threat on attentional processes and information processing through the stimulation of positive affect

6.3.4.1. Experiencing positive emotions – Broad Minded Affective Coping (BMAC)

The next stage in CBSP is to direct attention to memories associated with positive affect. As discussed in Chapter 3, there are strong theoretical reasons for doing so. According to the Broaden & Build theory (Frederickson & Branigan, 2005; Frederickson et al., 2008; Frederickson & Losada, 2005; Frederickson et al., 2000; Garland et al., 2010), emotions evolved to achieve important psychobiological goals. Threat-based emotions, with their own inherent thought-action repertoires,are concerned with safety-seeking, and focus attention, thoughts and behaviours on dealing with or escaping from threat. Positive emotions, on the other hand, evolved to promote approach behaviours and lead to a broadening of attention and thought-action repertoires. An increase in the retrievability of memories associated with positive emotions may therefore allow a person to activate such affect states more easily when they experience threat. The Broaden & Build theory suggests that repeated stimulation of positive affect, at a ratio of at least 3:1, can begin to attenuate the sensitivity of threat states in the long term (Garland et al., 2010). Applied early in therapy, such techniques may be used as a wedge to open the door and allow positive emotions to begin to attenuate pervasive experiences of threat. The BMAC is used continually throughout therapy in a formulation-based way, as discussed in more detail below and by Kelly et al. (in preparation).

In the Broad Minded Affective Coping (BMAC; Tarrier, 2010) technique, clients are asked to focus on a positive event from their past. Ideally, this is done in a state of relaxation, with the client closing their eyes and engaging all their senses. The client processes the memory deeply and savours the positive emotions associated with this memory. The client then processes the meanings associated with these feelings. This is a potentially powerful technique that can be used to achieve the following aims, depending on the formulation:

1. To facilitate access to a broader range of psychological resources and inhibit narrow threat-related attention.
2. To have the positive experience of recalling positive memories and positive emotions, which in itself will be intrinsically rewarding.
3. To increase awareness of the role of cognition and appraisal in determining emotion.
4. To act as a balance to the experience of negative emotions and negative appraisals.
5. To aid emotional regulation and stress management.
6. To develop a sense of control and improve self-efficacy.
7. To provide an emotional scaffold for alternative positive appraisal.
8. To learn to improve problem-solving capability by accessing past problem-solving success.
9. To increase appraisals of agency over memory recall.
10. To increase the retrievability of networks of positive memories, both drive- and affiliative-based.
11. To increase the retrievability of memories of suicide inhibition and increase appraisals of mastery over experiences linked to the suicide schema.

We have found that a 'positive affect memory interview' can be a useful precursor to the BMAC. This can generate a number of positive memories. We also suggest that it can prime the affect systems prior to more intense stimulation using the BMAC. Once a memory has been selected for the BMAC we carry out a brief interview of the details of the memory, to prime this memory further and to give the therapist important anchor points to draw upon when conducting the BMAC (see below). When the BMAC has been completed, the therapist explores the feelings and emotions and then the implications of this in terms of the formulation. Finally, the therapist generates other memories with the technique of 'chaining'. As discussed below, the therapist may then move into Broad Minded Affective Scheduling, generating plans to engage in similar activities in the future.

6.3.4.2. Positive affect memory interview

We have found that a short interview schedule may be used to understand naturally occurring experiences of positive affect in a person's life. The aims of this interview are as follows:

1. Identify natural experiences of positive affect (affiliative- or drive-based) that may form the material for the BMAC procedure.
2. To identify natural experiences of positive affect (affiliative- or drive-based) that may be further increased by listening to a recording of a previous BMAC.
3. To identify periods when a person may experience threat that may then be attenuated by the BMAC.

I'm going to ask you some questions about how your mood changes over the course of the day or week.

General information about positive mood fluctuations:

1. Do you have good days and bad days?
2. Does this follow a pattern?
3. What tends to be the best days of the week for you?
4. What happens on these days?
5. When are you at your happiest? Or when does your mood lift?
6. What events are linked to these experiences?
7. Elicit descriptions of events.
8. What is it about this experience that makes you happy? (Assessing meaning.)
9. If we think about the past week, can you identify times when you felt good or happy?
10. General questions:

    a.   What happened?

11. Specific questions:

    a.   Who was there?
    b.   What could you see?
    c.   What could you hear?
    d.   What could you smell?
    e.   Could you taste anything?
    f.   What could you feel?

12. Think now about the emotion; let it come back to you now. Let it wash over you.
13. What words would you use to describe this emotion(s)?
14. How long did the feeing(s) last for?
15. Then use TPAS to generate other feelings.
16. What did you do next? If chain of events, follow them.
17. How many more experiences can you think of like that?
18. Go back to question 9 until exhausted good memories.
19. Now think about times when you felt low or bad and something happened to cheer you up, make you feel better, stopped you feeling bad.

    a.   How did you feel?
    b.   What happened to make you feel like this?
    c.   What happened to make you feel better?
    d.   Who was there?
    e.   What could you see?
    f.   What could you hear?
    g.   What could you smell?
    h.   Could you taste anything?
    i.   What could you feel?

20. Think now about the emotion or emotions you felt; let it come back to you now. Let it wash over you.
21. What words would you use to describe this emotion(s)?
22. How long did the feeing(s) last for?
23. Then use TPAS to generate other feelings.

24. What did you do next? If chain of events, follow them.
25. How many more experiences can you think of like that?
26. Go back to question 19 until exhausted good memories.

6.3.4.3. BMAC preparation interview

The following interview was designed to establish the anchor points in a person's memory to aid the therapist in guiding the person through the memory. It also serves to prime recall and elicits information prior to the BMAC.

* Think of a recent memory that made you feel happy/good/excited/positive. Write down a short description.
* Where were you? Write down as many details of where you were. Who were you with? Write down all the people in the memory.
* Who were you with? Write down all the people in the memory.
* What happened? Write down in as much detail as possible.
* What happened? Write down in as much detail as possible.
* How did you feel? Write down your emotions/feelings – try and describe them in as much detail as possible.
* What went through your mind? Why was this good memory? What did you think? Write down the key thoughts that made you feel positive or good.
* What does this memory mean to you? What does it say about how other people think about you? What does it mean about how you think about yourself?
* What does this mean for your future? How do you think good memories can help you?

6.3.4.4. The procedure of Broad Minded Affective Coping (BMAC)

6.3.4.4.1. RATIONALE

The rationale for the BMAC procedure is explained as follows:

> 'Negative emotions, be they fear anxiety, depression, anger or shame, are almost always threat-related. They serve to focus and narrow attention to be vigilant or aware of threat, so that the constant experience of negative emotions creates a mental, tunnel vision. Positive emotions, on the other hand, are associated with a broader aspect and allow the person to be creative, content, curious and to develop social relationships. Positive emotions provide a broader psychological experience with all its advantages because they are not related to threat and danger. What we are going to try and do in these exercises is to allow you to re-experience positive memories, through mental imagery exercises, and to try to re-experience the positive emotions that went with these memories.'

The BMAC procedure is explained. Initially the procedure and its purpose are explained to the client. For example:

> 'I am going to ask you to think back to a specific time when you were happy or enjoying yourself, and I want you to focus on that memory and paint a picture in your mind of that event. I am going to ask you to make that mental image as vivid as possible and

to try and experience the positive emotion you had at the time. This may be difficult for you, but I would like you to try as hard as you can and to practise this regularly at home. The purpose of this exercise are (1) to learn to be able to focus your mind on a positive memory rather than a negative, unpleasant or traumatic memory and experience a balance of positive and negative memories; (2) to learn to be able to control your emotions and to enjoy positive emotions and the benefits they bring; (3) to learn to have more control over your attention and on what you think about; (4) to help you cope with stress and low moods; (5) to be more aware of how your thought processes may affect your emotions.'

Prior to commencing the exercise the client is asked whether they can remember an event or time when they enjoyed themselves, had a good time or felt happy. Although there are no hard-and-fast rules, it is usually best to start with a more recent event rather than one that occurred long ago.

6.3.4.4.2. PREPARATION

It is advisable to start the exercise by asking the client to close their eyes and relax themselves using a simple autogenic procedure and by then focusing on their breathing. (In many cases they will have been taught and practised these stress management procedures in an earlier session.) This aims to create a relaxed state, which will reduce stress and anxiety and facilitate the experience of positive emotions.

6.3.4.4.3. GUIDED IMAGERY OF POSITIVE MEMORIES

Once the client has relaxed then the clinician prompts them to recall the specific memory. They are asked to focus their attention on the memory and to 'paint a picture in their mind' of the event or situation. For this reason the elicited memory should be as specific as possible. The client can be asked to describe the scene out loud, although in most cases this may disturb attention and is not recommended unless the client has difficulty with visual imagery. They may also do this sub-vocally. The clinician, having previously obtained details of the event, can prompt the client to recall detail. They can be prompted to recall the situation and the environmental detail. With some clients preparatory work on quizzing these details into a script can facilitate this. The client can be asked to immerse themselves in a 'mental virtual world' and recall all the details of the place, people and situation by 'looking around' the memory or taking a different perspective or angle so as to view the detail of both foreground and background. The client is frequently prompted to try to make the memory as clear and as vivid as possible.

6.3.4.4.4. ENGAGING THE SENSES

Once the client has successfully created a vivid and clear mental image, they are prompted to recall any other sensory input from the memory. For example, were there any particular noises, either salient or background? Or did they recall any particular smells associated with the experience (such as of the sea or new-mown grass or of food, as appropriate)? Similarly with touch or sensation. Sometimes asking about the weather, as in 'can you recall the sun on your skin or the wind on your face?' can trigger the memory of this sensory information. The aim is to attempt to prompt the client to re-experience the memory by engaging and integrating all possible sensory information.

6.3.4.4.5. RE-EXPERIENCING THE ASSOCIATED EMOTION

Once the client has successfully created a vivid mental image and recalled any other relevant aspects of the memory in their other senses, they are asked to attempt to recall how they felt emotionally at the time. Clearly this may not be an easy task, although the memory may naturally evoke some positive emotional response. The client should be prompted to scaffold an emotional response through the use of verbal descriptors, that is, to describe to themselves how they felt and how the emotion was experienced, with prompting from the clinician. This is a useful practice of introducing appraisal and verbal descriptors, and flows naturally into the next stage of the exercise.

6.3.4.4.6. INTERROGATING THE MEMORY

Finally, the client is prompted to ask themselves what was it about the experience that caused them to feel happy, cheerful, what was it that made them feel positive? The aim here is to make the client aware of the interpretations and appraisals about the situation or experience that resulted in the positive emotion. This helps to further elicit a positive emotional response to the memory by explicitly sub-vocalising the positive interpretations associated with it and to increase awareness of how cognitions influence emotions. The client is asked to rehearse the association between memory, cognition/appraisal and emotion so as to strengthen that association and improve performance through practice and repetition.

6.3.4.4.7. FEEDBACK AND DEBRIEFING

Once sufficient practice has been performed, which usually takes about 20 to 30 minutes, the client is asked to open their eyes and to stretch. They are then asked how they are feeling. This usually elicits a positive response, as it is rare that clients do not feel at least a temporary positive feeling of well-being after performing this exercise. In some cases they are quite surprised at how positive they feel. This is immediately used by the clinician to exemplify the effects of focusing attention on positive memories and of positive appraisals of situations and events, even those in the past. Detailed feedback is then elicited from the client about their successful implementation of each stage of the procedure and of any difficulties they may have encountered.

The procedure is then repeated within the session and set as a daily homework exercise. It is advisable to have an array of different positive memories to practise in future sessions and as homework.

As discussed in more detail in the Chapter 10, positive memories may be upsetting as they might contrast with the client's current situation. Furthermore, it has been found that some clients have a fear of positive affect owingto previous threatening experiences with caregivers (Gilbert, 2010; Kelly BMAC PAPER). While such experiences may be difficult they represent another avenue for exploration and formulation development. Interventions examining emergent appraisals may be necessary before further work. It is important in all imagery work to ensure clients understand that they can stop the exercise at any time. Careful debriefing can help to identify any problems with this.

6.3.5. Chaining

The differential activation hypothesis suggests that stimulating nodes within a network would lead to the increased retrievability of information stored within that network (Teasdale & Barnard, 1993). The SAMS suggests that the network activating suicide as an escape plan becomes elaborated or broadened, increasing the probability that the network becomes activated (Johnson et al., 2008; Prattet al., 2010). It is suggested that the elaboration of this network serves to inhibit the network(s) containing positive memories, thoughts and emotions and memories of coping. Previously benign triggers may then become linked to the defeat network. We suggest that the aim of CBSPp is develop the strength of coping and positive networks to re-establish their links to alternative triggers and memories, reducing links to the defeat network. We suggest that an increase in a person's awareness of this burgeoning network of positive self-appraisals about beliefs about ability to cope can lead to further problem-solving behaviour, thus establishing a positive feedback cycle (see positive events scheduling).

The development of this technique in therapy was triggered by a number of clients who spontaneously discussed similar memories. For example, one client who was grieving for his father did a BMAC about a day out with his father. This prompted the spontaneous recall of a number of happy times with his father, and the client expressed joy in being able to remember these good times. This example demonstrated the power of these techniques in prompting memory recall but also the care needed when activating such memories.

An aim of the intervention is therefore to strengthen the ease of activation of the network containing positive memories and the connections between nodes within this network. The Broad Minded Affective Coping strategy (BMAC) was developed to increase the retrievability of specific memories. The Broad Minded Affective Coping chaining (BMAC-c) technique evolved out of the BMAC to further activate and strengthen links within the web of positive memories within a person's network. These questions can be asked after a BMAC.

Affective links

- Did this memory remind you of other memories that made you feel (name of emotion used by client).
- Spend a moment thinking of similar memories with this feeling.

    ○ Therapist notes, memories.

Sensory links

- Returning to the memory we have just reviewed, think about all the things you could see (therapist to list). Does this remind you of any other positive memories?
- Returning to the memory we have just reviewed, think about all the things you could smell (therapist to list). Does this remind you of any other positive memories?
- Returning to the memory we have just reviewed, think about all the things you could feel either in the environment remember touching (therapist to list). Does this remind you of any other positive memories?
- Returning to the memory we have just reviewed, think about all the things you could hear (therapist to list). Does this remind you of any other positive memories?
- Returning to the memory we have just reviewed, think about all the things you could taste (therapist to list). Does this remind you of any other positive memories?

Interpersonal links

• Returning to the memory we have just reviewed, think about all the people in the memory (therapist to list). Can you think of other memories with these people?

Meaning/cognitive links

• Think about what this memory meant to you. Can you think of other experiences or times in your life that have had similar meanings to you?

6.3.6. Amended BMAC for high threat sensitivity

We have found that some clients can't tolerate relaxation or imagery tasks. We have found that in such cases the therapist can engage the person in conversation and discuss positive memories, and apply the BMAC procedure without the client being in a state of deep relaxation. The therapist applies the same techniques used in the BMAC, but rather than savouring the experiences, the client is asked to acknowledge the emotions as they are triggered by recall. By combining this with the chaining procedure, the client may be able to discuss a number of memories.

The purpose of this technique is to begin to activate the breadth of the network linking positive memories rather than directly and intensely stimulate one memory within the network. We hypothesise that such 'network priming' is more favourable than focusing on a specific memory because this could activate the defensive, defeating network. This has not been tested empirically, but some clients who cannot tolerate the full BMAC have found this to be a positive experience.

6.3.7. Recall of successful problem-solving strategies

If this procedure follows on from BMAC the client will already have had practice in memory exercises, and it should be a straightforward procedure to move on to recall successful problem-solving.

The client should be asked to recall a problem they had in the past with which they successfully dealt or coped. As with the previous exercise, the client should be asked to recall the situation in detail and describe how they successfully dealt or coped with this situation. This should be carried out in imagination as though the client is reliving the memory. The memory should be elaborated on with emphasis given to:

• the positive affect in mastering the situation is elicited and details are attended to such as body language;
• the feeling of being competent;
• the impact of personal agency in successfully dealing with the situation.

The client can be asked how they felt about resolving their problem. How would it make them feel if this happened again? Self-statements and imagery should be used to increase the client's feeling of confidence in having dealt with difficulties successfully. This should be practised with a number of different memories. In a similar manner as before the client can write an account of the memory or make an audiotape describing the situation. Clients should also be asked to come up with a few words that describe the memory, which can be used to trigger or recall the positive memory and affect.

Care should be taken not to defeat the client and make them feel as though they have failed by having few positive memories. Rather than asking general questions that may elicit vague and over-generalised responses, questions should be asked around specified time-anchors, such as holidays, birthdays etc.

6.3.8. Generating specific problem-solving strategies for anticipated and potentially stressful situations in the future

In a similar exercise to that practised with past memories the client can be asked to identify possible future problems and to generate possible solutions thatcan be practised in imagination through guided imagery. Attention should be paid to the problem-solving process of defining the problem and generating a range of positive solutions, whichcan be prompted if necessary, but the aim is for the client to improve their problem-solving capabilities. Thus detailed accounts relating to personal agency within specific problem-solving situations will be described so that they are encoded in autobiographical memory.

It is possible to scaffold this exercise if necessary. The client can be given general, but easy, problems to solve first to build up their confidence. For example, you ask the client to solve the following problem which you set them: 'you need milk for breakfast. There are a number of shops closeby. One is a garage thatsells some groceries and is open all night. What would you do?' The therapist can prompt as appropriate to help the client resolve the task, and then practise and rehearse the solution in imagination as described above.

6.3.9. Recalling specific memories of suicide reduction

As discussed in Chapters 4 and 5 (Assessment and Formulation), a key component of CBSPp is to strengthen memories of the self as having coped with suicide. Also, the frame of the memory of suicidal experiences may be altered by including tangible, identifiable triggers and also to include the diminishment of suicidal thoughts and feelings. We hypothesise that this reduces the sense of a lack of control over suicide and makes it feel more preventable. These memories may be difficult to establish and the details become important. The clinician and client may work on a number of imagery tasks, switching from standard interview format to imagery. As discussed in the difficulties section, recalling of episodes through the BMAC can actually reduce tangential thinking or processes, such as worry and rumination, that can often make it hard for clients to focus on one thing without other thoughts competing for their attention.

6.4. Appraisals

Working on appraisals is a key aspect of CBSPp. Appraisals are thought to reflect a causal link to the activation of the suicide schema and to reflect the elaboration of the suicide schema, that is, in new and challenging situations, subjective appraisals of not being able to cope and that the situation is intolerable lead to suicide schema formation. Appraisals may also be patterned in a top-down fashion by the suicide schema. Appraisals about experiences of psychosis, of becoming ill and/or being hospitalised, and appraisals of previous experiences of mental catastrophe may lead to increased internal and threat-focused attention.

In a standard, sequential progression through CBSPp, the clinician may spend a number of sessions introducing the Cognitive Behavioural model to clients. The clinician and client may then work together to identify and challenge, through cognitive behavioural methods, the negative appraisals regarding situation, self, personal agency, future and external agency. This needs to take into account both the content and the process of appraisal so that the biases that direct the processing of negative and suicide associated information are rectified. This will involve the active awareness of the process and the use of cognitive and behavioural methods of change. Appraisal involves valued judgements and interpretation of situations, expectations of future situations and self-reflections on personal capability, which can be translated into specific beliefs thatcan be challenged, tested and disconfirmed. The following list, which is not exhaustive, can be used to prompt and access the client's appraisals.

1. Appraisal of current situation

    •   The current situation or experience is stressful and/or aversive and/or threatening.
    •   The situation results in distress or negative emotions, which are difficult to bear.
    •   Stress relates to psychotic symptoms or consequences of the illness.
    •   The situation is uncontrollable and inescapable, and personal agency is ineffective.
    •   The person's social position is perceived as subordinate to others, including the voices.
    •   Social support is not available, not helpful and/or not legitimate.
    •   The situation is punitive.
    •   The situation is persistent and relentless.
    •   The situation involves thwarted aspirations and reduced expectations.
    •   The situation is persistent and stable and unchangeable.
    •   The situation is burdensome.
    •   The situation is deserved or if undeserved then unjustly so.

2. Appraisal of past events

    •   These are traumatic.
    •   Past events elicit negative emotions or personal interpretations.
    •   They are humiliating or shameful.
    •   Past events are repeating themselves and are uncontrollable.
    •   Past events intrude or 'contaminate' the present and future.

3. Appraisal of the future

    •   An inability to generate solutions to future problems, lack of capacity for problem-solving, inability to formulate rules for generating solutions.
    •   Content of problem-solving solutions is negative, and inability to think flexibly and fluently about future.
    •   Agency of others to help, willingness to help, ability to help, agency of others to change situation (this may include reciprocity, that is, the perception that others may be willing to help depends on the capacity of the client to help others, hence the client must be able to help others or have done so in the past so that others will reciprocate).
    •   The availability of social resources.
    •   The future is uncontrollable and full of impediments to change.

- Failure to change is an indication of failure and personal worthlessness (self-reflection).

There will be a strong tendency to:

- personalise by reflecting back to reinforce negative characteristics of the self;
- selectively attend to information; interpret information to confirm established negative beliefs;
- search for confirmatory information; inhibit the generation of positive solutions and increasingly to reject or fail to consider appropriate escape options other than suicidal behaviour;
- increasingly evaluate the situation/future as aversive, intolerable, unchangeable and inescapable through normal appropriate means.
- implicate the ineffectiveness of personal agency (helplessness) and of the agency of others when it refers to active assistance, recognition, valuing, or other source of positive regard or action.

6.4.1. Explicit and implicit appraisal

The appraisal process will occur at a level of conscious awareness (explicit) and without awareness (implicit). In the former this will be apparent through spontaneous account or by direct questioning. Implicit appraisal is revealed by understanding the inferential process and by listening to the client's narrative and attributional statements. Thus a client's statement that 'life is not worth living' or 'there is no way out' or 'life is intolerable' or 'I have to do what I am commanded to do' is a conclusion that has been arrived at through the process of attribution or inferred judgement. Clarifying what has lead the person to arrive at that point or conclusion should reveal their inference or judgement (appraisal).

6.4.1.1. Change methods

- Increase awareness of current appraisal processes especially those that are automatic and below awareness and its consequences.
- Widen the range of appraisal and reduce the differential information filter.
- Use behavioural experiments to change appraisal and inferences and to understand the process.
- Use appropriate inferential processes to evaluate evidence and validation of current interpretations and beliefs.
- Identify interpretation and evaluative judgements and dispute their accuracy.
- Encourage social exchange – the client can be encouraged to engage in helpful behaviour towards others such as friends and family. In terms of reciprocity this social action is 'money in the bank' as far as social exchange is concerned. It allows the client to feel able to ask others for support and help as a reciprocal action, and also will make them feel worthy of social support. This explanation can be shared with the client.

6.4.1.2. Improve problem-solving capability

Problem-solving capacity is a specific technique that should be modelled throughout therapy and can be a powerful agent of change in CBSPp work. The conventional method of problem-solving is as follows:

1. List clearly the problems to be resolved.
2. Select a problem and clearly and simply define it.
3. Brainstorm as many solutions (without prejudice – that is, without evaluating at this stage their feasibility) as possible.
4. List the advantages and disadvantages of each solution (at this stage feasibility comes into play potentially).
5. Select and implement a solution on the basis of the evaluation.
6. Evaluate its effectiveness. If ineffective, select and implement an alternative, and repeat.

One of the advantages of this method is that as well as specifying possible solutions to difficulties specifying the problem can cut through much of the 'emotional fog' that tends to distract and impede positive action. Problem-solving training can be achieved by working through these stages in an abstract exercise such as a game of noughts and crosses or draughts and verbalising the various problem-solving stages for each turn or move. This helps internalise the problem-solving method. Training can continue with hypothetical problems, such as:

'You move into a new area where you do not know anybody, how do you make friends?'

Or

'You are on your way to a job interview and you spill coffee down yourself.'

As always, using the client's current difficulties or interests may make this technique more understandable. For example, with one client we used a football example:

'Sir Alex Ferguson (the renowned manager of Manchester United football team) recently had a situation where he had no defenders. What did he do?'

Define the problem: Having no defenders and needing someone else to play there.

The following examples were generated:

*   Sir Alex could play himself
    *   *Advantages:*
        *   *Previously a professional footballer, good knowledge of the game.*
    *   *Disadvantages:*
        *   *Too old.*
        *   *Played as a striker.*
*   Wayne Rooney (a famous Manchester United footballer, a striker/forward) could play in defence
    *   *Advantages*:
        *   *Professional footballer.*
        *   *Currently in squad.*

- ○ *Disadvantages*:
  - ▪ *Striker.*
  - ▪ *Maybe too short.*
  - ▪ *Less chance of scoring.*
- The client could play in defence
  - ○ *Advantages*:
    - ▪ *This would be very enjoyable.*
  - ○ *Disadvantages*:
    - ▪ *Not a professional footballer.*
    - ▪ *Too old.*
- The therapist could play in defence
  - ○ *Advantages*:
    - ▪ *This would be a dream come true.*
- ○ Disadvantages:
  - ▪ *None at first, although the client pointed out that the therapist wasn't a professional footballer!*
- A midfielder could play in defence
  - ○ *Advantages*:
    - ▪ *Professional footballer, currently in squad, role involves defending; midfielders have played there before, would have time to practise in training, team had a number of midfielders.*
  - ○ *Disadvantages*:
    - ▪ *Wouldn't be as good as regular defenders.*

Option chosen: Surprisingly, the therapist wasn't selected for the next match! The client decided the best option was to play a midfielder in defence.

6.4.1.3. Feedback and exploration of utility of problem-solving technique

The use of humour here and a hypothetical situation that overlapped with the client's knowledge base led to an enjoyable and fruitful session. The client spontaneously remarked that he was surprised with how many solutions he had generated. The client also thought that this was a technique they could use for future difficulties. The advantage of this example was also to engage the client's interest in contemporary events, in effect re-engaging him with his external environment.

6.4.2. Activity scheduling

The activation of the suicide schema can lead to a sense of inertia; the state of defeat can become so pervasive that a person can begin to find it difficult to initiate activities. As in depression work, the therapist may work with the client to identify previous activities that gave them a sense of achievement or were pleasurable. If the client is finding it difficult to generate a list of activities, worksheets are freely available on the internet with common activities. The therapist and client then work to schedule in activities for the following week. Appraisals of difficulties in completing tasks are then worked on in similar ways to other appraisals, the clinician remaining aware of the suicide formulation and making links to broader themes where appropriate.

6.4.3. Artwork

As discussed in the Chapter 10, some clients find expressing themselves verbally to be very difficult. It may be that clients can communicate ideas to the therapist by drawing pictures. This can then be used as a stimulus to prompt conversations about particular memories or emotions, how they see themselves and others. Often by labelling different elements of the pictures, the client can build up their own language for expressing themselves and their feelings – this is a key goal of CBSPp. Artwork can also be used to strengthen positive memories and is a good technique to cement a memory further as well as using the BMAC procedure. We have also used artwork as stimulus for coping cards, that is, a client can draw a picture to represent an event that demonstrated their internal resilience factors, for example, one client used a picture of a pressure cooker releasing steam to indicate that he had relaxed and felt less threatened and defeated.

6.5. Schema change

The final component of CBSPp is schema change work. The aim here is to deactivate, inhibit and/or change suicide-related schema through the adoption of new and appropriate schematic beliefs about the person's circumstances, self and future. The initial procedure is to understand the triggers that activate the suicide schema and then to build up positive alternative schema that will reduce the inhibitory effect of the suicide schema and also create alternative associative networks that produce an alternative set of active problem-solving responses.

6.5.1. Change methods

Alternative schemata are created through promoting behaviour inconsistent with suicide schema and consistent with new positive schema. This can be achieved in a number of ways:

6.5.1.1. Weaken current schema

The weakening of current suicide schemas by the introduction of new information incompatible with the current schema. This can be achieved by a demonstration that the perception of a situation or that the person's expectations of events are incorrect.

6.5.1.2. Strengthen alternative schema

Methods are used to promote beliefs about positive self-worth (Tarrier, 2002, 2007; Hall &Tarrier, 2004; Oestricht et al., 2007). The establishment of positive schema requires the strengthening of associations that link alternative and mutually exclusive goals and actions to those triggered by suicide schema. This involves reducing the strength of negative beliefs about current circumstances, self and future, and strengthening positive beliefs about these through conventional cognitive and behavioural methods. In addition, positive affective responses will be elicited and strengthened through the use of imagery and cognition and associated recall of specific thoughts, behaviour and events (as described earlier). Furthermore, alternatives to suicide as a goal-directed escape behaviour will be generated by developing change strategies and developing tolerance to currently poorly tolerated situations. This can be achieved by effective problem-solving strategies. In doing so the appraisal system will be actively redirected to attend to and process a wider range and more positive aspects.

- Generating positive and specific autobiographic memories of successful change strategies (problem-solving capacity).
- Generating specific autobiographical memories of time when suicidal thoughts have been more effectively dealt with, or the specific incidents that have led to these thoughts/ feelings being reduced.
- Generating specific future change strategies.
- Generating positive affect.
- Creating and strengthening associations between positive and specific change strategies and positive affect.
- Countering and weakening negative appraisals.
- Creating and strengthening alternative and positive schema.
- Strengthening the inhibitory capacity of newly established positive schema.
- Developing change strategies as an alternative to suicidal behaviour as a goal – direct escape response.
- Developing tolerance to poorly tolerated circumstances – habituation and restructuring.
- Developing feelings of positive self-worth and strengthening associations of positive self-worth.
- Reducing beliefs about negative self-worth.
- Strengthening associations by cuing aspects of the schema and eliciting others.

6.5.1.3. Integration of past problem-solving capability and current skills training

Having trained in the problem-solving method the client can be asked to think about how they overcame difficulties in the past, what process they went through and what was helpful. They can integrate past skills onto the explicit problem-solving framework as described above. Strategies for resolving current and future difficulties can be generated and rehearsed in imagination before being implemented. Mood and confidence can be enhanced by the practising of BMAC and past problem-solving successes prior to any practice or implementation.

6.5.1.4. Improving low self-esteem

Clients with experiences of psychosis frequently have a poor perception of themselves and low self-esteem. These global concepts can be hypothesised to be manifest in terms of a negative self-schema. This is postulated as being a consequence of suffering from a severe mental illness and all that goes with this. This can involve suffering the stigma of having a mental illness and even harassment and exclusion, the effects of social rejection and negative interpersonal environments and the projected sense of being valueless and devalued. Clients suffering depression and suicidal ideation may feel increased feelings of low self-worth because of their low mood. Furthermore, an attribution process can make them think that if they feel they want to kill themselves then they must be worthless and deserve to die.

The factors that potentially impact upon and maintain negative self-schema are represented in Figure 6.3. It can be seen that the factors that influence and maintain negative self-schema are strong, multiple and relentless. The consequence of suffering a severe mental illness is the formation of such negative self-schema, which then serves to bias the way information is assimilated so that these negative schemas are maintained and strengthened rather than being challenged and modified. Self-schemas can be incorporated into the suicide schema so that negative thoughts about the self can trigger thoughts of suicide as an appropriate and sole escape response. Furthermore, exposure to situations that negatively impact upon views of the self can then also lead to activation of the suicide schema.

Low feelings of self-worth can also inhibit the effective use of coping strategies and successful problem-solving by impairing beliefs in personal agency.

6.5.1.4.1. IMPROVING THE CLIENT'S SELF-ESTEEM

The aim of this set of techniques is to produce generalisations of positive attributes, challenge negative self-schema, improve global self-esteem and elicit positive emotional reactions. This method can be carried out in two stages. The first elicits positive cognitions about the self, and the second elicits a positive emotional response. Alternatively, the two stages can be combined so that the processes of cognitive and emotional responding occur together. The procedure for the two-stage process is described for convenience as follows:

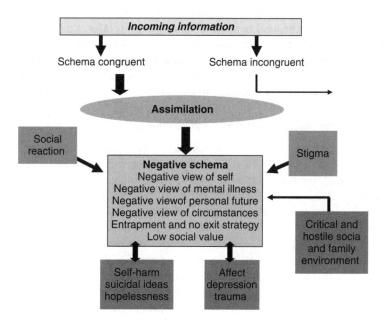

Figure 6.4 Maintenances of negative self-schemas

Stage 1. Cognitive responding

- Ask the client to produce up to 10 positive qualities about themselves (the number can be varied dependent on the client's capabilities – it is important not to have the client fail in generating the required number, so care has to be taken in selecting how many qualities to work with each client).
- Once the client has produced a list of these qualities, ask them to rate each one on how much they really believe it to be true on a 0 to 100 scale (where 0 = not at all and 100 = completely).
- Ask the client to produce specific examples of evidence of each quality. Prompt specifically for actions that have occurred recently and can be time-linked, such as "last week". Also use your knowledge of the client to elicit examples. Prompt as many examples as possible and list.
- Ask the client to rehearse the list of examples for each quality. This can be done through verbal description and mental imagery of the event. Then re-rate their belief that they believe that they possess this quality. (Usually the belief rating changes to show an increase. It should be emphasised to the client that their belief can change depending on what evidence they focus their attention upon.).
- The client is set a homework exercise of monitoring their behaviour over the next week and recording specific evidence to support the contention that they do have these qualities. The aim is to produce generalization and experiential learning of a number of positive attributes.
- At the next session provide feedback on examples and prompt further examples. Again ask the client to re-rate their belief that they actually do have these qualities and further point out any changes in these beliefs.
- Ask the client to reflect on the effect of eliciting and focusing on specific behaviours and evidence has on their beliefs about themselves and the qualities that they have and how this could affect their general opinion of themselves. Reinforce all positive attributes and the process whereby the client comes to a more positive view of themselves.
- Continue to repeat the above procedure. Continually emphasize that beliefs about themselves vary depending on what is the focus of attention, and self-esteem can be greatly affected by belief and is thus amenable to change.

Stage 2. Affective responding (positive affect generation)

Positive affect generation is a method in which the aim is to generate and experience a feeling of positive emotion or affect. This is achieved by describing and reliving a situation in which positive actions and outcomes occur and the client imagines and experiences the positive affect that would be concomitant on that situation. This can be achieved through *reciprocal interpersonal interaction*, that is, a good outcome happens to someone else because of the client's actions and agency, and the client is asked to imagine how that other person felt and then asked how they would feel having made the other person feel good. Or it can be done directly by asking the person to generate the positive emotional reaction in that situation in a way described in BMAC above. There are opportunities to identify, cue and build upon mediating cognitions to facilitate positive inference and interpretation. This task can be difficult for clients but effort should be put into reproducing positive emotional responses. This task is also important to help establish accurate anticipation of how others would respond and react emotionally to the client. This can be used to emphasise the negative effects self-harm or successful suicide would have on others, especially if the client believes they are a burden and others would be better off if they were dead.

The metaphor of 'social currency' can be made to help explain to the client the value of this. Doing things for others is similar to investing money: the more you do the more you save. Once you have money and savings in the bank you can spend it if you experience hard times. So receiving help or support from others is OK because you are spending the social currency you have saved by helping others at other times. Also helping others makes you feel good.

The client can be asked to explain the reasons why these qualities were important to them and the potential benefits of possessing them. Guided discovery and imagery can be used during this process to ensure the qualities selected were meaningful and important. The client can be asked to generate practical examples of this quality. Particular emphasis being placed on describing specific behaviours associated with the quality and the context in which they were carried out. Attention can be directed to the emotional experiences when acting in a way consistent with the quality, thus generating the positive affect associated with that experience. The client can be asked to imagine the positive emotional reaction that another person would experience as they interacted with them displaying a positive quality. They were asked to vividly imagine the other person's experience and describe how they would feel and attempt to mimic this experience. They can then be asked to describe how they themselves felt when they had evoked the positive emotion in the other person.

For example, in displaying generosity by helping out a friend the client was asked to imagine through guided imagery how that friend felt when they were so assisted. They were then asked to intensify and sustain this positive emotion. Through a similar process, they were asked to imagine and describe how they felt when they realized how positive their friend had felt in being helped out. Again they were asked to intensify and sustain this emotion. A similar process should be carried out for all positive characteristics and scenarios.

6.5.1.5. Guided imagery and confidence boosting

Positive imagery of the self-mastering different and difficult situations can be a powerful method to elicit and reinforce positive statements about self-worth and also to assist in initiating positive and appropriate goal-directed behaviour. Attention should be given to developing appropriate and positive body language and posture. For example, the client should be made aware of the body language associated with being anxious, defeated, depressed and subordinate, and in imagery change this to images of self-confident, self-assured and assertive posture and behaviour. Clients can be asked to imagine themselves growing in size, have their head up and shoulders back, walking in an assured manner and reacting to situations in a positive manner. Clients can be asked how behaving in this manner makes them feel, and trying to reproduce feelings of confidence and positive affect.

6.5.1.6. Developing positive schema and inhibiting suicide schema

Positive schema should be developed by linking this positive affect and imagery with real events and situations and by making as many associations as possible that are personally relevant to the client. Hopefully previous successes with BMAC and other imagery exercises will allow the client, with the therapist's assistance, to challenge any beliefs about ineffectiveness, poor personal agency, no control and so on. Changes in these beliefs and appraisals can be used to challenge beliefs incorporated within the suicide schema. This may also involve reliving past situations and imagining them happening again, but this time with positive and confident behaviour. In a similar way to that described above the client should generate positive descriptors of themselves and their behaviour, and then these should be linked to other situations and events in the client's life. Specific attention should be focused on developing and strengthening these associative links. Associations within the suicide schema should be weakened by challenging beliefs and assumptions by demonstrating inaccuracies and investigating inferences and interpretations through Socratic questioning. Behavioural experiments and observations can be used too, and new information introduced to weaken suicide schema.

There is a dual process of building up new schematic representations by developing positive associative (emotional and affective) links and by weakening suicide schema by direct challenge and interpretation. Clients should be encouraged to behave in a way that is inconsistent with suicide schema and consistent with new and appropriate schema, and then reflect back on the meaning of their behaviour and be cued into producing appropriate evaluation and inference. Positive biases can be set up through direct instruction such as instruction to focus on two positive aspects of a specific event or to magnify the positive interpretation of an event and then reflect these back in terms of positive self-worth.

6.5.1.7. Perspective taking

Further to generating positive affect clients can be asked about the effect their suicidal behaviour (and successful suicide) may have on others. This should only be embarked upon once the client's self-esteem has been raised, otherwise there is a danger that the client will respond that people would be better off without them. They need to be prompted to feel empathy towards others in states of distress and then be asked to describe and imagine how others would feel if they did commit suicide.

Potential inhibitors to self-harm and suicide, such as having children and/or family, should be identified and built into new positive schema. Suicide causing others distress should be reframed in terms of affection and interdependency needs that others have for the client. Specific examples of affection, love, help and other positive emotions others have for the client can be targeted, and through the use of imagery and positive affect generation can be integrated into positive schema.

6.5.1.8. Integration

The aim of this therapeutic intervention is to reverse the effects of the underlying psychological mechanisms and processes that lead to suicide behaviour as outlined in the theoretical model. The model emphasises the iterative interactions between the three elements of the model, processing bias, appraisal and schema. In therapy, this iterative process should be at the forefront so that any opportunity to use positive change in one element should be used to reinforce positive change in the other two. For example, identification of a bias in processing can be used to demonstrate how this is reflected in appraisal and suicide schema, and how a change to a more balanced or positive bias can have a profound influence to the good on appraisal and schema. Similarly, the effects of weakening and inhibiting suicide schema and the strengthening of alternative schema will influence appraisal and the way information is selected and processed. Examples of such interactions should be constantly generated and reinforced.

The treatment strategy is to build on methods that produce change through cognitive processes, through enhancement of positive affect and through cognitive and schematic change.

It should be recognised that these procedures and mechanisms are complementary but may have different speeds and durations of action. Homework exercises in the form of specific tasks are always to be encouraged but should not be burdensome.

It is unrealistic to expect change to be immediate or quick, and it will be necessary to go over old ground on many occasions. Each time this is done the suicide schema will be weakened, but this process will be facilitated only by the creation of alternative positive and inhibitory schema.

6.5.2. Past, present and future self perspectives

In order to aid integration and to facilitate the strength of positive schema, the following technique can be used. This technique uses reflections on change over time to generate goals and hope for the future.

6.5.2.1. Imagery exercise 1: Present-to-past self-reassurance

The purpose of this exercise is to strengthen the sense of positive changes over time that are often minimised by current activation of the suicide schema. This technique is also critical to informing the future-to-present self exercise, which is aimed at both strengthening positive future appraisals and an acceptance of uncertainty over the future (see exercise 2 below).

This exercise has optimum effects when done through imagery, although it can be done in conversation if a client can't tolerate this. It is, in essence, a summation of the meanings derived from the cognitive and BMAC interventions. Prior to the task, the client is asked to identify a particular period of difficulty in their life, optimally, a state that they found defeating and never ending. The client is then asked to speak to their past self and inform them of what happened and what resources they have drawn upon over time. They are asked to adopt a reassuring tone to themselves. They may talk about how they could have handled the situation differently, using problem-solving strategies. However, the key point is that regardless of how bad they felt, they are now in a position to look back with mastery and control over that situation and from the perspective of someone who has come through it.

6.5.2.1.1. POST-EXERCISE REFLECTION

The therapist asks the client what they made of the exercise. What do they make of the appraisals that they were thoroughly defeated? What personal resources did they draw upon? They are then asked to reflect on how it felt to reassure themselves, to provide themselves with knowledge that things were ok. Then they are asked what it felt like to be reassured, to be told with certainty that things turned out better than expected. They are asked to reflect on the fact they were being reassured by themselves. Finally, this is used to bridge to the future – how may this help with future difficulties?

6.5.2.2. Imagery exercise 2: Future-to-present self-reassurance

The second exercise involves taking the perspective of their future self, who can see how things work out. This is done in conversation first, discussing the things that the future self may say to the present self. The therapist then elicits similar conditions to the BMAC. The therapist asks the client to think about specific difficulties and encourages them to reassure

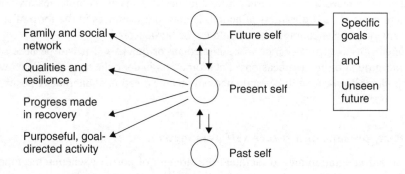

Figure 6.5 The past, present and future self

themselves in the same way as in exercise 1. Although they cannot see the future they can reassure themselves that they can draw upon the same resources that they have used in the past.

Figure 6.5 is a simple illustration that can be drawn out with a client. This shows the present self, with their current resources. The links to the past can be clearly seen, and the knowledge of how things turned out can be logged. The future self is depicted and this perspective can be adopted to reassure the current self.

6.5.3. Broad Minded Affective Scheduling (BMAS)

Some clients find the scheduling of activities very difficult. As discussed in Chapter 2, it has been suggested that in the group of people who experience psychosis, and those with negative symptoms in particular, people find it difficult to a get a felt sense of the reward that they expect from particular activities. Our attention was alerted to this by one client in particular who remarked after a successful BMAC, 'I need to do more things now, so I can remember them!' We developed a clinical technique to increase the links between savouring and anticipating events. Similar techniques can be found in the literature (Favrod, Giuliani, Ernst & Bonsack, 2010; Gard, Kring, Gard, Horan & Green, 2007; Gilbert, Allan, Brough, Melley & Miles, 2002; Kuha et al., 2011). This is called Broad Minded Affective Scheduling (BMAS). The following model is specific to prevention of suicide work.

6.5.3.1. Model for integrating BMAC with positive event scheduling

The basic proposition of this model is that when the therapist works with the client on a BMAC, they are activating the brain system(s) underlying the particular positive emotions experienced. As discussed in Chapter 2, stimulation of these brain systems also stimulates anticipation of future events with the same emotion although, for some people, this link is lessened (link to reward responsiveness). Once this brain system has been activated, the therapist and client may then turn to (1) generating future events that are similar to the past event and (2) imagining the event in detail, 'carrying over' the positive affect. Over time a feedback cycle is developed, where events resulting from the BMAS are then subject to the BMAC. This behaviour is designed to increase the predicted reward associated with events to be more in line with the actual reward experienced (see Figure 6.4).

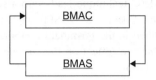

Figure 6.6 Imbuing future events with the emotions from past pleasures

This simple technique can evolve throughout therapy into a system for broadening the repertoire of behaviours a person engages in. Furthermore, this should not be a separate stream to work on the suicide schema, and the therapist should be alert to any opportunity to integrate increases in activity. We present the full model in Figure 6.5. As will be discussed, this provides the therapist with a schematic map to guide questioning of successful activity scheduling and to use this sequence with the aim of reducing hopelessness. Ultimately, we suggest that assisting clients in setting up this feedback loop is important in developing schema that may inhibit the suicide schema.

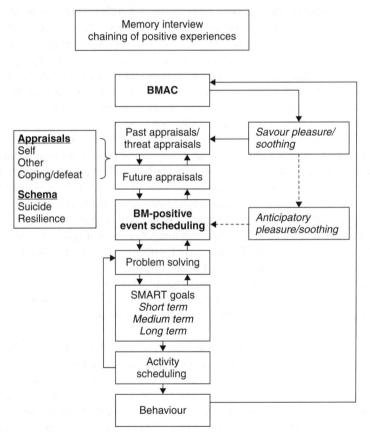

Figure 6.7 The Broad Minded Affective Scheduling procedure

1. The therapist begins with a positive memory interview as described above.
2. As described above, the BMAC technique leads into a savouring of positive emotion and an exploration of meaning. Specific to CBSPp, we tend to explore this in relation to the appraisal system established in the formulation, appraisals of the past, present and future. It can be important here to reflect on the *change to these appraisals* that may result in savouring a positive emotion.
3. Deeper/schematic beliefs may also be targeted, that is, the beliefs a person holds about themselves, other people, the world and about resilience from suicide.
4. The person is asked to hold and savour the positive emotion in mind and begin to imagine similar events that may occur in the future. The techniques listed in the 'chaining' section can be used here. The therapist pays particular attention to the specific cues that most likely lead to 'chains' of positive memories. These cues can then be built into the BMAC. In addition, these cues may be used to create a stimulus to be used *in-situ*. This is akin to grounding techniques (Linehan, 1993a,b) but with the added rationale that these cues trigger a network of memories with positive emotions attached to them.
5. The therapist and client then set a SMART goal, because as this system is developing, it is very important that the goals are achievable. We believe that it is important to start with a memory with a mild positive emotion attached to it and to schedule in a future event where the magnitude of positive emotions is similar. These events should not be particularly resonant with personal meaning to begin with. This is a very subjective process. For some people the initial memory/event was walking their dog while, for others, this may be too powerful a starting place. Rewarding oneself for making a cup of tea may be a good starting place, or even managing to turn the TV on. Strong positive emotions or events laden with personal meaning may trigger the suicide schema at this early stage, which may result in the cessation of the positive affect system. The therapist and client build this system slowly and steadily over time.
6. As in standard homework tasks, it is important to explore any barriers to this event occurring. This gives the client an opportunity to put their problem-solving skills into practice. The watchful CBSPp therapist also alerts the client to successful problem-solving and encourages them to take this into account in terms of their resilience schema.
7. The event is then scheduled. It is good to encourage the client to make a range of goals over different time courses, such as short, medium and long term.
8. The client then schedules in activities in a diary. Other techniques may help here, such as writing out an action plan. The therapist is encouraged to utilise their own repertoire of skills to increase motivation or deal with ambivalence.
9. Hopefully this will lead to the behaviour occurring. If so, this is then reviewed at the next session with the BMAC. It is important to also review the sense of mastery of the person has using this technique, of the changes that they have made, and of their impact on their resilience schema.
10. If the person did not engage in the behaviour, they did so partially, or in some other way failed, this is normalised. The therapist then explores the nature of the obstacle to carrying out the behaviour and develops a plan to help with this. If the client succeeded in changing their behaviour in some way but did not complete the whole activity or some element of the event led to them perceiving this as a failure, the therapist draws their attention to this, and cognitive change techniques aimed at reappraisal may then be applied.

11. As well as developing internal cues to behaviours (see point 4), the therapist also aims to solidify behaviours by increasing cues in the environment. By getting a person's family involved in helping with this and to provide cues in the day may help the client. The therapist must then remain curious about these social processes. If people around the client are critical and demanding that the client begins and maintain these activities, the model can be used for psychoeducation purposes – a useful analogy here can be one of an engine in need of a starter motor. The therapist also reflects with the client on the nature of their relationship with the people around them, as this may help to reduce appraisals of isolation and no rescue. The therapist also remains alert for barriers to engaging with others or negative consequences such as feeling like a burden to others, and internal/external shame. These barriers are discussed in more detail in the Chapter 9..

6.6. Summary

CBSPp is a formulation-based therapy. A thorough assessment and formulation can help guide this intervention, although sometimes there are significant barriers that makethis difficult. However, the formulation provides a constant barometer of change for interventions and evolves to incorporate the information gleaned from each intervention. Ideally, the interventions described above are delivered in sequence, systematically addressing attention and information processing, appraisals and then the suicide schema. This is married to a constructive process of building broad-minded attention, balanced appraisals and alternative schema about the self, world, future and of resilience to the suicide schema. Naturally occurring exits from the suicide schema are used as evidence of resilience, and the processes underlying these exits are drawn upon and strengthened. If the sequence described above cannot be delivered in this order, then the therapist works with the client to formulate the barrier to this (Chapter 9). This is often hugely informative and provides a clue to the factors that can lead a client to defeat. Decisions on intervention strategy should always bear engagement in mind, and developing ways of allowing the client to communicate their feelings to the therapist is extremely important. Artwork and metaphor are some of the techniques we have found to be useful.

Chapter 7

A case study in suicide prevention
Mark

7.1. Executive summary

The case of Mark draws attention to how to use a SAMS formulation-informed intervention of CBSP therapy within a window of opportunity in the absence of distressing experiences, and in the context of social communication difficulties. This case study describes the structured, constructive approach to therapy that could only be commenced once the working alliance between the therapist and client had been explicitly and collaboratively agreed. Mark's case highlights the common appraisal, held by many experiencing suicidal ideation, of being a failure, which is felt not only by the individual, but also inaccurately perceived to be held by others in their close family. Such appraisals of others impinge upon a person's willingness and motivation to seek support and help when most in need, thus elevating the likelihood of activating the suicide schema. Alternative, positive schemas linked with appraisals of others as caring and supportive needed to be reinforced, culminating in the inclusion of close family members in Mark's suicide prevention plan for the future: 'learning how to shine a light into a Dark Room'.

7.2. Background

Mark was a 27-year-old white British male who worked part-time as a store assistant in a local shop. Mark had previously attended college up to the age of 19 years, and achieved an average standard of educational qualifications. Mark was single but interested in starting a relationship with a girlfriend with a longer-term view of settling down and starting a family of his own. Mark lived with his parents and two younger sisters, whom he had previously been very close to and occasionally helped out with the household chores, when prompted to do so. Mark only had a few social friendships, although he saw these friends several times each week. Mark was under the care of an Early Intervention for Psychosis team that provided support to individuals for the first few years following initial onset of psychotic experiences.

7.3. Assessment

Information for the assessment of Mark's current difficulties was gained from semi-structured clinical interviews, following an assessment protocol for the first two or three sessions, complemented by the completion of psychometric measures. Mark was polite and appropriate throughout the assessment sessions, although he was very concise in his self-report – indeed, one-word answers to open questions were common. In response to several questions aimed to elicit historical information about Mark's feelings or thoughts about previous experiences, he would often state that he didn't know this detail or couldn't remember. While this was not experienced by the therapist as being deliberately obstructive, collating the pertinent data to inform the development of the formulation was a slow, and at times frustrating, process. A limited ability to reflect on previous experiences did call into question Mark's appropriateness for CBSP therapy, although Mark's clearly stated motivation to proceed with the therapy allayed the therapist's doubts somewhat.

7.3.1. Depression

Mark described a long-standing experience of recurrent depressive thoughts and prolonged low mood states. At the time of assessment, Mark rated the strength of his depression currently as 7 out of 10, where 1 out of 10 was no impact of depression and 10 out of 10 was a severe and profound impact of depression. Mark stated the onset of the depression, which was also when he had endured the most severe impact (8 out of 10), coincided with the death of his Aunt whom he had been especially close to. During his childhood, Mark had often visited his Aunt and, along with his sisters, he had enjoyed playing with his Aunt when they stayed overnight. Mark's Aunt died of natural causes when he was aged 17 years, and he felt this to be a deep loss. Ten years later, Mark would become tearful describing this loss and preferred to concentrate on the factual details with little emphasis on the emotional impact of this life event. Further questioning would often be responded to with responses of 'I don't know' or 'I can't remember'.

7.3.2. Experience of psychosis

Mark also reported experiences of psychosis, which he referred to as 'hallucinations', of an auditory, visual and tactile nature. Mark reported his first experience of a 'hallucination' was when he was aged 8 years. While saying overnight at his Gran's house, Mark saw a dark grey-black coloured silhouette in the shape of a figure approximately 3 feet tall walking across his bedroom. Mark has been asleep shortly before seeing this figure, and soon became frightened over who the figure was and what they may want from him. Mark decided against disclosing this experience to his family for fear of embarrassment and negative judgement. A similar experience occurred when Mark was 10 years old. In his own bed, half asleep, Mark saw a similar figure walk across his bedroom floor. Again, this experience frightened Mark, who thought it to be bizarre and therefore something to keep to himself. Mark has not seen this figure since.

Mark experienced a different visual 'hallucination' when he was aged 14 years. When half asleep in bed at his Gran's house, Mark woke to see and feel an emerald green lady's hand on his right shoulder, which frightened him considerably. In the morning, Mark told his Gran about this hallucination whose explanation was that it may have been a deceased relative trying to get in touch with him. Mark took some comfort from this explanation and felt less threatened by the hand when it reappeared to him on several further occasions before ceasing to appear within the subsequent few months.

About a year after his Aunt's death, when aged 20 years, Mark explained that he began hearing whispering voices for a year or so before they naturally subsided. The voices then returned to Mark around the time of his attempted suicide, when aged 27 years. Mark explained that he heard up to three 'fuzzy' whispering voices at a time. They were easy for him to hear but difficult to understand what they were saying.

For the past two years, Mark has also occasionally experienced hearing his mother call his name, but when Mark has asked his mother, she has denied doing so. This 'voice' tends to occur at about 9pm most evenings as Mark is getting ready to go to bed (which is usually before 10pm). Mark reported two possible explanations for hearing this voice: (1) he could have imagined hearing his mother's voice, (2) a para normal identity may have trapped his mother's voice, from earlier in the day, in the air and then releasing the voice for Mark to hear. Mark rated his conviction in each belief equally (50/50). Since it was his mother's voice that he heard, Mark did not report this experience to be distressing and it was not a problem for him.

At the time of the assessment, Mark was also experiencing a recurrence of the 'tactile hallucination' from his teenage years. On one or two occasions each month, Mark would become aware of the sensations of a hand resting on his shoulder, which belonged to a person who stood either behind him or above his head. Before noticing the hand on his shoulder, Mark would become aware of a build-up of anxiety 'swirling inside my body' and a build-up of tension and energy in his bedroom. On a few occasions, Mark would experience a 'tactile hallucination' of someone sitting upon his chest as he lay in bed, which severely restricted his breathing and prevented him from moving. These 'tactile hallucinations' only occurred when Mark was 'half-awake, half-asleep' lying in his bed.

7.3.3. History of suicidal behaviour

At the time of assessment, Mark rated his current intent to complete suicide as 5 out of 10; however, he had experienced a maximum 10 out of 10 rating, suggesting a full and committed intent, approximately two years previously. At this time, Mark was experiencing regular episodes of intense suicidal ideation lasting approximately 2–3 days, occurring every 4 weeks or so. During these episodes, Mark reported struggling to think of anything other than how he would end his life.

In the months leading up to Mark's one serious suicide attempt, he reported that he had become increasingly depressed by the fact that he was in another low-paid job that he did not enjoy and that he was struggling to hold on to. Mark recalled harbouring a desire to be in a different job but felt a financial pressure to remain in his current job. To cope with this continuing disappointment in where his life was going and the negative impact this was having on his self-esteem, Mark began to use gambling and alcohol as ways to cope, which he later recognised may have actually made the situation worse rather than better. At the time, Mark had also begun experiencing significant and strong headache pains, which he thought were a sign of stress and tension in relation to his job. Mark described the headaches as feeling like someone had his head in a vice, which was being increasingly tightened. Furthermore, Mark was regularly hearing the three 'fuzzy' voices for up to several days at a time, which were causing him considerable distress and anxiety, since he had no clear understanding why this was happening to him.

These three experiences (job dissatisfaction, headaches and voices) were explained by Mark to be the key triggers that led him to consider suicide as a 'way out'. For the attempt, Mark had planned to take his own life through an overdose of alcohol and aspirin. However, after drinking the alcohol, Mark found himself unable to swallow the aspirin tablets despite trying several times to do so. At the time of the attempt, Mark stated he was not aware of any protective factors or reasons to halt his attempt, and that he thought other people would be better off if he was dead. Since Mark did not feel the need for any subsequent hospital treatment, he decided against disclosing the details of the attempt to any of his close family members owing to a fear of embarrassment and perceived shame.

7.3.4. Related psychopathology

Prior to the initial assessment session with Mark, the therapist discussed the referral for CBSP treatment with Mark's care coordinator in the Early Intervention team. In addition to the usual risk-pertinent information routinely requested when working with suicidal clients, the therapist was also interested to hear that the care coordinator had recently invited Mark to complete the Autism-Spectrum Quotient (AQ; Baron-Cohen et al. 2001). Based on their previous contacts with Mark, the care coordinator had developed a suspicion that Mark may have been experiencing a number of social communication difficulties that appeared consistent with a profile of Asperger's Syndrome. Specifically, Mark appeared to present with limited social/communication skills, such as reduced eye contact and noticeably stunted conversations with others, a preference for solitary activities and a somewhat limited imagination. On the AQ, Mark achieved a score of 20 out of a maximum of 50. This score placed Mark in the average range for the general population and significantly below the cut-off score of 32, used to identify 80% of people diagnosable with Asperger's Syndrome. Hence, this screening measure did not indicate further assessment was necessary, although the therapist was aware of Mark's particular interpersonal style and his preference for a more concrete, rather than abstract, presentation of information. Also, throughout the course of the assessment, it became clear to the therapist that Mark appeared to struggle to recall memories of previous events in chronological order or in great detail, which was consistent with a diminished ability for recalling episodic autobiographical memories previously found among individuals with an Autistic Spectrum Disorder (Crane & Goddard, 2008).

7.3.5. Information processing

Mark and the therapist were able to collaboratively identify important information-processing biases that seemed to influence Mark's attention in his daily life. Mark tended to see the world through a 'negative lens' where he would pay particular attention to those aspects of a situation that seemed to confirm his negative predictions, especially in social situations at work when Mark was fearful of being criticised by others or of his performance being scrutinised. This expectation of criticism and scrutiny tended to cause Mark to become vigilant of any potential indications of negative judgements by others. Upon noticing any indicators of poor performance, Mark tended to 'jump to conclusions' and predict he would soon be criticised, or even rejected, by others as a result. These tendencies seemed to feed into Mark's increasing anxiety and distress in social situations, which he would subsequently feel the need to escape from through gambling and alcohol as a temporary exit and then thinking about suicide as a more permanent solution.

7.3.6. Significant life events

To develop a clearer understanding of the historical factors influencing Mark's current wellbeing, and allowing for the apparent difficulties in autobiographical memory recall, a pictorial timeline of significant life events was constructed, with the assistance of Mark's close family. In addition to the psychotic experiences already described, Mark also disclosed several events that were considered potential predisposing factors for his subsequent suicide attempt.

When he was 16 years old, Mark's mother explained to him that her current partner, whom Mark had always been lead to believe was his father, was not his biological father, and that his biological father had actually separated from his mother when she was pregnant with Mark. Mark recalled how this had been a difficult revelation for him to adjust to, since it undermined his trust of his mother and 'father', and it also revealed to Mark that his two sisters were actually half-sisters. While Mark recognised that he loved his family just the same, he struggled to understand why he had been misled in such a fundamental way. Mark seemed to have internalised this experience as evidence of him being gullible, stupid and 'different' from everyone else in his family. Mark later learned how his biological father had heavily abused alcohol, which elevated a deep-seated fear that he may be at risk of developing a similar problem and therefore become 'just like my real Dad'.

Aged 18 years and working at a local shop, Mark was physically attacked by a group of youths who stole Mark's wallet and phone. Mark was severely injured to his face and upper body, which required considerable hospital treatment. Understandably, for the next year or so following the attack, Mark became extremely cautious in social situations and avoided leaving the house alone after dark. Mark explained that this social anxiety eventually faded, although clear images from the time of the attack can intrude into Mark's attention upon occasion.

Another key life event considered for inclusion within the conceptualisation of Mark's suicidality was another disclosure of a family secret that his mother had been adopted when she was very young. When Mark learned of this fact, aged 19 years, he was extremely surprised and reminded of the previous revelation when he was 16, described above. Mark explained that the difficulty he experienced, at this time, was due to the realisation that the Gran, whom we was very close to as a young boy, was not actually a 'real relative' since she was his mother's adoptive mother. Again, Mark stated a recognition that family love did not necessarily have to be based on biological relations, although he seemed to find the lack of honesty about this information deeply unsettling and to be further evidence that he had been misled by people whom he had come to trust.

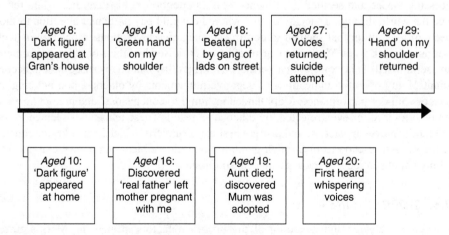

Figure 7.1 Timeline of significant life events

7.3.7. 'The dark room'

During the assessment sessions, Mark seemed to have difficulty in describing his experience in a direct manner, preferring instead to use metaphor and imagery. A common metaphor often referred to while conducting the assessment was 'the dark room'. When distressed with feelings of depression and loneliness, Mark described this experience as like being stuck in a dark room where he was not able to find the door handle to let himself out. In the dark room, Mark reported to feel trapped with no escape and unable to 'see' a way forward with his life. Mark could not explain how he came to find himself in the dark room.

7.3.8. Coping

In sessions with Mark, close attention was paid to any existing coping strategies utilised when he was experiencing distress or negative predictions about his future. Mark had developed a heavy use of alcohol as a way to 'numb the pain' he felt when caught thinking about his life and his disappointment in what he did with his time. Mark would frequently come home with several cans of strong lager and a bottle of vodka, and spend the night in his bedroom away from the rest of his family members. He would spend the rest of the day in his room drinking the alcohol until he became intoxicated and fell unconscious.

Alternatively, Mark would spend large parts of his day asleep as a way to escape his thoughts and feelings. Mark preferred to spend his time in the fantasy world of his dreams over the hopeless reality he felt he was facing in his day-to-day life.

7.3.9. Protective factors

At the time of the assessment, Mark had become more aware of potential buffering factors that may protect him from suicidal behaviour in the future. Mark rated the 'protection' offered by his close family was now 7 out of 10 (with 10 out of 10 being full protection against suicide), but he rated the percentage chance of him attempting suicide in the future still as 50%. An indicator of Mark's motivation to engage in the therapy was his belief that a better understanding of his suicidal ideation and how to cope with such thoughts would bring this percentage down considerably.

7.3.10. Summary of risk

At baseline assessment, Mark received a suicide probability score of 52%, which was rated within the moderate range, although on other measures of suicidal ideation Mark achieved scores in the mild range. A full assessment of suicidal risk was conducted in the initial sessions, which Mark fully engaged in (see Figure 7.2). Mark provided a detailed description of the one serious suicide attempt he had made approximately 18 months prior to referral. The overdose seemed to be a significant turning point in Mark's life. Following the attempt, Mark reported to have worked hard to challenge his negative self-appraisals and predictions for his future. Although Mark was unemployed, he expressed a renewed determination and optimism in securing a job that would suit his skills and preferences. He had begun to reduce his alcohol intake, a preferred suicide method and known disinhibitor of Mark's suicidal risk. Mark had also begun to actively develop his social network by joining new groups, which also seemed to improve his self-esteem. As such, Mark's level of suicidal risk throughout the course of therapy was assessed as low, although early warning signs of increased alcohol use, withdrawal from family, increased sleep and suicidal ideation were regularly monitored and used to inform a suicide prevention plan with his care team.

7.4. Formulation

The formulation of Mark's difficulties was developed in two stages (see Figure 7.2). The initial stage focused upon the potential triggers for a worsening of mood and feelings of loneliness. Once an understanding of Mark's daily experiences had been developed, a second stage looked to focus upon the function of suicidal ideation, planning and behaviour as the only solution to Mark's ongoing distress.

Mark identified three main events considered to be the precipitating factors leading to his day-to-day distress:

1. frequent occurrence of intense headaches, causing him considerable pain;
2. perceiving himself to be stuck in a job that he did not enjoy and where he was struggling to get along with other staff;
3. experiencing 'auditory hallucinations' in the form of whispering noises, which were too quiet to be heard clearly and therefore unable to be better understood.

Mark described his life, at this time, as 'like being stuck in a dark room with no way out'. While stuck in this dark room, Mark's distress would be further aggravated by ruminating on a series of challenging, existential questions such as 'What am I doing with my life?', 'Who am I?', and 'Why is this happening to me?' The outcome of this reflective thought process would be negative predictions about his future, where Mark visualised himself as being stuck in similar, unenjoyable jobs for the rest of his life, with a firmly held belief that he would eventually turn out like his biological father (whom Mark described as a 'jerk').

To cope with the feelings of depression and loneliness of being trapped in a dark room and the confusion as to why this was happening to him, Mark turned to alcohol as a way of coping and he developed a preference for spending more time asleep as a way of escaping the ruminative thoughts and negative predictions, with sleep offering a way of forgetting how difficult his life was at this time.

In order to better understand how and why these current difficulties were affecting Mark, the formulation also paid consideration to Mark's previous life experiences. Mark recalled having a fear of the dark when he was a young child. This fear developed in response to the occasions in his early and later childhood when he experienced visual hallucinations of seeing dark, shadowy figures walking across his bedroom floor and a green hand resting on his shoulder. Another important life experience was Mark's discovery that his biological father separated from his mother while she was pregnant with him. Mark was appalled at such an act of abandonment, which lead him to develop a grave fear that he may inherit such a personality flaw and turn out to be like his father. At the age of 18 years, Mark was a victim of an assault by a 'gang of lads' while walking along a quiet street at night. Mark did not know the identity of his attackers, and described the attack as unprovoked and happening at random. Mark received considerable facial injuries during this attack, which required hospital treatment. Less than a year later, Mark then discovered that his mother had been adopted at birth, and therefore his maternal grandmother was not his 'real Gran'. This caused Mark considerable confusion since he had developed a close relationship with his Gran during his early childhood.

These previous experiences enabled Mark to better understand the fear and loneliness he was experiencing when he felt his life was like 'being stuck in a dark room'. As a result of his childhood experiences of seeing shadowy figures and green hands at night time, it seemed likely that he developed a fear of the dark. Mark also harboured a strong fear that the

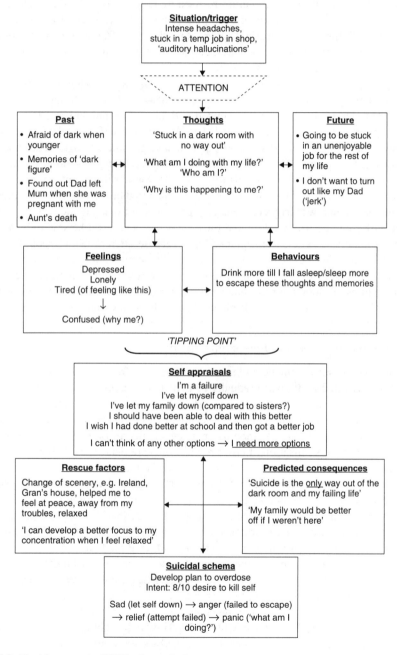

Figure 7.2 Mark's generic CBSPp formulation

abandonment of his pregnant mother by his biological father may have been passed down to himself somehow, despite Mark dreading this to have happened. Mark had also developed a growing belief that he was one of life's weak and vulnerable "victims" unable to cope with experiences that others are able to live with.

Once a clearer conceptualisation of the difficulties Mark experienced on a day-to-day level, the second stage of the formulation focused more upon the role and function of suicidality. Mark described experiencing a 'tipping point' approximately a month before his suicide attempt. Rather than a specific trigger, Mark described being gradually 'worn down by the weight of my problems' (headaches, employment problems, hallucinations, rumination and negative expectations for his future).

Mark had begun to try to make sense of his difficulties, which led him to view himself as a failure and having let himself down. Mark also considered himself to have let his family down, perhaps as a result of comparing himself with his sisters and their academic achievements and opportunities to go to university. Mark developed a series of self-critical thoughts that he should have done better at school, he should have got a better job, and he should have been better able to cope with the difficult time he was experiencing. Eventually, Mark began to lose hope of finding a way out of his difficult situation. At this point, Mark recognised that he became unable to think of any options other than to take his own life, at which point Mark's suicide schema was triggered. He developed a belief that suicide was the only way out of the dark room he was stuck in and the only way to end what he saw to be a "failing life". Acting upon this belief, Mark planned an overdose attempt using alcohol and pain-relief medication. After being unable to complete the suicide attempt, Mark experienced anger with himself for the failure, which soon turned to relief and then panic over what he was doing to himself. Soon after the suicide attempt, Mark was aware of how his behaviour would affect his family and how his death would have been devastating for them.

7.4.1. Process issues when developing formulation

Collaborating with Mark in the development of a formulation, a two-part diagram, referred to as the 'therapy route-map', was gradually constructed over several sessions. Each formulation session began with a summary of the work from the previous session, so that Mark was aware of what the new information, to be presented in the current session, was to be added to. A gradual process of addition and embellishment eventually allowed Mark and the therapist to develop a full conceptualisation of how previous life experiences and subsequent appraisals and behaviours had led to the development of suicidal ideation.

Mark clearly expressed a motivation for a more thorough understanding the development and maintenance of his suicidal ideation, and was particularly interested in how each aspect of the formulation linked to other aspects within positive feedback cycles. Despite this motivation, it became apparent that Mark seemed to struggle to 'emotionally align' himself to some of the content of the formulation, even though this referred to his own life experiences. Initially, this was hypothesised by the therapist to be indicative of an inaccuracy within the formulation, a strategy by Mark to protect himself from re-experiencing the emotional content of these experiences, or simply as an indicator of Mark's disinterest in the session. However, a more accurate explanation may come from the empathising-systemising theory of autistic spectrum disorders (Baron-Cohen, 2009), which highlights a drive to analyse, construct and understand the rules of systems over and above the appropriate emotional reaction to thoughts and feelings, referred to as affective empathy (Davis, 1994).

Since Mark disclosed a difficulty in holding the full formulation in his attention at any one time, it was agreed that, in subsequent treatment sessions, only the aspects of the formulation most pertinent to the current intervention work would be emphasised to Mark.

7.5. Goals for therapy

Mark had firm aims for undertaking a course of CBSP therapy, which were clearly stated to the therapist. These were:

- to develop a better understanding of depression and suicidality, and how these problems specifically affect him;
- to develop better ways of coping with depression and suicidal thoughts and feelings;
- to better understand the reasons behind the auditory and visual hallucinations that Mark experiences and to understand how these may contribute to his depression and suicidality.

Mark began the first assessment session with a firm belief that his previous suicidal attempt had been a result of his experiences of depression and the 'voices' he had been hearing at the time. Mark felt that by developing his understanding of depression and hallucinations he would be able to better respond to any subsequent thoughts about suicide as he would have more potential solutions to such problems.

7.6. Intervention

In order to achieve the goals agreed with Mark for the CBSP therapy, and to address the essential elements of the formulation, namely attentional biases, self-criticism and other negative appraisals, and a suicide schema with suicide as the 'only' escape, the plan for the intervention comprised:

- Attention broadening and reducing threat-based processing by developing Mark's control over the focus of his attention to external stimuli rather than internal cognitive events.
- Introducing Broad Minded Affective Coping (BMAC) as a new, helpful coping strategy when experiencing distressing thoughts, and to develop easier access to positive memories of rescue and relaxation.
- Psychoeducation of psychosis to reduce the need to respond to culturally unacceptable appraisals of unusual experiences, such as auditory and visual hallucinations.
- Improving ability for social problem-solving and to develop more accurate self-appraisals of coping with distress.
- Self-esteem work to improve Mark's image of himself and what his family think of him.

Following the sharing of the formulation with Mark and socialisation to the cognitive model and the subsequent stages of therapy, Mark explained to the therapist that he would view the intervention as an opportunity for him to discover more helpful ways out of the dark room he had previously felt trapped within. The new ways of coping that Mark would learn throughout the intervention stage were viewed as alternatives to the only exit from the dark room that he had previously been aware of, that is, suicidal behaviour.

7.6.1. Attention broadening

In order for Mark to develop an awareness of the negative mental filter he was perceiving events of his life through, the initial phase of the intervention focused upon the broadening of Mark's attention. The aim was for Mark to develop a more balanced view of himself, the world and others.

Working with the therapist using an unhelpful thinking styles sheet, Mark was able to recognise key information processing biases he was particularly prone to and how his biased thinking styles, or perceptions, impacted upon the likelihood of him recognising any success in his future.

Using the protocol presented in section 6.3, Mark began to practise attention broadening activities as homework between sessions, which were framed as 'concentration strengthening' tasks, with his attention likened to a muscle to be 'worked out' in the same way as the rest of his body when Mark was at the gym. Mark found these tasks to be easy to follow and reported being pleased with the perceived improvement in his concentration. Mark began to use the focused attention tasks, where he would choose to maintain an external focus on an object in his immediate environment, especially at times when he was experiencing distressing and unhelpful thoughts about himself and his future. Mark reported that the use of such tasks helped him to develop a confidence in his ability to cope better when such thoughts occurred to him, which also improved his perceived control over his response to such thoughts.

7.6.2. Broad-Minded Affective Coping

The Broad-Minded Affective Coping (BMAC) strategy was then implemented, with Mark experiencing a positive benefit in his immediate mood state following use of the strategy. The main foci of the BMAC strategies were times when Mark had enjoyed spending with his family (see Box 7.1), which served to reinforce the importance family had in Mark's view of himself and also to bolster his reasons for living and pursuing a way of coping with distress without suicidal behaviour.

After discussing and reflecting upon various positive memories that Mark was able to recall, two BMAC scripts were recorded onto a CD for Mark to follow and also remind himself of the meaning each of these memories had for him. Mark was enthusiastic about this work and regularly listened to the CD tracks each day between therapy sessions. Mark reported that he used the BMAC tracks to help himself achieve a more positive mood, to help him further broaden his attention and to enable easier access to a 'positive cycle' of thoughts and feelings. Once familiar with the procedure and the content of the BMAC tracks, Mark then decided to embellish the exercises by taking and collecting photographs of his route to his Gran's house. Mark explained that sight of these photographs acted as more immediate reminders of the positive affect he experienced while listening to the BMAC – a quick 'mood boost' that he could carry around with him. These photographs were complemented with other keepsakes and souvenirs from his family holidays to Ireland, which also supported a quick route into the feelings of happiness, peace and belongingness.

7.6.3. Psychoeducation about psychosis

A normalising approach was taken to expanding Mark's understanding of psychosis and, more specifically, his hallucinatory experiences when he was tired, in bed and close to sleeping. The aim for this stage of the therapy was to reduce Mark's self-reported fear of the auditory and visual hallucinations and to offer Mark an opportunity to discuss and reflect upon why this was happening to him. Information and materials written for service users about their experiences of psychosis was worked through by Mark, supported by his therapist. Mark soon began to develop an understanding of his previous psychotic experiences and how his vulnerability may have been particularly exposed when he felt tired and stressed after a busy day. With this new understanding Mark began to develop a more informed and helpful relationship with such experiences, whereby the images appearing at night time and the whispering voices occasionally heard when feeling stressed were more easily accepted as normal experiences. This new way of understanding reduced the need for Mark to engage with and respond to such experiences, based on a belief that the hallucinations were culturally unacceptable and a problem to be frightened of that required mental effort to resolve.

Box 7.1 Examples of BMAC

BMAC 1: Enjoying family time on holiday

Focus: On a family holiday to visit an Aunt's house in Ireland.

Affect: Happy, peaceful, calm, sense of belonging.

Meaning: There are times in Mark's life when he feels self-confident and able to please others without any pressure or expectation. Mark feels the love his family have for him, and this makes him feel happy. Mark also appreciated the benefit of fresh air and open spaces when motivating himself to lift out of darker moods.

Consequences: Reduced after-event processing that his family would not notice if he was gone.

BMAC 2: Walking to Gran's house

Focus: Walking to Gran's house along a country path through fields.

Affect: Happy, excited about seeing his Gran, proud of his willing visit.

Meaning: Making others happy makes me happy, I am kind, I love and care about my family.

Consequences: Reduced after-event processing about his lack of caring and connectedness with significant others in his life. Counter-evidence for appraisal that 'I've let my family down'.

7.6.4. Problem-solving

One of the key aspects of the formulation of Mark's suicidal behaviour was a lack of options generated when experiencing a distressing situation, that is, when Mark feels he is trapped in the dark room and looking for a way out. In order to draw on Mark's existing strengths on solving problems, and to bolster his self-esteem in problem-solving, Mark wrote a summary of a recent problem that he had successfully resolved himself. Mark reported a problem he had experienced a few months previously when he wanted to go out and socialise more with people of a similar age to himself. At the time, Mark was working in a charity retail shop with people aged significantly older than him, who did not share his interests in music and social activities. The appraisal of 'I'm alone with no friends to go out with' was seen to be pertinent to Mark's feelings of loneliness associated with the dark room, and subsequent negative self-appraisals, which may increase the likelihood of triggering Mark's suicide schema. In response to this problem situation, Mark decided to proactively seek out an appropriate opportunity to meet other young people. Among a range of possible venues, Mark decided to enrol at a local youth centre and enlist on a couple of their regular group activities, fro example, social night, computer club, etc. Despite the negative predictions Mark had in mind when planning this solution, he plucked up enough courage to challenge these thoughts by walking through the front door of the youth centre. After his first few visits, Mark soon began to feel more relaxed at the centre, happy to be there and interested in the other young people in the clubs they shared together; others seemed to express an interest in Mark's views. This experience of successful problem-solving provided Mark with the self-appraisal of 'I can feel comfortable with other young people' as a replacement to the previous feelings of loneliness with no friends.

With the memory of this success in mind, problem-solving training was then used to introduce Mark to a systematic approach comprising of several stages:

- identify and clearly define the problem to be resolved;
- clearly define the problem by breaking it down into management parts;
- generate as many potential solutions as possible (no matter how plausible);
- list the advantages and disadvantages of each potential solution;
- select the most preferred solution that seems most likely to be helpful;
- implement and evaluate the outcome;
- if solution was not effective, select and implement an alternative solution.

Mark was provided with a proforma to complete. listing each of the above steps, which he completed as homework on several occasions for current problems he was experiencing. Initial practices were conducted on less serious problems, such as running out of milk, before building Mark's confidence in using this approach with more important problems, including 'getting a new job', 'feeling better about myself', and 'working out what I want in life'.

Mark seemed very well suited to the structure offered by this approach and, once practised, was able to internalise the procedure without the need to use worksheets. Mark was also encouraged to involve his family in his solution generation, since this was a step Mark often had difficulty with, and also as this presented an opportunity for Mark to strengthen his family ties while collaborating on a positively focused task. By the end of this phase of the therapy, Mark began to view frustrations that he encountered as 'problems to be solved', and found that this approach helped him move forward more so than feeling stuck and a 'failure' in his life.

7.6.5. Activity scheduling

To bolster Mark's growing confidence in his ability to manage his mood, seen as a result of his continued practice of the Attention Broadening training and the BMAC strategy, a 'Managing My Mood' diary was also developed. The purpose of the diary was in keeping with traditional activity scheduling, with a list of existing activities shown to naturally improve Mark's sense of mastery and pleasure identified through the retrospective completion of a weekly schedule. Mark was able to recognise a number of activities that improved his mood, which included listening to his favourite music, watching a comedy DVD, going out for a walk, visiting his family and listening to BMAC tracks.

With this list of 'mood-booster' activities available to Mark, he then agreed to regularly self-monitor his mood, initially for up to three times a day (morning, afternoon, evening). At any time point that his mood was self-rated to be below an agreed level, Mark engaged in a 'mood-booster' activity and then re-rated his mood. He continued to draw upon this list of activities until his mood was lifted above the agreed level again. After a week or so, Mark had internalised the process of self-rating his mood and, if necessary, engaging in a 'mood-booster'. With his continued practice of using this approach, by the end of therapy, Mark had refined his selection process such that he was aware of the likely impact of each activity on his current mood given his current context. On this basis, Mark's decision-making improved with each iteration of the process, along with his belief in his ability to manage his mood and, therefore, look after himself even when he was feeling low.

7.6.6. Self-esteem

Some positive affect generation work had already been achieved through Mark's use of the BMAC strategy. The second BMAC track focused upon Mark walking to his Gran as a child. While Mark recalled enjoying spending time with his Gran very much, the most emotionally salient aspect of the positive memory was the initial moment when he walked through his Gran's door and saw the look of joy on her face at his arrival.

This positive memory was returned to when working with Mark to improve his self-esteem, since it demonstrated a reciprocal interpersonal interaction whereby Mark perceived that his effort in walking to his Gran's had resulted in a positive outcome for her. Through further elaborating his recollection of this positive memory, Mark described a great sense of personal pleasure in his visit 'making Gran's day', and he could imagine how his Gran would have felt in this situation – a joy at seeing her only grandson, and a sense of family belonging-ness. Upon realising the impact upon his Gran's feelings, which was a direct consequence of his own actions, Mark recognised a sense of pride in being a good grandson and a feeling of happiness for knowing his Gran knew he cared for her. Drawing upon the meaning contained within this BMAC, and through a process of guided discovery, Mark recognised the positive qualities this act demonstrated about him, which led to new appraisals of 'I show love and care to my family', 'I bring joy to other members of my family', and 'My family would miss me if I left'.

Since the time remaining in therapy was running short, Mark was encouraged to take this work further forward by surveying his family for current examples that also demonstrated these new appraisals about his self and his family. Mark invited his mother to attend one of the remaining sessions in order for her to feel informed about the work Mark had already achieved and to contribute to the plan for continuing this work alongside Mark.

7.6.7. Appraisals

Central appraisals within the formulation were Mark's beliefs that 'I'm a failure' and 'I've let myself down'. Mark would usually reach such conclusions following several days of low mood, feeling trapped in the dark room with no apparent way out, and considerable use of alcohol and sleep as a way to cope. According to the formulation, these self-appraisals would trigger the suicide schema and the planning of a serious suicide attempt as the way towards a solution. It was therefore considered important for these self-appraisals to be challenged with Mark provided the opportunity to consider counter-evidence for such conclusions. Drawing upon a standard technique of cognitive restructuring, Mark completed a daily thought record each time the appraisals occurred. Mark was able to provide several examples of evidence to support the conclusion that he must be a failure. However, with support from the therapist, Mark was also able to recognise examples that contradicted such a conclusion. For example, Mark's BMAC of an example of successful problem-solving was difficult to reconcile with the appraisals of being a failure when this example clearly demonstrated success, as well as perseverance, initiative and courage. The incongruence raised through this work weakened Mark's belief in 'I'm a failure' from 80% down to 20%.

Further reattribution work was conducted to restructure Mark's belief of 'I've let my family down'. To provide Mark with access to counter-evidence for this appraisal, he conducted a small survey of his family member's views of his top 5 qualities and characteristics, that is, 'What are the 5 things that you like or value most about Mark?' Mark predicted his family would have great difficulty completing this survey since 5 qualities would be too many for them to think of. However, Mark admitted considerable surprise when the survey responses came back, and his family had responded in full, with most of the survey sheets listing many more than 5 qualities. In summary, Mark's family saw him as a loving, caring and giving man whose efforts to contribute to the family were greatly appreciated and highly valued. This evidence served to weaken Mark's original belief that he had let his family down considerably, with an alternative view that, despite his faults, Mark was an important member of his family.

7.6.8. Positive schema work

The positive schema work was not a separately or distinctly defined part of therapy, rather a theme running throughout latter sessions. In addition to the self-esteem work, mood management and problem-solving training, towards the end of therapy a more explicit focus was placed on bolstering close links with Mark's family members. This served to undermine the potential belief that Mark's family would be better off without him, thus triggering access to his suicide schema. As described earlier, Mark was keen for his family links to be further strengthened within this work. Mark invited his mother to a session in the latter stages of the therapy in order to involve her in planning how his new role within the family could be developed. Mark also set himself the homework task of regularly spending time with his sisters. These opportunities enabled the integration of other key learning points and new coping strategies developed throughout the course of therapy into a broader context, importantly, outside of the therapist–client relationship. Regular contact and feedback from his family that they enjoyed and valued his company served to further strengthen a new positive schema that he was loved, cared for and would be sorely missed.

Additionally, Mark also further developed his ability to help himself by helping others. Social reciprocity within his family seemed to help Mark rediscover his role, and valued contribution, in relation to significant others in his life. As such, Mark's view of himself and his role within his family was positively updated. Mark recognised the importance of this work through his reflection on how his visit to his Gran led to an improvement in her mood and then a subsequent improvement in his own mood as well. Taking this learning forwards, Mark agreed to increase his contribution to the running of the family home by offering to help more with the household chores. This plan was met with gratitude by his mother and father, which pleased Mark and reinforced a new belief that he was a valuable member of his family who was happy to 'pull my weight'.

7.7. Process issues

As described within the assessment section of this chapter, a suspicion had been raised by Mark's care team that he appeared to present with limited social/communication skills and a particular interpersonal style of reduced eye contact and stunted, staccato conversations. Initially, Mark was extremely concise with his retorts, only providing 'yes/no/don't know' responses. Throughout the assessment sessions, the therapist adopted an open style of questioning to gain more detailed background information, although this was a slow process, which appeared to be frustrating to both Mark and the therapist.

A few sessions into the course of therapy, and once a therapeutic relationship had begun to be developed, Mark's interpersonal style was explicitly discussed. Mark recognised that he had always experienced some difficulty in starting and maintaining conversations with other people, and he often struggled to know what to say to people unless discussing topics he found particularly interesting, in which case he could talk in some considerable detail that often times did not seem to result in as much pleasure for the other person as it felt to Mark.

Another difficulty, referred to already, concerned Mar's ability to recall autobiographical information in a consistent and chronological order. Structured and systematic use of a timeline was introduced to allow Mark to 'get his bearings' with his memories of important events in his lifetime. Mark expressed a preference for making use of such structured approaches to tasks, which was always borne in mind when planning other in-session and homework activities. Instructions for homework tasks, and a brief practice attempt, were always collaboratively developed within session before any work was completed by Mark out of session.

Following the explicit discussion of Mark's interpersonal style, and having agreed a structured approach to therapy tasks, the in-session tension considered to have impeded Mark's contribution to discussion, gradually seemed to lessen. While Mark's interpersonal style remained stunted in places and the content of discussion always required a more concrete component, by the end of therapy both the therapist and Mark were able to recognise occasions where they enjoyed a more open and flowing conversation.

By the end of therapy, in discussion with the therapist, Mark had decided to ask his care team for a more thorough assessment of his social communication abilities. Consequently, a referral for a full diagnostic assessment with an Autistic Spectrum Disorder specialist unit was submitted.

7.8. Outcome

Psychometric assessments of suicidal ideation and Mark's experiences of psychosis did not indicate any significant change from baseline to the four- and six-month follow-ups, with all scores at each time point remaining within the non-clinical range. On measures assessing psychosis, Mark did not report any significant psychotic experiences or related distress, which seems to contradict Mark's self-report to the therapist that he experienced occasional auditory and tactile hallucinations, which he found to be distressing. This difference could potentially be explained by Mark's heightened anxiety when in social interactions with new people, such as the research assistant conducting the assessment, and his subsequent reluctance to discuss such experiences. Alternatively, Mark's observed difficulty in recollecting autobiographical events may have impacted upon his retrospective report of such experiences.

Outside of the somewhat restrictive assessment of experiences offered by psychometric measures, at the end of therapy, Mark reported that the therapy had been extremely helpful to him in overcoming future difficulties. In a repeat of a more subjective assessment of Mark's experience of depressive thoughts and low mood, Mark stated that the strength of his depression had fallen from 7 out of 10 at the start of therapy down to 2 out of 10 at the final session. Looking to the future, Mark expressed a confidence that he would not make a suicide attempt, and that if he was beginning to experience significant suicidal ideation, he would seek the immediate support of his family and care team. Mark described the therapy as being like a torch in his pocket, so that if he ever found himself in the dark room again, he would be able to use his torch to help him find a new way out. Mark's scores on the Beck Hopelessness Scale (Beck, 1988) reflected this new outlook, dropping from 9 at baseline down to 4 out of 20 at the six-month follow-up.

Upon completion of therapy, Mark was provided with a copy of the formulation diagram for him to remind himself of the route-map used to develop new ways of coping, a therapy blueprint summarising the techniques and learning points introduced during therapy, a pack of mood diary sheets to help Mark to continue to proactively manage his mood, and a CD containing the attention control training exercises and BMAC tracks developed at the start of the intervention work. Mark arranged to share this pack of materials with his family and his care team so that they were all aware of what helped Mark and to give them permission to assertively support him in any future difficulties.

7.9. Critical reflection

The case of Mark highlights the importance of individualising the delivery of the CBSP therapy to each client's presenting problem and interpersonal style. While the techniques and strategies described in previous chapters were appropriate to Mark's presenting problem list, the approach to their delivery had to be tailored to accommodate his interpersonal style. The development of a warm, empathic and non-judgemental therapeutic relationship between Mark and the therapist was of paramount importance before any intervention work could be contemplated. The therapist initially approached this case with some ambivalence about Mark's potential to engage with and benefit from the CBSP therapy, based on an awareness of Mark's existing social communication difficulties, his concise responses to open questions, and an apparent difficulty in making emotional contact with autobiographical memories of previous life events. Over time, and requiring effort and patience from both parties, a collaborative alliance was established with the 'rules of therapy' explicitly agreed between the therapist and Mark, summarising the roles and expectations of each person. The structured and systematic approach to assessment, formulation and the intervention tasks, which was clearly labelled by the therapist, enabled Mark to access the CBSP therapy.

Following the introduction of new coping strategies and Mark's committed level of homework practice, a key aspect of the later stages of therapy was the development of easier access to more positive schema. The formulation highlighted that the main pathway to suicidal ideation for Mark became available when experiencing frustration and stress in his daily life that he appraised as evidence of being a failure and disappointment to himself and his family. The earlier stages of therapy had enabled Mark to improve his ability to solve social problems and make friends, to recognise his previous successes and the impact this had on his self-esteem, and to develop the confidence needed to challenge his apprais-als of himself and other's perceptions of him. This gradual, constructive approach allowed Mark and the therapist to regularly reflect on progress to date and ensure that each new skill was being assimilated in the context of previous achievements. By integrating each positive experience into Mark's understanding of himself and others, access to positive schema was steadily improved. An indicator of success of this approach came near to the end of therapy when Mark proactively suggested involving key members of his family in the continuation of his work. Whereas previous appraisals of his family would have been of disappointment and even disgust in him, Mark had dared to believe that his mother and sisters would want to be more involved in supporting him and sharing their future lives together.

In the absence of frequent and regular suicidal ideation and other highly distressing expe-riences, the timing of the therapy window with Mark enabled the constructive approach to be taken, which focused almost entirely in developing new ways of coping with suicidal thoughts and feelings should they arise in the future. From the outset, Mark was motivated to learn more about his previous experiences of depression and suicidality, and to draw upon his more in-depth understanding to develop alternative ways of being with such problems. The opportunistic timing of the intervention and Mark's level of motivation and determina-tion to progress with this work were undoubtedly important determinants in the success of the therapy.

7.10. Summary

Mark was referred for CBSP therapy by an Early Intervention for Psychosis team. At the commencement of therapy, Mark was not experiencing any significant distress associated with suicidality or psychosis, although he did report some occasional hallucinations, which were ongoing. This presented a window of opportunity for Mark and the therapist to spend some time together developing an understanding of Mark's previous suicidal episode, which could be used to inform a set of resources for Mark to draw upon if any future times of need arose.

The initial development of a therapeutic alliance was delayed while a shared understand-ing of the expectations of therapy had been even agreed, which required explicit consider-ation of Mark's social communication style. Once these expectations had been made explicit, an idiosyncratic formulation of Mark's experience of suicidal ideation was collaboratively constructed. New coping strategies highlighted by the formulation were then implemented and, with considerable commitment from Mark, practised until competence was achieved.

Although not necessarily demonstrated in the psychometric measures, Mark considered the therapy to be a considerable success. He reported himself as pleased to be leaving therapy with new ways of coping with distress, a more positive approach to his loving family, and an optimism that he now had his own source of light to shine in the dark room.

Chapter 8

A case study in suicide prevention

Peter

8.1. Executive summary

Peter's case provides some useful insights into the challenge of implementing CBSPp. Distinctive features of this case were as follows:

- *Delivering CBSPp with current and distressing experiences of psychosis.*

- *Formulating suicide-specific processes.*

- *Strategies for working with clients with over general autobiographical memory.*

- *Strategies for working with clients who have fluctuating levels of distress and suicidal thoughts and intent.*

- *Attention broadening, Relaxation and BMAC can be used to manage in session threat.*

- *Reducing in session threat may lead to more balanced assessment and formulation information.*

- *CBSPp should focus on those aspects of experience of psychosis that are directly linked to suicide.*

- *Interpersonal difficulties need to be formulated and specific interventions implemented that reduce their impact on suicidal thinking.*

- *Future directions: momentary assessment and intervention tools may assist clients with rapid fluctuations on affect and with over general autobiographical memories.*

- *CBSPp should utilise and strengthen a client's existing coping repertoire and develop inhibitory schemata.*

8.2. Background

Peter was a 46-year-old white male. He had left school at 16 with no qualifications and had worked as a taxi driver in his twenties prior to becoming ill. At the age of 27 he was sectioned after a suicide attempt and then given a diagnosis of paranoid schizophrenia. Over the next 20 years he was hospitalised eight times but made no further suicide attempts. He was a Christian and had very strong religious beliefs. He believed himself to be one of God's Angels and/or God Himself. He currently lived alone, within 20 minutes' walk of his parents, his sister and one brother. He had four brothers and two sisters, and he was the third eldest. He also had 'about 5 or 6' nieces and nephews up to the age of 4 but he didn't see them that regularly. Peter had one daughter but had never had any contact with her; she was being brought up by her maternal grandmother. Peter said that he and the child's mother had been too ill to look after her at the time, but did not want to expand further on this, stating that it was a 'past issue' for him.

8.3. Assessment

8.3.1. Mode and process of assessment and difficulties

The assessment consisted of collecting information through both a semi-structured interview and psychometric data. Peter's accounts were notably vague, fragmentary and negative in content. This is therefore supportive of empirical investigations finding links between over-general autobiographical memories and suicidal thoughts and behaviours. Peter's recall also seemed to be influenced by his current mood state. The use of diaries to aid assessment was attempted, but Peter rarely completed these. Of particular note was the merit of beginning the intervention phases of reducing threat-based affect and associated information processing early in therapy. Attention broadening, relaxation and the BMAC were conducted at the start of each session, with drops in threat hypothesised to lead to more balanced recollections and appraisals of the previous week. The stages of Assessment, Formulation and Intervention were therefore cyclical throughout therapy, although they have been presented in sequential format for the reader's convenience.

8.3.2 Results of assessment

The assessment revealed significant experiences of suicidal thoughts and plans with variable intention to act, linked to fluctuations in threat-based affect. Peter's experiences of suicidal thoughts were found to be linked, in part, to his experiences of psychosis.

8.3.2.1. Suicidal experiences

Peter reported that he experienced suicidal ideation every 3 to 4 days, lasting 30 minutes to an hour, normally occurring at around 11 o'clock in the evening after going to bed at 10pm. Peter described how this was more likely on days when he had been worrying and that it was hard to switch off his worries. These worries focused on becoming ill again, his current difficulties, what was going to happen in the future and about whether he would be alive the following week. Peter believed that he coped with this by having conversations with God about his fate and about whether God wanted him to die. Peter reported that God was 100% sure he wanted Peter to die for 50% of the time and 100% sure he wanted Peter to live for the other 50% of the time. Peter described his own wishes to be in line with God's, and half of the week he was 100% sure he wanted to die and for the other half of the week he was 100% sure he wanted to live.

Peter's plan was to stab himself through the heart, and he had identified a specific knife in the kitchen for this purpose. This method was therefore considered by the therapist to be

(1) available and (2) highly dangerous. Peter had never gone into the kitchen to pick up the knife. Peter's views on the likelihood of completing his suicide plan changed from session to session, indicating ambivalence about killing himself. On some occasions, Peter stated that he would never actually act on his thoughts of suicide, while on others Peter was less confident but would wait until some landmark had passed, for example, his birthday.

In terms of hopelessness, Peter reported that he didn't see his life as worth much and that he wasn't happy with his life. Peter didn't think things would get any better for him. Peter also said that when he was suicidal he isolated himself and became consumed by his conversations with God. He no longer thought about protective factors, that is, the pain it would cause his family.

A high level of suicidal ideation was indicated by the Beck Suicidal Scale, Suicide Probability Scale and The Adult Suicidal Ideation Questionnaire. The BPRS indicated a high level of risk of suicide. Peter initially presented with high levels of Hopelessness, scoring 12 on the Beck Hopelessness Scale, which falls in the 'moderate' range, with a score of 15 indicating a severe risk.

Current problems serving to increase Peter's level of suicidality were financial difficulties (Peter was in a small amount of debt), conflicts caused by his brother, who would get into fights in local pubs when he was with Peter, and arguments with his siblings. These 'external' triggers led to 'internal' difficulties of worrying. Peter explained that he worried about his debts and about getting into conflicts and ending up in jail for harming others. Peter also reported that low mood was a difficulty, sometimes fluctuating across a day from 2/10 to 5/10, where 0 was the lowest it could be and 10 was the highest. Peter reported that his mood, experiences of psychosis and suicidality also fluctuated across the course of a week as a result of his depot injection; his mood would be more predominantly low in the days following the injection, becoming less so as the week progressed. Peter reported that when he believed he was conversing with God, his mood escalated to 8/10. This occurred more after his mood had dropped, and his mood could then rapidly cycle between 2/10 and 8/10.

8.3.2.2. History of suicide attempts

Peter explained that his suicide attempt occurred in the context of high levels of distress and had been an impulsive act. Peter had been drinking with his brother and had returned to his parent's house where his brother had continued to drink and was being 'loutish'. Peter had become angry with his brother for disrespecting their parents, and they had fought over this issue. Peter only had fragmentary memories of what followed but described leaving the fight and not being able to cope with the distress. He had then slit his wrists to escape from these feelings. Peter described this as an 'impulse', and that it was hard to recall further details or fully explain why this had happened.

Distal factors involved in this suicide attempt were identified by Peter. Over the course of his twenties, Peter had worked in retail. Peter described how this had been a good job, but it was difficult when he had male customers who were 'smart arses' and acted as if they were superior to him. Peter also explained how a local group of male customers had bullied him, calling him names and had 'put him down'. Peter interpreted their behaviour as arrogant, that they believed they were superior to him, and that they wanted him to know they viewed him as inferior. It was around this time that Peter had a daughter, but she was taken away from him and had gone to live with her maternal grandmother. Peter described these as background factors in increasing his stress levels, ultimately resulting in the physical fight with his brother and subsequent suicide attempt.

8.3.2.3. Experiences of psychosis

8.3.2.3.1. PSYCHOMETRICS

A psychometric assessment was completed by a research assistant prior to therapy com-mencing. The PANNS and PSYRATS indicated a high level of 'positive symptoms', in particular, auditory hallucinations and beliefs about being God. Negative symptoms were also high on the PANSS, indicating withdrawal from social situations and anhedonia. Gen-eral symptoms were also found to be pronounced on the PANNS, indicating a high level of general psychopathology such as depression and anxiety.

8.3.2.3.2. RESULTS OF SEMI-STRUCTURED INTERVIEW

The semi-structured assessment interview revealed that Peter's experiences of psychosis were linked to his experiences of suicidal thoughts, plans and intentions. Each experience is outlined below and the links to suicide highlighted.

Peter reported that he heard a voice approximately three times a day, for between 20 minutes and an hour. As therapy progressed, Peter's reports of the length, frequency and duration of voice-hearing experiences differed according to his level of threat and arousal in session. Sometimes Peter reported that these experiences lasted all night. Peter interpreted these experiences as hearing the voice of God. Peter engaged with the voice, believing he was speaking back to God. These conversations were about whether Peter was going to die or not, and, as stated above, Peter believed that God was undecided as to whether it was time for Peter to die yet.

Peter also experienced visual hallucinations and, again, the reports varied as to frequency and duration, ranging from a couple of times a week for 20 minutes at a time to lasting all night. Peter reported seeing his brother visiting him from heaven. Peter reported seeing Elvis Presley, who visited him from heaven; and Genghis Khan, Stalin and demons who visited him from hell. Peter believed the visits from heaven were arranged by his brother, who wanted to make him feel good and also because his brother wanted him to die and come to heaven. Peter believed that Genghis Khan and Stalin were jealous of him because he was one of God's angels or God himself, and that they would like to steal his soul. Peter saw 'demons' when he was trying to sleep, and also believed that they were coming to try and take his soul.

8.3.2.4. Information processing

The therapist worked with Peter to identify a number of information processing biases from the unusual thinking styles sheet. This indicated that Peter had a tendency to 'catastrophise' or to blow things out of proportion. Cues indicating either illness or rejection rapidly led to selective abstraction, that is, suicide schema-congruent information being selected and schema-incongruent information being neglected. This served to hasten the escalation into perceived relapse and imminent threat; and, in social situations, of immediate and total rejec-tion. These tendencies were found to be part of a positive feedback style with distressing emotions and threat-focused attention.

8.3.2.5. Current modulators/protective factors mitigating suicide

Peter reported that the main reason that he didn't kill himself was that it would hurt his parents' feelings and they would grieve for him. Peter did not think that his suicide would significantly hurt the feelings of his siblings, nieces or nephews. However, when questioned further, Peter acknowledged that his family would grieve for him. Another protective factor was Peter's belief that life was precious.

8.3.2.6. Process issues: Rejection and hostility

Depending on his affective state, Peter adopted a challenging questioning style with the therapist, asking him whether he believed he was an angel and whether he had danced with Elvis Presley. There was a tangible level of irritability at these times. Peter reported that he thought that the therapist would call his experiences 'hallucinations'. Peter viewed this term as a means of professionals attempting to assume their superiority over him, minimising him as a person. The therapist explained that it was his role to keep an open mind about all experiences as there was no way of knowing what was true or false, for sure. However, the therapist addressed the reasons Peter had asked why this was important. Peter explained that in his relationships both socially and with mental health professionals, he felt that people were dismissive of him, didn't believe his experiences were valid and used this to feel superior to him. Peter had wondered if the therapist would adopt the same approach. Over a number of sessions, these issues were linked to past experiences of believing that others, and particularly males, believed that they were superior to Peter.

8.3.2.7. Initial review of resources and coping

In the first few sessions, the therapist also worked with Peter to identify the ways he coped with his difficulties, in order to identify internal coping and resilience factors and also establish external resources that could be drawn upon to balance appraisals of low social currency, isolation and no-rescue.

In terms of personal qualities and resources, Peter had developed a repertoire of coping strategies that he used to 'exit' from his distressing cycles. He enjoyed listening to music and watching films. As well as enjoying these activities for their own inherent value, Peter said that they were important in taking his mind off his worries. Peter's 'natural exits' were utilised later as a rationale for attention broadening and in appraisal work to reduce beliefs about the need to worry. Peter reported that the most effective activity was to have a cup of tea, a cigarette and to 'forget about his worries'. Peter demonstrated a capacity to form a relationship with the therapist and to use this relationship to observe his hostility/rejection tendency. This suggested that Peter might benefit from addressing his tendency to jump to conclusions about being rejected by his sister and address his own behavioural responses to this.

In terms of external resources, Peter enjoyed a close relationship with his parents, although he didn't always feel well enough to go and see them. He had a good relationship with his sister, who cooked for him on occasion, either bringing food round to his house or inviting him over for tea. Peter enjoyed contact with her children, although he found them to be too lively at times. His family were a great source of support. However, Peter and his sister were prone to arguing and then rejecting each other, leading to a high level of expressed emotion in the family. This had the impact of increasing Peter's 'no-rescue' appraisals, triggering an acute sense of loneliness and disconnection.

8.3.2.8. Summary of risk

Current risk was assessed as low as, although Peter reported frequent suicidal ideation, this had followed the same pattern for a number of years and he had never acted upon it. Suicidal behaviour was inhibited by the protective factors of not wanting to hurt his family. It was also noted that, despite this relative stability, Peter seemed to be continually moving through a cycle that caused him distress, which might lead to cumulative stress over time. Peter also presented as being passively oriented to his mental experiences and had a history of acting impulsively. Peter was therefore considered to be potentially vulnerable to future stressors. The future risk of his parents dying was noted by the therapist, and this was returned to later in therapy. Peter was able to make a contract with the therapist to engage with the therapy for four months, to "give it a go". Early warning signs of increased alcohol consumption, deteriorating sleep, increases in voice hearing and self-harm were noted and informed a suicide prevention plan.

8.4. Initial engagement, formulation and goal setting

From the first session it was clear that Peter was keen to discuss experiences of suicide. The function of suicide was established as an escape from uncontrollable worry and intolerable feelings of distress. However, while suicide was beneficial in this aspect, it was also a distressing thought because of the harm it may cause to his family. These negative aspects of suicide seemed to provide Peter with the motivation to find an alternative option, and a shared goal was set; to reduce the uncontrollability and distress associated with suicide-focused worry. The subsidiary goal was to find ways of exiting from this state of uncontrollable worry. Peter was willing to engage with a shared process of identifying means of reducing worry, but had little confidence that worry and distress could be controllable. This initial formulation and shared agreement was represented in a diagram (see Figure 8.1).

8.5. CBSPp formulation

Formulation took three stages of development. The first was mapping out Peter's difficulties (Figure 8.1). This led into the development of the full CBSP formulation (Figure 8.2).

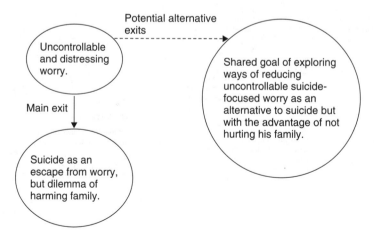

Figure 8.1 Initial engagement and goal setting

However, a summarised formulation with exit points was developed to help Peter anchor himself in the midst of his suicidal experiences and to provide a road map of natural and therapeutically derived exit points.

8.5.1. Mapping the factors leading to suicide

As can be seen in Figure 8.2, three core processes were hypothesised to be key elements of Peter's suicidal experience – suicide-focused attention, suicide-focused appraisals, and worry – and the key driver of the system, the suicide schema. The suicide schema was conceptualised to be a plan of Peter stabbing himself in the stomach, driven by positive beliefs about suicide ending his distress, preventing him from becoming ill and highly distressed again. This would enable him to be with God and his brother in heaven, and to be important in heaven as an angel. The negative beliefs about suicide, that it would harm his parents and that life was precious, created ambivalence about suicide.

It was hypothesised that the suicide schema was triggered by external sources such as setbacks, conflicts or somebody saying Peter looked ill. Voice-hearing experiences and appraisals of these experiences also triggered suicide-focused worry. A particularly pernicious positive feedback loop was formed between suicide-focused worry and low mood and motivation. Peter was hypervigilant to 'signs of illness', and the symptoms of depression such as anhedonia were specific triggers to a fear of relapse and of becoming suicidal again. This cycle was amplified by receiving the depot injection once a week, which would leave Peter feeling sedated, leading to an increase in low mood and a drop in energy. Interpersonal conflicts activated beliefs about others as being hostile, rejecting and assuming a superior position, leaving him feeling rejected, alone and inferior. Peter rejected the notion that he was inferior, however, believing himself to be an angel or God himself, and, in less acute

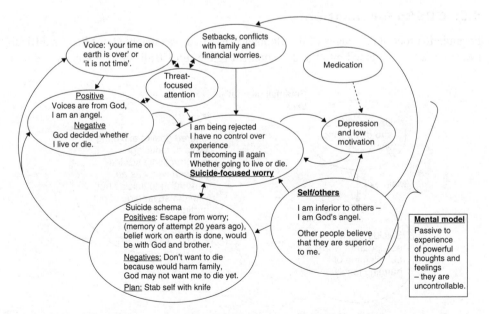

Figure 8.2 Mapping the relationship between Peter's experiences and his suicide schema

moments, as someone who described himself as always striving to be a 'better person'. However, it was hypothesised that latent core beliefs about the self being inferior may be externally attributed to guard against threats to self-esteem. The arrow joining the suicide schema to the voice-hearing experiences and the beliefs about voices represents the observation that Peter engaged with the voice of God as an alternative 'escape behaviour' to suicide. This was triggered by an urge to escape, but as a consequence of the negative beliefs about suicide, specifically, the impact it would have upon his family. Peter also experienced a temporary feeling of bliss and contentment when speaking to God. However, this was a short-term strategy, Peter gained no certainty from God that reduced his worry about suicide. He would then return to considering suicide, sometimes leading to rapid cycling between the two states, caught between a proverbial 'rock and a hard place'.

The aims of the 'mapping formulation' was to provide an initial roadmap as to the operation of the suicide schema and how Peter's different problems and psychological processes 'loaded' on to this. Peter reported that he did not think that he had any control over his experiences prior to this exercise, but it had given him a way of understanding how his different experiences were linked.

8.5.2. CBSPp formulation

The full CBSP formulation is presented here for convenience but was something that was developed throughout therapy. It provides a comprehensive overview of the mechanisms

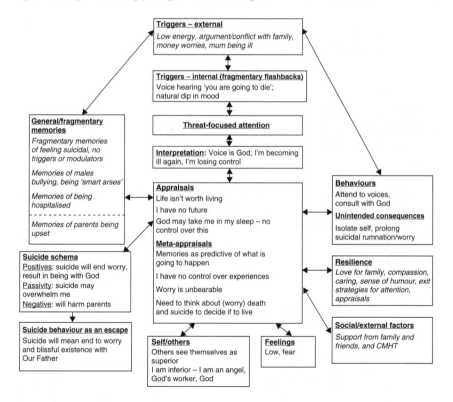

Figure 8.3 Peter's generic CBSPp formulation

exacerbating and reducing the experiences of suicide, therefore resulting in a homeostatic conceptualisation of these processes. Of particular note in addition to the mapping formulation is the inclusion of fragmentary memories of the previous suicide attempt, leading to a further sense of uncontrollability.

8.6. CBSPp intervention

The formulation suggested that the essential elements of CBSPp intervention of reducing threat-based processing, appraisals and the suicide schema, would be beneficial for Peter. Beliefs about others being rejecting and hostile also represented an important area of schema change. The following strategy was developed to guide the intervention:

1. Reduce threat-based processing

    a. Provide basis for switching attention away from worrying thoughts and distressing feelings.
    b. Increase positive emotions as natural regulators of threat and to broaden hitherto threat-focused attention.
    c. Address unhelpful thinking styles.

2. Appraisals

    a. Address appraisals of feelings of low mood and low motivation being indicative of 'being ill'.
    b. Address appraisals of feelings going to last forever.
    c. Address appraisals of no-rescue.
    d. Increase sense of agency over experiences.

3. Natural exits

    a. Enhance natural ways of switching attention.
    b. Enhance natural ways or reducing cycles of worry.
    c. Enhance natural ways of increasing positive affect.

4. Schema change

    a. Aggregate experiences of therapeutic change and natural exits to generalise appraisals of agency with regard to suicide prevention.
    b. Problem-solving training and appraisals of agency.
    c. Self-esteem continua work to reduce inferiority/superiority appraisals of self in relation to others.
    d. Switching to positive and inhibitory cycle of thoughts, feelings and behaviours.

8.6.1. Information biases and attention

The protocol presented in section 5.3 for reducing information processing biases was implemented from session 2 onwards. Peter responded well to the Attention Broadening protocol, finding the switch from internal experiences to elements of the external environment particularly useful, commenting that it would help when he was 'becoming ill' and experiencing voices. Difficulties in implementing these protocols in session were noted, again subject to the variability to Peter's affective state, that is, when Peter was experiencing a high level of anxiety/threat in session. Relaxation training helped to reduce these difficulties on some occasions. The Broad Minded Affective Coping (BMAC) strategy was implemented, and Peter reported that this was a good technique for reducing his sense of threat. The foci of the BMAC were predominantly visits to his parents and good experiences with his siblings (see Box 8.1), reinforcing the key element that Peter's volatile relationships with his family played in his suicidal schema.

Therapeutic techniques were bolstered by a careful analysis of Peter's natural exit points from suicidal cycles. Peter's usual method of resolving difficult experiences was to sit quietly, have a cup of tea and smoke a cigarette. Peter explained that by doing so he was attempting to clear his mind, while the savouring of the tea and the cigarette was another means of directing his attention away from his distressing experiences. This was incorporated into the attention-switching protocol, and Peter was encouraged to try this with other foods and drinks rather than relying on caffeine and as a substitute to nicotine/cigarette smoke. Of particular interest was Peter's use of putting on a comedy DVD such as Laurel and Hardy or the Pink Panther. Peter found any 'slapstick' humour incredibly funny, and this could rapidly end the cycle of worrying about his death. In fact, Peter became tearful with laughter when describing particular scenes that he could remember easily from these films. Barriers to doing this were noted as not having the motivation to put a film on or not remembering. The formulation was updated, and the strategy of triggering positive emotion cycles and humour in particular was added to the plan of therapy. Coping cards were developed to trigger humour and used as a catalyst for other activities.

Box 8.1 Examples of the use of the Broad Minded Affective Coping (BMAC) strategy to reduce threat-focused attention and information processing

BMAC 1: Visiting parents

- Focus: Walking to parents, seeing parents.
- Affect: Warmth at seeing patents.
- Meaning: Not alone. Reciprocal role taking: Peter able to acknowledge parents' warmth to him, making him feel less lonely.
- Reduced after-event processing about mother saying he looked ill.

BMAC 2: Going to the pub with his brother

- Focus: Walking to parents, seeing parents.
- Affect: 'Connected' being with brother.
- Meaning: Not alone. Reciprocal role taking: Peter able to acknowledge brother's warmth to him, making him feel less lonely.
- Reduced after-event processing about potential conflicts in pub.

The therapist and Peter used the 'unhelpful thinking styles' sheet, and Peter readily identified that he blew things out of proportion and jumped to conclusions, particularly when having an argument with his sister, when he often interpreted the smallest sign of disapproval as total rejection. Peter developed simple personal instructions such as, 'don't blow this out of proportion', 'go away and breathe', which he felt were effective in reducing these tendencies.

8.6.2. Appraisals

A number of key appraisals were addressed that were hypothesised to be shaped by the suicide schema and to maintain its activity. The strategic plan for appraisal work was as follows:

1. Address appraisals of feelings of low mood and low motivation being indicative of 'being ill'.
2. Address appraisals of feelings going to last forever.
3. Address feelings of no-rescue (prompting specific relational schema work).
4. Increase sense of agency.
5. Total breakdown of relationships and perceived hostility from others.
6. Others as viewing themselves as superior and self as inferior (implicitly held).

A voice-hearing experience, or someone saying to Peter that he didn't look well, led to the initial thought, 'I'm becoming unwell'. This could then trigger a positive feedback cycle of withdrawal and reduced activity, low energy and mood, and increased worry about becoming ill and suicidal. This escalated, and when Peter's mood dropped to 2/10 – indicating high distress levels – Peter began to consider suicide as an escape. This schematic appraisal system was triggered, and also triggered beliefs about other people as being hostile and implicit beliefs about the self as inferior.

8.6.2.1. The meaning of 'becoming ill'

Problematic appraisals were addressed using standard cognitive therapy techniques. Firstly, the underlying fear behind the appraisal 'I am becoming ill' was explored further with Peter, who stated that his key fear was returning to the state of total desperation he experienced at the time of his first suicidal attempt. Fragmentary memories of this episode were triggered, along with an associated sense of being overwhelmed and of having no personal agency over his internal experiences.

The first main intervention was a historical review. Despite possibly thousands of distressing experiences over the past 20 years, Peter stated that he had never got to the level of distress he had experienced on the occasion he became suicidal. An exploration of meaning of the appraisal 'I'm becoming ill' yielded the useful observation that this meant both a brief experience of psychosis and also becoming irrevocably ill to the point of hospitalisation. In short, despite the frequent, spontaneous cessation of distressing experiences, Peter still feared never-ending distress during such experiences. After the historical review, Peter was able to separate these eventualities out and reappraised a full relapse as much less likely. This led to a number of subsidiary reappraisals (see below), leading into the development of 'sayings' that Peter would repeat to himself when he was becoming distressed.

'I'm becoming ill again' means:

Never-ending illness   ⟶ It typically lasts about 2 hours.

I will end up in hospital.   ⟶ I can sit this out.

I can't stop becoming ill.   ⟶ I find having a cigarette and a coffee helps me to reduce these feelings.

8.6.2.2. Challenging the appraisal that low energy is a sign of illness

Peter interpreted signs of low energy and lethargy as strong indicators of becoming ill again. These appraisals were compounded by withdrawal from pleasurable, mastery and social experiences and, according to Broaden & Build Theory, the positive, regulatory emotions such experiences gave rise to. Peter was therefore provided with psychoeducation about depression and the positive feedback cycle between low mood leading to depressive rumination about what was wrong with him, leading to further low mood and how both factors were also linked with low energy/motivation. Verbal reattribution techniques then focused on alternative explanations for low energy. The review of Peter's weekly cycle made the links between medication and low energy/sedation more transparent. Peter observed that he was heavily sedated in the days following the injection. Peter reattributed the cause of the majority of his low energy levels to medication, which served to provide him with an exit point to worry about becoming ill. Behavioural reattribution techniques were also applied. For instance, Peter reported a love for watching comedy DVDs. A homework task was therefore set to watch a Laurel and Hardy and Pink Panther DVD for homework, and to score mood and energy levels prior to watching this DVD and afterwards. The results are summarised in Table 8.1.

Increases were noted in mood and, on one trial, there was a small increase in energy (Table 8.1). Peter had been surprised about this, and it served to increase his belief that energy levels were something that were subject to a number of influences, not just a sign of becoming ill again. The results of these experiments were incorporated into the verbal reattribution exercise of examining explanations for having low energy other then becoming ill, as depicted in Table 8.2.

With Peter's consent, the therapist wrote to Peter's mental health team, highlighting a high level of sedation. The letter also informed the care team that Peter had a tendency to believe that his feelings of sedation were a sign that he was becoming ill again and could trigger suicidal thoughts. This prompted a medication review, more careful monitoring and ultimately a change in medication.

8.6.2.3. Activity scheduling

Activity scheduling was used to increase Peter's positive experiences and also as a behavioural experiment to test whether increasing activity led to (1) further decreases in energy and increases in tiredness or (2) increases in energy and (3) an exit from the depressive/suicidal ruminative cycle. Over the course of therapy it was also used to address the following:

Table 8.1 Behavioural experiment to test the responsiveness of mood and energy to positive emotions stimulated by comedy DVDs

Trial 1: Laurel and Hardy	Prior to DVD	Post DVD
Mood	4	5
Energy	4	4

Trial 2: Pink Panther	Prior to DVD	Post DVD
Mood	6	8
Energy	5	6

Table 8.2 Evidence for and against the belief that low energy is a sign of becoming ill

Belief: Low energy = becoming ill again (100%)

For	*Against*
Low energy means I'm not looking after myself, which is a sign of becoming ill	A side-effect of medication is a high level of sedation
	If I haven't done anything stimulating, it will feel like I have no energy. I may have energy once I begin something
	Energy fluctuates naturally over the course of the day/week
	I can sometimes increase my levels of energy if I do pleasurable things, e.g. watch a comedy DVD/ or visit my parents

Belief: Low energy = becoming ill again (25%)

New belief: Low energy is most probably due to side effects to medication and I can increase my energy levels (80%)

1. Increase pleasure and mastery experiences – leading to increased positive emotions thought to help regulate threat.
2. Provide 'fuel' for links between BMAC and BMAS procedures to create tangible, achievable and pleasurable goals to increase hope.
3. To improve implicit self-esteem.
4. To increase level of activities in the day and create a routine to allow for better sleep hygiene at night.

A weekly schedule was put in place that matched Peter's natural level of energy after the depot injection, increasing in its level of activity across the week. This allowed Peter to schedule in more rest times and feel justified in doing so, allowing him to reattribute this to self-care rather than a sign of him becoming ill and, implicitly, failing at being a 'better person'. Also, the therapist and Peter worked to identify chains of events that led to increasing amounts of positive emotions and motivations. So, Peter would think about a comedy scene and make himself laugh. This would lead to him putting on a DVD and enjoying this. Peter would then have a shower and a shave, which would make him feel better, and then do something practical like cleaning his house for an hour. Peter also visited a local video rental shop to hire more comedy DVDs and also classic TV programmes he had enjoyed when growing up. Problem-solving techniques were utilised to help with these tasks, as addressed in section 8.6.3.

8.6.2.4. Appraisals of no-rescue

A critical component to Peter's suicidal experience was whether he felt connected to his family. The frequent arguments with his sister and other siblings seemed to be characterised by a mutual tendency to reject each other with hostility. For Peter, this led to a sense of being totally alone, in which he lost his sense of connection to others. According to the CBSPp formulation, this would trigger the suicide schema and the memory of the fight with his brother and subsequent suicidal attempt. It was therefore hypothesised that increasing Peter's sense of connection with his parents and other people in his network might be used to prevent his sense of isolation at such times. A historical review was conducted, and Peter noted that he had always restored his relationship with his sister after a couple of days. Also, Peter developed a list of around 10 to 12 people he cared about and who cared about him. This was used as evidence to challenge the appraisal that Peter was alone after an argument with his sister. This intervention was bolstered by use of the BMAC. This focused on specific memories of each person in his network in order to increase the retrievability of such memories at times when he was feeling rejected and alone.

8.6.2.5. Increased sense of agency over experiences

A consistent theme running throughout therapy was to reflect on how the developing formulation and intervention strategies provided Peter with a sense of agency over his experiences. Peter was both surprised and pleased to find that there were a number of strategies available to him to 'stop the suicidal cycle'. Another important discovery for Peter was that it was *his choice* to speak with God on many occasions, that this was often used as an exit or escape behaviour from high levels of distress. This was potentially difficult ground for the therapist to negotiate as it was clear that Peter still placed great importance on having a special relationship with God, and it was hypothesised that this was a source of self-esteem for him. However, Peter was willing to evaluate whether this was a useful thing for him to continue doing, leading to an 'advantages and disadvantages' analysis of engaging with God about whether he was going to live or die. This is summarised in Table 8.3.

After weighing up the advantages and disadvantages of engaging with God about whether he was going to die or not, Peter thought that it may be unhelpful because history had taught him that he never reached a decision and, in fact, on nights when he had been certain he

Table 8.3 Advantages and disadvantages of engaging with God about death

Engaging with God about whether going to die or not	
Advantages	Disadvantages
A way of seeking an answer to worry about dying	It was impossible to know God's wishes
Feelings of bliss and contentment when not feeling that in life	When he thought God wanted him to die it was very distressing
	He had been doing this for many years and he had not got an answer, so it may be making him more distressed than he needed to be
	Actually increased distress after initial feelings of bliss as sometimes led to certainty that he was going to die in his sleep, which then didn't happen
	Believed he needed to do this to know his fate or distress would never end – although remembered that it only lasts for 2 hours but did not know if due to communing with God

was going to die he had lived through the night. Although Peter attributed this to God changing his mind, he acknowledged that it was of little use if he never found out the answer. The therapist discussed ways forward with Peter, and reducing/banning communicating with God was attempted. This is similar to work in classical CBTp, where the behavioural experiment of banning engagement with a voice may then lead to a change in appraisal about the need to do so but with the added emphasis here on appraisals of (1) dying in the night, leading to (2) suicidal ideation. Peter attempted to ban communicating with God on nights when he was finding it hard to get to sleep, and found this to be effective approximately half of the time. However, Peter reported that on other nights he felt low and wanted to communicate with God, which then led to thoughts about death and suicide. Peter and the therapist then reviewed alternative exits points. Peter found that reminding himself to think about comedy clips and to visualise the scenes in detail made him laugh out loud both in session with the therapist but also when he was lying in bed experiencing high levels of distress. This was not ideal in terms of creating the conditions for sleep but provided a powerful exit from the hitherto all-demanding cycle of threat and suicide-related thoughts.

8.6.3. Problem-solving

The use of problem solving was reviewed with Peter. Firstly, the BMAC structure was used to review things he had done well (see Box 8.2).

Many other examples were used in therapy utilising the problem-solving technique. Peter reported that he could use these techniques to reduce the things he worried about, such as planning his finances.

8.6.4. Self-esteem

As has been discussed throughout the chapter, Peter had ostensibly high self-esteem, believing himself to be one of God's angels or even God himself. However, upon experiencing distress, Peter did experience the activation of a belief that he needed to be a better person, perhaps also implicitly believing at this time he was failing his parents or causing them distress, linked to the memory of how hurt they had been when he originally attempted suicide. It was therefore hypothesised that self-esteem work might increase Peter's implicit self-esteem. Both the continua method and the BMAC procedure for increasing a sense of reciprocal positive regard were used. Peter was able to generate a number of qualities such as thinking deeply (9/10), listening skills (9/10), caring about others (8/10), a sense of humour (8/10) and being tidy (8/10). Specific evidence was generated for each quality. For 'thinking deeply', Peter reported that he could solve problems such as retune his parents' TV, and for 'caring' Peter listed all the people he cared about. Interestingly, Peter's objective scores did not change on any of his scores following the elaboration of specific evidence, apart from 'caring'. The development of the list of people Peter cared about and who cared about him proved to be a powerful intervention, used to reduce appraisals of no-rescue (see section 8.9).

The therapist and Peter chose this memory after a discussing which memory would be most preventative of suicide, because it bolstered the sense of Peter being connected to his family, which tended to be lost at these times.

Box 8.2 BMACs aimed at increasing a sense of agency

BMAC 3: Problem-solving: Getting a taxi

Peter was shopping and felt very tired, but needed to get home.
Solutions considered:

1. Walking home

    a. Advantages: It was free.
    b. Disadvantages: It would make Peter more tired.

2. Get a taxi

    a. Advantages: He wouldn't have to carry his bags.
    b. Disadvantage: It cost £3.

Option chosen: Get a taxi.
Affect: Happiness.
Meaning: Was able to look after himself, put himself first and to think through a problem. In hindsight he could go shopping with his sister and her children – this became a part of Peter's routine.

BMAC 4: Problem-solving: Tuning in TV for parents

Peter had recently managed to sort out a problem with his parents' TV. He had followed a systematic plan in doing so, which was reviewed.

1. Check aerial – Peter tried another TV and found it worked so aerial ok.
2. Peter went through the menu on screen but didn't understand it.
3. Peter read the instruction manual and found out he needed to reset the aerial.
4. Peter used the menu system to reset the aerial.

Affect: Happiness, sense of mastery, warmth.
Meaning: Connection to parents, being a good son, capable of solving problems.

Box 8.3 BMACs aimed at reducing threat-focused attention/ information processing

BMAC 5: Peter looking after sister's children

1. Focus: Playing with niece and nephew.
2. Affect: Joy at seeing sister, niece and nephew happy.
3. Reciprocal affect: Joy at knowing that he was making sister and niece and nephew feel this way and that they felt that way to him.
4. Meaning: I care for them and they care for me.

8.6.5. Increasing hope and the Broad Minded Affective Scheduling (BMAS) technique

The Broad Minded Affective Scheduling (BMAS) technique was adopted to develop antici-pation of positive future events. For example, after Peter had been to his parents' he then arranged to see them again a few days later. He then savoured the original memory using BMAC principles and then imagined going again, while maintaining the emotions developed through savouring the memory. Peter responded well to this technique and implemented it naturally when planning his week. This was developed to incorporate all the elements of the intervention, with Peter running through suicide-incongruent appraisals associated with each activity, for example:

Think how each activity:

- Increases hope for the future.
- Connects you to your family (how you feel about them, hoe they feel about you).
- Gives you a sense of energy and of being well.
- Gives you a sense of control over your experience.
- Shows you can solve life's difficulties.
- Reduced thoughts of suicide.

8.6.6. Suicide schema

Formulating processes linked to suicide schema activation was at the core of therapy. Links to suicidal behaviour were explicitly sought during the integration part of each session. Use-ful questions after an intervention were as follows:

- How do you think this helps with times you have felt suicidal?
- [After a change in appraisal] If that is the case, does that increase or decrease desire to kill yourself?
- How may you take this forward and reduce fears of relapse, becoming ill and suicidal?

Explicit awareness of the nature of the suicide schema was engendered using Padesky's discrimination model. This was used to demonstrate how when the suicide schema was acti-vated, suicide-congruent information was attended to and non-congruent information was dismissed. The development of a 'positive cycle' with its own inherent triggers, thoughts, feelings and behaviours allowed Peter to observe that there were different schemas or modes in his mind that could be triggered, and that they were not congruent; the activation and strengthening of his positive cycle led to less time spent worrying, communicating with God and time spent considering suicide. The work on self-esteem was also drawn upon. The 'caring' section of self-esteem had revealed a rich network of people who Peter cared about. Peter was asked to consider each in turn and think about what they valued from him. This was used to reduce acute suicidality, increasing Peter's array of protective factors, as all these people would miss Peter if he killed himself and would grieve for him. It also broadened the base of people to minimise feelings of rejection from his siblings. Hope for the future and further generation of suicide schema-incongruent appraisals were amplified through the use of the BMAS. Finally, the idea of social currency was drawn upon, and Peter was encouraged to talk to people at times when he was feeling low or distressed because he offered this to others, which was more of a preventative strategy.

8.7. Outcome

At the end of therapy, Peter reported that he had much-reduced intent to kill himself. However, he reported still experiencing suicidal thoughts and plans, and that he still communicated with God about this issue. The fluctuations in distress were still present across daily and weekly cycles and, at times, it was still very difficult for Peter to 'exit' from them. However, the frequency had dropped to around two nights a week, and the duration had dropped to around 2 hours. When Peter looked to the future, he was confident that he wouldn't kill himself and that he would have things to look forward to, and that he could maintain a sense of connection with his family.

The psychometrics indicate that the intervention resulted in sustained drops in depression from baseline to the four- and six-month follow ups. Slight drops were noted in positive experiences of psychosis and, specifically, the amount of time spent thinking about delusions. Steady and sustained increases were noted in self-esteem. A mixed picture was noted for suicidal ideation. Scores on the BPRS indicated a slight drop in risk, and this was mirrored by sustained drops in ideation as measured by the ASIQ. However, the scores on the Beck Suicide Scale indicated a drop at four months as compared to baseline but a return to baseline levels at six months.

8.8. Critical reflection

Peter's case highlights a number of issues central to the delivery of a focused CBSPp intervention. His suicidal experiences were closely connected to his experiences of psychosis and to his interpersonal difficulties. The links to the suicide schema were therefore formulated, and these experiences were only addressed in therapy as they related to suicide. This seemed to be effective and actually fitted well with Peter as his experiences of voice hearing were highly valued and linked to his self-esteem. However, a longer-term therapeutic intervention drawing from CBTp and addressing his interpersonal difficulties as well as anxiety and depression may also have been beneficial to Peter. A number of past issues such as grief for the loss of his brother and of his relationship with his child may have also been linked to his current affective state, experiences of psychosis and suicide. Such issues may be focused upon in a longer-term therapy to bolster CBSPp.

Working with Peter and with other clients with high levels of fluctuations in suicidal thinking highlighted to the clinical team the need to develop ways of)1) assessing and (2) intervening at specific high-risk times. Peter found it difficult to recall the details of what had happened across the week, and in remembering when to introduce intervention techniques. We discuss the use of momentary assessments and interventions in Chapter 11. This leads us to a critical appraisal of the psychometric measures, as it is hard with an individual case to separate the natural baseline of experiences at each time point from the level of distress experienced on the day of assessment. These measures rely on retrospective memory and ability to aggregate experiences. However, the psychometrics do suggest a drop in suicidal ideation and planning, a drop in delusional beliefs and depression. This is corroborated by Peter's reports of an increasing sense of agency over suicidal experiences as therapy progressed.

8.9. Summary

The implementation of CBSPp to Peter's complex presentation was a challenge for the therapist. Peter presented with high levels of fluctuations in suicidal thinking and intent across daily and weekly cycles, which made it difficult to develop strategies for Peter to implement *in situ*. However, work with Peter led to a number of useful guidelines for working with people with such presentations. Strategies for reducing threat-based affect and suicidal thinking such as Attention Broadening and the BMAC can be used in session. CBSPp provides a model for isolating psychological processes linked to suicide specifically in the context of a number of other difficulties. The development of natural 'exit points' provides a template upon which to graft intervention techniques. The development of positive inhibitory cycles can move the focus beyond a 'within-schema perspective', that is, attenuating process involved with maintaining the suicide schema perspective to a 'between schema perspective', in which the therapist may spend time focusing on inhibitory cycles. Finally, future therapies should scaffold the flow of information from the client's natural environment to the therapy room and the implementation of therapeutically derived interventions back into the ebb and flow of everyday life, possibly utilising experience sampling and momentary intervention techniques.

Chapter 9

Overcoming difficulties in implementing CBSPp

Maintaining a hope for hope

9.1. Executive summary

- *A range of 'difficulties' or barriers may need to overcome to optimise the delivery of*
    - o *CBSPp.*
- *Therapy may need to address resistance or ambivalence to the prevention of suicide.*
- *Intrapersonal factors such as emotional regulation difficulties, beliefs about talking about suicide, voicehearing or alexithymia may need to be addressed when delivering CBSPp.*
- *Interpersonal factors such as suspiciousness or relationship difficulties may also need to be addressed.*
- *External difficulties beyond CBSPp may need to be addressed prior to, or during CBSPp.*
- *CBSPp may identify specific learning disabilities or neuro-developmental disorders that are implicated in suicide and which indicate specialist assessment and interventions.*
- *CBSPp is emotive and therapists need appropriate supervision.*
- *The therapist should adopt a stance of maintaining a hope for hope in the face of recurrent and persistent difficulties.*

9.2. Overview of difficulties in implementing CBSPp

One of the most difficult tasks for a clinician can be working with the client who is suicidal. In doing so, they are likely to work with the full range of mental health problems faced by clients. In addition, clients will have different profiles, histories and current environmental situations that must be considered in order to maximise the implementation of CBSPp. The present chapter provides an overview of the difficulties that may be faced by the clinician. It is not exhaustive. Rather, it has been written to engender a creative problem-solving approach within the clinician, an approach we hope will be transferred to the client who is currently feeling defeated. The topics covered in the present chapter are as summarised in Box 9.1.

Box 9.1 Guidelines for overcoming difficulties in delivering CBSPp

- Goal setting with the suicidal client:
  - o CBSPp as a systematic exploration of decision making.
- Ambivalence towards suicide:
  - o The suicide schema and inhibitory schemas
  - o Positive and negative beliefs about suicide.
- Psychological barriers to implementing CBSPp:
  - o Intrapersonal
  - o Interpersonal.
- External difficulties.
- Readiness for CBSPp.
- Impact upon the clinician and supervision.
- Final thoughts: A hope for hope.

9.3. Goal setting with the suicidal client

It may be that the client is ambivalent about reducing their suicidal behaviour or there is no doubt in their minds, they want to kill themselves. As covered in Chapters 3 and 4, the assessment and formulation establish the reasons a person has for seeking an end to their life. As we have learnt from the Cry of Pain model (Williams, 1997; Williams, Crane, Barnhofer & Duggan, 2005) and the SAMS (Johnson, Gooding & Tarrier, 2008) the client may view suicide as a means of escaping an intolerable situation from which they believe they cannot escape. The key point is that **suicidal behaviour serves a function**. It is therefore difficult for the client to set a goal to prevent suicide at this time. To do so is to accept the very situation that they find unacceptable. So, at this point, the therapist's goal, 'keeping the client from killing themselves', and the client's goal, 'wanting to kill myself', may be directly opposed.

Bordin (1979, 1994) identified such moments in therapy as a mismatch of goals and an obvious threat to the therapeutic alliance. According to Bordin, the therapeutic alliance is based on "three features: an agreement on goals, an assignment of a task, and the development of bonds" (Bordin, 1979, p.253). We have adjusted Bordin's model for the specific task of working with the suicidal client (see Figure 9.1).

The aim is to gain an understanding of the situation the client is in, and the nature of the appraisals that lead them to want to take their own life. The task is then to develop a shared understanding of the function of the escape or the suicidal behaviour. Once the reason for wanting to escape is established (for example, to reduce distress in relation to a hostile voice) the therapist and client may then agree on the goal of exploring ways of addressing this mechanism and to develop a functional alternative. At this stage, the goals may become aligned once more, such as reducing the distressing situation by other means. A bond can then be formed to work together towards this shared goal. Clients are often prepared to accept the premise that an alternative way of dealing with their difficulty would be advantageous for them, even if they cannot currently contemplate that such a strategy is possible. Bond setting can be based on a 'worth a try' premise, or 'what have you got to lose?', setting therapy up as an experimental approach, evaluating alternative solutions to suicide.

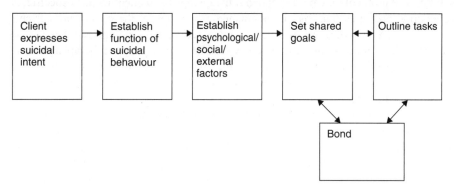

Figure 9.1   Tasks, bonds and goals in CBSPp

Box 9.2 Clinical example of resistance to suicide prevention

Carl became suicidal during the course of the therapy. The therapist established that the reason for this was because he was worrying uncontrollably and believed that this would result in psychological breakdown and a return to hospital, ultimately ending up in a vegetative state (the client had an image of sitting in a chair, rocking back and forth and foaming at the mouth) and rejected by his family and partner.

The therapist and client agreed on the following goals:

1) Reduce worry.
2) Reduce beliefs in uncontrollability of worry.
3) Reduce specific beliefs that he would become the image in his mind.
4) Increase confidence in others not rejecting him.

This collaboration between the therapist and client served to reduce the sense of defeat or entrapment by addressing his key fears. As Bordin discussed, once the **tasks** are outlined this offers the client **hope**, and a **bond** forms to work together towards these goals.

Sometimes the client may be so hopeless that they believe their situation is irrevocable and beyond the therapist's power to change. At such times, the therapist may outline the CBSPp model as a means of separating out the objective stressors in the client's life from those thoughts, feelings and psychological processes that we know can be triggered by highly stressful situations, but serve to maintain or even increase a person's stress. In this way, CBSPp may be looked upon as a means of being sure that the biggest decision a person may make in their lives is one that is free from such biases. As discussed at the end of the chapter, we believe that the therapist's position is one of hoping for hope. This allows the therapist to validate current hopelessness but to model a cautious optimism for positive change in the future. If the therapist can maintain this, even when the client faces the most extreme challenges, the client has the opportunity to explore their choices with the therapist. Of course, the full CBSP protocol may be suspended if the therapist and client identify specific, objective external pressures that may be attenuated. For instance, the client may currently be subject to a high level of physical abuse, or a very real threat of being assaulted, kidnapped, killed, etc. These are extreme cases, but may well be possible, and the therapist must remain open to these possibilities. In such cases, the therapist and client work to actively solve problems in the environment that are leading to high levels of distress, if this is possible, working alongside other agencies as necessary.

Ultimately CBSPp is a process that can reduce the positive feedback cycles between thoughts, behaviours and emotions that trigger and are triggered by the suicide schema. These processes were functional in reducing threat in response to situations that were beyond a person's coping potential. If the environment is currently within a person's coping potential, the schema may operate to maintain a sense of defeat. In such conditions, CBSPp is indicated.

9.4. Ambivalence towards suicide

A key aspect of the suicide schema is that it may contain both positive and negative beliefs about suicide. The function of suicide represents the positive beliefs and a person's protective factors; reasons for not killing themselves may represent negative beliefs about suicide. Once a person is no longer currently engaging in actively trying to kill themselves owing to internal protective factors, that is, they haven't killed themselves when they had an opportunity to do so, the full meaning of these 'protective factors' should be explored. The ambivalence resulting from the positive and negative beliefs about suicide should be acknowledged. Any increase in negative beliefs about suicide should be highlighted, and the client asked to reflect on these along with decreases in their certainty that killing themselves is the only solution. For instance, if a client begins to connect with the mental anguish their death would cause others, or suicide conflicts with their wish to see their children grow up, then these shifts should be explored and their meanings formulated.

The conceptualisation of protective factors as negative beliefs about suicide can prove to be a powerful intervention. For instance, a person may believe that they want to kill themselves but are not doing so because they don't want to hurt their family. This may be explored fully, with the aim of connecting a person with the emotions and meaning of what harming their family *causes them*. Socratic dialogue should always explore the full meaning of the negative consequences of suicide for each person. This may lead to a reduction in the externalisation of the consequences of suicide, and to the processing of suicide with reference to their own value base and belief system, factors that can be minimised at times of acute suicidality. Herein lies another important goal: to prevent the minimisation of the negative consequences of suicide and to maintain the negative consequences of suicide 'online' when people are in defeating situations.

It is also common for clients to *minimise* the harm suicide would cause other people. Client may make appraisals such as 'they won't miss me too much'. A mother of a teenager commented to the therapist, 'he'll be ok, he's got his own life now'. This decision can be based on a logic devoid of the emotional links a person has with others, and critically, a sense of the emotional links that person has with them. A number of strategies may help here. Reconnecting a client with their emotional connections to other people using the BMAC and a reciprocal perspective can help to reconnect people with their loved ones. Using the BMAS can help to stimulate a sense of positive future events with others. By stimulating the positive emotions a person feels towards another and the *felt sense* of the positive feelings that are reciprocated from the other person, the therapist may then work with the client to explore the feeling of loss and grief the other would feel if the person killed themselves. This is challenging work but sometimes necessary as such perspectives can be quickly lost when a person becomes defeated. They can serve as the basis for powerful negative beliefs about suicide, as highlighted by the case of Joseph (Box 9.3).

Box 9.3 The case of Joseph

Joseph was asked to imagine his feelings on the day of his daughter's graduation. This resulted in strong feelings of pride, warmth and love. The meaning of this was that Joseph had been a good Dad and was loved by his daughter. Joseph was also asked to reflect on his daughter's feelings about her Dad being there at her graduation. Joseph acknowledged the strong feelings of warmth and love his daughter would have for him. This led into a strong goal for living and reduced Joseph's immediate wish to kill himself.

The full range of this intervention is to encourage the client to process the emotions that other people would feel if the person killed themselves. This can be a powerful intervention. It may also be a risk to do this if the person has no other way of dealing with intolerable distress but then has no prospect of an escape. It must therefore be done alongside offering the person alternative and more functional ways of dealing with distress.

The therapist worked with Joseph to understand the resulting drop in suicidal feelings. Joseph explained that by remaining alive to be there at his daughter's graduation would mean he was being a good Dad. As discussed later in the chapter, this was a core theme to Joseph's experiences of suicide. The therapist then reviewed other evidence of being a good Dad, to bolster this belief. The therapist and Joseph then worked through phase 1 of CBSPp to provide him with means of reducing threatening emotions, increasing his beliefs that he could cope.

The therapist and Joseph then re-engaged with the emotions connected to his daughter's graduation. The therapist asked Joseph to dwell on the feelings his daughter would have if she lost her father. Joseph became tearful, acknowledging that his daughter would grieve for him, much as he was currently grieving for his father and granddaughter. This was formulated as a strong reason for living and a strong negative belief about suicide, 'suicide would harm my daughter and cause her overwhelming pain'. Later imagery concentrated further on his daughter's feelings on her graduation day if her father had killed himself. Joseph thought his daughter would feel tremendous loss and also pain and anger towards him. These solidified the negative beliefs about suicide, and strengthened Joseph's belief that being a good Dad meant tolerating difficult times so he could be there for his children. Joseph acknowledged that he had already tolerated extremely high levels of distress and had stayed alive for his children, further strengthening his beliefs of being a good Dad. Joseph was realistic in predicting difficult times in the future, but he could now find meaning in these experiences, that by tolerating them he was being a good father and a strong man.

9.5. Barriers to therapy

There may be specific barriers that are preventing a person from engaging with CBSPp, namely intrapersonal, interpersonal and external barriers.

9.5.1. Intrapersonal barriers

There may be a number of psychological or mental health difficulties that pose a barrier to working directly upon CBSPp. These may be more pressing problems that need to be addressed before CBSPp can be implemented, for example, a distressing experience of psychosis, panic disorder or post-traumatic stress disorder (PTSD). The barrier may also be a psychological barrier to talking about suicide itself, such as shame or stigma.

9.5.1.1. Putting out fires, dealing with immediate difficulties prior to commencing with CBSPp

The assessment process should screen for other psychological difficulties that may impede progress with CBSPp. The therapist has a number of choices here. Firstly, psychological difficulties may be listed and prioritised. Then specific evidence-based protocols can be implemented for each problem in turn (Persons, 2008; Tarrier, 2006). However, the therapist may seek to further formulate the underlying psychological mechanisms giving rise to the problems a person is experiencing (Harvey, 2004; Mansell, 2011; Persons, 2008; Tarrier, 2006). The role of each psychological mechanism is then considered in terms of its contribution to the suicidal experience. For instance, low self-esteem may give rise to both experiences of anxiety and depression (Fennell, 2009) and a potential activator of the suicide schema. Metacognitive beliefs about Thought Action Fusion may lead a person to experience difficulties with Obsessional Compulsive Disorder (Wells, 2000), for instance, believing that an intrusive image of harming others may lead to a fear that they will actually do this. The same underlying mechanism could lead the person to appraise a suicidal intrusion as evidence that they will kill themselves, leading to a further sense of hopelessness at reducing their urge to commit suicide. The therapist and client then proceed with specific interventions that attenuate the psychological mechanisms that (1) prevent direct CBSPp work, and (2) are actually involved in the maintenance of suicide itself.

The formulation should therefore guide the therapist in linking experiences to the suicidal schema. It may be that the problem facing the client is the product of processes separate to those involved in the suicide schema. However, if we adopt a threshold model of activation of the suicide schema, all problems are potential activators of the suicide schema if they lead to a level of distress and defeat sufficient to trigger the schema as an escape. It is important therefore to work on such difficulties before they become additional triggers to the suicide schema, that is, the suicide schema extends its function to this area of difficulty.

The therapist should also be mindful of falling into a pattern of continually 'putting out fires', or working on 'surface difficulties' with clients without reaching the core issues. If it becomes clear that this is the case, then the therapist may consider assessing whether this is a means of avoiding a specific focus on suicide, and to discuss this sensitively with the client. Clients may be unaware that they are not working on deeper psychological mechanisms; it is the role of the therapist to make this transparent through the formulation process to enable clients to make informed choices and assume equal responsibility in collaborative agenda setting and maintaining focus within session.

9.5.1.2. Addressing specific intra-individual barriers to suicide prevention work

There may be a number of barriers preventing a client from discussing their experiences of suicide. We have summarised some of the core issues below, but the therapist is encouraged to draw from their experiences outside of specific suicide prevention work, and from supervision, in order to formulate the mechanisms that are preventing direct work on suicidal memories and the suicidal schema.

- Metacognitive beliefs about the links between suicidal thoughts, images, memories and suicidal actions.
- Beliefs about overwhelming emotions.
- Shame-based memories.
- Experiences of psychosis:
    - Voice hearing
    - Suspiciousness
    - Motivation and negative symptoms.
- Fluctuating affect.

As stated in Chapters 4 and 5 (assessment and formulation) we have found that the barriers to talking about suicide often arise out of the same mechanisms that lead to the preservation of the suicide schema. Interventions to reduce a person's fear of talking about suicide may actually serve to reduce the valence of the suicide schema itself.

There is a common belief in society that talking about suicide will make a person want to kill themselves. This may also be a fear held by mental health professionals. This led us to conduct qualitative research to explore people's experiences of participating in suicide research and in talking about their experiences (Taylor et al., 2010). The main outcome of this research was that a number of people find this process cathartic, and may never have been offered the chance to do it before, maybe owing to the barriers professionals have about talking about suicide. However, we discovered that a significant number of people who find engaging with CBSPp difficult report being afraid of talking about suicidal experiences.

9.5.1.3. Fears of taking about suicide: Metacognitive beliefs

A fear of talking about suicide may be driven by specific metacognitive beliefs about the function between internal mental events and subsequent actions or environmental consequences (Wells, 2000). In essence, the person may believe that intrusive thoughts or images of harming themselves will lead to them returning to the state when they wanted to do so in the past. Furthermore, we suggest that for a number of people, suicidal ideation may be completely ego-dystonic in that they never actually want to kill themselves, but they report such intrusive images as evidence that they will do so. For others, these thoughts represent the underlying activation of a suicidal schema. Interestingly, in our clinical experience, intrusive thoughts and images of suicide remain ego-dystonic until some threshold has been reached and the person experiences distress beyond their appraised coping potential, at which point the positive beliefs about suicide may outweigh the negative and these thoughts become ego-syntonic. The advantage of working on metacognitive beliefs is that the therapist need not go into detail about the content of thoughts, but rather test predictions based on beliefs about thoughts (see Box 9.4).

Box 9.4 The case of Linda: Metacognitive beliefs as a barrier to therapy

Linda was terrified of her suicidal intrusions of stabbing herself, so much so that she avoided the kitchen. The therapist ascertained that this was based on a strong belief that when she experienced these thoughts she believed that she would be unable to resist then performing the action. The therapist worked with Linda to actively form images of benign actions, such as making a cup of tea, ringing a friend. Linda realised that images of performing actions did not reduce her choice of whether to act upon them. This is a good task therapeutically, because it is perceived to be 'safe' by many clients, but when framed correctly, can reduce fears about more fearful thoughts, images and experiences.

The therapist and Linda then proceeded with simple experiments of thinking about and holding images in her mind of knives and of stabbing herself. Linda was able to do this and reported a sense of these 'just being images'. Linda was also encouraged to manipulate her imagery, so she turned the image of stabbing herself into a cartoon, or made the knife into a baguette. This served to reduce Linda's belief that (1) images always led to actions, and (2) she had no control over the content of the images in her mind. Linda reported that she had been handling knives without difficulty as a spontaneous development between sessions. Linda found it much easier to talk about her suicidal experiences after this.

Interestingly, in retrospect, Linda reported that experimenting with benign images had been a tremendous relief, and the concept alone had led her to be (1) more aware of the images in her mind, and (2) to develop an alternative appraisal of them, that is, 'they are just images'. This effectively replaced the appraisals of 'I am going to kill myself' and 'I need to prevent myself from committing suicide' and the associated behaviour of avoiding certain objects.

For others, suicidal memories are linked to highly distressing experiences such as trauma, rape or abuse. Such experiences have been found to be elevated in populations of people with experiences of psychosis (Read & Argyle, 1999; Read & Hammersley, 2005). The therapist should draw upon the full range of their experiences in working with people who have had such experiences. Some clients may need to develop strategies for dealing with a high level of distressing affect before they can then address the memories that were linked to suicidal experiences. This may mean that the initial phase of CBSPp, of reducing threat-based affect and information processing biases is prolonged and specifically amended to the needs of each individual. Linehan's (1993a, b) work on grounding may be useful here. The client may then be able to talk about memories of suicidality, more confident in their ability to regulate the distress associated with them. It can be helpful to inform people that therapy need not involve discussion of particular experiences; it may focus on developing a person's capability of coping with such experiences and also in increasing a person's ability to experience and savour positive emotions despite such experiences. We have found that increasing a person's capacity to regulate distressing affect can lead to them naturally processing hitherto overwhelming emotions as a natural consequence. Often, focusing on Phase 1 of the CBSPp protocol with no explicit links to suicide can be then form the foundation to later work on addressing more traumatic memories of suicide and associated trauma memories.

A further difficulty can be strong feelings of personal shame attached to a specific memory or experience. This is reviewed by Gilbert (2006), who distinguished between internal shame and external shame. Internal shame is relevant to the present discussion, referring to a tendency to view the self as inferior or flawed and linked to a tendency to attack the self in order to punish the self (Gilbert & Irons, 2005). The reader is referred to specific therapies linked to addressing shame-based self-attacking (Gilbert & Irons, 2005; Gilbert, 2010). Such therapies involve understanding the nature of the shameful view of the self, to provide validation and normalising information as to how such experiences developed and to encourage the person to view their perceived flaws, mistakes and inadequacies compassionately (Gilbert, 2010). Again, the specific work of CBSPp is to link such processes to reducing the activation of the suicide schema. Cognitive behavioural strategies and schema change may also address specific self-attacking thoughts and core beliefs about the self.

9.5.1.4. Fluctuating affect, information processing biases and mode of therapy

CBT as delivered in the traditional setting of the clinic and in the traditional mode of the therapeutic hour has a number of advantages. It allows the client to take time away from their difficulties and to sit and reflect with the therapist about the nature of their experiences. The origins of these experiences can be carefully plotted on a timeline and formulated in terms of schema development (Beck, 1976). Within this setting, the client may develop a cognitive behavioural formulation of their difficulties and learn strategies that may help to attenuate them. The client may then use the formulation and the intervention strategies in the real-world setting, to allow them to become active agents of their experiences rather than passive recipients, and the active agent in implementing strategies that initially attenuate maintenance cycles, and then, as therapy progresses, begin to modulate the activation of the schematic appraisal systems that lead to problematic thoughts, feelings and behaviours.

The therapist delivering this 'detached' mode of therapy may have some difficulties to overcome. If we remind ourselves of the case of Peter (Chapter 8), some of these difficulties may become clear. Peter presented with highly variable cognitive, behavioural and affective cycles influenced by weekly and daily variables. Peter's account of specific events and of the week in general were often sparse, devoid of detail and tended to be flavoured by his current affective state. Peter and the therapist therefore faced the challenge of formulating the processes that led him to becoming suicidal over the week with a reduced or biased set of data about events in the week. The very processes of an over-general, and negative recall style and state dependent recall, which rendered Peter vulnerable to suicidal experiences, posed a barrier in session to the amelioration of such difficulties. This is an important point as fluctuations in affect, as experienced by Peter, have been found to be a key predictor of suicidal experiences in conditions such as borderline personality disorder (Nica & Links, 2009).

At this point it is worth reflecting on the task demands placed upon the client within CBT. For optimal results, clients rely on an autobiographical memory rich in details specific to each situation and a prospective memory that allows them to remember to implement strategies in future situations. They must be able to 'de-centre' from threatening affect sufficiently within sessions, and at the time of the difficulty to be able to implement these strategies. However, as we saw in Chapter 3, clients prone to suicidal thinking tend to have fragmentary memories that are charged with negative affect. The details of specific situations tend to be lost to long-term memory. Such clients report being passive to negative emotions, and find it difficult to 'de-centre' from them.

It is for these reasons that specific strategies are included within the CBSPp protocol to help reduce threat, switch attention to neutral elements of the environment and to encourage and stimulate the experience of positive emotions. Other strategies that can help are the development of momentary intervention strategies that can be used across daily and weekly cycles. We recorded sessions and provided client with copies. Furthermore, we broke the session into segments, so that clients had edited audio clips of relaxation techniques, BMACs and verbal reattribution techniques. We then attempted to link these to specific triggers, using an 'exit formulation' or 'staying well' plan. For instance, if a person was experiencing a hostile voice telling them that they were worthless, one option would be to develop an audio recording encouraging them to reconsider the advantages and disadvantages of listening to their voice, engaging in actively switching their attention away from the voice, initiating an activity such as walking or listening to their music. This could then be played when they hear the voice. Suicide specific strategies may remind the person of all the people in their support network and contain specific BMACs aimed at reconnecting them with their feelings towards such people and how people feel about them (Kelly et al., in preparation).

We are therefore attempting to reach out from the therapy room to the person's specific experiences of suicide, in their natural environments. We have argued elsewhere that the scaffolding of assessment, formulation and intervention from the therapy to the real world may benefit from momentary assessment and intervention strategies as well as learning algorithms that may maximise the timing of such interventions (Chapter 9; Kelly et al., in press). The therapist is encouraged to use a creative problem-solving approach, maximising the opportunity to use phone calls, text messages or even multi-media content, guided by the CBSPp formulation, in order to address the momentary difficulties experienced by the suicidal client.

9.5.2. Interpersonal barriers

It is possible that interpersonal barriers are preventing the person from fully engaging in CBSPp. The following factors may offer the therapist a checklist, but again, this is an area where the therapist is encouraged to draw from the breadth of their clinical experience and from supervision. As with other problematic areas, the clinician works with the client to formulate the ways such experiences are linked to the suicide schema.

- relationship difficulties;
- external shame;
- suspiciousness;
- hostility to others and homicidal ideation;

- fluctuating affect, information processing biases and mode of therapy;
- therapeutic relationship;
- no-rescue.

The client may not be able to engage with an individual mode of therapy, struggle to do so, or fail to see the relevance, when their main difficulties are perceived to be in the context of a problematic relationship. The therapist is faced with a number of options. It may be that family therapy can address difficulties in relationships that reduce the level of critical and hostile expressed emotion (Lobbanet al., 2009). However, the therapist working within a CBSPp framework remains alert to how a change in social processes may lead to changes in 'no-rescue appraisals' and underlying core beliefs and assumptions about the self and others. Furthermore, the links between such beliefs and the activation of the suicide schema should be explored. In essence, the therapist should be asking themselves how expressed emotions trigger suicide-related beliefs.

Box 9.5 Joseph's home environment

After returning to the family home, Joseph began to hear voices that were highly critical of him, and he began to see complex formulae he believed would allow him to purify the water system to cure cancer. He believed that the cure was present in part of his brain. His wife had no patience with him, branded his ideas as 'idiotic' and blamed him for the discord within the family, in which his son left his wife shortly after the death of their child.

Joseph reported that his wife was highly critical of him, and was almost continually verbally abusive towards him. This was exacerbating his desire to kill himself. The therapist worked along with other members of the care team to attempt to begin Family Therapy with Joseph and his wife. However, Joseph's wife did not attend these sessions, steadfast in her opinion that the relationship was over. The therapist worked with Joseph to implement strategies for acute suicide reduction and respite accommodation was found. Joseph was provided with alternative accommodation in the community and CBSPp was then delivered.

The case of Joseph was presented in order to highlight the challenges of delivering CBSPp in the context of a high level of interpersonal stress. The therapist can conceptualise the success of therapy like a see-saw. When the suicide schema is also compounded by such a high level of stress in the immediate environment, it may be that CBSP is not enough to counterbalance this. It is therefore better to attempt to address the interpersonal stressor (if possible) before beginning CBSPp.

The impact of difficult relationships may leave the person with a bias in their perceptions and beliefs about others, how they think others view them and beliefs about the self (Beck, 1976). As stated above, Gilbert (2006) delineates between internal and external shame. External shame refers to the sense that the person is held as flawed, damaged or inferior in the eyes of others. (Internal shame, as discussed above, refers to the person's own view of themselves.) This may present a specific barrier to direct CBSPp work if the client fears that telling the therapist about their experiences will result in the therapist rejecting and shaming them.

Box 9.6 Joseph's sense of failing as a man and as a father

Joseph's difficulties were triggered by the death of his granddaughter. He had put great pressure on being there for his son at this time, who he saw become 'uncontrollably distressed'. This led Joseph to question his role as a father who would always be able to protect his son. He ran away and considered suicide because he believed he had failed in this and had lost his identity of being a good father.

The therapist worked with Joseph to understand how his experiences of not being able to cope with his son's distress had impacted upon him. John explained that his father had died a year prior to the death of his grandchild. His father had been the 'strong silent type' and had been a formidable feature in his life growing up, but had always given Joseph an incredible level of support. Joseph developed strong rules of what it was to be a man and to be a father as a result of his experiences. Men should be strong and Fathers should *always* protect their children. In a tearful session, Joseph connected with the origins of his beliefs and acknowledged that he believed he had failed in his own father's eyes.

Joseph felt an incredibly strong sense of internal shame because of this – 'he was weak'. Joseph also felt a strong sense of external shame – to how his father would see him, to how his wife and family saw him and to how the male therapist would see him – leaving him feeling totally exposed. The therapist provided Joseph with normalising information about grief reactions and experiences of psychosis. The therapist acknowledged that he would have found the chain of events experienced by Joseph to be incredibly overwhelming. The therapy proceeded by Joseph acknowledging that his own father would have found this situation overwhelming and would have understood and not blamed Joseph for his reactions.

9.5.2.1. Suspiciousness and paranoia

A specific interpersonal difficulty that may impact upon the delivery of CBSPp is suspiciousness. The person may be suspicious of the therapist, making engagement with the therapist and with the therapy difficult. The person may be suspicious in a more general way, and even though they may trust the therapist, they may still not be ready to talk about their experiences. The therapist may then draw from their experiences of working within a CBTp perspective to address such difficulties. Excellent resources are available to guide the clinician when working with paranoia and persecutory beliefs (Freeman, Bentall & Garety, 2008). As always, the difference here is that the therapist remains mindful of links to CBSPp. Critically, does a person's suspiciousness lead to their suicidality? This may be directly, via 'no-rescue appraisals'. The route from suspiciousness to suicide may also be indirect, with suspiciousness setting in action a chain of events, for example, the person isolating themselves, becoming preoccupied with their internal world, lower opportunities to reality-check and an increase in threat, ultimately leading to defeat appraisals and the activation of the suicidal schema.

We have found that one option is to implement phase 1 of CBSPp without discussion of experiences of suicide or concerns regarding suspiciousness. The client may be engaged with the shared process of engaging with phase 1 of the protocol in order to *cope with the threat of their environment* without the need to discuss this threat specifically. Again, we return to the model of Bordin (1979, 1994): the shared goal of coping with distress can lead to the bond of working together on attention broadening, relaxation and the BMAC. Spontaneous drops in paranoia can then be explored as the potential result in a drop in distress or level of arousal. From this basis, the person may then be able to set a goal of working on paranoia and suspiciousness as it relates to their experiences of suicide within CBSPp.

9.5.2.2. Experiences of voice hearing

If the client experiences voice hearing, it may be useful to work with them to evaluate how this may impact upon therapy. It is useful to discern whether these experiences are going to be linked to the person's capacity to benefit from the session and/or whether it is going to be linked directly to the person's experiences of suicide.

If the experience of voice hearing does impact upon a person's attention and memory processes, the therapist may consider using techniques from CBTp to bolster phase 1 of CBSPp. So, for instance, techniques for 'coping' with voices may be used such as humming, speaking, listening to music. This may help the person to engage with tasks of attention broadening, relaxation and imagery tasks including the BMAC and the BMAS. The therapist should also establish whether voice hearing leads the client to appraisals that form a barrier to therapy:

• Does the content of the voice or beliefs about the voice threaten engagement with the therapy or the therapist?

Again, such barriers, by their very nature, can be difficult to access to formulate. Strategies for engagement within CBTp are useful here, and the application of phase 1 techniques can help to reduce the threat cycles linked to voice-hearing experiences if the client is reluctant to engage in a discussion about them. A client's appraisals about the therapy and the therapist may then be addressed using the techniques outlined in Chapter 6. Finally, the schematic appraisal networks underlying difficulties with voices may be addressed alongside suicide schema prevention work. For instance, Birchwood et al. (2004) suggested that a social rank schema influences both relationships with others and also the internal relationships with their voice. In such cases, the links between this schema and the suicide schema should be explored.

Finally, it is important not to jump in too quickly with CBSPp, assuming a client has received adequate information about experiences of hearing voices. For many clients, information about how common such experiences are and how they arise out of particular psychological mechanisms will be important information that naturally reduces distress. Resistance to looking at this information can then lead to a functional analysis of the importance of voice hearing. The case of Peter (Chapter 8) provides an example of how CBSPp was delivered without directly challenging the client's belief system about their voice.

9.5.2.3. Motivation and 'negative symptoms'

People with experiences of psychosis may present with marked anhedonia (Favrod, Giuliani, Ernst & Bonsack, 2010; Gard, Kring, Gard, Horan & Green, 2007; Kuha et al., 2011). As discussed in Chapter 5, such people may benefit from the Broad Minded Affective Scheduling

(BMAS) technique. However, the therapist must be careful to note any side effects of medication that may be interfering with motivation and energy levels (see Chapter 8, the case of Peter). Continuing with a psychological intervention may lead a client to blame themselves for their lack of motivation rather than acknowledging the effects of medication.

9.5.2.4. 'Recovery inertia': A fear of goal-directed behaviour leading to defeat and suicide

A number of clients presented with what we came to call 'recovery inertia', a psychological resistance to change to daily routines or the level of activities they wanted to engage in. A person's beliefs about their illness and also about goal-directed behaviour may therefore need to be elicited and addressed prior to engaging with CBSPp. For example, some people believed that restricting goal-directed behaviour was a way of not increasing the risk of relapse (Gumley & Schwannauer, 2006) and a fear of becoming suicidal again.

The information clients have received from mental health professionals may have compounded such beliefs. It was our experience was that clients who had experiences of psychosis had not received any messages of hope, normalising information or information about the many different pathways that could result in such experiences. Sometimes, the 'model of illness' people had been given to explain their experiences was one of a biological 'time bomb': people had been told that they had a disease and they could relapse *at any point*, *regardless of what they did*. This was reflected in a sense of hopelessness for the future, both in clients, their families and, in some cases, in mental health professionals. Furthermore, there was a resistance to change or to move away from living life at a much-reduced level of functioning. This was especially so when people had been in services for a longer time period. We therefore found it important to provide people with information about the bio-psychosocial model and about recovery, finding Pitt et al.'s (2007) paper on the concept of recovery a useful resource. We present the case of Brian to highlight the importance of this phase of therapy (Box 9.7).

Box 9.7 Recovery inertia: the case of Brian

Brian was a 40-year-old white British male. He lived with his mother and was in the process of decorating a flat he had recently bought, which he planned to move into. He reported becoming increasingly stressed over a number of years prior to becoming ill. He had worked as a builder and although he had enjoyed it, he had set very high standards for himself and those around him, such that anything less than these standards was unacceptable. This brought him into conflict with his workmates and his employers, who were more focused on output and productivity. As the stress escalated, Brian withdrew from work and his social circle and began to develop unusual thoughts about himself being in control of the world around him. When others did not comply with his wishes, he began to think a higher force was intervening, which made him very afraid. Concerned, his parents took him to his doctors and he was then diagnosed with schizophrenia. This was 15 years prior to being referred for CBSPp.

> *Brian was told that he had a brain disease and that it was a 'timebomb': he could relapse at anytime, and there was nothing he could do to prevent it. In fact, the best thing to do, according to his doctor at the time, was to do little in order not to become stressed. Brian accepted that he had an 'illness' and reduced his range of activities.*

At the beginning of therapy, Brian presented as difficult to engage, with set routines. However, he found the routine of attending appointments and treating himself for lunch afterwards to be very rewarding. This served as a catalyst for working on his flat later in the afternoon. This was contrasted to the days when he would sit in his flat and 'daydream'. He explained that he did not schedule any activities: he lived in the moment, a day-to-day existence, which he described as his 'bubble'. If he felt his stress levels rising at all, he would disengage, and 'drift'. He also believed that he could not turn a bad day into a good day. He would therefore monitor his feelings in the morning, and if he didn't feel 'good' or 'energised' he would then sleep, relax or do nothing so as not to get involved in stressful activities.

These conversations were prompted by the therapist's attempts to set goals. This approach to life was in stark contrast to how Brian had been living his life. The therapist therefore explored the appraisals Brian had about his illness and began gently exploring the information available about Recovery using Pitt et al.'s (2007) paper. Brian's initial reaction was one of anger at not receiving this information 15 years previously, and then one of grief for the time he had lost. Brian found it very difficult to engage with the process of goal setting, but was able to consider long-term goals such as going travelling to South America, which he had done in his late teens/early twenties. Short-term goals were set and he slowly began to extend his range of activities. The fear of suicide was latent, but connected to feelings of stress at 'doing too much'. Pacing was therefore extremely important. Problem-solving training was implemented to help with goal setting, and achievement and agency appraisals were revisited. Fears of relapse diminished. The therapist worked with Brian to develop a relapse plan with early warning signs, done in tandem to increased goal-focused behaviour. The therapist liaised with Brian's care co-ordinator, and they agreed to continue monitoring goals and pacing, along with developing a relapse prevention plan, to be used after CBSPp had finished.

9.5.3. External stressors and chronic difficulties

The external environment may need to be addressed before an individual model of suicide is applied. It may also be the case that the individual and the therapist cannot change an aversive external environment or only partially alter it. CBSPp then becomes a means of exploring together the choices a client has over their internal reactions to this environment. This results in a different path through the protocol. The initial attention and information processing section becomes strategically engaged with coping with threat responses to ongoing stressors. This may then lead into an exploration of how this has led to biases in appraisal but also to an exploration of the role of acceptance of the situation as it is (Hayes, Luoma, Bond, Masuda & Lillis, 2006). Similar work may be conducted if the person has some other ongoing stressor, as in the case of a chronic condition. This may be particularly the case for the client with chronic and unremitting experiences of psychosis or a client who has experienced a number of relapses.

9.6. Core capacities for CBSPp

The SAMS identifies modifiable psychological processes that are thought to (1) be influenced by experiences of defeat and suicide, and (2) further increase the likelihood of such experiences in the future. The CBSPp intervention presents a systematic, strategic intervention package for bringing balance back to these processes, to reduce their role in maintaining suicide. Furthermore, true to a homeostatic model of mental distress (Tarrier & Calam, 2002; Tarrier, 2006), experiences of suicide may result from a lack of resilience factors in the environment. CBSPp may also be viewed as a systematic assessment of how modifiable these processes are. If a person does not respond to interventions targeting specific processes, for example, attention, reasoning, perspective taking or emotional regulation, then the therapist may then go on to hypothesis test deficits to these areas and arrange specific assessments and interventions.

9.6.1. Alexithymia

A number of clients we have worked with presented with alexithymia, a difficulty to identify, describe or work with feelings. While some studies have found that alexithymia is not linked to suicidal thoughts or plans (Sayar, Acar & Ak, 2003), we have found that it can pose a barrier to the verbal processing of emotions and experiences that are important attributes in enabling clients to benefit from CBSPp.

We have found that it can be tremendously liberating for clients to be told that putting feelings into words is something we may all struggle with from time to time, and that for some this process is more difficult than others. This can then be identified as *one of the processes leading to defeat.* In particular, feelings can build in their intensity, and clients can feel totally overwhelmed by them. Without a way of classifying, labelling and understanding feelings, this process may seem even more uncontrollable. The therapist may then be tempted to address alexithymia. However, it is to be remembered that the purpose of CBSPp is to prevent suicide, as a focused therapy. The key questions are therefore:

- Is the client finding it difficult to talk about their experiences because they have no language to do so?
- If emotions and feelings are hard to express, how does this lead to overwhelm?
- How does this difficulty in identifying, classifying and understanding emotions lead to defeat and activation of the suicide schema?
- How can we work with this within the CBSPp protocol?
- What amendments may need to be made to the CBSPp protocol?

We have found that normalising and validating alexithymia can reduce a client's sense of there being an uncontrollable element within their mind. It provides an explanation to the groundswell of emotion. It may even be necessary to work with clients to explain emotions and that they are powerful systems in the brain that direct us to certain important goals and away from threat (LeDoux, 1998). For some, there may be a developmental difficulty restricting their ability to process emotions; for others, it may be that they have never had the experience of being in an environment where emotions are talked about. For others again, emotions are difficult to process owing to traumatic experiences. These processes can be shared with the client and validated.

We have found that helping clients to develop a language for their experiences, or a metaphor for the impact of overwhelming emotions can be helpful. Here, the first task need not be to meticulously note each emotion and process the memories associated with it. This may be beneficial in the long term. However, in the short term, the therapist may be better oriented to the focused nature of CBSPp if this helps a client to (1) spot the process of emotional overwhelm, (2) label it and (3) provide strategies to help reduce it. Phase 1 of the CBSPp protocol may therefore be adapted for this purpose.

Box 9.8 Alexithymia: Joseph's pressure cooker

Joseph found it tremendously difficult to describe his experiences of suicide. In session, he presented as extremely low in mood initially, and as if he was struggling to speak. When questioned about his experiences, he was able to communicate that it was to do with 'pressure'.

The therapist was able to ascertain that when a perceived setback occurred, such as a bill coming through the letter box, Joseph immediately got an image of arguing with his wife over money and an immediate overwhelming feeling in his body, which he described as 'like a wave'.

The therapist provided Joseph with information about emotions and how they may be linked to previous experiences. The therapist outlined alexithymia, and Joseph agreed that he had never been able to talk about his feelings. The therapist returned to John's use of pressure as a way of understanding this, and a goal was set to help Joseph 'relieve the pressure'. Joseph compared this to a pressure cooker, which became a metaphor for therapy and was included in Joseph's staying well plan (see Figure 9.2).

Joseph responded well to relaxation and use of the BMAC to reduce the surge of pressure he felt. John was then able to engage in problem-solving and contacting others. His friend Sam was a tremendous source of support, and talked through the situation slowly with him.

Joseph was able to put this in practice outside of the therapy. These experiences were reviewed in therapy, and Joseph was able to develop appraisals of control over situations within which he had previously felt powerless.

9.6.2. CBSPp as a screening tool for specific learning disabilities and neuro-developmental disorders

When the therapist is administering CBSPp, they should be mindful of whether the person has capacity to modify the processes involved in resilience from suicide. It would be problematic to maintain the assumption that factors associated with verbal, behavioural and emotional regulation are *modifiable* when the person has a reduced capacity for change. Adopting a wholly psychological approach to analysing the factors leading to suicide may lead both the client and the therapist to feel defeated when there may be other factors involved. We have

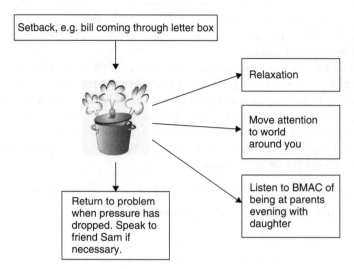

Figure 9.2   Joseph's staying well plan incorporating metaphor of pressure cooker 'release'

discussed the role of extreme environmental stressors, but here we are referring to the possibility that the client presents with a specific learning disability or a neuro-developmental difficulty such as anautistic spectrum disorder (ASD). The therapist must therefore be careful to balance a curiosity about psychological and emotional barriers to therapy with a preparedness to accept that clients do not come to therapy with the same underlying capacities. The client's responsiveness to the different elements of the CBSPp protocol may provide the basis for an assessment of their attentional, reasoning and emotional regulation skills that may be useful as a basis for further and more specialist assessments. Joint working or sharing of a detailed formulation with specialist services may be of particular benefit to the client.

9.7. Therapist barriers and impact upon clinician

We began this chapter by stating that working with the suicidal client may be one of the hardest tasks facing the clinician. As discussed by Wenzel, Brown & Beck (2009), it is therefore important to consider the impact such work has on the clinician. Pope and Tabachnik (1993) found that more than 97% of clinical psychologists answered that they fear their clients will kill themselves, and clinicians may feel anger towards their suicidal clients. As discussed in section 10.8, we suggest that the ideal theoretical orientation is to hope for hope, a stance that may be hard to maintain in such work. It is therefore extremely important to address the needs of clinicians. Supervision may focus on eliciting clinician's beliefs about suicide and any barriers they have to working with suicidal clients. Common barriers can be that the work may not be effective and the person will eventually kill themselves. Clinicians may experience grief, guilt or even external shame about this – how other clinicians will perceive them. Clinicians may also be afraid of their work being shown to be inadequate or negligent, resulting in a review of their practices, and ultimately, losing their licence to practise. These fears may result in a clinician reducing the scope for goal setting in session and making clinicians more risk averse, disrupting therapy sessions with frequent risk assessments. A common implicit goal of the clinician is for the client to reassure them that they have nothing to worry about, that they are not going to kill themselves. As discussed, clients may be in no position to give away the only mechanism they believe they have for dealing with their own experiences of horror or defeat.

We suggest that it may be useful for therapists to work through their fears of working with suicidal clients *hypothetically* in supervision, prior to seeing clients, in order to address any particular areas of sensitivity that may restrict their practice. Supervision should regularly address the emotional load on clients. As Wenzel et al. (2009) suggest, peer supervision can be particularly validating and normalising for therapists. Another difficulty can be taking on too much responsibility for a client's level of suicidal ideation, for suicidal attempts and for actual suicide. Factors outside of the sphere of influence of CBSPp may be operating upon a client, and these should be reflected upon in supervision. The 'see-saw' metaphor can be useful here.

9.8 Final thoughts: A hope for hope

The aim of CBSPp is to address the factors that maintain a person's current suicidality or predispose them to suicidal ideation, planning and behaviour in the future. This is complemented by the strengthening of specific factors that inhibit suicide. In this chapter we have discussed a number of potential difficulties that may need to be addressed in order to allow the effective delivery of CBSPp. It may be that these difficulties, or others beyond the scope of this chapter, seem insurmountable for the client and maybe for the therapist. We propose that the therapist proceeds with a systematic approach.

Firstly, CBSPp offers a strategic approach to evaluating a client's potential for change within their current situation. If individual change does not occur, the therapist and the client may proceed by exploring barriers to change; these may be psychological or due to underlying deficits that warrant specific assessment and interventions. Therapists also explore the scope for changing the external environment.

Secondly, if change is not possible at the moment, the therapist and client may shift towards an acceptance and commitment to tolerate the current situation (Hayes et al., 2006). This can be difficult work for both the therapist and the client. Regular supervision and peer supervision should be sought by the therapist to enable them to remain hopeful of change in the future – in essence, hopeful that the client will find hope. If the therapist maintains this while being available for clients and providing them with support at the most difficult times of their lives, we believe this lays the foundation for the alleviation of such difficulties and keeps alive the prospect of future change.

Ultimately, we believe that the central orientation a therapist brings to CBSPp is one of cautious optimism, a creative approach to problem-solving and an enduring perseverance. If we offer our clients nothing else, we may offer them this general orientation to their difficulties, which may be enough to prevent them from killing themselves.

Chapter 10

People and suicide

Lived experiences of suicidality and involvement in suicide prevention research

Yvonne Awenat: a personal account

In the time that it takes for you to read this paragraph one person will die by suicide somewhere in the world (World Health Organization, 2011). Statistics indicate around 1 million recorded suicides each year, equating to one death every 40 seconds. In the UK the most up-to-date data available at the time or writing reports 5,675 suicides for 2008 (Office for National Statistics, 2011). Even so, death by suicide is still a relatively rare event when compared to the other 500,000 non-suicidal deaths typically recorded in the UK each year (Anderson & Jenkins, 2005). However the psychological morbidity of suicidality is far higher than indicated by records of completed suicides. This is reflected in the Samaritans' national data showing evidence of telephone contact by a person experiencing suicidality every 57 seconds, amounting to almost 5 million contacts during 2010 (Samaritans, 2011).

Within general populations internationally it has been suggested that between 10 and 18% of people experience suicidal thoughts at some point in their lives, with 3 to 5% attempting suicide (Weissman, Bland, Canino, Greenwald, Hwu et al., 1999). Lakeman (2010) suggests that experiencing suicidal thoughts is fairly common, affecting between 15 and 25% of adolescents and up to 70% of acutely depressed people. Reliable data of suicidal behaviour in terms of contact with health services owing to expressed suicidal feelings, intent or actual attempts is difficult to obtain given the complexities of traditional methods of data recording, but for every completed suicide there are estimated to be at least 20 attempts (WHO, 2011). Windfuhr and Kapur (2011) have presented extensive information outlining the serious limitations of suicide statistics, indicating that lack of consensus regarding definitions of case ascertainment, levels of proof and cultural influences such as religious beliefs and many other factors all contribute to difficulties in interpretation of the real extent of death by suicide.

The picture is even more complex concerning classifying suicidal ideation and suicidal behaviour, as Silverman (2011) outlines in a comprehensive discussion of the challenges and consequent impaired utility of current data. Ultimately, however, official figures cannot reflect the impact of the distress felt by individuals, their families and professionals in association with any level of suicidality.

I write this chapter from the perspective of someone who had previously experienced over 15 years of serious mental health problems including personal experiences of being in situations where I felt and at times acted suicidally. When I joined the Suicide Research Group in 2009 as a service user consultant to assist the study that first tested use of CBSP in the study described in this book, I had absolutely no idea of what to expect in terms of what my role might be and how I would be received by the research team. This opportunity had been identified to me by my daughter, Dr Fairuz Awenat (herself a consultant clinical psychologist), who was aware of the pioneering work at Manchester in actively involving service users in the research process. Fairuz had met and was inspired by Liz Pitt, who was (and still is) a leading service user researcher, and Fairuz recognised the possibility of my involvement as an chance to engage in some meaningful therapeutic activity that might help me liberate myself (and my family) from the toxic confines of my situation. I had reluctantly retired from my previous role as a consultant nurse (RGN) in the NHS after 25 years in a job that I loved. Having had some experience of academia in education and research, Fairuz saw this as a way of helping me perhaps rekindle my research interests as I had to abandon my own PhD owing to my retirement from the NHS, as it was integral to my job in being funded as a Department of Health Research Fellowship.

I approached my first meeting with the research team with great anxiety, as I was still extremely unwell at that time. Based on my own earlier experiences of university life, I envisaged hushed tones of an insider closed technical language of complex psychological theory dominated by authoritative revered directions of the 'top man' to whom everyone would respectfully defer. I was therefore pleasantly surprised to encounter a well-organised, lively and inclusive debate. At times meetings were focused and 'businesslike' regarding deadlines for actions, but there was always time and enough flexibility for discussion around new avenues of enquiry. I was impressed at how democratic the meetings were, and how in particular Dr Trish Gooding (who I viewed as the organisational director!) always facilitated the input and contribution of even the most junior undergraduates and volunteers (even me!).

The limited precedents of this team's experience of service user involvement in research went in my favour, allowing me flexibility to shape my particular contribution. Although I was faced with a fairly steep learning curve to familiarise myself with psychological concepts of which I knew nothing and in particular of suicidology, which at that time I only had my own undisclosed experiences to draw on. At times I struggled in following technical discussions around quantitative methodological matters such as statistical analytical tests. as my prior experience was overwhelmingly in qualitative research and I had cultivated a long tradition of avoiding the quantitative lectures, particularly those on statistics, which I had never understood. I realise now that the quality of teaching was probably a major factor in alienating me from something that I now do not find quite so challenging.

I operationalised my role in the research by trying wherever possible to focus discussions on issues that might eventually generate a practical output of real benefit to people with mental distress. I drew on my experiences of using mental health services to illuminate possible avenues for accessing participants, and I hope helped to deepen researchers' understanding of the 'real-life' issues for ordinary mental health service users. I was particularly interested in optimising the safety, and care and concern and ethical needs of participants and contributed to the design and analysis of a small piece of qualitative research that sought to investigate people's views of being involved as a participant in suicide research (Taylor, Awenat et al., 2010). This revealed that far from being harmed or traumatised as often feared by ethics committees, within a carefully planned and supportive research study, participants identified several benefits. One of these benefits, interestingly, was 'therapeutic gain', as this was certainly not one of the stated aims of the research interviews carried out by the research assistants. Sadly, this may reflect the situation that even within a mental health setting, patients have very limited opportunities to just simply talk to someone who will actively listen. I sought out appropriate moments to either confirm or disconfirm academic views and research plans based not only on my own experiences but also those that I heard from other service users in my locality in connection with my voluntary work with a branch of Mind.

I recall a discussion at one research team meeting around trying to pin-point the precise trigger that for some people finally leads to the point of no return in either an attempted or completed suicide. The idea of a 'red light', representing perhaps a seemingly innocuous, unremarkable yet irresistible demand to act, possibly being only a relatively minor irritant in the midst of other serious stresses, resonated with not only my own past experiences but also with fellow patients that I had talked with. This might be an area of useful study for the future.

I discovered a whole new world of knowledge of mental health and psychology that was not just generally interesting but was in effect a catalyst in awakening my consciousness to the possibility of recovery after 15 years of absorbing psychiatric dictates that I had a life-long incurable disease. I now began to see that the alternative non-medical perspectives of not just aetiology but also treatment that my daughter had been persistently begging me to consider for several years made sense. As a nurse working in physical health where doctors prescribed drugs for people with less questionable disease entities, and where a significant part of my role was to administer such drugs to patients who on the whole responded and got better, I had not understood that psychiatry cannot emulate a similar medical speciality role akin to cardiology or gastroenterology etc.

I had for years been a willing uncritical recipient of medications, repeated courses of electro-convulsive treatment and frequent hospitalisations. Despite the pleas of my highly qualified clinical psychologist daughter, whom I had dismissed as just "my baby girl" who could not possibly know as much as the medics, it took me many years to be in a position of 'readiness' to critically appraise my rapidly deteriorating situation. With the re-emergence of a degree of mental clarity that had been clouded by so many years of heavy use of a complex cocktail of psychiatric drugs I could reach no other conclusion that they had not helped me. With a self-designed, very slow discontinuation process lasting over a year, despite medical cautions of relapse and impending doom, I feel better than I have felt in many years, my only regret being that I did not have the foresight to stop the drugs before I had been affected by some very unpleasant disabling side effects, which I now fear may be permanent.

Knowledge is truly empowering, and entering into the world of psychology research, studying topics and issues that I had previously believed were scientifically rigorous and beyond dispute, coupled with the welcoming acceptance and support of the research team, really boosted my dilapidated self-confidence. It would be untrue to suggest that my recovery is complete or that it has been a linear process, but my new-found direction in using my previous skills and experiences to contribute to improving mental health services mainly via research has been empowering, and my ambition is to see clinical psychology play a far more prominent role, particularly in in-patient settings, where psychologically informed practices are desperately needed.

The stigma around suicide reflecting societal attitudes of fear, hatred and disgust persists and is influential in preventing people from accessing help. One of the greatest fears of disclosing the feelings or intentions to end one's own life is the anticipated reaction of others. Let us not forget that as recently as 1961 'committing' suicide was a criminal offence in the UK, and remains so today in several predominantly religious states. Media portrayal of suicides always captures the headlines, and the manner in which it is reported ranges from the romanticised 'Van Gogh'-styled descriptions of a sad, lonely, misunderstood figure, rejected and rejecting of life, right across to the blatant raw anger, disgust and horror at 'the person who had everything' but selfishly and willingly abandoned loved ones.

Actually there is nothing romantic about experiencing suicidality. In simple pragmatic terms, it is just a very serious situation that faces individuals, their families and communities that could be handled better. A pragmatist perspective would be that preventable deaths, of which suicide is one example, should always be targeted to enhance methods of detection and management. Whether through the failings of staff in diagnosing a treatable cancer (one in every four cases of cancer is missed by GPs) or in the coroner's report that someone might have lived if obvious warning signs of impending suicide had been identified, all situations where life, and crucially *quality of life*, could be improved are worthy of attention.

Within the mental health community clinical psychology has been a pioneer in attempting to de-stigmatize language by prompting use of the word 'complete' instead of 'commit' in verbal and written communication. There are many other examples where changes of accepted terms of language have been instrumental in promoting more positive public attitudes, for example, racial and sexual prejudices. It is disappointing therefore that an otherwise excellent authoritative contemporary text did not harness the opportunity to lead by example and exclude the term 'commit' in favour of the less judgemental word 'complete' (O'Connor, Platt & Gordon, 2011).

In terms of NHS resource allocation for predominantly physical health conditions such as cancer, when compared to mental health issues such as suicide prevention, the latter always loses out, with lower levels of investment provided for research and service delivery. An example of such disparity is that each year over 5,500 people die by suicide and fewer than 1,000 die by cervical carcinoma. The latter figure has been achieved by widespread public health campaigns to raise awareness and encourage women to uptake screening opportunities, with corresponding investment in effective treatments for the disease if identified, and more recently a vaccine produced to prevent future cases. This is admirable, and is just the kind of approach that needs to be invested in for suicide prevention. The outcome of the recent Department of Health (2011) consultation on suicide prevention for England is imminent, and is eagerly awaited, but appears to have failed to address the need for effective psychological interventions, hence replicating earlier strategies that focus more on containment and reducing access to lethal means.

However, this is mitigated in part by the new guidelines from the National Institute for Clinical Excellence (NICE) for longer-term management of self-harm, which now recommend the provision of a targeted, suicide-specific form of CBT for patients experiencing suicidal episodes (NICE, 2011). The challenge now presented will be to negotiate a way through the complexities of financial limitations and poor-quality mental health commissioning that serves as a barrier to patients accessing recommended psychological therapies. An example of this is evident in the wide variation of eligible patients receiving NICE (2009) recommended CBT for schizophrenia, with evidence that in some areas only 6% of patients were ever offered this (Department of Health, 2009).

For a significant proportion of people with mental health problems repetitive episodes of periods of suicidality are common. Kapur and colleagues have identified substantial evidence illustrating the often repetitive nature of suicidal behaviour resulting in attendance at emergency departments and admission to hospital (Kapur, Cooper, King-Heles et al., 2006; Kapur, House & Creed, 1999). Furthermore, such treatment shows little evidence of efficacy, often invoking the 'revolving door' phenomenon with frequent re-presentations and re-admissions (Langdon, Yaguez et al., 2001), and in itself being linked to an escalated level of suicide soon after discharge (Meehan, Kapur, Hunt et al., 2006). A systematic review of repetition of deliberate self-harm for individuals who received hospital treatment indicates that

20 to 30% experience repeat episodes of deliberate self-harm within one year of the index event, with 2% going on to complete suicide within one year, rising to 7% within nine years (Owens, Horrocks & House, 2002). This type of data demonstrating a longitudinal, almost chronic health issue appears to resonate with the hypothesis of a suicide schema that at times lays relatively dormant but is readily activated by individual factors reflecting an ever-present remitting and relapsing disorder.

However, current clinical services and practices appear to reflect the fallacious view that patient presentations of suicidality are singular, self-limiting occurrences, which are therefore appropriately responded to with the typical 'fire-fighting', reactive approach that aims to dampen down but never really address the underlying psychological mechanisms that are likely to persist and drive future episodes. Reactive services usually comprise of short-term intensive staff activity, often involving community crisis resolution teams and often including hospitalisation. Considerable effort is invested into preventing physical access to lethal means of suicide alongside repetitive, almost obsessional risk assessment. For patients who are admitted to psychiatric wards this is accompanied by frequent or continuous formal 'observation', a practice known to be extremely stressful for patients. Such approaches may be driven by the desire to avoid medico-legal action by being able to provide documentary evidence of adherence to procedural risk assessment, but the reality is that assessment and even identification of risk does not provide protection from suicide without treatment to address the underlying psychological mechanisms of suicidality.

Unfortunately, all these labour-intensive actions do not guarantee prevention of suicide, as even in in-patient settings this still a regular event, as indicated by the recent (2011) experience of one NHS Trust in England where two separate patient incidences of suicide occurred on the same acute psychiatric ward within a two-week period. This indicates that containment with custodial care alone is ineffective, perhaps generally only providing a temporary relief from re-presentations or completed suicide at a later date. More numerous repetitions of attempted suicide proportionately increase the individual's likelihood of future completion of suicide.

The new NICE guidelines for self-harm (longer-term care) are to be welcomed in providing a long-overdue authoritative statement that standard suicide risk assessment tools should no longer be used and relied on to predict future suicide risk. Instead a more psychologically informed 'formulation' styled comprehensive assessment is recommended (NICE, 2011). This presents the opportunity for clinical psychologists to teach others and lead by example in a technique that forms the basis of their own contemporary practice.

Clinical psychology is an expensive but arguably cost-effective commodity whose contribution to mental health services has not yet been fully realised. The provision of clinical psychology to people with mental health problems remains restricted, being influenced by its relatively high unit cost, which limits the availability of qualified practitioners. This is coupled with a surprising lack of understanding and knowledge even within the wider professional mental health community concerning what clinical psychology actually is, how it works and the evolving evidence base that supports its use as an effective therapy. The lack of awareness of the potential benefits to patients is an important issue to address as within the NHS referral by another discipline is required for a patient to access psychological therapies.

Other mental health staff who function as 'gatekeepers' for access to clinical psychologists often fail to refer eligible patients. Common perceptions relate to unfounded generalisations applied to certain types of patients. For example older people may be assumed to be unable to benefit owing to discriminatory judgements arising more from prejudice than the genuine barriers of severe cognitive deterioration that might exclude a small minority. Where one profession accepts that they have little to offer, as in the case of psychiatry for people with the contentious label of 'personality disorder', there is a tendency to assume that noone else can help, which especially in this case is inaccurate.

Likewise there exists a commonly held belief that all patients who are judged to be acutely unwell would not wish to or would not be able to engage in therapy, perhaps explaining the present minimal input of clinical psychology for patients in acute psychiatric wards. The presumption that acuity of presentation is a contraindication to receiving therapy has been refuted in the recent Mind report aptly titled *Listening to Experience*, which depicts the results of their investigation into patients' and carers' views of the current acute and crisis care in mental health services (Mind, 2011). The review demonstrates that it is precisely at the time of suicidal crisis that people feel the most urgent need for help to 'make sense' of their situation, yet too often pleas for help are dismissed with insensitive platitudes, as evidenced by the statements of a suicidal patient calling an NHS Crisis Help-line who was told to "make a cup of tea or have a bath" (Mind, 2011).

These points are made to indicate the need for continued inter-professional information and training to ensure that unnecessary barriers to psychological therapies are challenged. However, merely increasing referrer demand will be ineffective without targeting commissioners and managers with budgetary responsibility. These issues will ultimately need to be addressed for CBSP to be available to those people who might benefit from this therapy.

Patient reports abound of poor experiences of healthcare provision in times of acute mental distress (Bee, Playle & Lovell 2008; Department of Health, 2005; Duffy & Ryan, 2004; Hawton, Taylor, Saunders & Madadevan, 2011; Healthcare Commission, 2008; Horrocks et al., 2005; Mind, 2004, 2011; National Audit Office, 2008; Rethink, 2005, 2006; Sainsbury Centre for Mental Health, 2005). While some patients do report satisfaction with care, there are many that do not. Negative experiences mainly relate to patient's perceptions of critical and hostile staff attitudes, but other issues such as poor communication between staff and patients, lack of information about their condition and treatment options, and difficulties in accessing aftercare services are also important (Hawton, Taylor & Madadevan, 2011).

The aforementioned issues of prior patient experiences are highly relevant to considering implementation of CBSP as such experiences inevitably affect patients' expectations, willingness and ability to engage in therapy, all of which are influential determinants of the outcomes of therapy. A starting point for successful therapy may need to acknowledge the trauma and damage caused by experiences of other mental health (and general) services to facilitate the trust, rapport and engagement crucial for a strong therapeutic alliance.

Expressing suicidal thoughts and feelings activated by an existential crisis not only challenges the self but also invokes unwanted distressing thoughts and feelings in staff who are in contact with the suicidal person. Morgan (1979) explained the complexities of the ensuing interpersonal relationship dynamics between suicidal patients and mental health staff as a process of 'malignant alienation'. Duffy (2003a, b), building on the work of Morgan (1979), investigated the occurrence of this process with mental health nurses and suicidal patients. For some patients the experience of in-patient hospital care in particular can be so additionally traumatic that their risk of suicide is heightened rather than relieved (Duffy, 2003). Here instead of being the solution, the ward and its staff become part of the problem. Malignant alienation involves a process in which therapeutic relationships deteriorate and become dysfunctional. High levels of distress presented by suicidal patients who may feel hopeless, helpless, dependent, frightened and altogether despairing can invoke negative feelings in staff who become patient-avoidant in an attempt to protect themselves from such distress. Some patients become angry by their own vulnerability, dependency and the acuity of their intolerable distress, and this can be interpreted by staff as being unreasonable, provocative and over-dependent. The consequent disengagement and failure to empathise by staff is felt as abandonment and rejection by the patient, a situation that in itself may serve to further drive and reinforce suicidal behaviour, thereby constituting an additional risk factor. Such wards have been described as 'dangerous places for suicidal patients' (Bowles, 2004, p77).

It is well known that some staff perceive the concept of deliberate self-harm with or without suicidal intent (which may be present but not disclosed for many reasons, not least of which is fear of enforced hospitalisation) to be particularly challenging to deal with as evidenced by the numerous reports of their unhelpful attitudes as perceived by individuals who present for treatment at Accident and Emergency departments (Brophy, 2006; Horrocks et al., 2005: Wicklander, Samuelsson et al., 2003). Indeed, the fear of staff disapproval, lack of understanding and sometimes even unmasked anger is well recognised among patients and is a strong barrier that negatively influences help-seeking behaviour. Having attempted to face and overcome the barriers to disclosure by openly asking for help when mental distress deteriorates to such a level, dismissive attitudes found in some staff actually reinforce accompanying feelings of self-rejection and failure, resulting in even greater determination to give up, escape and die.

Even when patients make direct attempts to actively seek help the staff response often manifests as repetitious episodes of dubious-quality 'risk assessments'. Organisational targets to provide documentary evidence of staff activity in recording risk override and divert staff attention away from addressing the identified risk factors with a therapeutic intervention aimed at reducing risk. So essentially problems may be identified, but little is done to provide meaningful help to address them.

Another issue relates to staff perceptions of their lack of training and feelings of insufficient confidence and competence in addressing the particular needs of suicidal patients. Droughton, Gask et al. (2004) challenge the common assumption that professional staff will have received sufficient training in their basic preparation. It may surprise some readers that even within mental health settings many experienced staff do not feel confident to talk with patients who are suicidal, and even when clearly indicated the dreaded 'death question' is evaded. The acclaimed 'Skills Training on Risk Management' (STORM, 2004) programme developed by the University of Manchester for multidisciplinary suicidal crisis management is recognised to reflect 'best practice' (although there is very little research of what constitutes 'best practice'). Although it is reported to be a good course of study and is well received by those who complete it, the evidence of its use and application in clinical practice together with any effects on patient outcome is lacking. It is nevertheless very disappointing for patients that despite having received some specialist training, many of the professionals that they are likely to come into contact with during times of overwhelming mental distress do not appear able to help them.

It is to be hoped that the content of future staff education will have a stronger evidence base to draw upon in terms of knowing what interventions are likely to contribute to suicide prevention, along with research demonstrating the patient outcomes of staff delivering evidence-based interventions.

Certainly the organisational cultures and practices that prioritise non-clinical activity and thus impose barriers to the availability of staff for therapeutic care are influential (Department of Health, 2005). However, the situation is inherently more complex than merely being a case of too much work and too little staff to do the work. It is not even entirely explained by the oft-cited staff 'burnout', although this is known to be relatively common in mental health staff (Johnson, Wood, Paul et al., 2010).

This situation arises within the wider context of other general stressors well recognised to be problematic to front-line mental healthcare staff (Royal College of Psychiatrists, 2011). So, overall, for many suicidal patients current services are neither well received nor effective.

The inherent barriers of open disclosure imposed by the societal stigma associated with suicide, together with fear of the actions likely to be instigated by mental health professionals (i.e. hospitalisation and increased medication), creates a situation where some people in distress feel that they have to cope alone. Actively seeking help despite such barriers when met with superficial containment approaches only serves to amplify a patient's feelings of no hope, no rescue, defeat, entrapment and failure, perhaps creating an even stronger perception of suicide as the only solution. Sometimes the last bastion of control during the suicidal crisis may be the sense of still having the ability to end one's own life if all else fails. Paradoxically this remaining fine thread of sense of control and power of self-determination may serve as a protective factor, which if removed by incarceration may actually heighten risk.

In terms of informal or enforced admission to a psychiatric ward (most of which have now returned to being 'locked' wards), the suicidal person is not only psychologically 'trapped' but is physically trapped by enforced confinement. Staff shortages and other factors often result in in-patients being refused accompanied breaks to spend some time off the ward, which creates a feeling of desperation to escape from a toxic environment devoid of human communication. It is not surprising therefore that the majority of in-patient suicides occur when they have managed to leave the ward without permission. I personally recall a period around two years before writing this chapter when as an in-patient for four weeks I was not allowed any time at all to spend even a few minutes away from the ward.

Irrespective of the suicide risk issues, the overall level of absconsions from psychiatric wards is recognised as a major organisational problem. However, if wards were perceived as supportive environments, with the availability of skilled and compassionate care that provided a welcome sanctuary at a times of desolation and hopelessness when all else has failed, this might not be so. For some patients the confirmation of realisation that there is no help forthcoming (no rescue) and that the situation really is hopeless combines to arouse inventive methods of escape from the ward, leading to enactment of what now is the only remaining final solution of suicide. This theory would appear to have a good 'fit' with the statistics demonstrating escalated levels of the post-discharge suicide rate, especially within the first 24-hour period.

Among some mental health staff presented with a potentially suicidal patient, particularly where there is a history of previous suicide attempts, the inevitable debate about whether the patient is 'genuinely' suicidal or merely 'attention-seeking' plays out. Failure to take the patient seriously and respond appropriately to the expressed distress is a potentially dangerous gamble with that person's life. The personal attitudes of the staff carrying out formal risk assessment scales inevitably influence their subjective interpretation and rating of several items. Bentall (2010) has presented extensive examples of evidence suggesting that personal expectations of researchers administering quantitative measurement tools impacts on their scoring of participants' clinical status.

Additionally there is evidence to demonstrate the poor validity and reliability of even the better suicide risk assessment instruments in that for most cases of completed suicide professionals had scored patients at either 'no risk' or 'low risk' (National Confidential Inquiry into

Suicide & Homicide by People with Mental Illness, 2010). Indeed, experts in suicidology have recently called for urgent attention to the need to develop better suicide risk prediction screening measures with greater power of sensitivity and specificity (O'Connor, Platt & Gordon, 2011).

The new NICE guidelines for Self-harm longer-term care (NICE, 2011) have now recognised the serious limitations of standard risk assessment checklists and have advised that their use to predict suicide should be abandoned, and a more 'formulation' style assessment is recommended. This is a major breakthrough in traditional practice, and with it presents an opportunity for clinical psychologists to take the lead in pioneering more meaningful psychologically informed approaches that can be used by a range of mental health staff.

Returning to the issue of negative dismissive attitudes associated with clinicians' pre-judgements, I recall being interviewed by a psychiatrist at our first meeting as he laboured through the monotony of the usual psychiatric assessment protocol. The point came where I was asked if I had ever attempted suicide. On being informed that indeed I had, his next question was whether I had been admitted to an intensive care unit (general, not psychiatric), to which I replied that I had not. The indulgent grin and rolling of his eyes made it abundantly clear to me (as I think was intended) that he was totally unimpressed with what he obviously decided was merely an insignificant gesture warranting dismissal. This is an illustration of yet another arbitrary, subjective and ill-founded distortion of science.

Admission to an intensive care unit is typically indicated by the patient's inability to inde-pendently maintain vital organ functions such as respiration, thereby necessitating artificial mechanical ventilation. In the case of self-poisoning the raw quantity of toxin needed to induce this level of organ failure varies considerably between individuals being influenced by age, sex, pre-existing health status, and many other idiosyncratic variables of physiologi-cal biochemical absorption, metabolism and excretion related to liver and kidney function. For one person serious multi-organ failure could arise from consuming, for example, a box of paracetamol; for someone already tolerant to regular doses of various combinations of psychotrophic drugs it might only result from large overdose of these drugs; or for an elderly person with sub-optimal metabolism even a relatively small overdose of toxic tricyclics may cause a life-threatening situation.

I am perhaps labouring this point in excess of its relevance here and would not wish to imply any unwarranted credibility to those concerned, but I feel it is an important illustration of the unscientific floundering of some (but by all means not all) highly qualified profession-als who are in positions of leadership of mental health teams with public trust and perhaps misplaced confidence. Dismissal and failure to validate the distress of someone who has made a non-fatal suicide attempt – a term that can only ever have retrospective validity – is not only insensitive and arrogant but can sometimes be interpreted by the individual as a challenge to do 'a proper job' next time.

No doubt much labelling of some patients suicidal behaviour as 'attention-seeking' by the more intellectually challenged staff groups arises from ignorance due to lack of understand-ing of the purpose and function of such behaviour as a fundamental mechanism of expres-sion of extreme mental distress and self-survival. The drive for self-survival is the strongest instinct in all living creatures, being a major determinant of continued existence of the spe-cies. When this is not just lost but superceded by a conscious determination to self-destruct, surely something must have gone very badly wrong? If someone feels so mentally distressed as to purposely harm themselves, being unable to access more socially accepted mechanisms of relief of that distress, then surely this indicates the need to respond professionally and compassionately to that 'cry for help'?

The research presented in this book depicting the formation and chronicity of the suicide schema (Pratt et al., 2010) in conjunction with development of the Schematic Appraisal Model of Suicide (SAMS) brings new hope for patients whose lives are blighted by suicidality. The concept of the influence of a 'suicide schema' as a preformed, lingering persistent semantic memory mechanism that is easily and frequently triggered into action by a set of individually defined stressors resonates with patients. It has a good 'fit' with the lived experience of susceptible individuals, offering the possibility to understand, make sense of and gain some control over a previously inane situation. It also contributes to the empowerment so essential for people to challenge a situation where feelings of powerlessness, shame and guilt may have been prominent features within the experiences of suicidality. Perhaps more importantly, this new knowledge and theory generation have operationalised the ideal of translational research for patient benefit. For the first time ever we now have a theoretically driven and clinically relevant purpose-designed suicide prevention *intervention* in Cognitive Behavioural Suicide Prevention (CBSP) therapy. For patients this turns the 'cry of pain' into a tangible feature of which the contributory individual psychological processes can be examined, deconstructed where necessary and rebuilt to offer improved quality of life and a better outcome. Specifically, CBSP offers the chance to really tackle underlying issues that have and will probably continue to reappear without such help. In itself the *structural* existence of CBSP offers hope, and application of the therapeutic *process* harnesses opportunities for learning how to rebuild hope and optimism to achieve the *outcome* of a better life. It therefore fulfils all the components of a quality health intervention (Donabedian, 1980).

Emerging qualitative data of the experiences of CBSP elicited from patients with experience of psychosis in a community setting are encouraging as they describe a treatment that is well received and valued. This work is described in more detail in other chapters of this text. The main benefits described by participants in qualitative interviews carried out to elicit patient perceptions of their experience of CBSP therapy focus strongly on the quality of the relationship with the therapist. Additional influences associated with positive meaningful outcomes of importance were feelings of the restoration of hope and improved confidence to reinvest and engage in life. People have cited several examples of how this has helped the development of better family and other social relationships that may have deteriorated as a result of the patient's previous suicidal behaviour. Social functioning, by perhaps being able to leave the house or live independently where previously this had been problematic, was perceived as empowering. Reports of improved self-esteem and self-care (both personal and environmental) are linked to achievements evidenced by getting involved in work-related and other meaningful activities. In some cases, even quite some time after therapy, people reported still valuing and using the techniques of invoking positive memories, concentration, problem-solving and distraction skills taught by their therapist. The particular value of being given personalised resources such as tape recordings and written information by their therapist was evident, and these were still being used months later. Although realistically noone reported CBSP as a miracle cure, people who often entered therapy with little or no expectations gained tangible, self-defined benefits. While perhaps not entirely eliminating ongoing suicidal thoughts the intervention was perceived to help reduce these to a much less disabling level in which the individual had an array of skills and tools to challenge and prevent acting on such thoughts.

The future is looking bright, and there are now plans to build on our earlier studies in suicidology to further investigate and refine understanding of the precise psychological mechanisms of suicidality. Ideas abound concerning new, more innovative methods of delivering suicide preventative therapy to open up access to more people. Specific modalities such as e-technologies may offer acceptable user-friendly treatments, particularly for populations that are more challenging to engage, and in particular young people, especially men.

Other future directions for further study are to examine the application of CBSP to other populations of patient groups. As alluded to earlier, acute psychiatric wards are an obvious target owing to the ultra-high-risk environment as most in-patients are admitted precisely because they are seriously suicidal and judged to be so unsafe as to require 24-hour supervision. Sadly, that is generally exactly what they receive – supervision and containment without any evidence-based interventions to address the underlying psychological mechanisms responsible for suicidal behaviour. Therefore a proposal for a randomised controlled trial to introduce CBSP as an early intervention in acute psychiatric wards is currently being prepared (Awenat, 2012), the first stage of which will be a feasibility study to address several areas of uncertainty associated with contextual complexities of the setting.

Preliminary investigations of informally surveying the professional clinical psychology community and mental health patients suggests there to be only sporadic minimal (if any) input of clinical psychologists to acute psychiatric wards. There are some notable exceptions in the work of Drury (2000), who showed positive patient outcomes arising from a longitudinal study of CBT for in-patients experiencing acute psychosis, along with Durrant (2007) who reported on a pilot study of delivering psychological therapies to acute in-patients. However, no evidence of use of interventions specifically targeting suicide prevention was found, leading to the conclusion that the provision of psychological interventions in acute psychiatric wards remains extremely limited.

The recent report by Mind (2011) investigating conditions in acute wards identified strong public demand for psychological therapies for in-patients, recommending their use for suicidal patients. Although there appears to be a popular (untested) opinion in some quarters that acutely unwell patients would not be able to benefit from psychological therapy, patient testimonies within the Mind report refute this idea, suggesting that psychological therapies are likely to be valued and well received at precisely this time in order for acutely suicidal patients to make sense of their crisis and start to recover.

An additional arm of the proposed study will examine the health economics of cost-effectiveness of CBSPp compared to usual treatment. As mentioned earlier, the work of Kapur (1999, 2006) and others has illuminated some parts of the huge public health costs of the full burden of illness arising from all forms of suicidality, demonstrating that in addition to the humanitarian issues large amounts of public funds are used to little effect. Therefore a study testing the delivery of psychological therapy for in-patients is a priority, and targeting suicidal ideation and behaviour is likely to have a significant positive impact on patients' wellbeing and on service costs.

Personally my role over the past few years has evolved from suicidal in-patient to leading the research proposal development of an application for a major study to address an issue that I feel very strongly about. The support and encouragement I have received from all members of the Manchester Psychological Suicide Research Group has contributed to my 360-degree transformation facilitated by this proposal, which is my 'passion project'. In many ways the hard work required for this project has been therapeutic and has contributed to a welcome reawakening of my previous interests and abilities with consequent liberation from years of unproductive psychiatric dependency. (I say this with caution lest the American Psychiatric Association jump on this as an opportunity to add "Psychiatric Dependency Disorder" to DSM-V!)

A further reason why I am committed to working towards advancing higher levels of clinical psychology involvement into acute wards, which in some areas are psychologically toxic environments, is that I believe there to be many untapped benefits for both patient and staff groups of the strategic input of clinical psychologists working with ward teams to train, role-model, mentor and supervise enhanced psychologically informed practice. The necessary shift in culture and the change agent role that clinical psychologists could play is well described by Holmes (2002).

An interesting and useful area for future is the challenge of developing a service user-defined measure of recovery from suicidality. My experiences of being involved with the analysis of a qualitative study of community patients' experience of CBSP therapy indicated that many of the perceived benefits that participants identified as being beneficial outcomes for them were not evident within existing suicide and wider mental health evaluation instruments. From a research and clinical perspective this presents two problems: firstly, we do not currently have a scale that elicits outcomes that are relevant and meaningful to people; and secondly, the current outcome measures that are available are not recognising the issues of importance to them. There is therefore a need and clinical utility in undertaking some qualitative work to determine recognised recovery factors and indicators of progress or relapse leading to formation and validation of a quantitative measure with clinical and research utility.

The development of meaningful service user-defined outcome measures was an important component of other work undertaken within the Recovery Programme series of studies, in which the suicide studies described in this text were conducted. Haddock and colleagues worked closely with service user researchers and people with experience of psychosis to develop the Subjective Experience of Psychosis Scale (SEPS), described in more detail in Haddock et al. (2011). A further example of the successful development of user-defined scales is the Questionnaire about the Process of Recovery (QPR) developed by Neil and colleagues, which reflects substantial dissonances found between psychiatric views of indicators of progress or relapse and the views of people with 'lived experience' of the situation (Neil, Kilbride, Pitt et al. 2009).

Another area of unmet need relates to the situation of close family and friends of people who are suicidal. Constraints attributed to confidentiality and conflicting interests and needs often mean that the closest people to the suicidal individual are excluded from involvement in clinical decisions and rarely receive any personal support to address their own fears and needs. The dynamics of balance between family and friends being a protective as opposed to a driver for suicide is a precarious one. While social inclusion and good relationships are known to be positively influential in preventing suicide, there are also situations where a person is acutely aware of the stress and distress that they unintentionally place on loved ones, and genuinely feel that it would be in everyone's best interest if they killed themselves. Here the huge sense of being a burden, and the desire to protect loved ones from further distress, often perceived by the suicidal person at the time of suicidal crisis as likely to be permanent and unremitting, constitutes a powerful driver for suicide. This is an area of need of further study.

I am very aware of the impact of family stress arising from my own long period of mental distress, and it was only recently that I was heartbroken to learn how badly affected my own family had been during times when I did not even openly disclose that I felt suicidal and as such was unaware that they really knew the depth of my distress. This became apparent when I learned that one of my closest family members reflected that they were indeed aware of and understood my perceptions of intolerable unrelenting distress to the degree that they admitted to seriously questioning their own moral and ethical stance in constantly urging me to keep going.

They knew that I was only staying alive for their sake, having lost all hope and reason to want to live for myself, and battling with the inner conflict of wishing to die and convincing myself that they would have a better life without me, yet truly not wanting to hurt them. The question was whether it was fair to pressurise me to stay alive for their sake when it was apparent that I was suffering so much. The ability to mentalise is a gift but can also a burden, as evidenced here.

I am saddened to think that someone so very close to me experienced such a depth of insight into a situation that I tried to conceal from them that they really did share my suffering. I am so grateful for the unfailing support of my family without which I would definitely not be here to write this now. My family received absolutely no help or support from the statutory mental health services. The cost in terms of family mental and physical health morbidity for those bereaved by suicide is well known, even to the extent of the heightened risk of their own eventual death by suicide (Grad, 2011), but an area in need of urgent future research attention must be family needs.

Note: Throughout this chapter I make reference to people who have experience of mental distress by a number of terms, none of which are particularly satisfactory nor universally accepted within the professional and lay community. I hold major personal reservations of affiliation with the term 'service user' (which will be described in more detail elsewhere), but in the absence of an alternative have used it. This is my own view and may not necessarily be shared by other co-authors.

Chapter 11

Future directions in clinical research and new technologies

11.1. Executive summary

- *Intelligent Real Time Therapy:*
  - *Momentary assessments may provide the clinician with richer data to enhance the CBSPp formulation.*
  - *Momentary intervention strategies may offer situation specific methods of preventing or reducing suicidal states.*
  - *Momentary assessment and intervention strategies may confer specific advantages for clients with poor autobiographical and prospective memories.*
  - *A Reinforcement Learning algorithm may be utilised to coordinate the timing of the delivery of momentary interventions based on momentary assessment data.*

11.2. Intelligent Real Time Therapy (iRTT)

Our experiences of delivering CBSPp have led us to critically evaluate the delivery of CBT generally and to search for creative solutions to these difficulties. As discussed in Chapter 10, one of the difficulties in implementing CBSPp is that clients may struggle to remember and accurately render their experiences for standard retrospective assessment procedures and may struggle to remember to implement intervention strategies in their everyday lives. For this reason, we looked to technological solutions to (1) conduct momentary assessments, (2) enable momentary interventions and (3) optimise the timing of such interventions towards the goal of reducing suicidal ideation, intent and planning. We have outlined a conceptual framework for this elsewhere (Kelly et al., accepted) and summarise the important points below.

11.2.1. Momentary assessments

Experience Sampling Methodology (ESM; Csikszentmihalyi & Larson, 1987; Delespaul, 1995; Palmier Claus et al., 2011) has emerged as an important research and clinical tool. ESM takes a number of measurements over the course of a day to 'sample' the person's experience at different time points. Respondents answer in accordance to how they currently feel or how they have felt since the last beep, a time period not normally longer than a couple of hours. Respondents may do this by filling in a paper diary, using a Palm Pilot or by using a specialised phone application made possible by SMART phones. The diary can sample a number of different elements of experience. So, in the case of suicide, a client may answer questions about their current affective state, the level to which they endorse key suicidal appraisals and behaviours, and general coping strategies or safety behaviours that they have employed. Experiences of psychosis may also be measured.

This level of data collection allows for an analysis of change over time and a more complex modelling of relationships between core variables that amplify or attenuate the suicidal experience. The data is collected in a person's natural environment and does not suffer from difficulties related to an over-general and negatively focused recall style.

Summaries of momentary data may be used to explore the role of memory in connection to appraisals in therapy. For example, a person may not remember any positive experiences and thus predict no future positive events. An analysis of ESM data allows such statements to be tested for their validity. Clients may well discover that their memories are over-general and influenced by how they are currently feeling, which may loosen the grip of hopelessness; positive experiences may happen again.

Such assessments may provide data on the times when suicide may become particularly likely, leading to specific suicide reduction strategies. An example may be verbal prompts linked to exercises exploring and broadening negative beliefs about suicide. Also, following Broaden & Build theory (Frederickson & Branigan, 2005; Frederickson, Cohn, Coffey, Pek & Finkel, 2008; Garland et al, 2010), periods of naturally occurring positive emotions may be identified and then amplified with momentary interventions, with the purpose of regulating threat-based affect, for example, a video clip of a warm moment with a friend.

In summary, momentary assessments seem to offer a number of advantages in the more accurate assessment of experiences pertinent to suicide and provide data to form the basis for a strategic implementation of momentary intervention strategies. Such data can also be used to test model-driven hypotheses to test the SAMS model and further develop the theoretical understanding of suicide.

11.2.3. Momentary interventions

The advent of SMART phones has led to increased access to mobile, portable, computer technology with the capability to deliver multimedia content to people in their natural environments. This clearly offers the CBSPp therapist a number of new avenues to explore in the delivery of 'ecological momentary interventions' (Heron & Smyth, 2010). Other areas of technological development have further closed the gap between the therapy room and a person's natural setting. These have included desktop computer programs that can be used at home or in the clinic, virtual reality (Gregg & Tarrier, 2007), interactive voice systems (Newman et al., 2011), palmtop computer programs (Depp et al., 2010; Heron & Smyth, 2010), SMS messages and mobile phones (Bang et al., 2007; Depp et al., 2010; Flynn et al., 1992; Free et al., 2011).

The SMART phone has two main advantages as a technology to exploit in future therapies. Firstly, as stated, it can deliver multimedia content. This allows the client and therapist to develop media that can be accessed 'in-situ', taking the form of SMS messages, audio clips, music, photos or videos. BMACs may be used that invoke imagery of specific memories and that elicit suicide-incongruent appraisals. The client may develop their own media, and ask those around them to contribute. This may provide them with a rich array of moments captured from the course of their everyday life that can be reviewed at times of need. For instance, a person may develop a video clip of their mother saying how much she loves them; an audio clip of a friend telling a joke; a photo of the client with a newborn baby, to whom they are related or closely linked. These media can then be assessed in therapy and their specific role in moderating suicidal processes can be evaluated, enabling them to be used at specific times to prevent suicide.

11.2.4. Optimising momentary interventions: Reinforcement learning

Momentary interventions seem to offer much to the client experiencing suicidal experiences, and may offer means of increasing access to natural moderators of specific suicidal experiences, that is, reminding a person about their negative beliefs about suicide, reasons to live and hope for the future. Such media may also be used to maintain or even amplify 'suicide-incongruent' states characterised by positive emotions that could, over time, come to increase resilience to suicide (Frederickson, 2005, 2008). In fact, Garland et al. (2010) suggest that if a person experiences positive emotions and negative emotions at a ratio of 3:1, long-term regulation of the threat-based emotions will begin to occur.

The data made available from momentary assessments, and the wide range of interventions made possible by the advent of portable devices capable of delivering multimedia content, leads to an important question: how do the client and therapist identify what interventions should be administered, and when should they be administered? As discussed in our paper on intelligent Real Time Therapies (iRTT; Kelly et al., in press), we believe that a third component may be functioning to optimise this process, namely, a reinforcement learning algorithm (Sutton & Barko, 1998).

We suggest that the development of a learning algorithm will allow us to achieve a process whereby interventions are rewarded for their impact on reducing experiences of suicidality. Ongoing momentary assessments and frequent use of validated measures of suicide can be used to evaluate the interventions for their effectiveness for each individual. An example can help to elucidate this process. If a person is experiencing increased suicidal ideation, a multimedia clip may be triggered containing a text-based affirmation to 'breathe and switch attention away from their experiences', followed by a video clip of them at a recent family party. If this happens a number of times, data is available on subsequent momentary assessments to evaluate the effectiveness of the intervention in reducing suicidal ideation. This data alters the reward value attached to the intervention, that is, decreased suicidal ideation results in a higher reward. A higher reward value then increases the possibility that this media will be administered in similar situations in the future. A lower reward value decreases the possibility that this intervention will be triggered.

Interventions may be classified for their functionality, for example, to boost positive affect, or as an acute method of reducing current suicidal thoughts, rules may be developed as to when to administer them. A process called 'bootstrapping' (Sutton & Barko, 1998) then allows the system to test these rules and amend them to each person. A fascinating prospect is that the more people the algorithm is exposed to, the more sensitive it should become. If such a system were allowed to mature, it may be able to implement an intervention strategy found to be effective for individuals with similar ESM data profiles, and then vary the delivery of interventions for each individual. This captures the essential elements of a psychological formulation: drawing from an empirical, nomothetic, evidence base as to what interventions work to ameliorate specific disorders or psychological mechanisms, and then adjusting this based on ongoing, idiosyncratic, data collection from the individual in therapy. We therefore suggest that developments in applying the power of machine learning and reinforcement learning in particular (Sutton & Barko, 1998) may offer much in the optimisation of the strategic delivery of momentary intervention strategies in reducing suicide (Kelly et al., in press).

11.3. Appendix

The following are some materials you might find helpful:

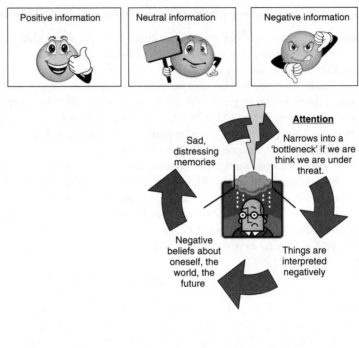

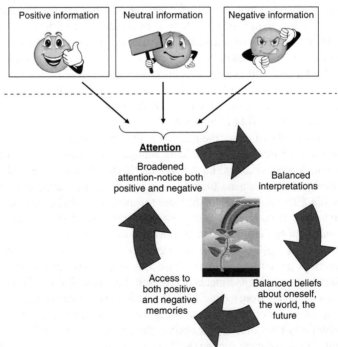

This sheet can help you to focus on neutral memories. You can discuss this further with your therapist.

Think of a recent event in your life that did not have strong emotions connected to it. Write down a short description below:

Where were you? Write down as many details of where you were.

Who were you with? Write down all the people in the memory.

What happened? Write down in as much detail as possible.

How did you feel? Write down your emotions/feelings – try and describe them in as much detail as possible.

What went through your mind?

11.4. Generic BMAC procedure

In combination with the Positive Memory Interview, the following procedure may be followed by the client for their own use. The therapist may record themselves reading this out at an appropriate pace so the client can use this by themselves.

- Think about past week. Think about a good memory, an event or person.
- Write down the details of the memory using the sheet:
  - Relaxation.
  - Breathing.
  - Attention to body.
- Allow your attention to move to positive experience.
- Where were you?
  - Inside our outside?
  - Try and focus on what you can see:
    - Move around memory – build the scene in your mind.
- Outside – what was weather like?
  - Ground?
  - What could you see?
  - Focus on each thing around you.
- Inside
  - Floor.
  - Walls.
  - Furniture.
    - Was there anybody else in the image?
- For each person:
  - Person 1: Focus on their faces:
    - What was their expression?
- Look at their eyes – the colour.
- Look at their nose.
- Look at their mouth.
    - What were they wearing?
- Focus on their clothes – the colour.
    - What were they doing?
- Recreate the image of what they were doing in your mind.
  - Person 2: Focus on their faces:
    - What was their expression?
- Look at their eyes – the colour.
- Look at their nose.
- Look at their mouth.
    - What were they wearing?
- Focus on their clothes – the colour.
    - What were they doing?

- Recreate the image of what they were doing in your mind.
  - o Try and focus on what you could hear.
    - ▪ Allow the sounds to fill your mind.
- If there were people in the memory, try and focus on their voice, the tone.
- What did they say? Try and recreate the sound of the words.
    - ▪ Other sounds in environment:
- Think through each sound and allow it to fill your mind.
  - o Try and focus on the smells in the memory.
    - ▪ Any food/drink?
    - ▪ Perfume/Aftershave?
    - ▪ If you're outside, are there any smells in the scene, fresh grass?
  - o Try and focus on any taste in this memory.
    - ▪ Did you eat or drink anything?
    - ▪ Really savour the taste of this, allow the memory to fill your mind.
  - o Try and focus on the feel of things in the memory.
    - ▪ Did you touch anything? How did it feel?
- You are free to move around this image at your will.
- May be choose a strongest point you can return to if it begins to fade.
- Think of a word to bring you back at any point.
- Focus now on the strongest bit and the most positive bit of this memory.
- How did it make you feel?
  - o Allow the feelings to wash over you, to fill your mind.
  - o Really savour this feeling.
- Think of a word to bring you back at any point.
- Think about what this memory means to you.
- What went through your mind?
- Why was it important to you?
- Think of a word to bring you back at any point.
- If there were other people in this memory, how did they feel?
- How does that make you feel – that they feel like this?
- What does it mean to you that other people think or feel this way about you?
- What does this memory mean about your life?
- How can this memory help?
- How does it show your positive qualities? Think about these qualities.
- Once again think about the feeling and allow it to fill your mind. You can come back to this at any time. Think of the word that could bring you back here at any time you want to.
- Just begin to become aware of the room you are in.
- When you are ready, open your eyes.

Maybe you want to add more details to your sheet or write a new one. You may want to write down a word you thought of.

References

Preface

Bolton, C., Gooding, P., Kapur, N., Barrowclough, C. & Tarrier, N. (2007) Developing psychological perspectives of suicidal behaviour and risk in people with a diagnosis of schizophrenia: We know they kill themselves but do we understand why? *Clinical Psychology Review, 27*, 511–536.

Johnson, J., Gooding, P. & Tarrier, N. (2008) Suicide risk in schizophrenia: Explanatory models and clinical implications: The Schematic Appraisal Model of Suicide (SAMS). *Psychology & Psycho-therapy, 81*, 55–77.

Johnson, J., Gooding, P.A., Wood, A.M. & Tarrier, N. (2010) Resilience as positive coping appraisals: Testing the Schematic Appraisals Model of Suicide (SAMS). *Behaviour Research & Therapy, 48*, 179–186.

Johnson, J., Wood, A., Gooding, P., Taylor, P. & Tarrier, N. (2011) Resilience to suicidality: The Buffering Hypothesis. *Clinical Psychology Review, 31*, 563–591.

Panagioti, M., Gooding, P.A. & Tarrier, N. (2009) Post-traumatic stress disorder and suicidal behaviour: A qualitative review. *Clinical Psychology Review, 29*, 471–482.

Picken, A. & Tarrier, N. (2011) Trauma and co-morbid PTSD in individuals with schizophrenia and substance abuse. *Comprehensive Psychiatry, 52*, 490–497.

Pratt,D., Gooding, P., Johnson, J., Taylor, P. & Tarrier, N. (2010) Suicide schemas in non-affective psychosis: An empirical investigation. *Behaviour Research and Therapy, 48*, 1211–1220.

Tarrier, N. & Gooding P. (2007) Treatment Manual: Cognitive Behavioural Suicide Prevention for Psychosis (CBSPp). University of Manchester: Unpublished treatment manual.

Tarrier, N. & Picken, A.(2011) Co-morbid PTSD and suicidality in individuals with schizophrenia and substance abuse. *Social Psychiatry & Psychiatric Epidemiology, 46*, 1079–1086.

Tarrier, N., Taylor, K. & Gooding, P. (2008) Cognitive-behavioural interventions to reduce suicide behaviour: A systematic review and meta-analysis. *Behavior Modification, 32*, 77–108.

Tarrier, N., Gooding, P., Gregg, L., Johnson, J., Drake, R. & The Socrates Trial group (2007) Suicide schema in schizophrenia: The effect of emotional reactivity, negative symptoms and schema elaboration. *Behaviour Research and Therapy, 45*, 2090–2092.

Taylor, P.J., Wood, A.M., Gooding, P., Johnson, J. & Tarrier, N. (2009) Are defeat and entrapment best defined as a single construct? *Personality & Individual Difference, 47*, 795–797.

Taylor, P.J., Gooding, P., Wood, A.M., Johnson, J. Pratt, D. & Tarrier, N. (2010a) Defeat and entrapment in schizophrenia: The relationship with non-lethal suicide behaviour and positive psychotic symptoms. *Psychiatry Research, 178*, 244–248.

Taylor, P.J., Wood, A.M., Gooding, P.A. & Tarrier, N. (2010b) Appraisals and suicidality: The mediating role of defeat and entrapment. *Archives of Suicide Research, 14*, 236–247.

Taylor, P.J., Gooding, P.A., Wood, A.M. & Tarrier, N. (2010c) Memory specificity as a risk-factor for suicidality in non-affective psychosis: The ability to recall specific autobiographical memories is related to greater suicidality. *Behaviour Research and Therapy, 48*, 1047–1052.

Taylor, P.J., Gooding, P.A., Wood, A.M. & Tarrier, N. (2011) The role of defeat and entrapment in depression, anxiety and suicide. *Psychological Bulletin, 137*, 391–420.

1 Suicide: the problem

American Psychiatric Association (2000) *Diagnostic and Statistical Manual for Mental Disorders*, 4th edition (text revision). Washington, DC: APA.

Appleby, L., Shaw, J., Sherratt, J., Amos, T., Robinson, J., McDonnell R., McCann K., Parsons, R., Burns, J., Bickley, H., Kiernan, K., Wren, J., Hunt, I., Davies, S. & Harris, C. (2001) *Safety First: National Confidential Inquiry into Suicide and Homicide by People with Mental Illness*. London: Department of Health.

Babor, T., Higgins-Biddle, J., Saunders, J., de la Fuente, J.R. & Grant, M. (2001) *AUDIT: The Alcohol Use Disorders Identification Test: Guidelines for use in Primary Care*, 2nd edition. Geneva: World Health Organisation.

Barraclough, B., Bunch, J., Nelson, B. & Sainsbury, P. (1974) A hundred cases of suicide: Clinical aspects. *British Journal of Psychiatry, 125*, 355–373.

Beautrais, A.L., Joyce, P.R., Mulder, R.T., Ferguson, D.M., Deavoll, B.J. & Nightingale, S.K. (1996) Prevalence and comorbidity of mental disorders in persons making serious suicide attempts: A case-control study. *American Journal of Psychiatry, 153*, 1009–1014.

Breslau, N., Kessler, R.C., Chilcoat, H.D., Schultz, L.R., Davis, G.C. & Andreski, P. (1998) Trauma and Posttraumatic Stress Disorder in the community: The 1996 Detroit Area Survey of Trauma. *Archives of General Psychiatry, 55*, 626–632.

Caces, F.E. & Harford, T. (1998) Time series analysis of alcohol consumption and suicide mortality in the United States, 1934–1987. *Journal of Studies on Alcohol, 59*, 455–461.

Caldwell, C.B. & Gottesman, I.I. (1992) Schizophrenia – A high risk factor for suicide: Clues to risk reduction. *Suicide and Life Threatening Behaviour, 22*, 479–493.

Cavanagh, J.T.O., Carson, A.J., Sharpe, M. & Lawrie, S.M. (2003) Psychological autopsy studies of suicide: A systematic review. *Psychological Medicine, 33*, 395–405.

Charlton, J., Kelly, S., Dunnell, K., Evans, B., Jenkins, R. & Wallis, R. (1992) Trends in suicide deaths in England and Wales. *Population Trends, 69*, 10–16.

Cheng, A.T., Mann, A.H. & Chan, K.A. (1997) Personality disorder and suicide: A case-control study. *British Journal of Psychiatry, 170*, 441–446.

Cheng, A.T.A. (1995) Mental illness and suicide. *Archives of General Psychiatry, 52*, 594–603.

Cheng, A.T.A. & Lee, C.-S. (2000) Suicide in Asia and the Far East. In K. Hawton & C. Van Heeringen (eds) *The International Handbook of Suicide and Attempted Suicide*. Chichester: John Wiley & Sons, 29–48.

Conwell, Y., Duberstein, P.R., Cox, C., Herrmann, J.H., Forbes, N.T. & Caine, E.D. (1996) Relationships between age and axis I diagnoses in victims of completed suicide: A psychological autopsy study. *American Journal of Psychiatry, 153*, 1001–1008.

Conwell, Y., Duberstein, P.R., Cox, C., Herrmann, J.H., Forbes, N.T. & Caine, E.D. (1998) Age differences in behaviors leading to completed suicide. *American Journal of Geriatric Psychiatry, 6*, 122–126.

Cooper, J., Kapur, N., Webb, R., Lawlor, M., Guthrie, E., Mackway-Jones, K. & Appleby, L. (2005) Suicide after deliberate self-harm: A 4 year cohort study. *American Journal of Psychiatry, 162*, 297–303.

Crombie, I.K. (1989) Trends in suicide and unemployment in Scotland, 1976–1986. *British Medical Journal, 298*, 782–784.

De Hert, M. & Peuskens, J. (2000) Psychiatric aspects of suicidal behaviour: Schizophrenia. In K. Hawton & C. Van Heeringen (eds) *The International Handbook of Suicide and Attempted Suicide*. Chichester: John Wiley & Sons, 121–135.

Diekstra, R.F.W. & Garnefski, N. (1995) On the nature, magnitude, and causality of suicidal behaviors: An international perspective. *Suicide and Life Threatening Behavior, 25*, 36–57.

Duberstein, P.R., Conwell, Y., Conner, K.R., Eberly, S., Evinger, J.S. & Caine, E.D. (2004) Poor social integration and suicide: Fact or artifact? A case-control study. *Psychological Medicine, 34*, 1331–1337.

Dumais, A., Lesage, A.D., Alda, M., Rouleau, G., Dumont, M., Chawky, N., Roy, M., Mann, J.J., Benkelfat, C. & Turecki, G. (2005) Risk factors for suicide completion in major depression: A case-control study of impulsive and aggressive behaviors in men. *American Journal of Psychiatry, 162*, 2116–2124.

Durkheim, E. (1897) *Le Suicide*. Translated in 1952 as *Suicide: A Study in Sociology*, by J.A. Spalding & G. Simpson. London: Routledge & Kegan Paul.

Ferrada-Noli, M., Asberg, M., Ormstad, K., Lundin, T. & Sundbom, E. (1998) Suicidal behavior after severe trauma. Part 1: PTSD diagnoses, psychiatric comorbidity, and assessments of suicidal behavior. *Journal of Traumatic Stress, 11*, 103–112.

Foster, T., Gillespie, K., McClelland, R. & Patterson, C. (1999) Risk factors for suicide independent of DSM-III-R Axis I disorder: Case-control psychological autopsy study in Northern Ireland. *British Journal of Psychiatry, 175*, 175–179.

Frans, O., Rimmo, P.A., Aberg, L. & Fredrikson, M. (2005) Trauma exposure and post-traumatic stress disorder in the general population. *Acta Psychiatrica Scandinavica, 111*, 291–299.

Gradus, J.L., Qin, P., Lincoln, A.K., Miller, M., Laweler, E., Sorensen, H.T. & Lash, T.L. (2010) Posttraumatic Stress Disorder and completed suicide. *American Journal of Epidemiology, 171*(6), 721–727.

Gunnell, D., Lopatatzidis, A., Dorling, D., Wehner, H., Southall, H. & Frankel, S. (1999) Suicide and unemployment in young people: Analysis of trends in England and Wales 1921–1995. *British Journal of Psychiatry, 175*, 263–270.

Gunnell, D., Middleton, N., Whitley, E., Dorling, D. & Frankell, S. (2003) Why are suicide rates rising in young men but falling in the elderly? – A time series analysis of trends in England and Wales 1950–1998. *Social Sciences and Medicine, 57*, 595–611.

Harkary-Friedman, J.M., Restifo, K., Malaspina, D., Kaufman, C.A., Amador, X.F., Yale, S.A. & Gorman, J.M. (1999) Suicidal behavior in schizophrenia: Characteristics of individuals who had and had not attempted suicide. *American Journal of Psychiatry, 156*, 1276–1278.

Harris, E.C. & Barraclough, B. (1997) Suicide as an outcome for mental disorders: A meta-analysis. *British Journal of Psychiatry, 170*, 205–228.

Hawton, K. (2000) Sex and suicide: Gender differences in suicidal behavior. *British Journal of Psychiatry, 177*, 484–485.

Hawton, K., Appleby, L., Platt, S., Foster, T., Cooper, J., Malmberg, A. & Simkin, S. (1998) The psychological autopsy approach to studying suicide: A review of methodological issues. *Journal of Affective Disorders, 50*, 269–276.

Hawton, K., Harriss, L., Hadder, K., Simkin, S. & Gunnell, D. (2001) The influence of the economic and social environment on deliberate self harm and suicide: An ecological and person-based study. *Psychological Medicine, 31*(5), 827–836.

Hawton, K. & van Heeringen, K. (eds) (2000) *The International Handbook of Suicide and Attempted Suicide*. New York: Wiley.

Heikkinen, M.E., Isometsä, E.T., Marttunen, M.J., Aro, H.M. & Lönnqvist, J.K. (1995) Social factors in suicide. *British Journal of Psychiatry, 167*, 747–753.

Heila, H., Isometsa, E.T., Henriksson, M.M., Heikkinen, M.E., Martinnen, M.J. & Loonqvist, J.K. (1997) Suicide and schizophrenia: A nationwide psychological autopsy study on age and sex specific clinical characteristics of 92 suicide victims with schizophrenia. *American Journal of Psychiatry, 154*, 1235–1242.

Henriksson, M., Aro, H.M., Martunnen, M.J.m Heikkinen, M.E. Isometsa, E.T., Kuoppasalmi, K.I. & Loonqvist, J.K. (1993) Mental disorders and comorbidity in suicide. *American Journal of Psychiatry, 150*, 935–940.

Isometsa, E.T. & Lonnqvist, J.K. (1998) Suicide attempts preceding completed suicide. *British Journal of Psychiatry, 173*, 531–535.

Jenkins, G.R., Hale, R., Papanastassiou, M., Crawford, M.J. & Tyrer, P. (2002) Suicide rate 22 years after parasuicide cohort study. *British Medical Journal, 325*, 1155.

Kendell, R.E. & Zealley, A.K. (eds) (1993) *Companion to Psychiatric Studies.* Edinburgh: Churchill Livingstone.

Kessler, R.C., Borges, G. & Walters, E.E. (1999) Prevalence of and risk factors for lifetime suicide attempts in the National Comorbidity Survey. *Archives of General Psychiatry, 56*(7), 617–626.

Kessler, R.C., Sonnega, A., Bromet, E., Hughes, M. & Nelson, C.B. (1995) Posttraumatic stress disorder in the National Comorbidity Survey. *Archives of General Psychiatry, 52*, 1048–1060.

Kposowa, A.J. (2000) Marital status and suicide in the National Longitudinal Mortality Study. *Journal of Epidemiology and Community Health, 54*, 254–261.

Lester, D. (1997) An empirical examination of Thomas Masryk's theory of suicide. *Archives of Suicide Research, 3*, 125–131.

Lester, D. & Yang, B. (1991) The relationship between divorce, unemployment and female participation in the labour force and suicide rates in Australia and America. *Australian and New Zealand Journal of Psychiatry, 25*, 519–523.

Lester, D., Curran, P.S. & Yang, B. (1991) Time regression results of suicide rates by social correlates for the USA and Northern Ireland. *Irish Journal of Psychological Medicine, 8*, 26–28.

Low, A.A., Farmer, R.D., Jones, D.R. & Rohde, J.R. (1981) Suicide in England and Wales: An analysis of 100 years, 1876–1975, *Psychological Medicine, 11*, 359–368.

Luoma, J.B. & Pearson, J.L. (2002) Suicide and marital status in the United States, 1991–1996: Is widowhood a risk factor? *American Journal of Public Health, 92*(9), 1518–1522.

McCloud, A., Barnaby, B., Omu, N., Drummond, C. & Aboud, A. (2004) Relationship between alcohol use disorders and suicidality in a psychiatric population: In-patient prevalence study. *British Journal of Psychiatry, 184*, 439–445.

McClure, G.M.G. (2000) Changes in suicide in England and Wales, 1960–1997. *British Journal of Psychiatry, 176*, 64–67.

Makela, P. (1996) Alcohol consumption and suicide mortality by age among Finnish men, 1950–1991. *Addiction, 91*, 101–112.

Mann, J.J. (2002)A current perspective of suicide and attempted suicide. *Annals of Internal Medicine, 136*, 302–311.

Mann, J.J., Waternaux, C., Hass, G.L. & Malone, K.M. (1999) Toward a clinical model of suicidal behaviour in psychiatric patients. *American Journal of Psychiatry, 156*(2), 181–189.

Meltzer, H.J. & Fatemi, H. (1995) Suicide in schizophrenia: The effects of clozapine. *Clinical Neuropharmacology, 18*(s), 18–24.

Mortensen, P.B., Agerbo, E., Erikson, T., Qin, P. & Westergaard-Nielsen, N. (2000) Psychiatric illness and risk factors for suicide in Denmark. *Lancet, 355*, 9–12.

Neeleman, J. Halpern, D., Leon, D. & Lewis G. (1997) Tolerance of suicide, religion and suicide rates: An ecological and individual study in 19 Western countries. *Psychological Medicine, 27*(5), 1165–1171.

Neria, Y., Bromet, E.J., Sievers, S., Lavelle, J. & Fochtmann, L.J. (2002) Trauma exposure and post-traumatic stress disorder in psychosis: Findings from a first-admission cohort. *Journal of Consulting and Clinical Psychology, 70*, 246–251.

Norström, T. (1995) Alcohol and suicide: A comparative analysis of France and Sweden. *Addiction, 90*, 1493–1469.

Office for National Statistics (2010) *Social Trends, No.40.* London: Office for National Statistics.

Office for National Statistics (2011) *Mortality Statistics: Deaths Registered in England and Wales (Series DR).* London: Office for National Statistics.

Owens, D., Horrocks, J. & House, A. (2002) Fatal and non-fatal repetition of self-harm. *British Journal of Psychiatry, 181*, 193–199.

Palmer, B.A., Pankratz, S. & Bostwick, J.M. (2005) The lifetime risk of suicide in schizophrenia. *Archives of General Psychiatry, 62*, 247–253.

Panagioti, M., Gooding, P. & Tarrier, N. (2009) Post-traumatic stress disorder and suicidal behavior: A narrative review. *Clinical Psychology Review, 29*, 471–482.

Pritchard, C. (1992) Is there a link between suicide in young men and unemployment? A comparison of the UK with other European Community Countries. *British Journal of Psychiatry, 160*, 750–756.

Qin, P, Agerbo, E. & Mortenson, P.B. (2003) Suicide risk in relation to socio-economic, demographic, psychiatric and familial factors: A national register-based study of all suicides in Denmark, 1981–1997. *American Journal of Psychiatry, 160*, 765–772.

Qin, P., Agerbo, E., Westergård-Nielsen, N., Eriksson, T. & Mortensen, P.B. (2000) Gender differences in risk factors for suicide in Denmark, *British Journal of Psychiatry, 177*, 546–550.

Ramstedt, M. (2001) Alcohol and suicide in 14 European countries. *Addiction, 96* (Supplement 1), S59–S75.

Rossau, C.D. & Mortensen, P.B. (1997) Risk factors for suicide in patients with schizophrenia: Nested case-control study. *British Journal of Psychiatry, 171*, 355–359.

Roy, A. (1982) Risk factors for suicide in psychiatric patients. *Archives in General Psychiatry, 39*, 1089–1095.

Sareen, J., Cox, B.J., Goodwin, R.D. & Asmundson, G.J.G. (2005) Co-occurrence of posttraumatic stress disorder with positive psychotic symptoms in a nationally representative sample. *Journal of Traumatic Stress, 18*, 313–322.

Sareen, J., Houlahan, T., Cox, B. & Asmundson, G. (2005) Anxiety disorders associated with suicidal ideation and suicide attempts in the National Comorbidity Survey. *Journal of Nervous & Mental Disease, 193*, 450–454.

Schmidtke, A., Bille-Brahe, U., DeLeo, D., Kerkhof, A., Bjerke, T., Crepet, P., Haring, C., Hawton, K., Lonnqvist, J., Michel, K., Pommereau, X., Querejeta, I., Phillipe, I., Salander-Renberg, E., Temesvary, B., Wasserman, D., Fricke, S., Weinacker, B. & Sampaio-Faria, J.G. (1996) Attempted suicide in Europe: Rates, trends and sociodemographic characteristics of suicide attempters during the period 1989–1992. Results of the WHO/EURO Multicentre Study on Parasuicide. *Acta Psychiatrica Scandinavica, 93*(5), 327–338.

Schneidman, E. (1981) The psychological autopsy. *Suicide and Life Threatening Behavior, 11*, 325–340.

Seedat, S. & Stein, M.B. (2001) Post-traumatic stress disorder: A review of recent findings. *Current Psychiatry Reports, 3*, 288–294.

Skog, O.J. (1991) Alcohol and suicide: Durkheim revisited. *Acta Sociologica, 34*, 193–206.

Southall, H. (1998) Working with historical statistics on poverty and economic distress. In D. Dorling & S. Simpson (eds) *Statistics in Society*. London: Arnold, 350–358.

Stack, S. (1983) The effect of religious commitment on suicide: A cross-national sample. *Journal of Health and Social Behaviour, 24*, 362–374.

Stack, S. & Lester, D. (1991) The effect of religion on suicide ideation. *Social Psychiatry and Psychiatric Epidemiology, 26*, 168–170.

Strauss, J.L., Calhoun, P.S., Marx, C.E., Stechuchak, K.M., Oddone, E.Z., Swartz, M.S. & Butterfield, M.I. (2006) Comorbid posttraumatic stress disorder is associated with suicidality in male veterans with schizophrenia or schizoaffective disorder. *Schizophrenia Research, 84*, 165–169.

Suominen, K., Isometsa, E.T., Suokas, J., Haukka, J., Achte, K. & Lonnqvist, J.K. (2004) Completed suicide after a suicide attempt: A 37 year follow-up study. *American Journal of Psychiatry, 161*(3), 563–564.

Tarrier, N. & Picken, A. (2010) Co-morbid PTSD and suicidality in individuals with schizophrenia and substance and alcohol abuse. *Social Psychiatry and Psychiatric Epidemiology, 46*, 1079–1086.

Tarrier, N., Khan, S., Cater, J. & Picken, A. (2007) The subjective consequences of suffering a first episode psychosis: Trauma and suicide behaviour. *Social Psychiatry and Psychiatric Epidemiology, 42*, 29–35.

van Heeringen, K. (2001) *Understanding Suicidal Behaviour: The Suicidal Process Approach to Research, Treatment and Prevention*. London: Wiley.

Verbrugge, L.M. (1979) Marital status and health. *Journal of Marriage and the Family, 41*, 267–285. In A.J. Kposowa (2000) Marital status and suicide in the National Longitudinal Mortality Study. *Journal of Epidemiology and Community Health, 54*, 254–261.

Walsh, E., Harvey, K., Whire, I., Higgitt, A., Fraser, J. & Murray, R. (2001) Suicidal behaviour in psychosis: Prevalence and predictors from a randomised controlled trial of case management. *British Journal of Psychiatry, 178*, 255–260.

Warnes, H. (1968) Suicide in schizophrenics. *Diseases of the Nervous System, 29*(5), Supplement, 35–40.

Weyerer, S. & Wiedenmann, A. (1995) Economic factors and the rates of suicide in Germany between 1881 and 1989. *Psychological Reports, 76*, 1331–1341.

World Health Organisation (1999) *Figures and Facts about Suicide*. Geneva: World Health Organisation.

World Health Organisation (2002) *Suicide Prevention in Europe: The WHO European Monitoring Survey on National Suicide Prevention Programmes and Strategies*. Geneva: World Health Organisation.

Wulsin, L.R., Vaillant, G.E. & Wells, V.E. (1999) A systematic review of the mortality of depression. *Psychosomatic Medicine, 61*, 6–17.

WVS Study Group (1994) World Values Survey (1981–1984 and 1990–1993) (computer file). Institute for Social Research (producer) and Inter university Consortium for Political and Social Research (distributor): Ann Arbor. In J. Neeleman, D. Halpern, D. Leon & G. Lewis (1997) Tolerance of suicide, religion and suicide rates: An ecological and individual study in 19 Western countries. *Psychological Medicine, 27*(5), 1165–1171.

Yen, S., Shea, M.T., Pagano, M., Sanislow, C.A., Grilo, C.M., McGlashan, T.H., Skodol, A.E., Bender, D.S., Zanarini, M.C., Gunderson, J.G. & Morey, L.C. (2003) Axis I and Axis II disorders as predictors of prospective suicide attempts: Findings from the Collaborative Longitudinal Personality Disorders Study. *Journal of Abnormal Psychology, 112*(3), 375–381.

2 A theoretical approach to understanding suicide

Addington, J. & Addington, D. (2008) Social and cognitive functioning in psychosis. *Schizophrenia Research, 99*(1–3), 176–181. doi: 10.1016/j.schres.2007.07.004.

Barrowclough, C. & Hooley, J.M. (2003) Attributions and expressed emotion: A review. *Clinical Psychology Review, 23*(6), 849–880.

Baumeister, R.F. (1990) Suicide as escape from self. *Psychological Review, 97*(1), 90–113.

Beattie, N., Shannon, C., Kavanagh, M. & Mulholland, C. (2009) Predictors of PTSD symptoms in response to psychosis and psychiatric admission. *Journal of Nervous and Mental Disease, 197*(1), 56–60.

Beck, A.T. (1986). Hopelessness as a predictor of eventual suicide. *Annals of the New York Academy of Sciences, 487*, 90–96.

Beck, A.T., Steer, R.A., Beck, J.S. & Newman, C.F. (1993) Hopelessness, depression, suicidal ideation, and clinical-diagnosis of depression. *Suicide and Life-Threatening Behavior, 23*(2), 139–145.

Birchwood, M. & Spencer, E. (2001) Early intervention in psychotic relapse. *Clinical Psychology Review, 21*(8), 1211–1226.

Birchwood, M., Iqbal, Z. & Upthegrove, R. (2005) Psychological pathways to depression in schizophrenia – Studies in acute psychosis, post psychotic depression and auditory hallucinations. *European Archives of Psychiatry and Clinical Neuroscience, 255*(3), 202–212.

Birchwood, M., Meaden, A., Trower, P., Gilbert, P. & Plaistow, J. (2000) The power and omnipotence of voices: Subordination and entrapment by voices and significant others. *Psychological Medicine, 30*(2), 337–344.

Birchwood, M., Trower, P., Brunet, K., Gilbert, P., Iqbal, Z. & Jackson, C. (2007) Social anxiety and the shame of psychosis: A study in first episode psychosis. *Behaviour Research and Therapy, 45*(5), 1025–1037.

Blankstein, K.R., Flett, G.L. & Johnston, M.E. (1992) Depression, problem-solving ability, and problem-solving appraisals. *Journal of Clinical Psychology, 48*(6), 749–759.

Blumenthal, S.J. (1988) Suicide –Aguide to risk-factors, assessment, and treatment of suicidal patients. *Medical Clinics of North America, 72*(4), 937–971.

Blumenthal, S.J. & Kupfer, D.J. (1988) Overview of early detection and treatment strategies for suicidal-behavior in young-people. *Journal of Youth and Adolescence, 17*(1), 1–23.

Bolton, C., Gooding, P., Kapur, N., Barrowclough, C. & Tarrier, N. (2007) Developing psychological perspectives of suicidal behaviour and risk in people with a diagnosis of schizophrenia: We know they kill themselves but do we understand why? *Clinical Psychology Review, 27*(4), 511–536.

Brezo, J., Paris, J. & Turecki, G. (2006) Personality traits as correlates of suicidal ideation, suicide attempts, and suicide completions: A systematic review. *Acta Psychiatrica Scandinavica, 113*(3), 180–206. doi: 10.1111/j.1600-0447.2005.00702.x.

Broome, M.R., Johns, L.C., Valli, I., Woolley, J.B., Tabraham, P. & Brett, C. (2007) Delusion formation and reasoning biases in those at clinical high risk for psychosis. *British Journal of Psychiatry, 191*, S38–S42. doi: 10.1192/bjp.191.51.s38.

Buchy, L., Woodward, T.S. & Liotti, M. (2007) A cognitive bias against disconfirmatory evidence (BADE) is associated with schizotypy. *Schizophrenia Research, 90*(1–3), 334–337. doi: 10.1016/j.schres.2006.11.012.

Chernomas, W.M., Clarke, D.E. & Chisholm, F.A. (2000) Perspectives of women living with schizophrenia. *Psychiatric Services, 51*(12), 1517–1521.

Cohen, S., Lavelle, J., Rich, C.L. & Bromet, E. (1994). Rates and correlates of suicide attempts in first-admission psychotic-patients. *Acta Psychiatrica Scandinavica, 90*(3), 167–171.

Compton, M.T., Carter, T., Kryda, A., Goulding, S.M. & Kaslow, N.J. (2008) The impact of psychoticism on perceived hassles, depression, hostility, and hopelessness in non-psychiatric African Americans. *Psychiatry Research, 159*(1–2), 215–225.

Diaz-Asper, C., Malley, J., Genderson, M., Apud, J. & Elvevag, B. (2008) Context binding in schizophrenia: Effects of clinical symptomatology and item content. *Psychiatry Research, 159*(3), 259–270. doi: 10.1016/j.psychres.2007.02.018.

Dick, D.M., Smith, G., Olausson, P., Mitchell, S.H., Leeman, R.F. & O'Malley, S.S. (2010) Understanding the construct of impulsivity and its relationship to alcohol use disorders. *Addiction Biology, 15*(2), 217–226. doi: 10.1111/j.1369-1600.2009.00190.x.

Drake, R.J. (2008) Insight into illness: Impact on diagnosis and outcome of non affective psychosis. *Current Psychiatry Reports, 10*(3), 210–216.

Dumais, A., Lesage, A.D., Lalovic, A., Seguin, M., Tousignant, M. & Chawky, N. (2005) Is violent method of suicide a behavioral marker of lifetime aggression? *American Journal of Psychiatry, 162*(7), 1375–1378.

Elizabeth Sublette, M., Carballo, J.J., Moreno, C., Galfalvy, H.C., Brent, D.A. & Birmaher, B. (2009) Substance use disorders and suicide attempts in bipolar subtypes. *Journal of Psychiatric Research, 43*(3), 230–238.

Ensum, I. & Morrison, A.P. (2003) The effects of focus of attention on attributional bias in patients experiencing auditory hallucinations. *Behaviour Research and Therapy, 41*(8), 895–907. doi: 10.1016/s0005-7967(02)00102-x.

Fawcett, J., Busch, K.A., Jacobs, D., Kravitz, H.M. & Fogg, L. (1997) Suicide: A four-pathway clinical-biochemical model. In D.M.M.J.J. Staff (ed.) *Neurobiology of Suicide – From the Bench to the Clinic*. New York: New York Academy of Sciences, 288–301.

Fialko, L., Freeman, D., Bebbington, P.E., Kuipers, E., Garety, P.A. & Dunn, G. (2006) Understanding suicidal ideation in psychosis: Findings from the Psychological Prevention of Relapse in Psychosis (PRP) trial. *Acta Psychiatrica Scandinavica, 114*(3), 177–186.

Fortune, G., Barrowclough, C. & Lobban, F. (2004) Illness representations in depression. *British Journal of Clinical Psychology, 43*, 347–364.

Fredrickson, B.L. (2004) The broaden-and-build theory of positive emotions. *Philosophical Transactions of the Royal Society of London, Series B–Biological Sciences, 359*(1449), 1367–1377.

Fredrickson, B.L. & Levenson, R.W. (1998) Positive emotions speed recovery from the cardiovascular sequelae of negative emotions. *Cognition & Emotion, 12*(2), 191–220.

Freeman, D. (2007) Suspicious minds: The psychology of persecutory delusions. *Clinical Psychology Review, 27*(4), 425–457. doi: 10.1016/j.cpr.2006.10.004.

Freeman, D., Pugh, K. & Garety, P. (2008). Jumping to conclusions and paranoid ideation in the general population. *Schizophrenia Research, 102*(1–3), 254–260. doi: 10.1016/j.schres.2008.03.020.

Fritzsche, A., Dahme, B., Gotlib, I.H., Joormann, J., Magnussen, H. & Watz, H. (2010) Specificity of cognitive biases in patients with current depression and remitted depression and in patients with asthma. *Psychological Medicine, 40*(5), 815–826.

Garrett, M., Stone, D. & Turkington, D. (2006). Normalizing psychotic symptoms. *Psychology and Psychotherapy–Theory Research and Practice, 79*, 595–610. doi: 10.1348/147608306x96947.

Gilbert, P. (2001) Evolutionary approaches to psychopathology: The role of natural defences. *Australian and New Zealand Journal of Psychiatry, 35*(1), 17–27.

Gilbert, P. (2006) Evolution and depression: Issues and implications. *Psychological Medicine, 36*(3), 287–297.

Gilbert, P. & Gilbert, J. (2003) Entrapment and arrested fight and flight in depression: An exploration using focus groups. *Psychology and Psychotherapy – Theory Research and Practice, 76*, 173–188.

Gilbert, P., Gilbert, J. & Irons, C. (2004). Life events, entrapments and arrested anger in depression. *Journal of Affective Disorders, 79*(1–3), 149–160.

Gilboa-Schechtman, E., Ben-Artzi, E., Jeczemien, P., Marom, S. & Hermesh, H. (2004) Depression impairs the ability to ignore the emotional aspects of facial expressions: Evidence from the Garner task. *Cognition & Emotion, 18*(2), 209–231.

Glockner, A. & Moritz, S. (2009) A fine-grained analysis of the jumping-to-conclusions bias in schizophrenia: Data-gathering, response confidence, and information integration. *Judgment and Decision Making, 4*(7), 587–600.

Gollan, J.K., Pane, H.T., McCloskey, M.S. & Coccaro, E.F. (2008) Identifying differences in biased affective information processing in major depression. *Psychiatry Research, 159*(1–2), 18–24.

Gotlib, I.H., Krasnoperova, E., Yue, D.N. & Joormann, J. (2004) Attentional biases for negative interpersonal stimuli in clinical depression. *Journal of Abnormal Psychology, 113*(1), 127–135.

Grover, K.E., Green, K.L., Pettit, J.W., Monteith, L.L., Garza, M.J. & Venta, A. (2009) Problem solving moderates the effects of life event stress and chronic stress on suicidal behaviors in adolescence. *Journal of Clinical Psychology, 65*(12), 1281–1290. doi: 10.1002/jclp.20632.

Hackmann, A. & Holmes, E. (2004) Reflecting on imagery: A clinical perspective and overview of the special issue of *Memory* on mental imagery and memory in psychopathology. *Memory, 12*(4), 389–402. doi: 10.1080/09658210444000133.

Hawton, K. (2010) Completed suicide after attempted suicide. *British Medical Journal, 341*. doi: 10.1136/bmj.c3064.

Hawton, K. & van Heeringen, K. (2009) Suicide. *Lancet, 373*(9672), 1372–1381.

Hawton, K., Sutton, L., Haw, C., Sinclair, J. & Deeks, J.J. (2005) Schizophrenia and suicide: Systematic review of risk factors. *British Journal of Psychiatry, 187*, 9–20.

Hoff, A.L. & Kremen, W.S. (2003) Neuropsychology in schizophrenia: An update. *Current Opinion in Psychiatry, 16*(2), 149–155. doi: 10.1097/01.yco.0000058615.61505.37.

Holmes, E. & Hackmann, A. (2004) A healthy imagination? Editorial for the special issue of *Memory*: Mental imagery and memory in psychopathology. *Memory, 12*(4), 387–388. doi: 10.1080/09658210444000124.

Holmes, E.A. & Arntz, A. (2008) Special issue: Imagery rescripting in cognitive behaviour therapy: Images, treatment techniques and outcomes. *Journal of Behavior Therapy and Experimental Psychiatry, 39*(2), 101–101.

Holmes, E.A., Crane, C., Fennell, M.J.V. & Williams, J.M.G. (2007) Imagery about suicide in depression –'Flash-forwards'? *Journal of Behavior Therapy and Experimental Psychiatry, 38*(4), 423–434.

Huisman, A., van Houwelingen, C.A.J. & Kerkhof, A. (2010) Psychopathology and suicide method in mental health care. *Journal of Affective Disorders, 121*(1–2), 94–99.

Hunt, I.M., Kapur, N., Windfuhr, K., Robinson, J., Bickley, H. & Flynn, S. (2006) Suicide in schizophrenia: Findings from a national clinical survey. *Journal of Psychiatric Practice, 12*(3), 139–147.

Hunter, E.C. & O'Connor, R.C. (2003) Hopelessness and future thinking in parasuicide: The role of perfectionism. *British Journal of Clinical Psychology, 42*, 355–365.

Jacobs, J. (2010) Suicide prevention on the Golden Gate Bridge. *American Journal of Psychiatry, 167*(4), 473–473.

Janssen, I., Versmissen, D., Campo, J.A., Myin-Germeys, I., van Os, J. & Krabbendam, L. (2006) Attribution style and psychosis: Evidence for an externalizing bias in patients but not in individuals at high risk. *Psychological Medicine, 36*(6), 771–778. doi: 10.1017/s0033291706007422.

Johnson, J., Gooding, P. & Tarrier, N. (2008) Suicide risk in schizophrenia: Explanatory models and clinical implications, the Schematic Appraisal Model of suicide (SAMS). *Psychology and Psychotherapy – Theory Research and Practice, 81*, 55–77.

Johnson, J., Tarrier, N. & Gooding, P. (2008) An investigation of aspects of the Cry of Pain model of suicide risk: The role of defeat in impairing memory. *Behaviour Research and Therapy, 46*(8), 968–975.

Johnson, J., Gooding, P., Wood, A.M., Fair, K. & Tarrier, N. (In press) A therapeutic tool for boosting mood: The Broad-Minded Affective Coping Procedure (BMAC). *Behaviour Research and Therapy.*

Joiner, T.E., Van Orden, K.A., Witte, T.K., Selby, E.A., Ribeiro, J.D. & Lewis, R. (2009) Main predictions of the Interpersonal-Psychological Theory of Suicidal Behavior: Empirical tests in two samples of young adults. *Journal of Abnormal Psychology, 118*(3), 634–646.

Joormann, J. & D'Avanzato, C. (2010) Emotion regulation in depression: Examining the role of cognitive processes. [Review]. *Cognition & Emotion, 24*(6), 913–939. doi: 10.1080/02699931003784939.

Joormann, J. & Gotfib, I.H. (2008) Updating the contents of working memory in depression: Interference from irrelevant negative material. *Journal of Abnormal Psychology, 117*(1), 182–192.

Joormann, J. & Gotlib, I.H. (2010) Emotion regulation in depression: Relation to cognitive inhibition. *Cognition & Emotion, 24*(2), 281–298.

Joormann, J., Teachman, B.A. & Gotlib, I.H. (2009) Sadder and less accurate? False memory for negative material in depression. *Journal of Abnormal Psychology, 118*(2), 412–417.

Joormann, J., Yoon, K.L. & Zetsche, U. (2007) Cognitive inhibition in depression. *Applied & Preventive Psychology, 12*(3), 128–139.

Karparova, S.P., Kersting, A. & Suslow, T. (2007) Deployment of attention in clinical depression during symptom remission. *Scandinavian Journal of Psychology, 48*(1), 1–5.

Kinderman, P., Setzu, E., Lobban, F. & Salmon, P. (2006) Illness beliefs in schizophrenia. *Social Science & Medicine, 63*(7), 1900–1911.

Lau, M.A., Segal, Z.V. & Williams, J.M.G. (2004) Teasdale's differential activation hypothesis: Implications for mechanisms of depressive relapse and suicidal behaviour. *Behaviour Research and Therapy, 42*(9), 1001–1017.

Law, C.K., Yip, P.S.F., Chan, W.S.C., Fu, K.W., Wong, P.W.C. & Law, Y.W. (2009) Evaluating the effectiveness of barrier installation for preventing railway suicides in Hong Kong. *Journal of Affective Disorders, 114*(1–3), 254–262.

Lawson, C., MacLeod, C. & Hammond, G. (2002) Interpretation revealed in the blink of an eye: Depressive bias in the resolution of ambiguity. *Journal of Abnormal Psychology, 111*(2), 321–328.

Lejoyeux, M., Huet, F., Claudon, M., Fichelle, A., Casalino, E. & Lequen, V. (2008) Characteristics of suicide attempts preceded by alcohol consumption. *Archives of Suicide Research, 12*(1), 30–38.

Lepage, M., Sergerie, K., Pelletier, M. & Harvey, P.O. (2007) Episodic memory bias and the symptoms of schizophrenia. *Canadian Journal of Psychiatry – Revue Canadienne De Psychiatrie, 52*(11), 702–709.

Levine, E., Jonas, H. & Serper, M.R. (2004) Interpersonal attributional biases in hallucinatory-prone individuals. *Schizophrenia Research, 69*(1), 23–28. doi: 10.1016/s0920-9964(02)00493-0.

Lobban, F., Barrowclough, C. & Jones, S. (2004) The impact of beliefs about mental health problems and coping on outcome in schizophrenia. *Psychological Medicine, 34*(7), 1165–1176.

Lobban, F., Haddock, G., Kinderman, P. & Wells, A. (2002) The role of metacognitive beliefs in auditory hallucinations. *Personality and Individual Differences, 32*(8), 1351–1363.

Mawson, A., Cohen, K. & Berry, K. (2010) Reviewing evidence for the cognitive model of auditory hallucinations: The relationship between cognitive voice appraisals and distress during psychosis. [Review]. *Clinical Psychology Review, 30*(2), 248–258. doi: 10.1016/j.cpr.2009.11.006.

McDowell, E.E. & Stillion, J.M. (1994) Suicide across the phases of life. *New Directions for Child Development; Children, Youth, and Suicide: Developmental Perspectives*, 7–22.

Montross, L.P., Kasckow, J., Golshan, S., Solorzano, E., Lehman, D. & Zisook, S. (2008) Suicidal ideation and suicide attempts among middle-aged and older patients with schizophrenia spectrum disorders and concurrent subsyndromal depression. *Journal of Nervous and Mental Disease, 196*(12), 884–890.

Moritz, S., Woodward, T.S., Jelinek, L. & Klinge, R. (2008) Memory and metamemory in schizophrenia: A liberal acceptance account of psychosis. *Psychological Medicine, 38*(6), 825–832. doi: 10.1017/s0033291707002553.

Moritz, S., Veckenstedt, R., Randjbar, S., Hottenrott, B., Woodward, T.S. & Eckstaedt, F.V.V. (2009) Decision making under uncertainty and mood induction: Further evidence for liberal acceptance in schizophrenia. *Psychological Medicine, 39*(11), 1821–1829. doi: 10.1017/s0033291709005923.

Morrison, A.P., Bowe, S., Larkin, W. & Nothard, S. (1999) The psychological impact of psychiatric admission: Some preliminary findings. *Journal of Nervous and Mental Disease, 187*(4), 250–253.

Morrison, A.P., Nothard, S., Bowe, S.E. & Wells, A. (2004) Interpretations of voices in patients with hallucinations and non-patient controls: A comparison and predictors of distress in patients. *Behaviour Research and Therapy, 42*(11), 1315–1323.

Moses, T. (2009) Self-labeling and its effects among adolescents diagnosed with mental disorders. *Social Science & Medicine, 68*(3), 570–578.

Nielssen, O.B. & Large, M.M. (2009) Untreated psychotic illness in the survivors of violent suicide attempts. *Early Intervention in Psychiatry, 3*(2), 116–122.

Nordstrom, P., Schalling, D. & Asberg, M. (1995) Temperamental vulnerability in attempted-suicide. *Acta Psychiatrica Scandinavica, 92*(2), 155–160.

O'Connor, R.C. (2007)The relations between perfectionism and suicidality: A systematic review. *Suicide and Life-Threatening Behavior, 37*(6), 698–714.

O'Connor, R.C. & Cassidy, C. (2007) Predicting hopelessness: The interaction between optimism/pessimism and specific future expectancies. *Cognition & Emotion, 21*(3), 596–613.

O'Connor, R. C. & O'Connor, D.B. (2003) Predicting hopelessness and psychological distress: The role of perfectionism and coping. *Journal of Counseling Psychology, 50*(3), 362–372.

O'Connor, R.C., Fraser, L., Whyte, M.C., MacHale, S. & Masterton, G. (2009) Self-regulation of unattainable goals in suicide attempters: The relationship between goal disengagement, goal reengagement and suicidal ideation. *Behaviour Research and Therapy, 47*(2), 164–169.

Odonnell, I., Farmer, R. & Catalan, J. (1996) Explaining suicide: The views of survivors of serious suicide attempts. *British Journal of Psychiatry, 168*(6), 780–786.

Panagioti, M., Gooding, P. & Tarrier, N. (2009) Post-traumatic stress disorder and suicidal behavior: A narrative review. *Clinical Psychological Review, 29*(6), 471–482.

Panagioti, M., Gooding, P. & Tarrier, N. (2012) An empirical investigation of the effectiveness of the Broad-Minded Affective Coping Procedure (BMAC) to boost mood among individuals with Post-traumatic Stress Disorder (PTSD). *Behavioural Research and Therapy*.

Panagioti, M., Gooding, P.A., Dunn, G. & Tarrier, N. (2011) Pathways to suicidal behavior in Posttraumatic Stress Disorder. *Journal of Traumatic Stress, 24*(2), 137–145. doi: 10.1002/jts.20627.

Pollock, L.R. & Williams, J.M.G. (2004) Problem-solving in suicide attempters. *Psychological Medicine, 34*(1), 163–167.

Pratt, D., Gooding, P., Johnson, J., Taylor, P.J. & Tarrier, N. (2010) Suicide schemas in psychosis. *Behaviour Research and Therapy.*

Prescott, T.J., Newton, L.D., Mir, N.U., Woodruff, P.W.R. & Parks, R.W. (2006) A new dissimilarity measure for finding semantic structure in category fluency data with implications for understanding memory organization in schizophrenia. *Neuropsychology, 20*(6), 685–699. doi: 10.1037/0894-4105.20.6.685.

Radomsky, E.D., Haas, G.L., Mann, J.J. & Sweeney, J.A. (1999) Suicidal behavior in patients with schizophrenia and other psychotic disorders. *American Journal of Psychiatry, 156*(10), 1590–1595.

Ran, M.S., Xiang, M.Z., Mao, W.J., Hou, Z.J., Tang, M.N. & Chen, E.Y.H. (2005) Characteristics of suicide attempters and nonattempters with schizophrenia in a rural community. *Suicide and Life-Threatening Behavior, 35*(6), 694–701.

Rasmussen, S.A., O'Connor, R.C. & Brodie, D. (2008) The role of perfectionism and autobiographical memory in a sample of parasuicide patients: An exploratory study. *Crisis–the Journal of Crisis Intervention and Suicide Prevention, 29*(2), 64–72.

Raust, A., Slama, F., Mathieu, F., Roy, I., Chenu, A. & Koncke, D. (2007) Prefrontal cortex dysfunction in patients with suicidal behavior. *Psychological Medicine, 37*(3), 411–419.

Ribeiro, J.D. & Joiner, T.E. (2009) The Interpersonal-Psychological Theory of Suicidal Behavior: Current status and future directions. *Journal of Clinical Psychology, 65*(12), 1291–1299.

Robinson, J., Harris, M.G., Harrigan, S.M., Henry, L.P., Farrelly, S. & Prosser, A. (2010) Suicide attempt in first-episode psychosis: A 7.4 year follow-up study. *Schizophrenia Research, 116*(1), 1–8.

Rooke, O. & Birchwood, M. (1998) Loss, humiliation and entrapment as appraisals of schizophrenic illness: A prospective study of depressed and non-depressed patients. *British Journal of Clinical Psychology, 37*, 259–268.

Saarinen, P.I., Lehtonen, J. & Lonnqvist, J. (1999) Suicide risk in schizophrenia: An analysis of 17 consecutive suicides. *Schizophrenia Bulletin, 25*(3), 533–542.

Selby, E.A., Anestis, M.D., Bender, T.W., Ribeiro, J.D., Nock, M.K. & Rudd, M.D. (2010) Overcoming the fear of lethal injury: Evaluating suicidal behavior in the military through the lens of the Interpersonal-Psychological Theory of Suicide. *Clinical Psychology Review, 30*(3), 298–307.

Shneidman, E.S. (1993)Suicide as psychache. *Journal of Nervous and Mental Disease, 181*(3), 145–147.

Shneidman, E.S. (1998) Perspectives on suicidology – Further reflections on suicide and psychache. *Suicide and Life-Threatening Behavior, 28*(3), 245–250.

Tarrier, N. (2010)Broad Minded Affective Coping (BMAC): A 'positive' CBT approach to facilitating positive emotions. *International Journal of Cognitive Therapy, 3*(1), 64–76.

Tarrier, N. & Gooding, P. (2007) Treatment Manual: Cognitive Behavioural Suicide Prevention for Psychosis (CBSPp) [Unpublished treatment manual].

Tarrier, N., Barrowclough, C., Andrews, B. & Gregg, L. (2004) Risk of non-fatal suicide ideation and behaviour in recent onset schizophrenia – The influence of clinical, social, self-esteem and demographic factors. *Social Psychiatry and Psychiatric Epidemiology, 39*(11), 927–937.

Tarrier, N., Gooding, P., Gregg, L., Johnson, J., Drake, R. & Socrates Trial Group (2007) Suicide schema in schizophrenia: The effect of emotional reactivity, negative symptoms and schema elaboration. *Behaviour Research and Therapy, 45*, 2090–2097.

Taylor, P.J., Gooding, P., Wood, A.M. & Tarrier, N. (2011)The role of defeat and entrapment in depression, anxiety, and suicide. *Psychological Bulletin, 137*(3), 391–420. doi: 10.1037/a0022935.

Taylor, P.J., Gooding, P.A., Wood, A.M., Johnson, J. & Tarrier, N. (2011) Prospective predictors of suicidality: Defeat and entrapment lead to changes in suicidal ideation over time. *Suicide and Life-Threatening Behavior, 41*(3), 297–306. doi: 10.1111/j.1943-278X.2011.00029.x.

Taylor, P.J., Wood, A.M., Gooding, P., Johnson, J. & Tarrier, N. (2009) Are defeat and entrapment best defined as a single construct? *Personality and Individual Differences, 47*(7), 795–797.

Taylor, P.J., Awenat, Y., Gooding, P., Johnson, J., Pratt, D. & Wood, A. (2010) The subjective experience of participation in schizophrenia research: A practical and ethical issue. *Journal of Nervous and Mental Disease, 198*(5), 343–348.

Taylor, P.J., Gooding, P.A., Wood, A.M., Johnson, J., Pratt, D. & Tarrier, N. (2010) Defeat and entrapment in schizophrenia: The relationship with suicidal ideation and positive psychotic symptoms. *Psychiatry Research, 178*(2), 244–248. doi: 10.1016/j.psychres.2009.10.015.

Van Orden, K.A., Witte, T.K., Cukrowicz, K.C., Braithwaite, S.R., Selby, E.A. & Joiner, T.E. (2010) The Interpersonal Theory of Suicide. *Psychological Review, 117*(2), 575–600.

Warman, D.M., Lysaker, P.H., Martin, J.M., Davis, L. & Haudenschield, S.L. (2007) Jumping to conclusions and the continuum of delusional beliefs. *Behaviour Research and Therapy, 45*(6), 1255–1269. doi: 10.1016/j.brat.2006.09.002.

Weishaar, M.E. & Beck, A.T. (1992) Hopelessness and suicide. *International Review of Psychiatry, 4*(2), 177–184.

Williams, J.M.G. (1997) *Cry of Pain*. Harmondsworth: Penguin.

Williams, J.M.G., Barnhofer, T., Crane, C. & Beck, A.T. (2005) Problem solving deteriorates following mood challenge in formerly depressed patients with a history of suicidal ideation. *Journal of Abnormal Psychology, 114*(3), 421–431.

Williams, J.M.G., Crane, C., Barnhofer, T. & Duggan, D.S. (2005) *Psychology and Suicidal Behaviour: Elaborating the Entrapment Model*. Oxford: Oxford University Press.

Williams, J.M.G., Chan, S., Crane, C., Barnhofer, T., Eade, J. & Healy, H. (2006) Retrieval of autobiographical memories: The mechanisms and consequences of truncated search. *Cognition & Emotion, 20*(3–4), 351–382.

Wojnar, M., Ilgen, M.A., Czyz, E., Strobbe, S., Klimkiewicz, A. & Jakubczyk, A. (2009) Impulsive and non-impulsive suicide attempts in patients treated for alcohol dependence. *Journal of Affective Disorders, 115*(1–2), 131–139.

Wolkwasserman, D. (1986) Suicidalcommunication of persons attempting suicide and responses of significant others. *Acta Psychiatrica Scandinavica, 73*(5), 481–499.

3 Does Cognitive Behavioural Therapy for suicide work?

Baca-Garcia, E., Perez-Rodriguez, M.M., Keyes, K.M., Oquendo, M.A., Hasin, D.S. & Grant, B.F. (2011) Suicidal ideation and suicide attempts among Hispanic subgroups in the United States: 1991–1992 and 2001–2002. *Journal of Psychiatric Research, 45*(4), 512–518. doi: 10.1016/j.jpsychires.2010.09.004.

Bateman, A. & Fonagy, P. (2009) Randomized controlled trial of outpatient mentalization-based treatment versus structured clinical management for Borderline Personality Disorder. *American Journal of Psychiatry, 166*(12), 1355–1364. doi:10.1176/appi.ajp.2009.09040539.

Borenstein, M., Hodges, L.V., Higgins, J.P. & Rothstein, H.R. (eds) (2009) *Introduction to Meta-Analysis*. Chichester: Wiley.

Brown, G.K., Have, T.T., Henriques, G.R., Xie, S.X., Hollander, J.E. & Beck, A.T. (2005) Cognitive therapy for the prevention of suicide attempts: A randomized controlled trial. *Journal of the American Medical Association, 294*, 563–570.

Cartright, N. (2007) Are RCTs the gold standard? *Biosocieties, 2*, 11–20.

Cottraux, J., Note, I.D., Boutitie, F., Milliery, M., Genouihlac, V. & Yao, S.N. (2009) Cognitive Therapy versus Rogerian Supportive Therapy in Borderline Personality Disorder: Two-year follow-up of a controlled pilot study. *Psychotherapy and Psychosomatics, 78*(5), 307–316. doi: 10.1159/000229769.

Davidson, K.M., Tyrer, P., Norrie, J., Palmer, S.J. & Tyrer, H. (2010) Cognitive therapy v. usual treatment for borderline personality disorder: Prospective 6-year follow-up. *British Journal of Psychiatry, 197*(6), 456–462. doi: 10.1192/bjp.bp.109.074286.

Dick, D.M., Smith, G., Olausson, P., Mitchell, S.H., Leeman, R.F. & O'Malley, S.S. (2010) Understanding the construct of impulsivity and its relationship to alcohol use disorders. *Addiction Biology, 15*(2), 217–226. doi: 10.1111/j.1369-1600.2009.00190.x.

Hvid, M., Vangborg, K., Sorensen, H.J., Nielsen, I.K., Stenborg, J.M. & Wang, A.G. (2011) Preventing repetition of attempted suicide-II: The Amager Project, a randomized controlled trial. *Nordic Journal of Psychiatry, 65*(5), 292–298. doi: 10.3109/08039488.2010.544404.

Johnson, J., Gooding, P. & Tarrier, N. (2008) Suicide risk in schizophrenia: Explanatory models and clinical implications, the Schematic Appraisal Model of Suicide (SAMS). *Psychology and Psychotherapy – Theory Research and Practice, 81*, 55–77.

Liberman, R.P. & Eckman, T. (1981) Behavior therapy vs insight-oriented therapy for repeated suicide attempters. *Archives of General Psychiatry, 38*,1126–1130.

Linehan, M.M., Schmidt, H., Dimeff, L.A., Craft, J.C., Kanter, J. & Comtopis, K.A. (1999) Dialectical behavior therapy for patients with borderline personality disorder and drugdependence. *American Journal of Addictions, 8*, 279–292.

March, J.S. & TADS Team (2004) Fluoxetine, Cognitive-Behavioral Therapy, and their combination for adolescents with depression: Treatment for Adolescents with Depression Study (TADS) randomized controlled trial. *Journal of the American Medical Association, 292*, 807–819.

McMain, S.F., Links, P.S., Gnam, W.H., Guimond, T., Cardish, R.J. & Korman, L. (2009) A randomized trial of Dialectical Behavior Therapy versus general psychiatric management for Borderline Personality Disorder. *American Journal of Psychiatry, 166*(12), 1365–1374. doi: 10.1176/appi.ajp.2009.09010039.

Moher, D., Pham, B., Jones, A., Cook, D.J., Jadad, A.R. & Moher, M. (1998) Does quality of reports of randomized trials affect estimates of intervention efficacy reported in meta analyses? *Lancet, 352*, 609–613.

Nordentoft, M., Jeppesen, P., Abel, M., Kassow, P., Petersen, L. & Thorup, A. (2002) OPUS study: Suicidal behaviour, suicidal ideation, and hopelessness among patients with first-episode psychosis: One-year follow-up of a randomised controlled trial. *British Journal of Psychiatry, 181*(Suppl. 43), 98–106.

Pasieczny, N. & Connor, J. (2011) The effectiveness of dialectical behaviour therapy in routine public mental health settings: An Australian controlled trial. *Behaviour Research and Therapy, 49*(1), 4–10. doi: 10.1016/j.brat.2010.09.006.

Peters, E., Landau, S., McCrone, P., Cooke, M., Fisher, P. & Steel, C. (2010) A randomised controlled trial of Cognitive Behaviour Therapy for psychosis in a routine clinical service. *Acta Psychiatrica Scandinavica, 122*(4), 302–318. doi: 10.1111/j.1600-0447.2010.01572.x.

Rathus, J.H. & Miller, A.L. (2002) Dialectical Behavior Therapy adapted for suicidal adolescents. *Suicide and Life-Threatening Behavior, 32*, 146–157.

Rhee, W.K., Merbaum, M., Strube, M.J. & Self, S.M. (2005) Efficacy of brief telephone psychotherapy with callers to a suicide hotline. Suicide and Life-Threatening Behavior, 35, 317–328.

Rosenthal, R. & Dimatteo, M.R. (2001) Meta-analysis: Recent developments in quantitative methods for literature reviews. *Annual Review of Psychology, 52*, 59–82.

Schmidt, U. & Davidson, K. (2004) *When Life is Too Painful: Finding Options after Self Harm.* London: Psychological Press.

Schulz, K.F., Chalmers, I., Hayes, R.J. & Altman, D.G. (1995) Empirical evidence of bias: Dimensions of methodological quality associated with estimates of treatment effect in controlled trials. *Journal of the American Medical Association, 280*, 178–180.

Scocco, P., de Girolamo, G., Vilagut, G. & Alonso, J. (2008) Prevalence of suicide ideation, plans, and attempts and related risk factors in Italy: Results from the European Study on the Epidemiology of Mental Disorders–World Mental Health study. *Comprehensive Psychiatry, 49*(1), 13–21. doi: 10.1016/j.comppsych.2007.08.004.

Simon, S. (2001) Is the randomised clincial trial the gold standard of research? *Journal of Andrology, 22*(6), 938–943.

Simpson, G.K., Tate, R.L., Whiting, D.L. & Cotter, R.E. (2011) Suicide prevention after traumatic brain injury: A randomized controlled trial of a program for the psychological treatment of hopelessness. *Journal of Head Trauma Rehabilitation, 26*(4), 290–300. doi: 10.1097/HTR.0b013e3182225250.

Tarrier, N. (2002) Yes, Cognitive Behaviour Therapy may well be all you need. *British Medical Journal 324*, 291–292.

Tarrier, N. & Wykes, T. (2004) Is there evidence that Cognitive Behaviour Therapy is an effective treatment for schizophrenia: A cautious or cautionary tale? *Behaviour Research and Therapy, 42*, 1377–1401.

Tarrier, N., Taylor, K. & Gooding, P. (2008) Cognitive-Behavioral interventions to reduce suicide behavior: A systematic review and meta-analysis. *Behavior Modification, 32*(1), 77–108.

Tarrier, N., Gooding, P., Gregg, L., Johnson, J., Drake, R. & Socrates Trial (2007) Suicide schema in schizophrenia: The effect of emotional reactivity, negative symptoms and schema elaboration. *Behaviour Research and Therapy*, 45, 2090–2097.

Tarrier, N. & Wykes, T. (2004) Is there evidence that Cognitive Behaviour Therapy is an effective treatment for schizophrenia: A cautious or cautionary tale? *Behaviour Research and Therapy, 42*, 1377–1401.

ten Have, M., de Graaf, R., van Dorsselaer, S., Verdurmen, J., van't Land, H. & Vollebergh, W. (2009) Incidence and course of suicidal ideation and suicide attempts in the general population. *Canadian Journal of Psychiatry – Revue Canadienne De Psychiatrie, 54*(12), 824–833.

van Beek, W., Kerkhof, A. & Beekman, A. (2009) Future oriented group training for suicidal patients: A randomized clinical trial. *BMC Psychiatry, 9*. doi: 6510.1186/1471-244x-9-65.

Weinberg, I., Gunderson, J.G., Hennen, J. & Cutter, C.J. (2006) Manual assisted cognitive treatment for deliberate self-harm in borderline personality disorder patients. *Journal of Personality Disorders, 20*, 482–492.

Yoder, K.A., Whitbeck, L.B. & Hoyt, D.R. (2008) Dimensionality of thoughts of death and suicide: Evidence from a study of homeless adolescents. *Social Indicators Research, 86*(1), 83–100. doi: 10.1007/s11205-007-9095-5.

4 Pre-therapy: engagement and assessment

Beck, A.T. (1979) *Cognitive Therapy of Depression*. New York: Guilford Press.

Beck, A.T. & Steer, R.A. (1988a) *Manual for the Beck Hopelessness Scale*. San Antonio, TX: Psychological Corporation.

Beck, A.T. & Steer, R.A. (1988b) *Manual for the Beck Scale for Suicidal Ideation*. San Antonio, TX: Psychological Corporation.

Beck, A.T., Davis, J.H., Frederick, C.J., Perlin, S., Pokorny, A., Schulman, R. et al. (1972) Classification and nomenclature. In H.L.P. Resnik & B. Hathorne (eds) *Suicide Prevention in the Seventies*. Washington, DC: US Government Printing Office, 7–12.

Birchwood, M., Iqbal, Z., Chadwick, P. & Trower, P. (2000) Cognitive approach to depression and suicidal thinking in psychosis I: Ontogeny of post-psychotic depression. *British Journal of Psychiatry, 177*, 516–521.

Bolton, C., Gooding, P, Kapur, N., Barrowclough, C. & Tarrier, N. (2007) Developing psychological perspectives of suicidal behaviour and risk in people with a diagnosis of schizophrenia: We know they kill themselves but do we understand why? *Clinical Psychology Review, 27*(4), 511–536. doi: DOI: 10.1016/j.cpr.2006.12.001.

Cukrowicz, K., Smith, P. & Poindexter, E. (2010)The effect of participating in suicide research: Does participating in a research protocol on suicide and psychiatric symptoms increase suicide ideation and attempts? *Suicide & Life-Threatening Behavior, 40*(6), 535–543. doi: 10.1521/suli.2010.40.6.5 3510.1521/suli.2010.40.6.535 [pii].

Cull, J.G. & Gill, W.S. (1988) *Suicide Probability Scale (SPS) Manual*. Los Angeles: Western Psychological Services.

De Hert, M. & Peuskens, J. (2000) Psychiatric aspects of suicidal behaviour: Schizophrenia. In K. Hawton & C. Van Heeringen (eds) *The International Handbook of Suicide and Attempted Suicide*. Chichester: John Wiley & Sons, 121–134.

Dick, D.M., Smith, G., Olausson, P., Mitchell, S.H., Leeman, R.F., O'Malley, S.S. & Sher, K. (2010) Understanding the construct of impulsivity and its relationship to alcohol use disorders. *Addiction Biology, 15*(2), 217–226. doi: 10.1111/j.1369-1600.2009.00190.x.

Drake, R., Haddock, G., Tarrier, N., Bentall, R. & Lewis, S. (2007)The Psychotic Symptom Rating Scales (PSYRATS): Their usefulness and properties in first episode psychosis. *Schizophrenia Research, 89*(1–3), 119–122. doi: S0920-9964(06)00213-1 [pii].

Dumais, A., Lesage, A.D., Lalovic, A., Seguin, M., Tousignant, M., Chawky, N. & Turecki, G. (2005)Is violent method of suicide a behavioral marker of lifetime aggression? *American Journal of Psychiatry, 162*(7), 1375–1378.

Goldstein, R.B., Black, D.W., Nasrallah, A. & Winokur, G. (1991) The prediction of suicide: Sensitivity, specificity, and predictive value of a multivariate model applied to suicide among 1906 patients with affective disorders. *Archives of General Psychiatry, 48*(5), 418–422.

Gumley, Andrew & Schwannauer, Matthias (2006) *Staying Well after Psychosis: A Cognitive Interpersonal Approach to Recovery and Relapse Prevention.* Chichester, UK and Hoboken, NJ: Wiley.

Haddock, G., McCarron, J., Tarrier, N. & Faragher, E.B. (1999) Scales to measure dimensions of hallucinations and delusions: The Psychotic Symptom Rating Scales (PSYRATS). *Psychological Medicine, 29*(4), 879–889.

Harris, E.C. & Barraclough, B. (1997) Suicide as an outcome for mental disorders: A meta-analysis. *British Journal of Psychiatry, 170*, 205–228.

Hawton, K., Sutton, L., Haw, C., Sinclair, J. & Deeks, J.J. (2005) Schizophrenia and suicide: Systematic review of risk factors. *British Journal of Psychiatry, 187*, 9–20.

Hunter, E.C. & O'Connor, R.C. (2003) Hopelessness and future thinking in parasuicide: The role of perfectionism. *British Journal of Clinical Psychology, 42*, 355–365.

Johnson, J., Gooding, P. & Tarrier, N. (2008) Suicide risk in schizophrenia: Explanatory models and clinical implications, the Schematic Appraisal Model of Suicide (SAMS). *Psychological Psychotherapy, 81*(Pt 1), 55–77. doi: 10.1348/147608307X244996.

Jorm, A.F., Kelly, C.M. & Morgan, A.J. (2007) Participant distress in psychiatric research: A systematic review. *Psychological Medicine, 37*(7), 917–926. doi: S0033291706009779 [pii].

Kapur, N., Cooper, J., Hiroeh, U., May, C., Appleby, L. & House, A. (2004) Emergency department management and outcome for self-poisoning: A cohort study. *General Hospital Psychiatry, 26*(1), 36–41. doi: S0163834303000999 [pii].

Kay, S.R., Fiszbein, A. & Opler, L.A. (1987) The Positive and Negative Syndrome Scale (PANSS) for schizophrenia. *Schizophrenia Bulletin, 13*(2), 261–276.

Krupinski, M., Fischer, A., Grohmann, R., Engel, R., Hollweg, M. & Moller, H.J. (1998) Risk factors for suicides of inpatients with depressive psychoses. *European Archives of Psychiatry and Clinical Neuroscience, 248*(3), 141–147.

Kuyken, W., Padesky, Christine A. & Dudley, Robert (2009) *Collaborative Case Conceptualization: Working Effectively with Clients in Cognitive-Behavioral Therapy.* New York: Guilford Press.

Linehan, M.M. (1993a) *Cognitive-Behavioural treatment of borderline personality disorder.* New York: Guilford Press.

Linehan, M.M. (1993b) *Skills Training Manual for Treating Borderline Personality Disorder.* New York: Guilford Press.

Masten, A.S. (2001) Ordinary magic: Resilience processes in development. *The American Psychologist, 56*(3), 227–238.

Morrison, A.P., Renton, J.C., Dunn, H., Williams, S. & Bentall, R.P. (2004) *Cognitive Therapy for Psychosis: A Formulation Based Approach.* Hove, East Sussex: Brunner-Routledge.

Murphy, G.E. & Wetzel, R.D. (1982) Family history of suicidal behavior among suicide attempters. *The Journal of Nervous and Mental Disease, 170*(2), 86–90.

Neil, S., Kilbride, M., Pitt, L., Nothard, S. & Morrison, A. (2009) The questionnaire about the process of recovery (QPR). *Psychosis, 1*, 145–155.

Persons, J.B. (2008) *The Case Formulation Approach to Cognitive-Behavior Therapy*. New York: Guilford Press.

Pitt, L., Kilbride, M., Nothard, S., Welford, M. & Morrison, A.P. (2007) Researching recovery from psychosis: A user-led project. *Psychiatric Bulletin, 31*, 55–60.

Pratt, D., Gooding, P., Johnson, J., Taylor, P. & Tarrier, N. (2010) Suicide schemas in non-affective psychosis: An empirical investigation. *Behavioural Research and Therapy, 48*(12), 1211–1220. doi: S0005-7967(10)00179-8 [pii].

Rachman, S. & de Silva, P. (1978) Abnormal and normal obsessions. *Behavioural Research and Therapy, 16*(4), 233–248. doi: 0005-7967(78)90022-0 [pii].

Reynolds, W.M. (1991) *Suicide Ideation Questionnaire: Professional Manual*. Odessa, FL: Psychological Assessment Resources.

Shafran, R. & Rachman, S. (2004) Thought–action fusion: A review. *Journal of Behavior Therapy and Experimental Psychiatry, 35*(2), 87–107. doi: 10.1016/j.jbtep.2004.04.002.

Shafran, R., Teachman, B.A., Kerry, S. & Rachman, S. (1999) A cognitive distortion associated with eating disorders: Thought–shape fusion. *The British Journal of Clinical Psychology, 38* (Pt 2), 167–179.

Sorenson, S.B. (1991) Suicide among the elderly: Issues facing public health. *American Journal of Public Health, 81*(9), 1109–1110.

Tait, L., Birchwood, M. & Trower, P. (2003) Predicting engagement with services for psychosis: Insight, symptoms and recovery style. *British Journal of Psychiatry, 182*, 123–128.

Tarrier, N., Barrowclough, C., Andrews, B. & Gregg, L. (2004) Risk of non-fatal suicide ideation and behaviour in recent onset schizophrenia – The influence of clinical, social, self-esteem and demographic factors. *Social Psychiatry and Psychiatric Epidemiology, 39*(11), 927–937.

Taylor, P.J., Awenat, Y., Gooding, P., Johnson, J., Pratt, D., Wood, A. & Tarrier, N. (2010) The subjective experience of participation in schizophrenia research: A practical and ethical issue. *The Journal of Nervous Mental Disease, 198*(5), 343–348. doi: 10.1097/NMD.0b013e3181da8545.

Teasdale, J.D. (1988) Cognitive vulnerability to persistent depression. *Cognition and Emotion, 2*(3), 247–274.

Wenzel, A., Brown, G.K., & Beck, A.T. (2009) *Cognitive Therapy for Suicidal Patients: Scientific and Clinical Applications*, Washington, DC: American Psychological Association.

Williams, J.M.G. (1997) *Cry of Pain*. Harmondsworth: Penguin.

Williams, J.M.G., Crane, C., Barnhofer, T. & Duggan, D.S. (2005) *Psychology and Suicidal Behaviour: Elaborating the Entrapment Model*. Oxford: Oxford University Press.

Zerler, H. (2009) Motivational interviewing in the assessment and management of suicidality. *Journal of Clinical Psychology, 65*(11), 1207–1217. doi: 10.1002/jclp.20643.

5 Formulating the prevention of suicide

Beck, A.T. (1979) *Depression: Clinical, Experimental, and Theoretical Aspects*. New York: Hoeber.

Clark, D.M. (1986) A cognitive approach to panic. *Behavioural Research and Therapy, 24*(4), 461–470. doi: 0005-7967(86)90011-2 [pii].

Davey, G.C.L. & Levy, S. (1998) Catastrophic worrying: Personal inadequacy and a perseverative iterative style as features of the catastrophising process. *Journal of Abnormal Psychology, 107*, 576–586.

Depue, R.A. & Morrone-Strupinsky, J.V. (2005) A neurobehavioral model of affiliative bonding: Implications for conceptualizing a human trait of affiliation. *Behavioral Brain Science, 28*(3), 313–350; discussion 350–395. doi: S0140525X05000063 [pii].

Gilbert, Paul (2010) *Compassion Focused Therapy: Distinctive Features*. London and New York: Routledge.

Harvey, Allison G. (2004) *Cognitive Behavioural Processes across Psychological Disorders: A Transdiagnostic Approach to Research and Treatment*. Oxford and New York: Oxford University Press.

Holmes, E.A., Crane, C., Fennell, M.J.V. & Williams, J.M.G. (2007) Imagery about suicide in depression –'Flash-forwards'? *Journal of Behavior Therapy and Experimental Psychiatry, 38*(4), 423–434.

Johnson, J., Gooding, P. & Tarrier, N. (2008) Suicide risk in schizophrenia: Explanatory models and clinical implications, the Schematic Appraisal Model of Suicide (SAMS). *Psychological Psychotherapy, 81*(Pt 1), 55–77. doi: 10.1348/147608307X244996.

Johnson, J., Tarrier, N. & Gooding, P. (2008) An investigation of aspects of the Cry of Pain model of suicide risk: The role of defeat in impairing memory. *Behavioral Research and Therapy, 46*(8), 968–975. doi: S0005-7967(08)00089-2 [pii].

Johnson, J., Gooding, P.A., Wood, A.M. & Tarrier, N. (2010) Resilience as positive coping appraisals: Testing the Schematic Appraisals Model of Suicide (SAMS). *Behavioral Research and Therapy, 48*(3), 179–186. doi: S0005-7967(09)00248-4 [pii].

Johnson, J., Wood, A.M., Gooding, P., Taylor, P.J. & Tarrier, N. (2011) Resilience to suicidality: The buffering hypothesis. *Clinical Psychological Review.* doi: S0272-7358(11)00002-X [pii].

Johnson, J., Gooding, P.A., Wood, A.M., Taylor, P.J., Pratt, D. & Tarrier, N. (2010) Resilience to suicidal ideation in psychosis: Positive self-appraisals buffer the impact of hopelessness. *Behavioral Research and Therapy, 48*(9), 883–889. doi: S0005-7967(10)00109-9 [pii].

Joiner, T.E., Brown, J.S. & Wingate, L.R. (2005) The psychology and neurobiology of suicide. *Annual Review of Psychology, 56,* 287–314.

Kuyken, W., Padesky, Christine A. & Dudley, Robert (2009) *Collaborative Case Conceptualization: Working Effectively with Clients in Cognitive-Behavioral Therapy.* New York: Guilford Press.

Masten, A.S. (2001) Ordinary magic: Resilience processes in development. *American Psychologist, 56*(3), 227–238.

Morrison, A.P., Haddock, G. & Tarrier, N. (1995) Intrusive thoughts and auditory hallucinations: A cognitive approach. *Behavioural and Cognitive Psychotherapy, 23,*265–280.

Persons, J.B. (2008)*The Case Formulation Approach to Cognitive-Behavior Therapy.* New York: Guilford Press.

Pratt, D., Appleby, L., Piper, M., Webb, R. & Shaw, J. (2010) Suicide in recently released prisoners: A case-control study. *Psychological Medicine, 40*(5), 827–835.

Pratt, D., Gooding, P., Johnson, J., Taylor, P. & Tarrier, N. (2010) Suicide schemas in non-affective psychosis: An empirical investigation. *Behavioral Research and Therapy, 48*(12), 1211–1220. doi: S0005-7967(10)00179-8 [pii].

Rachman, S. (1981) Part 1: Unwanted intrusive cognitions. *Advances in Behavior Research and Therapy, 3,* 89–99.

Read, J. & Argyle, N. (1999) Hallucinations, delusions, and thought disorder among adult psychiatric inpatients with a history of child abuse. *Psychiatric Services, 50*(11), 1467–1472.

Read, J. & Hammersley, P. (2005) Child sexual abuse and schizophrenia. *British Journal of Psychiatry, 186,* 76; author reply 76.

Rudd, M.D. (2004) Cognitive therapy for suicidality: An integrative, comprehensive, and practical approach to conceptualization. *Journal of Contemporary Psychotherapy, 34,* 59–72.

Salkovskis, P.M., Clark, D.M. & Hackmann, A. (1991) Treatment of panic attacks using cognitive therapy without exposure or breathing retraining. *Behavioral Research and Therapy, 29*(2), 161–166. doi: 0005-7967(91)90044-4 [pii].

Tarrier, N. (2006)*Case Formulation in Cognitive Behaviour Therapy: The Treatment of Challenging and Complex Cases.* New York: Routledge.

Tarrier, N. & Calam, R. (2002) New developments in Cognitive-Behavioural case formation: Epidemiological, systemic and social context: An integrative approach. *Cognitive & Behavioural Psychotherapy, 30,* 311–328.

Tarrier, N., Barrowclough, C., Andrews, B. & Gregg, L. (2004) Risk of non-fatal suicide ideation and behaviour in recent onset schizophrenia – The influence of clinical, social, self-esteem and demographic factors. *Social Psychiatry and Psychiatric Epidemiology, 39*(11), 927–937.

Vasey, M. & Borkovec, T.D. (1992) A catastrophising assessment of worrisome thoughts. *Cognitive Therapy and Research, 16*, 505–520.

Wells, A. (2000) *Emotional Disorders and Metacognition: Innovative Cognitive Therapy*. Chichester: Wiley.

Wells, A. & Morrison, A.P. (1994) Qualitative dimensions of normal worry and normal obsessions: A comparative study. *Behavioral Research and Therapy, 32*(8), 867–870.

Wenzel, Amy, Brown, Gregory K. & Beck, Aaron T. (2009) *Cognitive Therapy for Suicidal Patients: Scientific and Clinical Applications*. Washington, DC: American Psychological Association.

Williams, J.M.G. (1997) *Cry of Pain*. Harmondsworth: Penguin.

Williams, J.M.G., Crane, C., Barnhofer, T. & Duggan, D.S. (2005) *Psychology and Suicidal Behaviour: Elaborating the Entrapment Model*. Oxford: Oxford University Press.

6 Clinical techniques and implementation of CBSPp protocol

Beck, A.T. (1979) *Depression: Clinical, Experimental, and Theoratical Aspects*. New York: Hoeber.

Favrod, J., Giuliani, F., Ernst, F. & Bonsack, C. (2010) Anticipatory pleasure skills training: A new intervention to reduce anhedonia in schizophrenia. *Perspectives in Psychiatric Care, 46*(3), 171–181. doi: PPC255 [pii]10.1111/j.1744-6163.2010.00255.x.

Fredrickson, B.L. & Branigan, C. (2005). Positive emotions broaden the scope of attention and thought-action repertoires. *Cognition & Emotion, 19*(3), 313–332.

Fredrickson, B.L. & Losada, M.F. (2005) Positive affect and the complex dynamics of human flourishing. *American Psychologist, 60*(7), 678–686.

Fredrickson, B.L., Mancuso, R.A., Branigan, C. & Tugade, M.M. (2000) The undoing effect of positive emotions. *Motivation and Emotion, 24*(4), 237–258.

Fredrickson, B.L., Cohn, M.A., Coffey, K.A., Pek, J. & Finkel, S.M. (2008) Open hearts build lives: Positive emotions, induced through loving-mindness meditation, build consequential personal resources. *Journal of Personality and Social Psychology, 95*(5), 1045–1062.

Gard, D.E., Kring, A.M., Gard, M.G., Horan, W.P. & Green, M.F. (2007) Anhedonia in schizophrenia: Distinctions between anticipatory and consummatory pleasure. *Schizophrenia Research, 93*(1–3), 253–260. doi: S0920-9964(07)00125-9 [pii].

Garland, E.L., Fredrickson, B., Kring, A.M., Johnson, D.P., Meyer, P.S. & Penn, D.L. (2010) Upward spirals of positive emotions counter downward spirals of negativity: Insights from the broaden-and-build theory and affective neuroscience on the treatment of emotion dysfunctions and deficits in psychopathology. *Clinical Psychological Review*. doi: S0272-7358(10)00042-5 [pii].

Gilbert, P., Allan, S., Brough, S., Melley, S. & Miles, J.N. (2002) Relationship of anhedonia and anxiety to social rank, defeat and entrapment. *Journal of Affective Disorders, 71*(1–3), 141–151. doi: S0165032701003925 [pii].

Hall, P.L. & Tarrier, N. (2004) The durability of a cognitive behavioural intervention for self-esteem in psychosis: Effects from a pilot study at 12 month follow-up. *Behavioural & Cognitive Psychotherapy, 32*, 117–121.

Johnson, J., Gooding, P. & Tarrier, N. (2008) Suicide risk in schizophrenia: Explanatory models and clinical implications, the Schematic Appraisal Model of Suicide (SAMS). *Psychological Psychotherapy, 81*(Pt 1), 55–77. doi: 10.1348/147608307X244996.

Johnson, J., Tarrier, N. & Gooding, P. (2008) An investigation of aspects of the Cry of Pain model of suicide risk: The role of defeat in impairing memory. *Behavioral Research and Therapy, 46*(8), 968–975. doi: S0005-7967(08)00089-2 [pii]10.1016/j.brat.2008.04.007.

Johnson, J., Gooding, P.A., Wood, A.M. & Tarrier, N. (2010) Resilience as positive coping appraisals: Testing the Schematic Appraisals Model of Suicide (SAMS). *Behavioral Research and Therapy, 48*(3), 179–186. doi: S0005-7967(09)00248-4 [pii]10.1016/j.brat.2009.10.007.

Johnson, J., Wood, A.M., Gooding, P., Taylor, P.J. & Tarrier, N. (2011) Resilience to suicidality: The buffering hypothesis. *Clinical Psychological Review*. doi: S0272-7358(11)00002-X [pii]10.1016/j.cpr.2010.12.007.

Johnson, J., Gooding, P.A., Wood, A.M., Taylor, P.J., Pratt, D. & Tarrier, N. (2010) Resilience to suicidal ideation in psychosis: Positive self-appraisals buffer the impact of hopelessness. *Behavioral Research and Therapy, 48*(9), 883–889. doi: S0005-7967(10)00109-9 [pii]10.1016/j.brat.2010.05.013.

Kuha, A., Suvisaari, J., Perala, J., Eerola, M., Saarni, S.S., Partonen, T. & Tuulio-Henriksson, A. (2011) Associations of anhedonia and cognition in persons with schizophrenia spectrum disorders, their siblings, and controls. *Journal of Nervous Mental Disorders, 199*(1), 30–37. doi: 10.1097/NMD.0b013e3182043a6d00005053-201101000-00006 [pii].

Linehan, M.M. (1993a) *Cognitive-Behavioral Treatment of Borderline Personality Disorder*. New York: Guilford Press.

Linehan, M.M. (1993b) *Skills Training Manual for Treating Borderline Personality Disorder*. New York: Guilford Press.

Oestrich, I., Austin, S.F., Lykke, J. & Tarrier, N. (2007) The feasibility of cognitive behavioural intervention for low self-esteem within a dual diagnosis inpatient population. *Behavioural & Cognitive Psychotherapy, 35*, 403–408.

Pratt, D., Gooding, P., Johnson, J., Taylor, P. & Tarrier, N. (2010) Suicide schemas in non-affective psychosis: An empirical investigation. *Behavioral Research and Therapy, 48*(12), 1211–1220. doi: S0005-7967(10)00179-8 [pii].

Tarrier, N. (2002) The use of coping strategies and self-regulation in the treatment of psychosis. In A. Morrison (ed.) *A Casebook of Cognitive Therapy for Psychosis*. Cambridge: Cambridge University Press.

Tarrier, N. (2010) Broad Minded Affective Coping (BMAC): A 'positive' CBT approach to faciliating positive emotions. *International Journal of Cognitive Therapy, 3*(1), 64–76.

Tarrier, N., Khan, S., Cater, J. & Picken, A. (2007) The subjective consequences of suffering a first episode psychosis: Trauma and suicide behaviour. *Social Psychiatry & Psychiatric Epidemiology, 42*, 29–35.

Teasdale, J. & Barnard, P. (1993) *Affect, Cognition and Change*. Hove, UK: Lawrence Erlbaum Associated Ltd.

Wells, A. (2000) *Emotional Disorders and Metacognition: Innovative Cognitive Therapy*. Chicherster: Wiley.

Wenzel, Amy, Brown, Gregory K. & Beck, Aaron T. (2009) *Cognitive Therapy for Suicidal Patients: Scientific and Clinical Applications*. Washington, DC: American Psychological Association.

7 A case study in suicide prevention: Mark

Baron-Cohen, S. (2009) Autism: The Empathizing–Systemizing (E-S) Theory. The year in cognitive neuroscience 2009. *Annals of the New York Academy of Sciences, 1156*, 68–80.

Baron-Cohen, S., Wheelwright, S., Skinner, R., Martin, J. & Clubley, E. (2001) The Autism-Spectrum Quotient (AQ): Evidence from Asperger Syndrome/high-functioning autism, males and females, scientists and mathematicians. *Journal of Autism and Developmental Disorders, 31*, 5–17.

Crane, L. & Goddard, L. (2008) Episodic and semantic autobiographical memory in autism spectrum disorders. *Journal of Autism and Developmental Disorders, 38*(3), 498–506.

Davis, M.H. (1994) *Empathy: A Social Psychological Approach*. Boulder, CO: Westview Press.

9 Overcoming difficulties in implementing CBSPp

Beck, A.T. (1979) *Depression: Clinical, Experimental, and Theoratical Aspects*. New York: Hoeber.

Bordin, E.S. (1979) The generalizability of the psychoanalytic concept of the working alliance. *Psychotherapy: Theory, Research and Practice, 16*, 252–260.

Bordin, E.S. (1994) Theory and research on the therapeutic alliance: New directions. In A.O. Hovarth & L.S. Greenberg (eds) *The Working Alliance: Theory, Research and* Practice. New York: John Wiley & Sons, 13–37.

Birchwood, M., Gilbert, P., Gilbert, J., Trower, P., Meaden, A., Hay, J. & Miles, J.N.V. (2004) Interpersonal and role-related schema influence the relationship with the dominant 'voice' in schizophrenia: A comparison of three models. *Psychological Medicine, 34*(8), 1571–1580.

Favrod, J., Giuliani, F., Ernst, F. & Bonsack, C. (2010) Anticipatory pleasure skills training: A new intervention to reduce anhedonia in schizophrenia. *Perspectivaes of Psychiatric Care, 46*(3), 171–181. doi: PPC255 [pii]. 10.1111/j.1744-6163.2010.00255.x.

Fennell, Melanie J.V. (2009) *Overcoming Low Self-Esteem: A Self-Help Guide Using Cognitive Behavioral Techniques*. New York: Basic Books.

Freeman, Daniel, Bentall, Richard P. & Garety, Philippa A. (2008) *Persecutory Delusions: Assessment, Theory, and Treatment*. Oxford & New York: Oxford University Press.

Gard, D.E., Kring, A.M., Gard, M.G., Horan, W.P. & Green, M.F. (2007) Anhedonia in schizophrenia: Distinctions between anticipatory and consummatory pleasure. *Schizophrenia Research, 93*(1–3), 253–260. doi: S0920-9964(07)00125-9 [pii]. 10.1016/j.schres.2007.03.008.

Gilbert, P. (2006) A biopsychosocial and evolutionary approach to formulation with special reference to shame. In N. Tarrier (ed.) *Case Formulation in Cognitive Behaviour Therapy: The Treatment of Challenging and Complex Cases*. New York: Routledge

Gilbert, P. (2010) *Compassion Focused Therapy: Distinctive Features*. London & New York: Routledge.

Gilbert, P. & Irons, C. (2005) Focussed therapies and compassionate mind training for shame and self-attacking. In P. Gilbert (ed.) *Compassion: Conceptualisations, Research and Use in Psychotherapy*. Hove, UK: Routledge, 263–325.

Gumley, Andrew & Schwannauer, Matthias (2006) *Staying Well after Psychosis: A Cognitive Interpersonal Approach to Recovery and Relapse Prevention*. Chichester, UK & Hoboken, NJ: Wiley.

Harvey, Allison G. (2004) *Cognitive Behavioural Processes across Psychological Disorders: A Transdiagnostic Approach to Research and Treatment*. Oxford & New York: Oxford University Press.

Hayes, S.C., Luoma, J.B., Bond, F.W., Masuda, A. & Lillis, J. (2006) Acceptance and commitment therapy: Model, processes and outcomes. *Behavioral Research and Therapy, 44*(1), 1–25. doi: S0005-7967(05)00214-7 [pii].10.1016/j.brat.2005.06.006.

Johnson, J., Gooding, P. & Tarrier, N. (2008) Suicide risk in schizophrenia: Explanatory models and clinical implications, the Schematic Appraisal Model of Suicide (SAMS). *Psychological Psychotherapy, 81*(Pt 1), 55–77. doi: 10.1348/147608307X244996.

Kelly, J.A. & Welford, M. (in preparation) Broad Minded Affective Coping: Reflections on the use of positive emotions and naturally occurring coping strategies in the prevention of suicide in psychosis.

Kelly, J.A., Gooding, P., Pratt, D., Ainsworth, J., Welford, M. & Tarrier, N. (accepted) Intelligent Real Time Therapy (iRTT): Harnessing the power of machine learning to optimise the delivery of momentary cognitive-behavioural interventions. *Journal of Mental Health*.

Kuha, A., Suvisaari, J., Perala, J., Eerola, M., Saarni, S.S., Partonen, T. & Tuulio-Henriksson, A. (2011) Associations of anhedonia and cognition in persons with schizophrenia spectrum disorders, their siblings, and controls. *Journal of Nervous Mental Disorders, 199*(1), 30–37. doi: 10.1097/NMD.0b013e3182043a6d.

Le Doux, J. (1998) *The Emotional Brain: The Mysterious Underpinnings of Emotional Life*. London: Weidenfeld & Nicolson.

Linehan, M.M. (1993a) *Cognitive-Behavioral Treatment of Borderline Personality Disorder*. New York: Guilford Press.

Linehan, M.M. (1993b) *Skills Training Manual for Treating Borderline Personality Disorder*. New York: Guilford Press.

Lobban, Fiona & Barrowclough, Christine (2009) *A Casebook of Family Interventions for Psychosis*. Chichester, UK & Malden, MA: Wiley-Blackwell.

Mansell, W. (2012) Working with comorbidity in CBT. In Windy Dryden (2011). *The CBT Handbook*. Thousand Oaks, CA: Sage Publications.

Nica, E.I. & Links, P.S. (2009) Affective instability in borderline personality disorder: Experience sampling findings. *Current Psychiatry Reports, 11*(1), 74–81.

Persons, Ja. B. (2008) *The Case Formulation Approach to Cognitive-Behavior Therapy.* New York: Guilford Press.

Pitt, L., Kilbride, M., Nothard, S., Welford, M. & Morrison, A.P. (2007) Researching recovery from psychosis: A user-led project. *Psychiatric Bulletin, 31*, 55–60.

Pope, K. & Tabachnik, B. (1993) Therapists' anger, hate, fear, and sexual feelings: National survey of therapist responses, client characteristics, critical events, formal complaints, and training. *Professional Psychology: Research and Practice, 24*, 142–152.

Read, J. & Argyle, N. (1999) Hallucinations, delusions, and thought disorder among adult psychiatric inpatients with a history of child abuse. *Psychiatric Services, 50*(11), 1467–1472.

Read, J. & Hammersley, P. (2005) Child sexual abuse and schizophrenia. *British Journal of Psychiatry, 186*, 76; author reply 76.

Sayar, K., Acar, B. & Ak, I. (2003) Alexithymia and suicidal behavior. *Israeli Journal of Psychiatry Related Science, 40*(3), 165–173.

Tarrier, Nicholas (2006) *Case Formulation in Cognitive Behaviour Therapy: The Treatment of Challenging and Complex Cases.* New York: Routledge.

Taylor, P.J., Awenat, Y., Gooding, P., Johnson, J., Pratt, D., Wood, A. & Tarrier, N. (2010) The subjective experience of participation in schizophrenia research: A practical and ethical issue. *Journal of Nervous Mental Disorders, 198*(5), 343–348.

Wells, A. (2000) *Emotional Disorders and Metacognition: Innovative Cognitive Therapy.* Chichester: Wiley.

Wenzel, Amy, Brown, Gregory K. & Beck, Aaron T. (2009) *Cognitive Therapy for Suicidal Patients: Scientific and Clinical Applications.* Washington, DC: American Psychological Association.

Williams, J.M.G. (1997) *Cry of Pain.* Harmondsworth: Penguin.

Williams, J.M.G., Crane, C., Barnhofer, T. & Duggan, D.S. (2005) *Psychology and Suicidal Behaviour: Elaborating the Entrapment Model.* Oxford: Oxford University Press.

10 People and suicide

Anderson, M. & Jenkins, R. (2005) The challenge of suicide prevention: An overview of national strategies. *Disease Management and Health Outcomes, 13*, 245-253.

Awenat, Y. in association with Manchester Psychological Suicide Group (2011) NIHR RfPB application: A pilot study to assess the feasibility of a cognitive behavioural suicide prevention therapy for people in acute psychiatric wards, submitted Jan. 2012.

Bee, P., Playle, J., Lovell, K., Barnes, P., Gray, R. & Keeley, P. (2008) Service user views and expectations of UK registered mental health nurses: A systematic review of empirical research. *International Journal of Nursing Studies, 45*(3), 442–457.

Bentall, R. (2010) *Doctoring the Mind: When Psychiatric Treatments Fail.* London: Penguin Books.

Bowles, N. (2004) Mental health in-patient settings. In D. Duffy & T. Ryan (eds) *New Approaches to Preventing Suicide: A Manual for Practitioners.* London: Jessica Kingsley Publishers.

Brophy, M. (2006) *Truth Hurts: Report of the National Inquiry into Self-Harm among Young People.* London: Mental Health Foundation.

Department of Health (2005) *Chief Nursing Officer's Review of Mental Health Nursing.* London: HMSO.

Department of Health (2009) *No Voice.* London: HMSO.

Department of Health (2011) *Consultation on Preventing Suicide in England: A Cross-Government Strategy to Save Lives.* London: HMSO.

Donabedian, A. (1980) *Exploration in Quality Assessment and Monitoring*, Vol 1: *The Definition of Quality and Approaches to its Assessment.* Ann Arbor, MI: Health Administration Press.

Droughton J., Gask L., Green G., & Dixon C. (2010) in Duffy D. & Ryan T. (2004) *New Approaches to Preventing Suicide: A Manual for Practitioners*, Jessica Kingsley publishers.

Drury, V., Birchwood, M. & Cochrane R. (2000) Cognitive therapy and recovery from acute psychosis: A randomised controlled trial 3: Five-year follow-up. *British Journal of Psychiatry, 177*, 8–14.

Duffy, D. (2003a) The therapeutic relationships of mental health nurses and suicidal mental health patients. Unpublished PhD Thesis, University of Manchester.

Duffy, D. (2003b) Exploring suicide risk and the therapeutic relationship. *Nursing Times Research, 8*(3), 185–199.

Duffy, D. & Ryan, T. (2004) *New Approaches to Preventing Suicide: A Manual for Practitioners.* London: Jessica Kingsley Publishers.

Durrant, C., Clarke, I., Tolland, A. & Wilson, H. (2007) Designing a CBT service for an acute inpatient setting: A pilot evaluation study. *Clinical Psychology and Psychotherapy, 14*, 117–125.

Grad,O. (2011) The sequelae of suicide. In R.C. O'Connor, S. Platt S & J. Gordon (eds) *International Handbook of Suicide Prevention: Research, Policy and Practice.* Chichester: Wiley-Blackwell, 561–577.

Haddock, G., Wood, A., Watts, R., Dunn, G., Morrison, A. & Price, J. (2011) The Subjective Experience of Psychosis Scale (SEPS): Psychometric evaluation of a scale to assess outcome in psychosis. *Schizophrenia Research, 133*(1–3), 244–249.

Healthcare Commission (2008) *The Pathway to Recovery: A Review of NHS Inpatient Health Services.* London: Commission for Healthcare Audit & Inspection.

Holmes, J. (2002) Acute wards: Problems and solutions. Creating a psychotherapeutic culture in acute psychiatric wards. *Psychiatric Bulletin, 26*, 383–385.

Horrocks, J., Hughes, J., Martin, C., House, A. & Owens D. (2005) *Patient Experiences of Hospital Care Following Self-Harm: A Qualitative Study.* Leeds: University of Leeds.

Johnson, S., Wood, S., Paul, M., Osborn, D., Wearn, E., Lloyd-Evans, B. et al. (2010) *Inpatient Mental Health Staff Morale: A National Investigation. Final Report.* London: NIHR Service Delivery & Organization Programme.

Kapur, N., Cooper, J., King-Heles, S., Webb, R., Lawlor, M., Rodway, C. & Appleby, L. (2006) The repetition of suicidal behavior: A multi-center cohort study. *Journal of Clinical Psychiatry, 67*(10), 1599–1609.

Kapur,N., House, A., Creed, F., Feldman, E., Friedman, T. & Guthrie, E. (1999) General hospital services for deliberate self-poisoning: An expensive road to nowhere? *Postgraduate Medical Journal, 75*(888), 599–602.

Lakeman R. (2010) What can qualitative research tell us about helping a person who is suicidal? *Nursing Times*, 106(33) 23–26.

Langdon, P., Yaguez, L., Brown, J. & Jope, A. (2001) Who walks through the 'revolving door' of a British psychiatric hospital? *Journal of Mental Health, 10*(5), 523–533.

Mind (2004)*Ward Watch: Mind's Campaign to Improve Hospital Conditions for Mental Health Patients.* London: Mind.

Mind (2011) *Listening to Experience: An Independent Inquiry into Acute and Crisis Mental Healthcare.* London: Mind.

Morgan, H. (1979) *Death Wishes? The Understanding and Management of Deliberate Self-Harm.* Chichester: John Wiley & Sons.

National Audit Office (2008) *Helping People through Mental Health Crisis: The Role of Crisis Resolution and Home Treatment Teams. The Service User and Carer Experience.* London: National Audit Office.

National Confidential Inquiry into Suicide & Homicide by people with Mental Illness (2010) *Annual Report for England and Wales.* Manchester: University of Manchester.

National Institute for Clinical Excellence (NICE) (2009) *Schizophrenia.* CG82. http://www..nice.org.uk/CG822113 [accessed 28 October 2011].

National Institute for Clinical Excellence (NICE) (2011) *Self-Harm (Longer Term Management).* CG133 www.nice.org.uk/guidance/CG133 [accessed 10 December 2011].

National Institute for Mental Health in England (NIMHE) (2003) *Preventing Suicide: A Toolkit for Mental Health Services.* London: NIMHE.

Neil, S., Kilbride, M., Pitt, L., Welford, M., Northard, S., Sellwood, W. & Morrison, A. (2009) The Questionnaire about the Process of Recovery (QPR): A research instrument developed in collaboration with service users. *Psychosis, 1,* 145–155.

O'Connor, R.C., Platt, S. & Gordon, J. (2011) Achievements and challenges in suicidology: Conclusions and future directions. In R.C. O'Connor, S. Platt S. & J. Gordon (eds) *International Handbook of Suicide Prevention: Research, Policy and Practice.* Chichester: Wiley-Blackwell.

Office for National Statistics (ONS) (2011) *Suicide Rates in the United Kingdom, 2000–2009.* Newport: ONS.

Owens, D., Horrocks, J. & House, A. (2002) Fatal and non-fatal repetition of self-harm: Systematic review. *British Journal of Psychiatry, 181,* 193199.

Rethink (2005) *Future Perfect? Outlining an Alternative to the Pain of Psychiatric In-Patient Care.* London: Rethink.

Rethink (2006) *Behind Closed Doors: Acute Mental Healthcare in the UK.* London: Rethink.

Royal College of Psychiatrists (2011) *Do the Right Thing: How to Judge a Good Ward. Ten Standards for Adult In-Patient Mental Healthcare.* Occasional Paper OP79. London: RCP.

Sainsbury Centre for Mental Health (2005) *Acute Care: A National Survey of Adult Inpatient Psychiatric Wards in England.* London: Sainsbury Centre for Mental Health.

Samaritans (2011) www.samaritans.org.

Silverman R. (2011) in O'Connor R. Platt S. & Gordon J. (2011) *International Handbook of Suicide Prevention, Research, Policy and Practice,* Wiley-Blackwell, Chichester.

STORM (2004) Skills based training in risk management. Manchester: University of Manchester.

Taylor, P., Awenat, Y., Gooding, P., Pratt, D., Wood, A. & Tarrier, N. (2010) The subjective experience of participation in schizophrenia research: A practical and ethical issue. *Journal of Nervous and Mental Disease, 198,* 343–348.

Taylor, T., Hawton, K., Fortune, S. & Kapur, N. (2009) Attitudes towards clinical services among people who self-harm: A systematic review. *British Journal of Psychiatry, 194*(2), 104–110.

Weissman, M., Bland, R., Canino, G., Grenwald, S., Hwu, H., Joyce, P., Karam, E., Lee, C., Lellouch, J., Lepine, J., Newman, S., Rubio-Stipec, M., Wells, J., Wickramaratne, P., Wittchen, H. & Yeh, E. (1999) Prevalence of suicide ideation and suicide attempts in nine countries. *Psychological Medicine, 29,* 9–17.

Wicklander, M., Samuelsson, M. & Asberg, M. (2003) Shame reactions after suicide attempt. *Scandinavian Journal of Caring Sciences, 17,* 293–300.

Windfuhr, K. & Kapur, N. (2011) International perspectives on the epidemiology and aetiology of suicide and self-harm. In R.C. O'Connor, S. Platt & J. Gordon (eds) *International Handbook of Suicide Prevention: Research, Policy and Practice.* Wiley-Blackwell. Chichester, 27–57.

World Health Organization http://www.who.int/mental_health/prevention/suicide_rates/en/index.html [accessed 18 October 2011].

11 Future directions in clinical research and new technologies

Bang, M., Timpka, T., Eriksson, H., Holm, E. & Nordin, C. (2007) Mobile phone computing for in-situ cognitive behavioral therapy. *Studies in Health Technology and Informatics, 129*(Pt 2), 1078–1082.

Csikszentmihalyi, M. & Larson, R. (1987). Validity and reliability of the Experience-Sampling Method. *Journal of Nervous Mental Disorders, 175*(9), 526–536.

Delespaul, P.A.E.G. (1995) *Assessing Schizophrenia in Daily Life: The Experience Sampling Method.* Rijksuniversitet van Limburg (Maastricht, The Netherlands).

Depp, C.A., Mausbach, B., Granholm, E., Cardenas, V., Ben-Zeev, D., Patterson, T.L. & Jeste, D.V. (2010) Mobile interventions for severe mental illness: Design and preliminary data from three approaches. *Journal of Nervous Mental Disorders, 198*(10), 715–721. doi: 10.1097/NMD.0b013e3181f49ea3.

Flynn, T.M., Taylor, P. & Pollard, C.A. (1992) Use of mobile phones in the behavioral treatment of driving phobias. *Journal of Behavioral Therapy and Experimental Psychiatry, 23*(4), 299–302.

Fredrickson, B.L. & Branigan, C. (2005) Positive emotions broaden the scope of attention and thought-action repertoires. *Cognition & Emotion, 19*(3), 313–332.

Fredrickson, B.L., Cohn, M.A., Coffey, K.A., Pek, J. & Finkel, S.M. (2008) Open hearts build lives: Positive emotions, induced through Loving-Kindness Meditation, build consequential personal resources. *Journal of Personality and Social Psychology, 95*(5), 1045–1062.

Free, C., Knight, R., Robertson, S., Whittaker, R., Edwards, P., Zhou, W. & Roberts, I. (2011) Smoking cessation support delivered via mobile phone text messaging (txt2stop): A single-blind, randomised trial. *Lancet, 378*(9785), 49–55. doi: S0140-6736(11)60701-0 [pii].

Garland, E.L., Fredrickson, B., Kring, A.M., Johnson, D.P., Meyer, P.S. & Penn, D.L. (2010) Upward spirals of positive emotions counter downward spirals of negativity: Insights from the broaden-and-build theory and affective neuroscience on the treatment of emotion dysfunctions and deficits in psychopathology. *Clinical Psychological Review, 30*(7), 849–864. doi: S0272-7358(10)00042-5 [pii].

Gregg, L. & Tarrier N. (2007) Virtual reality in mental health: A review of the literature. *Social Psychiatry & Psychiatric Epidemiology, 42*(5), 343–354.

Heron, K.E. & Smyth, J.M. (2010) Ecological momentary interventions: Incorporating mobile technology into psychosocial and health behaviour treatments. *British Journal of Health Psychology, 15*(Pt 1), 1–39. doi: bjhp696 [pii].

Kelly, J.A., Gooding, P., Pratt, D., Ainsworth, J., Welford, M. & Tarrier, N. (accepted) Intelligent Real Time Therapy (iRTT): Harnessing the power of machine learning to optimise the delivery of momentary cognitive-behavioural interventions. *Journal of Mental Health.*

Neumann, M., Edelhauser, F., Tauschel, D., Fischer, M.R., Wirtz, M., Woopen, C. & Scheffer, C. (2011) Empathy decline and its reasons: A systematic review of studies with medical students and residents. *Academic Medicine, 86*(8), 996–1009. doi: 10.1097/ACM.0b013e318221e615.

Palmier, Claus J. (2011) The negative and positive self: A longitudinal study examining self-esteem, paranoia and negative symptoms in individuals with first-episode psychosis. *Early Intervention in Psychiatry, 5*(2), 150–155.

Sutton, Richard S. & Barto, Andrew G. (1998) *Reinforcement Learning: An Introduction.* Cambridge, MA: MIT Press.

Index